An Amish Paradox

Young Center Books in Anabaptist & Pietist Studies

Donald B. Kraybill, *Series Editor*

An Amish Paradox

Diversity & Change in
the World's Largest Amish Community

Charles E. Hurst *and* David L. McConnell

THE JOHNS HOPKINS UNIVERSITY PRESS
Baltimore

© 2010 The Johns Hopkins University Press
All rights reserved. Published 2010
Printed in the United States of America on acid-free paper

2 4 6 8 9 7 5 3 1

The Johns Hopkins University Press
2715 North Charles Street
Baltimore, Maryland 21218-4363
www.press.jhu.edu

Library of Congress Cataloging-in-Publication Data

Hurst, Charles E.
An Amish paradox : diversity and change in the world's largest Amish community /
Charles E. Hurst and David L. McConnell.
    p.   cm. — (Young Center books in Anabaptist and Pietist studies)
Includes bibliographical references and index.
ISBN-13: 978-0-8018-9398-8 (hardcover : alk. paper)
ISBN-10: 0-8018-9398-4 (hardcover : alk. paper)
ISBN-13: 978-0-8018-9399-5 (pbk. : alk. paper)
ISBN-10: 0-8018-9399-2 (pbk. : alk. paper)
1. Amish—Ohio—Holmes County—Social life and customs. 2. Amish—Ohio—
Holmes County—Social conditions. 3. Amish—Education—Ohio—Holmes County.
4. Amish—Health and hygiene—Ohio—Holmes County. 5. Amish—Ohio—Holmes County—
Economic conditions. 6. Technology—Religious aspects—Amish. 7. Holmes County (Ohio)—
Social life and customs. 8. Holmes County (Ohio)—Social conditions.
I. McConnell, David L., 1959–   II. Title.
F497.H74H87 2010
305.83'1077164—dc22   2009018181

A catalog record for this book is available from the British Library.

*Special discounts are available for bulk purchases of this book. For more information, please contact
Special Sales at 410-516-6936 or specialsales@press.jhu.edu.*

The Johns Hopkins University Press uses environmentally friendly book materials,
including recycled text paper that is composed of at least 30 percent post-consumer waste,
whenever possible. All of our book papers are acid-free, and our jackets and covers are
printed on paper with recycled content.

Contents

Figures, Maps, and Tables

Figures

Maps

Tables

Preface

Studying the Amish is like undertaking a great detective adventure. There are detours, hidden treasures, unexpected discoveries, and clues to Amish culture and lifestyle lying all around. But as soon as you think you have a firm grasp on an issue, it slips away. You find exceptions and differences, and you begin to realize how misleading it is to jump to conclusions. You learn that it is dangerous to enter the study with a know-it-all attitude or a fixed theoretical framework. The research humbles but excites you because you become increasingly aware of the richness and depth of this living culture.

One of the many joys experienced in our exploration of the Amish in the Holmes County Settlement has been the twists and turns encountered on our journey. Because of the complexity and changing face of this settlement, the adventure has never been boring. Popular treatments of the Amish too frequently generalize inappropriately, focus on sensationalist incidents, or merely slide along the surface without ever penetrating the reality of Amish society. And while there are numerous excellent scholarly books on the Amish, they have tended to focus on other settlements, such as those in Pennsylvania and Indiana, even though the Holmes County Settlement in Ohio is the largest and perhaps the most complex in the world. It is on the latter community that our study focuses. (For convenience and because the settlement is centered around Holmes County, we use the term *Holmes County Settlement* throughout the book. In other works, the same settlement is sometimes referred to as the "Wayne-Holmes Settlement" or the "Wayne-Holmes-Tuscarawas Settlement."

In fact, it includes small parts of Wayne, Stark, Tuscarawas, Coshocton, Knox, and Ashland counties.)

To be Amish means to keep oneself separate from the wider society while at the same time being able to negotiate with it. This is an interminable struggle, one that contributes mightily to the dynamism of the Holmes County Settlement. This struggle has numerous faces and manifests itself in many forms. Among these are the ongoing negotiations between the individual and the community, between freedom and regulation, and between tradition and modernity. It is within the crucible of these cross-cutting and conflicting forces that Amish behavior and culture are generated. Like the polarities of a magnet, the elements within these pairs often repel each other but also often reach accommodation and create fascinating mixtures.

During the early months of our fieldwork and on numerous other occasions, we experienced these unlikely mixtures and the sense of paradox that accompanied them. Sitting quietly next to an Amish friend on our way to the Heritage Historical Library in Aylmer, Canada, we were startled when the sound of his cell phone broke the silence in the car. Eagerly awaiting the arrival of parents who were bringing a hot lunch to schoolchildren, we were surprised when a pizza delivery truck pulled into the schoolyard, followed minutes later by a horse and buggy loaded with soft drinks and salad. In another instance, an Amish teacher, hearing of our interest in a particular lesson plan, opened a cupboard and proceeded to run off a color copy of it on his battery-powered copy machine. In this community that so often emphasizes cooperation and mutual dependence, we also watched Amish boys and girls go head to head in front of the class in a timed competition to solve math problems. And when students arrived for a school campout, we noticed that they sported the latest Nike and Adidas travel bags, footwear, and camping gear (but only in dark colors).

Such surprises, of course, said as much about our own expectations of the Amish as they did about the realities of Amish life. Mixtures like these are not anomalies; they are interwoven throughout the fabric of Amish culture and characterize our substantive discussions of religion, family, education, economy, and health care. The central focus of our book is the diversity created by these seemingly unlikely combinations and the border work that they require between Amish affiliations and between Amish and English (non-Amish) societies. Challenging a singular view of

Amish culture and identity, we show how the interplay of internal tensions and external pressures affects integration and separation in different contexts.

The Holmes County Settlement is rife with diversity, internal disagreements, and varying adaptations to the conflicting forces that members must face. We find self-made Amish millionaires alongside struggling dairy and produce farmers; successful female entrepreneurs next door to stay-at-home wives; fervent adherents of public schooling and of homeschooling as well as supporters of parochial education within the same church district; and Amish youth who "run wild" even as their peers reject the period known as *rumspringa* altogether. Much of this diversity is caused by the coexistence of Swartzentruber, Andy Weaver, Old Order, New Order, and even New New Order affiliations within the Holmes County setting.

Over the past few decades, the tensions created by all these pressures have intensified as Amish settlements across America have undergone a remarkable economic transformation. To the surprise of many, as Amish enterprises and other forms of nonfarming employment have prospered, the retention rates of Amish youth have grown to an all-time high. To date, however, there has been no comprehensive analysis of the cultural negotiations, tensions, and contradictions unleashed by these changes in Ohio's Holmes County Settlement. Based on more than ten years of experience with the local Amish community and seven years of systematic field research, including extensive interviewing and survey data, our book analyzes cultural continuities and changes in the world's largest and most diverse Amish community. For those who are interested, we describe our methods of data collection more fully in appendix A.

In addition to our primary focus on the diversity and tensions within the Holmes County Settlement, a second emphasis in our analysis is on the far-reaching cultural implications of greater Amish involvement in the marketplace for changes in Amish religious convictions, family practices, educational choices, occupational shifts, and health care options. As a large and fundamental part of Amish lives, economics in all its particularities has impressed itself on even the most personal aspects of their lifestyles.

To our Amish readers, we are keenly aware that our book will not reflect the same spiritual tone that an Amish writer would strike. Ours is

a social-scientific study; following the standards of our respective disciplines, we have tried to put our personal beliefs aside and to avoid judgments that are not supported by the data we collected. At the same time,
we have tried to write with respect, and we hope that our admiration
for the many positive qualities in Amish life comes through. Walking
the tightrope between being outside analysts and participant observers,
as outsiders inside, we have tried to view Amish culture through Amish
eyes while trying to maintain somewhat of an objective stance. Neither
of us speaks Pennsylvania Dutch, and so the differences in language required us to be especially sensitive to the insider's point of view so as to
get a more accurate picture of the Amish lifeworld. Along the way, we
made use of Amish insiders, outsiders who had been insiders (ex-Amish),
and total outsiders (English) as informants. To ensure anonymity, we have
not used any individual names except where names have been published
in the news media or for those individuals whose names are associated
with Amish affiliations.

Researchers who work with the Amish usually end up with a great deal
of respect for what Amish communities are trying to accomplish. As Marc
Olshan notes, one side effect of this process is that many accounts have
treated the Amish with "kid gloves" and have examined their lifestyle
through "rose-colored glasses."[1] We too greatly admire certain aspects of
Amish society. But we have tried to look at Amish society with a critical
eye and have not hesitated to point out contradictions and conflicts. As a
living, prospering cultural community, the Amish wrestle with the same
problems of finding adequate health care, staying true to their principles,
teaching their children, and making a living as does everyone else. We
hope we have portrayed the Holmes County Settlement as a complex, dynamic, contemporary, and creative community and have dispelled the image of Amish life as a vestige of a bygone era.

WE HAVE ORGANIZED THIS BOOK around six substantive chapters that, taken
together, tell a multifaceted story about diversity and change in the Holmes County Settlement. Chapters 1 and 8 are the bookends to this story.
In chapter 1 we take readers on a cultural tour of the Holmes County Settlement, provide background information on common cultural and historical threads that unify the Amish, and lay out the central puzzle and guid-

ing concepts for our study. In chapter 8 we attempt to tie together many of the specific patterns associated with religion, family, education, work, and health care to construct a coherent framework for understanding the Holmes County Settlement as a community.

Chapters 2 and 3 explore the origins and consequences of religious diversity among the Amish.[2] The Amish have not been immune to religious conflict, and chapter 2 delves in some detail into the various factors—doctrinal disagreements, technology use, personality clashes—that have given rise to the four main church affiliations in the settlement. In chapter 3 we ask, How far-reaching are these religious divisions in shaping patterns of interaction in the Holmes County Settlement? Specifically, we focus on three key barometers of religious life—mission and outreach efforts, rumspringa, and excommunication and shunning.

In chapter 4 we explore an area that would seem to be the most resistant to change: family life. To be sure, the structure of the family has not been completely altered by the move to nonfarming occupations. But even this most stable of Amish institutions is showing signs of new stresses and challenges. We discuss the various meanings surrounding family and home, continuities and changes in relations between parents and children and between husbands and wives, and the re-shaping of leisure time and consumption.

Chapter 5, on Amish education, looks at the new set of choices and challenges facing Amish parents, teachers, and school board members as they try to ensure that children are both socialized into the Amish worldview and trained in the skills they will need to make a living. The Holmes County Settlement is distinctive for the diversity of educational choices made by Amish parents. This chapter examines the educational options available to Amish parents—parochial schools, public schools, and home-schooling—and asks why some Amish parents choose public schools even though they are well aware of the excessive competition, individualism, and other cultural baggage found within the public school terrain. We also explore recent trends in vocational training and education for special-needs children.

Chapter 6 takes up the variety of occupational niches available to the Holmes County Amish and asks what kinds of social and cultural consequences stem from particular occupational choices. Unlike other large Amish settlements, where the shift away from farming has resulted in more widespread adoption of micro-enterprises and factory labor, the Holmes County Settlement can be described as a "mixed economy." The challenges raised by the tourist industry continue to be an issue, as does growing concern about social class inequalities among the Amish themselves. This chapter also examines emerging occupations such as dog and deer raising and organic farming and businesses such as greenhouses and produce auctions.

The Holmes County Settlement offers a useful window on diverse responses to health care among the Amish, which we examine in chapter 7. With major hospitals in nearby cities and with world-class health care services available at the Cleveland Clinic and at Akron Children's Hospital, the Amish have access to the finest doctors and the latest surgical techniques. However, one does not have to travel far to find midwives, reflexologists, chiropractors, natural foods proponents, and other nontraditional forms of health care. In this chapter we explore the role of church guidelines, cost, access, and knowledge in health care decisions across the life cycle, including where to give birth, how to address physical health problems, how to deal with mental illness, and how to die with dignity.

Ultimately, we argue that the notion of the Amish as "separate from the world" overlooks the fact that, to varying degrees, the Amish have come to see and to forge connections between themselves and outsiders. But the Amish have resisted complete assimilation into the English world. In the wake of the Amish economic transformation, which cultural meanings and practices have remained conventional and taken for granted, which have been discarded, and which have become troublesome or contested?[3] It is our hope that, through a fine-grained analysis of religion, family, education, work, and health care, we will be able to shed some light on these important questions.

Acknowledgments

We have many people to thank. First and foremost, we could have accomplished little without the cooperation and insights of many local Amish contributors, including members and ordained leaders from many church affiliations, as well as farmers, businessmen and businesswomen, committee chairs, teachers, factory employees, and homemakers. Several of these individuals read drafts of chapters and submitted comments to us that added to the reality and richness of our presentations or corrected errors. The directors of the Heritage Historical Library in Canada and the Ohio Amish Library graciously made all their resources available to us. Many Amish spent hours with us and welcomed us into their homes. We are truly appreciative of their tolerance and openness to us as strangers and outsiders.

Many other, mostly non-Amish (English), residents consented to interviews, sometimes repeatedly. They occupy a variety of pivotal positions within the local area, and among them were the executive directors of the Holmes County Chamber of Commerce and the Holmes County Education Foundation, the community development director of the Ohio State University Extension, principals at public elementary schools, and local historians who are Mennonite or Amish. English people who were business partners with Amish individuals or who worked often with Amish businesses also participated. Many ex-Amish from different affiliations also offered their ideas. For the health care chapter, we consulted with a wide variety of counselors and medical professionals, licensed and unlicensed. We are grateful for all the time these individuals gave to our project.

We also received support and comments from inside the academy. We owe a huge debt of gratitude to Donald Kraybill for his wise counsel and useful suggestions at every stage of the process. Richard Stevick, Karen Johnson-Weiner, Larry Greksa, David Luthy, and David Weaver-Zercher, all important analysts of the Amish, made very helpful suggestions for different parts of our study. An anonymous reviewer provided thought-provoking and constructive comments. We are also indebted to Richard Moore, Elizabeth Cooksey, and Myra Katz for sharing their work on the Holmes County Amish with us. Our colleague Jennifer Graber clarified many of the nuances of religion among the Amish and how their views contrast with those of evangelical and other Protestant churches. Anne Nurse provided methodological assistance, and Heather Fitz Gibbon and Christa Craven critiqued our comments on gender. Catherine Grand-george and Mary Schantz gave invaluable assistance in constructing fig-ures and maps. The following Amish individuals read drafts of all or parts of our book and/or provided helpful and detailed comments: Ed Kline, Marvin Wengerd, David Kline, Wayne Wengerd, Rob Schlabach, Ernie Hershberger, Monroe Beachy, and Jacob Beachy. Others providing assist-ance were Bruce Glick, David Wiesenberg, Owen and Pat McConnell, and Paul Hostetler. Any errors of fact or interpretation remain our own.

Numerous students assisted in gathering literature and transcrib-ing interviews, including Wil Burton, Megan Ammon, Andrea Brown, Julie Todd, Rachel Libben, Kate Matthews, Whitney Goodwin, Anne Richardson, Emily Sacher, and Amy Dupper. We are also grateful for the grants we received for our research from the Spencer Foundation of the Woodrow Wilson Fellowship Foundation. In addition, financial sup-port from the College of Wooster's Faculty Development Fund and the Luce Fund for Distinguished Scholarship, as well as a generous sabbatical program, allowed us to attend several programs and conferences on the Amish and to finish our writing. We are extremely grateful to Lois Crum for her expert editorial assistance.

Finally, it goes without saying (but we'll say it anyway) that we have been fortunate to have the full support and love of our spouses, Mary El-len and Cathy. Their continued encouragement and patience have made our work much easier.

An Amish Paradox

CHAPTER 1

Discovering the Holmes County Amish

You can drive down any north-south road in the settlement and in a span of just a
few miles you might pass Amish families from five or six different affiliations.
—An Old Order Amish man

Ohio's Amish Country

Just sixty miles south of Cleveland and seventy miles northeast of Columbus, in the center of the triangle formed by interstates 70, 71, and 77, lies the largest contiguous Amish community in the world. Over the past five years, we have driven thousands of miles crisscrossing this settlement as we gathered information for our study. Many times we had the good fortune to be accompanied by Amish friends and acquaintances who generously shared their intimate knowledge of the region's social and physical terrain. We invite you to join us, in this chapter, for a journey through the Holmes County Settlement; we'll explore a few of the places that have special meaning to the thirty thousand Amish who call it home.

It's a sunny day in early June 2007, and we begin our trip on the outskirts of Orrville, Ohio, heading south down Kansas Road. Just a stone's throw to the west is the Wayne County Speedway, where Amish youth sometimes gather at night to sneak a glimpse of the local auto racing scene. Almost immediately we come to the new U.S. 30 bypass, running from Wooster to Canton, and on this day the big story is road construction.

Kansas Road is temporarily closed because the Ohio Department of Transportation is building a bridge with a special buggy bypass over the highway to allow Amish families to travel safely to Orrville and other points north for health care and shopping. Partly because the area is home to the most conservative sect of Amish, the Swartzentrubers, who depend on buggy transport far more than do the other affiliations, the bridge was approved after extensive consultations between state and local officials and Amish residents.

Having navigated the detour, we proceed south past Riceland Golf Course and several dozen non-Amish homes, their identity betrayed by the electrical wires from the grid and the vehicles in the driveways. Within minutes, however, we are in an area that is filled with historical significance for the Amish. It includes the site of the oldest continuously operating school in Ohio and the original location of a major schism in the settlement that created another conservative branch, the Andy Weaver affiliation. By the time we pass the intersection with Lautenschlager Road, gently rolling farmland stretches east and west and the telltale signs of Amish homes emerge: windmills that power the pumps for the water wells, white purple martin houses that look like tiny apartment complexes on a pole, dark-colored clothes drying on clotheslines, and mailboxes with names such as Miller, Raber, and Hershberger. Some houses are crowded up against the road on small lots, whereas others are set back, accessible only by a long lane. More than a few can accurately be called "self-contained estates," since they include numerous outbuildings—a shop, a barn, an attached house for the elderly grandparents. Amish farms in this area generally range from 80 to 140 acres, with the land and buildings valued between three hundred thousand and a half million dollars.[1]

Soon, however, we realize that farms are not the only businesses in the area. Dotting the roadside are small shops with names like Kidron Woodcraft, Y and M Chair, and Yoder Hardwood. Misty Ridge Woodcraft makes entertainment centers and computer furniture, items never used by the Amish. The number of shops specializing in wood products is especially noticeable, but on closer inspection, a surprising variety of occupational niches appear, such as the Kansas Road Tarp Shop, Hostetler Welding, and Chupp's Powder Coating. We pass several Swartzentruber homesteads, identified by their dark red barns (white is considered too worldly) and dirt lanes, that sell products out of the house, advertised by

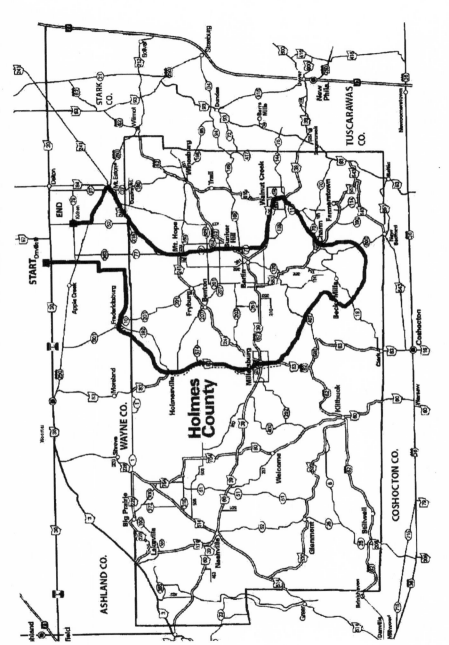

Holmes County tour. The solid black line on this map shows the route of our cultural tour through the heart of the settlement, which spans six counties but is centered in Holmes County. Courtesy of Mary Schantz.

handwritten signs, "Eggs for Sale" and "Hand-Woven Baskets." Just before we cross U.S. 250, we pass Yoder's Greenhouse, a large and tremendously successful Amish enterprise that involves extended family members—men, women, and children—in roles similar to life on the farm.

Buggy traffic is fairly light at this midmorning hour, but we pass one buggy with a bright yellow Little Tykes slide tied onto its top, a new jungle gym in the making. Coming down the other side of the road is a boy no more than ten years old, gripping the reins earnestly as he drives a halflinger, a golden chestnut-colored horse with white flowing mane and tail that is known for its friendly temperament. The boy's older sister appears to be coaching him from her side in the surrey. Three school-aged children play at the edge of a pond, enjoying their long summer recess. A middle-aged man emerges from one of the many phone shanties that dot the roadside, having checked his voicemail and perhaps placed a few calls. Many of the people we pass raise their hand in greeting, a common form of communication between those on foot, in buggies, and in vehicles on the less-traveled roads.

During our drives through the settlement with Amish friends, it became apparent to us that the landscape is not only alive with relatives and personal acquaintances but is deeply etched with memories of past events, some of them tragic. We pass near the site of a horrific accident that occurred in 1994, when a speeding motorist swerved off the road, plowed into a group of Amish schoolchildren, and killed five as they were walking home in the late afternoon. Later, we pass the spot where Steven Keim, age twenty-three, a young man who grew up Amish, was shot and killed on September 1, 2003, by Marion Weaver, fifty-eight, the owner of a car that had been hit with tomatoes in a typical rumspringa prank.[2] Returning with a shotgun late at night and firing into the cornfield in anger, Weaver accidentally killed the young man, with whom he had family ties. Such collective memories are vivid reminders of the ever-present dangers of maintaining a horse-and-buggy culture amid the unpredictable technologies and behaviors of non-Amish neighbors.

After turning onto County Road 363 and heading south toward Maysville, we stop to buy two quarts of fresh strawberries from a Swartzentruber family alongside their parked buggy. Soon we pass two Amish private schools, one on each side of the road, a visible reminder of the accidental burning of a school in 2001 and the ensuing conflict

Like many of their peers, this New Order Amish boy and girl have learned how to handle a pony cart at a very young age. Photograph by Doyle Yoder.

between Swartzentruber and Old Order parents. When the groups were unable to agree on the size of the basement for the new school, the Swartzentrubers built their own school no more than three hundred yards away, with a more modest basement and with hooks and shelves instead of cubbies for coats and lunch pails. As we come into the community of Maysville, the increase in pedestrian traffic and activity level is noticeable. Several children, clasping handfuls of dandelions, enjoy a ride in a wagon pulled by their mother, while nearby an older man in suspenders and rubber boots pushes a power mower.

At Salt Creek Road we turn sharply west and drive through a beautiful stretch of farmland, with the road crossing back and forth over the

Members of the Swartzentruber affiliation often sell fruits, vegetables, and
hand-woven baskets on roadsides in the Holmes County Settlement. Photograph by
Doyle Yoder.

Salt Creek, before it passes the entrance to the Yoder Bargain Store on our
right. Locals refer to this two-story shop adjacent to a house as the "Amish
Wal-Mart" for its vast supply of goods that cater to the Amish—from
clothing and housewares to books and children's toys. Only here can one
find an entire collection of rurally oriented board games with names such
as Horsopoly (a version of Monopoly), Deer Hunter's Challenge, Fish On,
and Life on the Farm. As we pull into the sleepy town of Fredericksburg,
passing the Village Car and Buggy Wash, we notice fliers advertising the
upcoming Fourth of July parade, an event that brings Amish and non-
Amish together to watch the parade, eat chicken barbecue, and play softball. As we pass the Horse and Harness Pub on our way out of town, we
are reminded that although Prairie Township, which encompasses most
of Fredericksburg, is dry, the local watering hole is conveniently located a
few feet over the township line.

Heading toward Millersburg, we follow the route of Rails to Trails, a twelve-mile "path" from Fredericksburg to the Millersburg Wal-Mart. A coalition of Amish and non-Amish worked for years to bring more than $3 million in state and federal grants to the county to create a two-lane road—one lane asphalt for bicycles, rollerblades, wheelchairs, and hikers and one lane "chip and seal" for buggies and horseback riding. Former governor Bob Taft attended the Grand Opening in 2005, which included a buggy ride with local Amish author David Kline, who was then serving as chair of the nonprofit Rails to Trails Coalition. Arriving in Holmesville, we make a beeline south on U.S. 83 to the county seat, Millersburg, which is a place of some ambivalence in the Amish psyche. It is true that Millersburg welcomes many Amish shoppers and that Pomerene Hospital has added the Amish House to house family members tending the ill. But the courthouse in the center of town has been the scene of numerous legal cases that have angered and, in some instances, split the Amish community. To a lesser extent than Wooster to the north, which has a reputation among the Amish for snobbishness, Millersburg is seen as oriented more toward the descendants of its Scots-Irish and English settlers.

Driving south out of Millersburg, we angle to the east on Route 39, and before we know it, the sights and sounds of the city disappear. Now the land breaks into a series of valleys and ridges, much of it planted in grass and hay rather than corn. It is the kind of hilly terrain that the Amish view as especially fit for their communities because it responds so well to hard work and loving care. Once in a while, however, we pass ornate non-Amish houses, occupied by city folk who want to escape or retire to the countryside. The area south of Route 39, mostly Old Order, is known and envied for having never experienced a church division, in contrast to the northern part of the settlement, where we began our tour. After angling west, we cut sharply east again as we turn onto a narrow gravel road and into the heart of Panther Hollow, a favorite spot for Amish birders seeking owls and rare species on the Millersburg Christmas Bird Count. This road can be dangerously icy in the winter.

We emerge dramatically from the stand of hardwoods and find ourselves in the fertile Doughty Valley. This area was not originally settled by Amish, as evidenced by one imposing brick mansion, known as the old Conrad place, that was built from the bounty of the early farmland. Today, however, the valley is home to young Amish families who are moving back into dairy and crop farming, and doing so quite successfully—some even

Back roads throughout the area provide opportunities for recreational activities such as rollerblading and bicycling. Photograph by Doyle Yoder.

venturing into organic farming. As we loop around the valley and crest a ridge heading northeast, Amish farms and shops stretch to the horizon. We pass one home that only ten years ago marked the southernmost point in the settlement. This family knew that if they heard a horse and buggy coming down the lane, they were about to receive visitors. Now the southern frontier has moved ten miles farther south, in Coshocton and Tuscarawas counties, and is advancing at a rate of nearly one-half mile a year.

Just before passing Flat Ridge Elementary School, a public school whose student body is 100 percent Amish, we stumble onto a funeral gathering. There are dozens of buggies and a few cars parked around an Amish home for the viewing and a message from the ministers; the procession to the cemetery will follow. Amish cemeteries typically occupy a small rectangular plot on a farm, and some of them hold clues to the first Amish settlers. Pulling into Yoder Nylon Works, a small harness shop, we get permission from the elderly proprietor to drive out through a field to the cemetery on his farm. The view is breathtaking, and we learn that ten generations of Amish are buried here, feet facing east, ready for the

Resurrection. Their graves are marked by simple headstones. After some searching, we find the resting place of Christian Schlabach. The letters "IMM" are carved in the headstone to denote that he was an immigrant; born in Germany in 1751, he died in 1840 at the age of eighty-nine.

Schlabach's grave is of particular interest because he was implicated in an intriguing story that still circulates in the Amish community about the group's earliest Holmes County ancestors from Somerset County, Pennsylvania. As the story goes, Henry Yoder had eyes for John Hochstetler's hired girl, who was John's wife's sister. One day, she was cooking sugar water and left the house through the back door as Henry was approaching. Believing he had been spurned, Henry murdered John's six-month-old baby, whom the girl had been caring for, smothering the child under the crib. But John's brother Solomon, who was something of a maverick in the community, was blamed, because he had a red hunting coat similar to one the girl identified on a man she had seen earlier looking in the window. The evidence was circumstantial, and the case was ruled a mistrial, but the incident cast a pall over the family's reputation. Solomon left the Amish church, still proclaiming his innocence, and near the end of his life was taken in and baptized on his word by "Big Mose" Miller at Walnut Creek Mennonite Church. At this gesture of kindness, Solomon reportedly wept like a baby. Eventually, Henry Yoder's father approached his friend Christian Schlabach with a proposal: he would give 640 acres of land near Walnut Creek, the very farm on which we now stood, to Christian's sons Jacob and Daniel if they would marry his two daughters (Henry Yoder's sisters). They agreed to this proposal and moved to Ohio. Imagine everyone's shock when, years later, Henry became ill and, thinking he was on his deathbed, confessed to the murder of the baby![3]

We then make our way into the heart of Walnut Creek, passing the original house of Jonas Stutzman, the first Amish settler in 1810. Stutzman believed so intently that Christ's Second Coming was imminent that he prepared for the event by dressing in white every day and building a large wooden chair to accommodate Jesus.[4] At the intersection with U.S. 39, we pass Carlisle Printing, the publishing company that prints the nine-hundred-page *Ohio Amish Directory* every five years. It is a comprehensive snapshot of occupations, births, marriages, and deaths for every family in the settlement except for the Swartzentrubers, who do not participate. Here in Walnut Creek, we are in one of several New Order Amish church districts in this region. The buggies we pass have more amenities, such as sliding doors; and some of the homes, with stone facades and carefully manicured lawns, are hard to distinguish from those of the non-Amish.

We are also in the heart of the settlement's multi-million-dollar tourist industry, as the busloads of people eating at the popular Der Dutchman Restaurant attest. Proceeding quickly on U.S. 39 through Walnut Creek and heading toward Berlin, we pass countless shops and restaurants that market the Amish brand to tourists, a sign that they are probably not owned by Amish themselves. At Troyer's Country Market, which specializes in Amish wedding foods, we turn north on County Road 77 and pass more Amish shops with names such as 77 Woodcraft, 77 Houseware, and Refrigerator 77. A pickup truck pulling a nondescript white trailer directly in front of us, one of the settlement's ubiquitous "furniture haulers," illustrates how the Ohio Amish country's thriving furniture business is competing with Lenoir, North Carolina, for the title "furniture capital of the United States." Approaching Bunker Hill, we pass the Amish-Mennonite Heritage Center, which houses a cyclorama 265 feet by 10 feet, a dramatic painting of Amish and Mennonite histories from their beginnings in Zurich to the present.

Next, we traverse a series of big hills known as the "Amish rollercoaster" and make our way past 77 Coach Supply Ltd., one of the premier makers of bent wood in the settlement. Just before we enter Mount Hope, we pass near a shop that served as the venue for a Drug and Alcohol Awareness seminar for more than two hundred Amish parents, featuring the sheriff and the head of the local affiliate of a federal drug task force. However, Mount Hope is best known to outsiders as the home of Wayne-Dalton, one of the largest garage door manufacturers in the United States. Wayne-Dalton, the Keim Lumber Company, and Weaver Leather are three of the main English employers of Amish in the settlement. Wayne-Dalton's gleaming headquarters seem strangely incongruous with the town's mostly Amish clientele. Even on this weekday, Mount Hope is abuzz with activity. On Saturdays the town really comes alive, as its huge auction grounds on the southwest side of town feature events such as the Horse Sale, the Mid-Ohio Exotic Animal and Bird Sale, and the Farm Machinery Sale. One of our Amish friends describes the Mount Hope auction as not only the best deal in town, but as the "Amish CNN," the hub of the Plain grapevine.[5]

As we exit Mount Hope, we pass a natural foods store and a chiropractor. Such health-related enterprises, which occupy a central place in Amish approaches to wellness, dot the countryside. On our left is Amish-owned Homestead Furniture, whose twenty-seven-thousand-square-foot showroom includes a map showing the location of customers in all fifty states. Now we bear sharply northeast on Route 241 and follow a five-mile stretch of road where one can count the non-Amish farms on one hand. As we approach Mount Eaton, we pass near the Mount Eaton Care Center, a special birthing facility; it serves Amish women who would like a childbirth option that is somewhat between the home and the hospital. We also drive by Mount Eaton Elementary School, where the principal has built a program adapted for Amish parents who prefer a public school education for their children. The K–6 school includes a special seventh-and-eighth-grade addition for the Amish pupils. Although it offers special classes in German, just like the Amish private schools, it also gives Amish youngsters computer skills and a high level of comfort in interacting with their non-Amish peers.

Following U.S. 250 west out of Mount Eaton, we see the sprawling complex of Coblentz Lumber and Furniture, started by an Old Order Amish man but now owned by a non-Amish man who hires a managerial staff and workforce that is almost entirely Amish. We are reminded that this area is populated by numerous Old Order families who are progressive in their outlook and savvy in their business acumen. One insider estimated that he could count more than a dozen Amish millionaires within a one-mile radius in this region. We also pass by the quilt shop where Charles Knowles, who died in 2007 in his early nineties, used to work. Having fallen in love with an Amish widow while in his sixties, Knowles was one of the few outside converts who survived his "testing period" and was accepted as a full member of an Old Order church.

As we approach Apple Creek, having almost completed a full circle, our growling stomachs prompt us to make a detour to Kidron, known for its outdoor flea market and a livestock auction frequented by the Amish. It is also the home of Lehman's Hardware, a popular source of nonelectric home products, which experienced an extraordinary surge in business before the year 2000. As in Mount Hope, buggies seem to outnumber cars, and Amish of all affiliations mingle with one another and with non-Amish in the marketplace. Nearby Central Christian High School serves as the venue each August for the Ohio Mennonite Relief Sale and Auction, to which many Amish contribute quilts, furniture, and other goods to benefit the Mennonite Central Committee in its mission work.

Our destination, however, is the Kidron Town and Country Store, which not only sells Amish hats, bonnets, and clothing but has a small restaurant in the basement. After our meal we indulge in fresh strawberry pie. Well fed, we get up to leave and notice an Amish teenager at the check-out register with five videos in his hand. It is a fitting note on which to end our tour, since it illustrates the ongoing challenges of keeping the Amish way of life meaningful to the next generation. Such an apparently rural and small-town setting belies the potential tensions and temptations facing the Amish as they attempt to navigate between two worlds.

In approximately three hours, we have covered nearly a hundred miles and crossed through several counties and nearly a dozen townships. We have witnessed firsthand a remarkable degree of diversity within the Amish community: socioeconomic, religious, educational, and occupational. Most importantly, our drive has raised a host of interesting sociological questions.

The Puzzle

Our trip through the Holmes County Settlement illustrates many unexpected features of Amish life, but none more vividly than what Donald Kraybill and Steven Nolt have called the "mini-industrial revolution" among the Amish.[6] Although farming remained the central means of economic livelihood for most Amish through the 1970s, high birthrates coupled with the shrinking availability of land, rising land prices, and technological changes in the larger society have made nonmechanized farming increasingly problematic.[7] As a result, many Amish have adopted economic alternatives such as micro-enterprises, mobile work crews, and factory employment. Today, more than three-quarters of the Holmes County Amish work in occupations other than farming.

On the eve of these sweeping economic changes, more than one Amish scholar offered dire predictions about the fate of a people who were seen as irrevocably tied to an agrarian lifestyle. Noted Amish specialist John Hostetler and his colleagues, for example, warned not only that the Amish viewed cultivation of the soil as a "moral directive" but that the very fabric of Amish culture was largely maintained by the ability of parents to establish their children in farming. Their sobering conclusion? Those who "cannot obtain a farm may find it hard to remain Amish."[8]

Yet the Amish surprised the pundits on two counts. First, the move "from plows to profits" was surprisingly successful when measured in economic terms.[9] The failure rate of Amish enterprises is far below the national average, and Amish entrepreneurs have shown a knack for creativity, on-the-job learning, and low-key but savvy niche marketing.[10] As it turned out, the gap between running a farm and managing a small business was not so large after all. The cultural constraints on business, such as the eighth-grade limit on formal schooling, were more than offset by a formidable repertoire of cultural resources, including a strong work ethic, a ready pool of family labor, and low overhead costs.

Second, and perhaps even more remarkable, retention rates of Amish youth have climbed to an all-time high over the past few decades. In most settlements, nearly 90 percent of Amish young people join the church. In one study of the Geauga Settlement in Ohio, the retention rate of children who grew up in nonfarming households was slightly higher than the rate for those in farming families.[11] Paradoxically, then, the entrance of the Amish into market-oriented enterprises, which often brings them in closer daily contact with the English world, seems to have made the Amish faith and lifestyle even more attractive to its young people. By almost any measure, the Amish today are thriving as never before.

The compromises made in the shift to nonfarming occupations have clearly transformed the style and substance of Amish life, but scholars and lay observers alike disagree on the scope and magnitude of these changes. Some argue that cottage industries and factory labor are like a "Trojan horse" that has ushered in an Amish cultural revolution.[12] For others, the "mini-industrial revolution" is more akin to an unusually large "blip" on the radar screen of incremental and selective adaptation that has been a hallmark of Amish life in the United States for nearly three centuries.[13] Similarly, scholars disagree about whether the growing interaction with non-Amish has led to the breakdown of traditional boundaries or whether it has only reinforced Amish skepticism about the outside world.[14]

In this book, we argue that it makes little sense to talk about one unified Amish response to change. Instead, we show that the combination of new outside pressures and internal distinctions has given rise to increasingly diverse decisions about religious and family life, school and work, and even health care. Our overall goal is thus to illuminate the complex causes of diversity and change among the Amish as well as the increasingly varied social outcomes of the Amish struggle "to save their cultural souls while turning their backs on the pastures of their past."[15]

Ours is not the first attempt to understand the social and cultural dynamics of diversity and change among the Amish.[16] It is, however, the first comprehensive analysis of that process in the Holmes County Settlement. In spite of its size, the Holmes County Settlement is decidedly understudied.[17] The paucity of scholarly attention is unfortunate because the Holmes County Settlement is not only the world's largest Amish community but also the most complex. As such, it offers a rich laboratory for exploring how external pressures and internal tensions have given rise to diverse patterns of accommodation.

The Amish Commonality

We acknowledge, along with our emphasis on diversity and change, the considerable stock of shared heritage and common outlook that characterizes all Amish in this settlement and elsewhere. Although the Amish are most accurately described as a sectarian group, with membership open to all who are willing to submit themselves to adult baptism and the rules of the church, they share many features of ethnic groups, including a common history, language, symbols, rituals, and beliefs.

The Amish trace their heritage back to the Swiss Anabaptists who emerged in the aftermath of the Protestant Reformation in Europe in the early 1500s.[18] In the years after Martin Luther's protest of practices within the Roman Catholic Church, some young reformers in Zurich, Switzerland, became impatient with the pace of change and called for a sharper break with Catholic tradition. Nicknamed Anabaptists, or "re-baptizers," because they insisted on baptizing only those adults who were willing to live a life of obedience to Scripture, they were severely persecuted by civil authorities for refusing to take up arms, swear oaths, or acknowledge infant baptism, which, not coincidentally, was used to confer citizenship and determine taxation and conscription for war. The subsequent bloody persecution of Anabaptists, which is chronicled in both the solemn hymns still sung in Amish church services and in the *Martyrs' Mirror*, an eleven-hundred-page book kept in many Amish homes, created a skeptical and even fearful view of the outside world.

Over the next 150 years, the Swiss Anabaptist movement successfully spread into northern Europe, but in 1693 a serious breach occurred within the church. Jakob Ammann, a recent but bold convert, proposed a series of measures to tighten up church discipline. Most controversial was his call to extend the ban on Communion for excommunicated members to an all-out shunning in daily life of those who had been excommunicated. In the aftermath of a heated showdown between Ammann and Hans Reist, a senior Swiss Anabaptist bishop, the followers of Ammann's version of shunning became known as Amish.[19] Facing social turmoil, intermittent persecution, and land shortages over the next few decades, the first wave of about five hundred Amish settlers sailed to the United States during the 1700s, settling in Pennsylvania. A second, larger wave of Amish immigrants came in the early to mid 1800s. All faced danger and hardship in adapting to life on the frontier. Curiously, the Amish no longer exist in Europe, as those who remained ended up joining more progressive churches.[20] By 2009, the Amish in North America numbered nearly two hundred fifty thousand in twenty-eight states and Ontario, Canada. These contemporary Amish communities all share the same compelling and unifying story of persecution in Europe, migration to the New World, and the challenges of frontier life.

Perhaps the most powerful symbol of the cultural distinctiveness of the Amish is the use of Pennsylvania Dutch, or Deitsch, one of a handful of minority languages in the United States that is neither endangered nor supported by continual arrivals of immigrants.[21] Of the original Pennsylvania Dutch speakers in the United States, less than 4 percent were Amish (most were Lutheran immigrants from Germany), but Mark Louden estimates that in another twenty years the Amish will likely be the sole speakers of the language.[22] Not to be confused with the Dutch spoken in the Netherlands, Pennsylvania Dutch retains the morphology, phonology, and syntax of its Palatine roots in spite of influence from the English lexicon.

Today, almost all Amish are functionally bilingual in Pennsylvania Dutch and English; however, domains of usage are sharply separated.[23] Pennsylvania Dutch dominates in most in-group settings, such as the dinner table and preaching in church services. In contrast, English is used for most reading and writing. English is also the medium of instruction in schools and is used in business transactions and often, out of politeness, in situations involving interactions with non-Amish. Finally, the Amish read prayers and sing in Standard, or High, German (Hoch Deitsch) at church services.[24] The distinctive use of three different languages serves as a powerful conveyor of Amish identity.

The basic organizational units of Amish society foster oral communication and face-to-face interaction. Perhaps the most social encompassing institution apart from the extended family is the church district. Each church district is comprised of twenty-five to forty families who live in relatively close proximity and attend church services, including weddings and funerals, in family homes instead of in a separate meetinghouse. Based on passages in the New Testament, ordained leaders greet each other at church services with a kiss on the lips, known as the Holy Kiss or the kiss of peace.[25] With some exceptions, a church district is typically presided over by a bishop, two ministers, and a deacon, all of whom are married male church members who have been selected by the casting of lots.[26]

Each church district is governed by an *Ordnung*, which serves as the "Amish blueprint for expected behavior."[27] Containing both prescriptions and proscriptions, the Ordnung is an understanding of expectations that is usually handed down orally through the generations and reviewed and modified twice a year before Communion. Congregational votes are taken on important matters, but they usually follow the bishop's recommendation, a system John Hostetler has dubbed the "patriarchal democratic" type.[28] Because each church district has flexibility to construct its own Ordnung, interesting variations arise between congregations. But the church district is clearly the institution that controls social change in the Amish community.

A cluster of church districts that share similar Ordnung are said to be "in fellowship" with each other and are called an affiliation. Full fellowship means that districts can exchange ministers at church services and funerals and that members can take Communion in one another's church. Amish Communion services still include foot-washing as a sign of continued commitment to the belief that, as one bishop put it, "I need you and you need me."

In the Holmes County Settlement, four affiliations account for approx-

Males and females sit facing one another in church services, which are usually held in a member's barn or shop every other Sunday. Photograph by Doyle Yoder.

imately 97 percent of all church districts: the Swartzentrubers, the Andy Weavers, the Old Order, and the New Order. Of these, the Old Order districts are by far the most numerous. Since each affiliation defines non-conformity in different ways, this dimension of religious life is one of the key sources of variation within an Amish settlement. The term *settlement* is widely used to refer to a geographically contiguous cluster of church districts, regardless of affiliation. In any given settlement, however, non-Amish homes are likely to be interspersed, to varying degrees, with those of Amish families.

Amish of all persuasions share a general set of orienting beliefs that distinguish them from their non-Amish neighbors. First is the belief in the necessity of living a life modeled after Jesus Christ and based in Scripture. Ideally, the Amish try to live out their faith in their daily lives. In this endeavor, they are guided by a strong belief in *Gelassenheit*, which is best translated as a spirit of selflessness, humility, or meekness. Kraybill describes Gelassenheit as the "master disposition" of the Amish and argues that the "yielded self" of Gelassenheit "stands in contrast to the bold, aggressive individualism of modern culture."[29] The sharp contrast between the dangers of "high-mindedness" (*Hochmut*) and the virtues of humility (*Demut*) is captured in a slogan and song (sung to the tune of "Jingle Bells") whose lyrics are "J-O-Y, J-O-Y, J-O-Y must be . . . Jesus first, Yourself last, Others in between."

A second key pillar of the Amish worldview is the notion of separation from the world, which finds expression in the clear distinction Amish draw between "our people" and "the English," between the church and the world. This dualistic mind-set, forged during the years of persecution and still acquired by children at a very young age, is usually traced to biblical passages such as Romans 12:2, which warn that believers should not conform to the world. It also gives rise to other dualisms that characterize the Amish worldview, such as the distinctions between obedience and disobedience, hard work and idleness, purity and impurity.

The beliefs in Gelassenheit and in separation from the world find expression in numerous cultural practices that serve as visible symbols of Amish identity to both insiders and outsiders. Plain dress (including head coverings for males and females and beards but no mustaches for married male church members) and horse-and-buggy transportation (or, more specifically, rejection of ownership of automobiles) are the two most obvious signs of nonconformity in daily life. The doctrine of nonresistance is another important feature, which distinguishes the Amish from sectarian groups in other parts of the world that have been engulfed in violent confrontations. Because they believe in avoiding force and excessive competition in social relations, the Amish do not file lawsuits or hold political office, and they do not serve in the military, in police departments, or on juries. In addition, all affiliations still place a cap on formal schooling at eighth grade, and one- or two-room schoolhouses have increasingly dotted the terrain in Amish settlements over the past fifty years. Both nonresistance and the limit on formal schooling are designed to combat the sin of pride, which one bishop defined succinctly as "when I think I'm a better person than you." The fact that Amish of all affiliations still try to live simply and to place limits on technology is also a powerful offshoot of the basic doctrine of nonconformity to the world.

From a bird's-eye view, this panoply of shared history and culture has created one of the most remarkable stories of cultural persistence in American history, perhaps in the world. Like a high-quality filter, these cultural dispositions seem to have insulated the Amish from the most detrimental aspects of modernity while ensuring an enviable level of community-mindedness. To many non-Amish, the costs—limitations on educational and job opportunities, sharply prescribed gender roles, and provincialism, among others—are too high, but it is indisputable that the Amish approach demonstrates how security and quality of life can accrue to people who collectively have the courage to rein in the negative excesses of personal freedoms and ambitions.

A worm's-eye view, however, provides a picture that is somewhat at odds with conventional accounts that portray Amish culture through a series of generalizations about "core values." For one, in spite of the success of micro-enterprises and the high retention rate of young people staying in the church, the Amish themselves continue to worry about the internal state of their faith. It is increasingly difficult to get the youth to appreciate the hardships suffered by earlier generations. The English language is being used in more and more situations, and learning high German is not always a top priority for the young people. For another, the range of practices included under the tent of Gelassenheit or under the umbrella injunction to remain separate from the world is increasingly diverse. There may be agreement in theory that all Amish maintain a "spirit" of nonconformity, but in practice there is a huge cultural chasm, for example, between those Amish groups that can own computers (with some restrictions on use), at one end of the spectrum, and those who are not even allowed to buy processed Velveeta cheese, at the other. Amish definitions of what is "worldly" have evolved over time, but such definitions have also become increasingly differentiated within the Amish community. As usual, the proof is in the details, for the realities of Amish life are far more complicated than the idyllic portraits in tourist guidebooks would suggest.

Central Concepts and Guiding Questions

The central argument of this book is that the Holmes County Amish are involved in an unprecedented and complex process of change that is driven both by external (global, national or regional, and local) forces and by internal social and cultural distinctions. This dialectic results in "border work" that transforms everyone, but not in the same way. Unraveling how and why the process of change is unfolding similarly and differently across families, church districts and affiliations, workplaces, schools, and health care institutions is one of our major goals. In telling this story, we have tried to dispense with scholarly jargon in favor of a more readable account. Still, we believe it is important at the outset to introduce three key components of the conceptual model we use to explain dynamism and diversity in the Amish community.

First, we see social change and difference among the Amish as a product of crosscutting external and internal forces.[30] In the Amish case, the external conditions and pressures come in many forms but include economic competition from abroad, federal regulations, and land pressures created by tourism and urban sprawl.[31] But most external pressures in the Holmes County Settlement have their origins at the state or local level (for example, highway safety, zoning, or health regulations) and affect different segments of the Amish in different ways. At the local level, the health department's concern over "gray water" primarily affects the Swartzentruber Amish,[32] while a school board decision about whether to "cater to the Amish" may affect Amish of all affiliations who live in a particular school district. At the state level, the attempt to establish a streamlined sales tax primarily affects Amish furniture makers who ship outside the county, whereas the decision to require that assistance for the mentally and physically handicapped be channeled through Medicaid forces accommodations in the financial strategies of Amish families who have special-needs children. Assuming that both outside pressures and internal responses are multidimensional, our study takes a fine-grained approach by asking which external pressures lead to what kinds of responses.

Although many Amish practices are shaped by outside forces, the seeds of change sometimes lie within. Internal characteristics such as settlement type (age, location, size, and history) and the number and distribution of affiliations within a settlement shape responses to external forces in powerful ways. Internal doctrinal disagreements, sometimes triggered by personality conflicts and hidden from outsiders, lead to different degrees of separation from the world among Amish church districts and affiliations. In the Holmes County Settlement, disputes over the application of shunning, the use of tobacco, control over the young folks, and the assurance of salvation have been at the center of several high-profile schisms.

These external and internal forces interact in complex ways. The increasing entanglement with the market economy, for example, has lead to greater socioeconomic disparities in a "flat" society that has long downplayed differences in wealth. One New Order man we interviewed referred to Amish who focus on educational and economic attainment as the "uppity-class Amish." His comment, though atypical, raises questions: how widespread are the seeds of class consciousness, and how do Amish millionaires and other wealthy individuals use their money in culturally appropriate or inappropriate ways? Our study examines how the growing purchasing power of the Amish has created new hobbies, patterns of consumption, access to health care, ways of thinking about leisure time, and forms of influence within Amish church districts.

Similarly, the new occupational niches occupied by the Holmes County Amish have created new challenges for family life. The shared labor and rhythms of daily life on the farm, which created a coherent, if not uniform, worldview among the Amish, have given way to a multiplicity of work situations with very uneven cultural implications. A husband who takes his lunch pail and "works away" may leave his wife at home alone with the children, while his own day may involve interaction with primarily Amish co-workers at a local factory or working side-by-side with non-Amish on a construction crew in a nearby town. Alternatively, he may wake up and simply walk next door to his furniture shop; its proximity keeps the family together but potentially brings new technologies closer to the home. Or the entire family may participate in running a greenhouse business, just as everyone would have pitched in on the farm. Each of these work situations has different implications for gender roles and for the socialization of children, as well as for contact with worldly values such as individualism, pride, and competition. A framework in which social change is viewed as a product of crosscutting external and internal forces allows us to ask how the Amish negotiate cultural boundaries in a context of competing pressures for integration and separation.

A second key component of our theoretical model is a focus on border work, the redefinition and defense of cultural boundaries that goes on at cultural margins. Periods of rapid social and economic change often involve the deployment of new symbols and practices to distinguish one group from another.[33] Rather than seeing only one cultural border between the Amish and the non-Amish, however, we believe the various Amish affiliations themselves function as status groups in the Weberian sense, namely, that "above all else a specific style of life is expected from all those who wish to belong to the circle."[34] Each group, the Swartzentruber Amish, the Andy Weaver Amish, and the Old and New Order Amish, can be seen as trying to exercise its status privilege by monopolizing certain material goods, dress, and even potential marriage partners.

In some cases, the construction and defense of boundaries become more significant than the cultural practices that differentiate two groups. The difference between Old Order buggies with steel-clad wheels and New Order buggies with rubber on the rims, for instance, is usually interpreted as a result of different value orientations. Yet the Old Order Amish have adopted other technologies that are far more progressive than rubber tires. A more probable explanation was offered by one Amish man: "The only reason the Old Order don't have rubber wheels is because the New Order did it first."

Our study thus explores the status rankings among Amish affiliations and the contemporary symbols of purity and pollution that are used to maintain boundaries both within the Amish community and with the non-Amish world. We look especially closely at the edges of community, which are defined by rules and rituals that designate who belongs, who has authority, and who can communicate with whom.[35] For example, we analyze the experiences of the ex-Amish as a window on the struggle to maintain the integrity of community, as well as teenagers who are in the rumspringa period and hold a "liminal" status in Amish society.[36] On the one hand, this focus leads us to ask very specific questions about which cultural boundaries are relatively permeable, which ones are fixed, and under what circumstances. On the other hand, it allows us to raise more general questions about the development of internal contradictions within a group and whether regular breaches of cultural rules should be seen as problematic (the Amish are sometimes accused of hypocrisy, for example) or as a key component of cultural renewal.[37]

The third and final piece of our conceptual model involves the notion of terrains of tension, which we define as the broad cultural dilemmas that are triggered by the interaction of internal and external forces. We argue that these dilemmas generally center on competing interpretations of the relative importance of community and the individual and, more specifically, on how to weigh values and interests, structure and agency, and freedom and security. At the broadest level, the relationship between the community and the individual is open to different interpretations. To some, community is seen as smothering rather than providing security for the individual. In this image, the community and the autonomous individual are in an antagonistic rather than complementary relationship. To others, the relationship is positive because the individual reaches perfection through the community, with the community providing economic, social, and religious security, thereby eliminating the danger of the loss of freedom that can come from insecurity. Advocates echo the sentiment related by the poet William Watson: "The stars of heaven are free because in the amplitude of liberty their joy is to obey the laws."[38]

The sociologist Emile Durkheim conveyed a similar view of the relationship between the requirements of community and the freedom of the individual: "The individual submits to society and this submission is the condition of his liberation. For man freedom consists in deliverance from blind, unthinking physical forces; he achieves this by opposing against them the great and intelligent force of society, under whose protection he shelters."[39] This latter view is one that is often attributed to all Amish by outside observers, but we argue that internal debate about the relative importance of the individual and the community is a recurring feature of Amish life.

More specifically, the relative weight given to values or interests may vary by affiliation, by church district, and even by particular circumstances. Like the rest of us, Amish individuals often make decisions that are informed by a mixture of cultural-religious values and material interests. The weight of community traditions, rules, and organization may also vary in the extent to which it limits the agency of individuals and their ability to freely choose particular paths of action. The connection between freedom and security is equally complex. Some define freedom in terms of choices and independence (i.e., freedom "to"), while others privilege a Rooseveltian view of freedom, freedom "from" insecurity, want, and fear.

Taken together, these terrains of tension suggest that viewing the modern and the traditional as singular opposing forces is far too simplistic to capture the dynamics of change in Amish communities. We assume rather that Amish groups experience "modernity" and "tradition" in different ways.[40] It is certainly true that, in general, the Amish do not adhere to key dimensions of modernity such as specialization, pluralism, rationalization, individuation, and choice.[41] But if the "modern" emerges in the form of "customary practice" (that is, if "new" cultural practices become routine and are perceived as "the way we've always done it" in a relatively short period of time), then it is hard to overlook the multiple interpretations of tradition and modernity that exist among the Holmes County Amish.[42] We must ask how and why each affiliation and each church district has made different choices in defining separation from the world. We must also inquire about the consequences of these competing definitions of tradition for interaction among the Amish themselves and for their integration with the larger world.

One outcome of our theoretical model is that we view Amish cultural identity in plural terms. The popular notion that the Amish are "plain and simple" has perpetuated the myth of a homogeneous people that is increasingly at odds with the complexity and diversity of Amish identities. It is no longer a secret that Amish church districts of every persuasion have negotiated compromises with worldly influences ranging from telephones and state bureaucracy to the modern health care system, tourism, and transportation by motor vehicle.[43] In emphasizing change and diversity, we do not deny the continuities with the past, nor do we disagree that all Amish share certain cultural inclinations and sensibilities. But we believe that many popular and academic accounts of the Amish have overstated the degree of coherence and integration in Amish communities, failing to even raise questions about the points of conflict and convergence between cultural knowledge and practices produced in the different contexts of work, family, church, and school. Thomas Meyers and Steven Nolt's image of Amish culture as "a patchwork quilt that combines different colors and shapes with a common thread" aptly captures this diversity amid unity, though perhaps not the accompanying tensions.[44]

The Origins and Growth of the Holmes County Settlement

Though centered in Holmes County, the Holmes County Settlement actually includes small parts of Wayne, Stark, Tuscarawas, Coshocton, Knox, and Ashland counties, as shown in the map of Ohio Amish settlements. The Holmes County Settlement is both the oldest and the largest in Ohio, but it is by no means the only one. More than fifty smaller Amish settlements have been established in other parts of the state, including the Geauga Settlement, the fourth-largest in the world (see appendix B for the location, the date of origin, and the affiliation of each settlement and the number of church districts each has). The roughly thirty thousand Amish who live in the Holmes County Settlement are about one-seventh of the total population of the Amish in the United States, well ahead of the population estimates for the two next-largest settlements, those in Lancaster County, Pennsylvania, and in Elkhart and LaGrange counties, Indiana. The large size of a settlement has many implications, but in the Holmes County context, it means that most Amish live relatively close to a town and that they have ample opportunity to interact with Amish from several affiliations as well as with non-Amish tourists and locals.

Amish settlements throughout the United States and Canada show considerable variation in not only size and age but also migration history, regional and local context, and mix of church Ordnung.[45] Like all Amish settlements, the Holmes County Settlement is distinctive in several ways, including its history. According to local historians, "Ohio fever" began running high among the Amish in the early 1800s. The first Amish settlers arrived in the Sugarcreek and Walnut Creek areas from Somerset County in southwestern Pennsylvania around 1809 as part

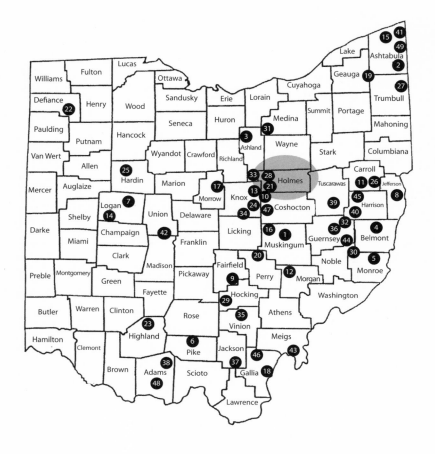

1. Adamsville
2. Andover
3. Ashland-Shiloh
4. Barnesville
5. Beallsville
6. Beaver
7. Belle Center
8. Bergholz
9. Bremen
10. Brinkhaven-Danville
11. Carrollton
12. Chesterhill-Stockport
13. Danville-Butler

14. De Graff
15. Dorsett–Cherry Valley
16. Frazeysburg
17. Fredericktown–Bellville
18. Gallipolis
19. Geauga
20. Glenford-Somerset
21. Glenmont-Brinkhaven
22. Hicksville
23. Hillsboro-Leesburg
24. Howard–East Knox
25. Kenton–Mt. Victory
26. Kilgore

27. Kinsman
28. Lakeville–Big Prairie
29. Laurelville
30. Lewisville
31. Lodi-Homerville
32. Londonderry
33. Loudenville-McKay
34. Martinsburg-Utica
35. McArthur
36. Middlebourne
37. Oak Hill
38. Peebles
39. Peoli–Port Washington

40. Piedmont
41. Pierpont-Conneaut
42. Plain City
43. Pomeroy
44. Salesville–Quaker City
45. Scio
46. Vinton
47. Walhonding-Warsaw
48. West Union–Winchester
49. Williamsfield

Ohio Amish settlements, 2008. Ohio is home to nearly fifty Amish settlements that vary
in age, number of church districts, affiliation, and community of origin. Adapted from *Ohio
Amish Directory*; and Luthy, "Amish Settlements across America." Compiled by Mary Schantz.

of the westward expansion of the first wave of migrants who settled in Lancaster County. President Thomas Jefferson signed deeds for land near Walnut Creek settled by a young Amish man named Jonas Stutzman. Several years later other Amish moved to Smithville in Wayne County, a settlement that eventually died out. Although the Amish clearly benefited from the systematic and violent expulsion of native peoples by the U.S. government, no reports exist of Amish settlers joining in the aggression; in fact, in the early days of the Holmes County Settlement, Indian and Amish farmers lived side by side on peaceful terms along the Sugar Creek.[46] By 1835, roughly two hundred fifty Amish families were living in the Holmes County Settlement.[47]

The years between 1850 and 1870 are known as a time of division between conservative-minded and progressive Amish in the large settlements in Pennsylvania, Ohio, and Indiana; however, the conflict in Holmes County was particularly bitter. Members differed over whether the church Ordnung was to be changed only in rare cases or whether it was to be used as a tool of adaptation, "a necessary means of remaining relevant."[48] In Wayne and Holmes counties, for example, some leaders argued over whether stream baptism was acceptable. Change-minded Amish such as Bishop Jacob D. Yoder, who also engaged in other "worldly" practices such as mule racing and horse trading, argued that stream baptism should be as valid as traditional baptism as part of an indoor church service. But other issues of adaptation to the world lurked behind the conflict over mode of baptism. To try to achieve reconciliation, leaders organized a national ministers' meeting attended by seventy-two ordained leaders from five states and held in Wayne County in June 1862. But most of the attendees were progressives, and the reports were disappointing to conservatives, leaving one bishop to lament, "If we wish to destroy a weed, we must pull it up by the roots; otherwise, it will just keep growing."[49]

Over the next few years, tensions persisted, and in 1865 the ministers met again in Wayne County. Before the meeting, however, thirty-four tradition-minded leaders from Holmes County drew up a manifesto staking out their position against such things as carnivals, fancy clothing, commercial insurance, unnecessary household furnishings, and "the singing of catchy, popular hymns with spiritually shallow lyrics."[50] The majority of the more moderate ministers largely ignored their concerns, and the conservatives withdrew, formalizing the two paths that mid-nineteenth-century Amish interaction with the wider world ultimately produced. The Amish-Mennonite majority took a variety of paths toward the American mainstream, whereas the minority Old Order Amish clung to a more conservative understanding of the Ordnung.

The Amish divided several more times in the first half of the twentieth century over such issues as farm technologies, telephones, and cars. The actions of the young people and relations with excommunicated individuals also entered into these heated debates. In these years, several high-profile conflicts with the U.S government also occurred. For example, many Amish were harassed as "German sympathizers" during World War I for their refusal to join the army and buy war bonds. Federal officials pressured Rudy Yoder, a local Amish man, to report to Camp Jefferson, Missouri, and then threatened him with death if he refused to begin rifle training.[51]

During the 1940s and 1950s, serious conflicts over schools emerged when Wayne County officials tried to enforce the Bing Act mandating public school attendance until age sixteen. The subsequent arrests and trials in Wooster contributed to an Amish skepticism of Wayne County administrators that continues to this day. Other conflicts arose when local Amish men served in hospitals or in other forms of alternative (I-W) service during and after World War II. Holmes County native Aden A. Miller was even featured in a *New York Times* article when he was sent to a federal work camp prison for three years because he refused I-W employment.[52] And the shocking murder in 1957 of an Old Order man, Paul Coblentz, by two recently released convicts led to a formal plea to the governor for a stay of execution and to letters of forgiveness sent to the cell of one of the men convicted of the murder[53]—an Amish response strikingly similar to that seen after the 2006 Nickel Mines school shooting in Pennsylvania.[54]

In spite of these conflicts with the outside world, most Amish found respite from their troubles on their farms. The soil and climate of the Holmes County Settlement proved to be very conducive to Amish farming techniques and to supporting large families. Indeed, the growth in the Amish population in the settlement over the past three decades should put to rest once and for all the misperception that the Amish are on the verge of extinction. Population studies estimate the doubling time for the Holmes County Settlement to be a mere 22.5 years.[55] From 1981 to

2005, for example, the number of church members increased from 6,751 to 12,537, while the total population (including children) increased from 13,994 to 26,722.[56] The growth to 221 church districts in 2009 is also remarkable, considering that there were only 9 church districts in the Holmes County Settlement in 1913.

These rates for the Holmes County Settlement far exceed the population growth rates for most countries in the world and, insofar as they mirror trends in Amish communities across the nation, support the claim that the Amish are one of the fastest-growing groups in the United States. As of December 2008, there were 410 Amish settlements in twenty-eight states and Ontario, more than half of which had been founded since 1990. In 2008 alone, 16 new settlements were founded, an average of one every twenty-three days.[57]

The Amish Flavor of Holmes County

Today the Amish account for approximately 45 percent of Holmes County's population and lend a distinctive flavor to life in this region of northeastern Ohio. Consider, for example, that out of the eighty-eight counties in the state of Ohio, Holmes County is among the seven lowest in per capita income;[58] the western portion of Holmes County is even designated as an "Appalachian" district, qualifying the county for federal and state assistance. Yet many of the other demographic and economic indicators that typically cluster with low per capita incomes are absent. In 2007 Holmes County had the third-lowest unemployment rate (4.1%) of all Ohio counties.[59] The crime rate was among the lowest in the state as well. Moreover, in 2005 Holmes County had the highest rate of exports to imports of all Ohio counties, testimony to the hundreds of wholesale woodworking shops run by Amish entrepreneurs. At the same time, it led the state in the number of licensed dairy farms and the number of acres planted in oats.[60]

Ohio's "Amish country" has also become a popular tourist destination, an important reminder of how outside perceptions of the Amish have markedly changed since the mid-1900s. One local historian remembers that in the 1950s and 1960s the Amish were considered unpatriotic, backward, and obstructionist. "I remember well when the Amish weren't popular. If you wanted to insult someone, you'd call him a 'dumb Amishman,' and that was the worst." Today, such sentiments are rarely heard. Tourists are especially inclined to see the Amish in positive terms, either as a saving remnant of bygone days or, more pragmatically, as a source of high-quality wood products, quaint crafts, or savory food. The director of the Holmes County Chamber of Commerce and Tourism Bureau put it this way: "Our number one industry is manufacturing. Number two is tourism. And number three is agriculture. Tourists wouldn't come here if it weren't for the beautiful agricultural scene: the shocks of wheat and corn and the pastoral, rolling hills with the laundry out on the lines. And if we didn't have the tourism, we wouldn't have all that furniture manufacturing going on. So those three cannot exist without each other." There is no question that Holmes County officials and the non-Amish business community highly value the Amish presence as vital to the area's economic base.

Despite their growing numbers, the Amish presence throughout the settlement is uneven. The large majority of Amish church districts, private schools, successful Amish businesses, and tourist destinations are in the eastern part of the settlement, represented by a crescent of towns stretching from Kidron, Mount Eaton, and Mount Hope in the north to Berlin, Walnut Creek, and Sugarcreek in the south. The western portion of the settlement is far more sparsely populated with Amish, as the map of Amish schoolhouses in Holmes County shows (see chapter 5). Route 83 from Wooster to Millersburg and south is an unofficial dividing line separating the mostly Amish and mostly non-Amish sides of the county. The roots of this division go back to the tendency of families of German descent to settle in the eastern areas.

Amish affiliations are also unevenly distributed across the settlement. Ironically, the majority of the more conservative Swartzentruber and Andy Weaver districts tend to be located in Wayne County, toward the northern end of the settlement, closer to the thoroughly "English" towns of Orrville and Wooster. The New Order and most Old Order districts cluster in the central and southern parts of the settlement, from Mount Hope south to Berlin and beyond. To some extent, these residential patterns shape the frequency of interaction between Amish affiliations and between the Amish and the non-Amish.

From the time of its incorporation, Holmes County itself has always been a relatively conservative and homogeneous community, with most

Each year millions of tourists visit Amish-themed shopping destinations in Berlin, Walnut Creek, and Sugarcreek, Ohio. Tourist establishments are rarely owned by the Amish. Photograph courtesy of Charles Hurst.

inhabitants originally coming from Germany, Switzerland, England, Scotland, and Ireland. Census figures show that in 2000 the composition of the county was 98.8 percent white, making it one of the most racially homogeneous counties in the United States.[61] Holmes County is also known for its political conservatism. In a state where George Bush edged John Kerry by a 53−47 percent margin in the 2004 presidential election, the returns in Holmes County showed 75.5 percent supporting Bush and 24 percent voting for Kerry. Although most Amish do not vote unless a local issue affects them directly, the overwhelming majority sympathize with positions held by the Republican Party's older conservative wing, which, as one Amish bishop put it, believes that "a true conservative is a person who conserves what is good." An Old Order Amish man, now deceased, used to joke that he could count the Amish who supported Democrats on one hand.

In terms of the broader religious context, most of the mainline Christian churches are represented in the Holmes County Settlement, but so too are more assimilated Anabaptist churches such as the Brethren, the Beachy Amish, and various Mennonite congregations. Together, these Anabaptist churches make up a large group of non-Amish people who have Amish roots or share enough theological similarities that they are sympathetic to Amish concerns. The Brethren, represented in the area by several distinctive offshoots of the German Baptist Brethren, for the most part have become too political, evangelical, and nonpacifist for Amish tastes.[62] The Beachy Amish, however, are literally "one step up" from the most liberal Amish group, the New Order Christian Fellowship. Sometimes called the Beachy Amish Mennonite Fellowship, they originated in Pennsylvania in the 1920s. In addition to driving cars, most Beachy Amish install electricity in their homes, use computers and phones, and dress less plainly than Old Order and New Order groups. Yet in spite of their name, the Beachy Amish are not considered Amish by most people in the Holmes County Settlement, primarily because they allow ownership of cars (though dark-colored ones only).[63]

Still, many Amish feel an affinity with these other Anabaptist groups born of shared history and theology. This is especially true of the large Mennonite population in the Holmes County Settlement, most of whom have parents or grandparents who are or were Amish. Some former Amish are deeply critical of the Amish lifestyle, but when taken together, members of other Anabaptist churches can be seen as part of a sizable "Amish cocoon," to use a phrase coined by Robert Kidder and John Hostetler.[64] These persons sympathetic with Amish life partially insulate the Amish from outside pressures, provide legal, medical, and other assistance when necessary, and are one of the definite attractions of the Holmes County Settlement to many Amish families.

The presence of more evangelical churches is a final feature of the local religious context. Most of these churches are small, but a few actively seek converts among the Amish population by having their members volunteer as drivers when the Amish want to use a motor vehicle rather than a horse and buggy for errands, visiting, or trips. It is tempting to lump the Amish in with such "fundamentalist" churches because of their shared belief in a literal interpretation of the Bible and in divinely ordained gender roles, including the restriction of women's roles in the ministry and hierarchy of the church.[65] However, with some exceptions, the Amish are uncomfortable with overt proselytizing, with individual interpretations of the Bible, and with the more charismatic and emotional aspects of fundamentalism. And they do not actively channel their religion into politics. The Amish are also far more likely to restrict the use of technology than are evangelical fundamentalists, who may drive nice cars, live in stately houses, and use television, radio, and the Internet.

At first glance, the Holmes County Settlement appears to represent a homogeneous Amish population nestled in a relatively insular and conservative region. Consistent with this view, tourists visiting Berlin, Walnut Creek, and surrounding areas are offered a return to a supposedly authentic premodern world in which Amish behavior is traditional, communal, and unreflective. Upon closer inspection, however, the Amish in the Holmes County Settlement could stand as the poster children for "plain diversity." Moreover, their lives are filled not with uncritical thought but with complex choices and trade-offs that are integral to the attempt to maintain a viable sectarian community in the midst of postindustrial American society. In the following two chapters, we explore Amish dynamism and diversity in the key institution that regulates modernity—the church.

CHAPTER 2

The Origins of Religious Diversity

Why do churches split? Seldom for the reasons stated.
—A New Order businessman

The Anabaptist Escalator among the Holmes County Amish

Out of the two major waves of Amish immigration to the United States in the eighteenth and nineteenth centuries, at least nineteen Anabaptist groups have sprung up.[1] Roughly half have formed the relatively progressive Mennonite or Beachy churches, but the remainder still classify themselves as Amish. This multiplicity of Amish identities is the result of disagreements about "where to draw the boundary between the church and the outside world and how to define nonconformity."[2] While each affiliation considers itself to be true to Anabaptist ideals, each has defined those ideals in different ways. In Holmes County, the result is widely differing cultural and religious practices within a single settlement. The reality of church schism stands in sharp contrast to the outside perception of the Amish as a unified people and has raised serious questions about the meaning and limits of community even within Amish circles.

As we survey this landscape of fracture in the Holmes County Settlement, several questions emerge. What factors lie at the root of these splits? Disagreements over theology? Acceptable use of new technologies? Personality conflicts among religious leaders? What are the breaking-off points and the corresponding talismans of identity that are seen as non-negotiable by different groups? And what are the consequences of these schisms for the interaction between Amish groups?

For all the talk about the dangers of pride in the Amish community, the groups that have resulted from these schisms share many features of status groups. As noted earlier, the Amish themselves use the terms *low* and *high* to classify churches and affiliations in terms of their degree of worldliness. In general, the lower, or more conservative, churches observe stricter discipline, separation from the world, and social avoidance, whereas the higher, or more progressive, churches have made more compromises with technology and emphasize a more personal and reflective religious experience. Value judgments are deeply embedded in the use of these terms as well. The more conservative churches see themselves as humble adherents to the religious core and criticize what they see as "drift" in the higher-church communities. By contrast, the more liberal churches often chide the lower churches for what they perceive as devotion to "man-made traditions" rather than "true spirituality."[3] However, the notion of a single continuum—running from conservative to progressive—along which every Amish affiliation can be conveniently placed somewhat oversimplifies the realities of Amish life. For example, the New Order affiliation is technologically progressive but morally and doctrinally conservative.

Two aspects of the broader context bear mentioning before we look at the specifics of the schisms. First, the defining dynamic in the Holmes County Settlement is the "sandwich effect" created by the existence of sizable and viable Amish affiliations at both ends of the spectrum. Nearly 50 conservative districts and 25 liberal districts stand as bookends for the roughly 140 church districts that comprise the main body of the Old Order. The presence of large numbers of Swartzentruber and Andy Weaver Amish, on the one hand, and New Order and New New Order Amish, on the other, represent the opposite ends of what Donald Kraybill has called the "Anabaptist escalator" and serve as constant reminders to the main body of Old Order Amish that they have both conservative and progressive choices. In total, eleven separate affiliations represent the Amish in the Holmes County Settlement, but several of these groups have only one or two church districts. Table 2.1 shows the relative size of the Holmes County Amish affiliations, running from the most conservative to the most liberal.

Second, church schism has been a recurrent feature of religious life in

Table 2.1. Amish church districts by affiliation, Holmes
County Settlement, 2009

Affiliation	Number
Swartzentruber–Andy Weaver	2
Swartzentruber–Mose Miller	3
Swartzentruber–Joe Troyer	14
Stutzman-Troyer	1
Roman	1
Andy J. Weaver	30
Old Order	140
Old Order Tobe	4
New Order	18
New Order Tobe	4
New Order Christian Fellowship	4
Total	221

Sources: Stephen Scott, Research Associate, Young Center for Anabaptist and Pietist
Studies, Elizabethtown College, Elizabethtown, PA; based on the 2009 *Raber's
New American Almanac.*

the Holmes County Settlement ever since the early 1900s, as shown in
figure 2.1. The cultural gap between the Amish and the non-Amish
in rural Ohio was fairly narrow in the early part of the twentieth century. As the speed of change in the wider society began to increase, Amish
church districts found themselves confronting a bewildering array of decisions about everything from appropriate farm technology to the activities of the young people to the conditions under which excommunication would be lifted. Most of the resulting controversies involved such a
thorny mixture of technology, doctrine, and personalities that they taxed
the resilience of Amish mechanisms for informal conflict resolution.

It is not easy to become familiar with the details of these church schisms,
because the Amish are reluctant to talk with outsiders about "church matters" and because the names of the protagonists can be as confusing as the
stories are complicated. As a result, these internal distinctions are usually
glossed over by the non-Amish. They are embedded in the Amish experience, however, and if we are to determine the very human causes and
consequences of church divisions, there can be no substitute for a case-by-
case approach. This chapter therefore provides an overview of the origins

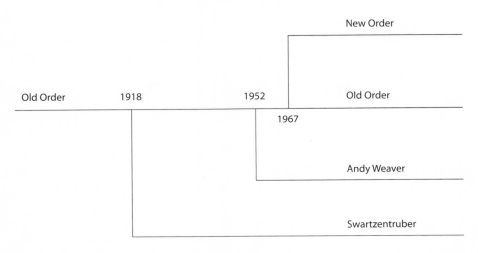

Fig. 2.1. The four main Amish affiliations in the Holmes County Settlement. Church schism has been a recurring feature of Amish religious life since the turn of the century. Courtesy of Mary Schantz.

and growth of the four largest affiliations, those shown in figure 2.1. (For a more detailed schematic of church schism in the Holmes County Settlement, see appendix C). We conclude the chapter by asking why certain issues sometimes lead to disciplinary action against church members and create schisms among church districts.

The "Ultraconservative" Amish: The Swartzentrubers

The Holmes County Settlement is the birthplace of the Swartzentruber Amish, the most conservative group, which emerged between 1913 and 1920. The Swartzentrubers have become legendary for their stubborn traditionalism, reflected in their windowless, no-frills carriages, large bonnets for women, wide-brimmed hats and untrimmed beards for men, and spartan homes. Most Swartzentruber men farm, even as many Amish in other affiliations have started small businesses. Moreover, the Swartzentrubers' construction of time and space is distinctive.[4] For example, they have refused to adopt "fast time" (daylight savings time) and have tried to stem the tide of modernity by flatly rejecting such conveniences as indoor plumbing, power mowers, weed-eaters, milking machines, linoleum floors, and community phone booths. In addition, customs such as smoking and bed courtship continue in most Swartzentruber church districts.[5]

Because the Swartzentruber Amish do not participate in the Amish directories and typically maintain a wall of silence toward outsiders, it is difficult to trace their growth.[6] According to David Luthy, however, they have established more than sixty-five settlements in twelve states and Ontario and are among the fastest-growing Amish affiliations.[7] In the Holmes County Settlement, the Swartzentrubers have nineteen church districts, concentrated in northern Wayne County. One Swartzentruber elder told us that because the price of land has gone up tremendously, "more than half of our children live outside the settlement."

Although the Swartzentrubers are best known for their minimalist approach to material conveniences, they have undergone several complex church divisions. Most scholars trace the split that created the Swartzentruber group back to Bishop Samuel E. Yoder of Apple Creek. In 1913 Yoder argued that members who joined the church and then left should be shunned until they repented and returned to the church. This strict interpretation of shunning was not supported by the main Old Order group, which wanted to allow the option of lifting the ban if the ex-member joined another Amish or Mennonite congregation and procured a letter saying the person was in "good standing." Such a description, however, hides more than it reveals.

Even in the first decade of the 1900s, when there were only nine church districts in the entire settlement, "cracks were beginning to appear" in the unity of the Old Order Amish. In 1913, two bishops from other settlements were called in to search out the trouble, which "proved to be a serious difference of opinion concerning 'Bann und Meidung' (excommunication and shunning)." The bishops recommended that members wishing to leave should be duly admonished not to, but if they departed, "we should feel we have done our duty and leave the matter to each church and to God." If the member "was disobedient and excommunicated by the church and later in a scriptural way taken out of the 'Bann' by the church he has now united with, then the original 'Bann und Meidung' should be removed."[8] All of the ministers except Sam Yoder accepted these recommendations. Yoder opposed any possible loopholes for leaving.

An even closer analysis by local historians reveals that the matter was further complicated because of Sam Yoder's personal and family prob-

These Swartzentruber girls help their parents sell hand-woven baskets by the roadside.
Photograph by Doyle Yoder.

lems. By 1919 Yoder had a following of 107 families in two districts. That
same year, a man in the Geauga Settlement confessed that he had had sexual relations with Yoder's daughter. Pressed to discipline her, Yoder stood
by his daughter. Believing he had been too lenient, roughly half (53) of
the families formed a separate group with Dan Wengerd, a co-minister
of Sam's, as their leader.[9] A three-day ministers' meeting, attended by
more than four dozen ordained leaders from four states, was then held in
Holmes County in November 1919 to resolve the conflict. When Yoder
did not show up at the meeting, Wengerd presented his view of the problems: (a) Sam Yoder does not want to commune with churches who do
not share his view of shunning; (b) he renounced communing with Ben
Yoder's church without consultation; (c) he did not carefully investigate
and discipline his daughter's conduct; (d) he did not bring to light that he
received compensation for his deceased son [who died in an Army camp];
and (e) his wife was not "abiding in her calling."[10]

   On the second day of the meeting, a group of five bishops was sent to
mediate with Yoder, but he would not meet with them. Finally the bish-

ops were able to have a lengthy conversation with him, but Yoder refused to have the differences examined, saying "the only way for them to attain peace was to call his things right." As a result, the five bishops concluded: "Therefore, we consider it inappropriate to continue to have fellowship with him, or to give him the kiss of peace at this time, unless he agrees to have the controversy thoroughly examined."[11] Ironically, Yoder's refusal to make peace bears striking resemblance to the circumstances under which Jacob Ammann broke from the Swiss Mennonite community in 1693.[12]

Given these personal difficulties, why did Yoder have a following at all? It appears he tapped into a wave of conservative sentiment on the part of Amish who had been wary of increased liberalism within the Old Order ever since the major split in the 1850s and 1860s that saw roughly two-thirds of the Amish join the Amish-Mennonites.[13] After the Yoder split was finalized, there were attempts to get the groups back together, and eventually the Dan Wengerd faction rejoined with the Old Order in 1934. Sam Yoder had died in 1932, but his group by then had formed distinctive practices and never rejoined the main body. Shortly after his death, rumors began to circulate that Sam Yoder had committed suicide by hanging himself in the chicken house, although Luthy finds evidence to the contrary.[14] The name Swartzentruber finally became attached to this group because after Yoder's death the bishops of both districts had that surname.[15]

For the first eighty years after the Sam Yoder incident, the Swartzentrubers in Wayne and Holmes Counties were unified, with one exception. In 1931 Abe Troyer and Jacob Stutzman led a small splinter group that became known as the Stutzman-Troyer Amish (or more commonly, the Troyer Amish).[16] The Troyer split created a ripple effect, however. First, a group led by a minister named Tobias Hochstetler broke off from the Troyer church in 1940 to form the Tobe affiliation.[17] Then in 1967, a group that came to be known as the New Order Tobe split with the Tobe and began affiliating with the Berlin district of the New Order Christian Fellowship.[18] Because the Tobe groups grew out of idiosyncratic conflicts that did not revolve around central doctrinal issues, neither has drawn more than a handful of supporters. The Stutzman-Troyer group has a larger following, though the large majority of its church districts are outside the Holmes County Settlement.

In the early 1990s, however, the Swartzentrubers experienced what insiders have described as one of the most difficult and painful schisms in Amish history. Once again, the controversy was centered in Wayne County, where the seeds of friction had been growing steadily for a decade or more before 1993. The major issue was control of the young folks.

Over time, a small number of Swartzentruber parents and church leaders had become concerned about the increasingly rowdy nature of youth activities and the passive stance taken by parents. Known by the term *demütig* [day-mee-tig], which means "low" or "humble," these individuals clamped down on the activities of the young people. For example, they would try to prohibit their teenagers from listening to radios, attending big parties, going to professional sporting events or rodeos, altering their hats to give them a cowboy flair, or smoking cigarettes instead of pipes or cigars. In many cases, demütig families were members of the very same church district as those they considered *lass* ("unconcerned"), families who tacitly condoned the "running around." But in several districts in the Holmes County Settlement, and in eight or nine districts in the nearby Lodi Settlement, the demütig families made up the majority and had strong backing from their bishops.[19] By the early 1990s, virtually every bishop, church district, and family were reputed to be in one of these two camps, or at least on a continuum of permissiveness with respect to youth activities. The situation was waiting to explode.

The "final straw" incident began one night in the early 1990s when several youth from one of the "wilder" groups went to a demütig minister's house to provoke him by playing loud music on the radio. The minister tried several tactics to establish the identity of the boys: shining his flashlight on the boys' faces (they hid them), spray-painting their buggies (they later washed the paint off), and unhitching their horses so that they couldn't get away. At this point, one of the boys struck the minister with a jockey stick, causing him to run to a neighbor's house and call the sheriff.

At first the minister said he did not know who the perpetrators were, but in the ensuing weeks, and after a passing milk-truck driver said he had seen the boys, the minister accused one of them. This boy was about to join church, and the accusation effectively held up his baptism. In the meantime, a church member stepped forward and confessed that he was actually one of the five responsible (the other four had not yet joined the church) and that the accused boy was innocent. Believing that the church member was covering for the other boy, the minister refused to accept his confession. The church congregation then split over whether to support their minister's subsequent recommendation to excommunicate the church member and hold up the other youth's baptism. In retaliation for his perceived lack of forgiveness, some of the boys returned to the minister's house at night, held him down, and cut his hair, an action that had tremendous symbolic implications.[20]

There were numerous attempts to resolve the conflict informally and locally. Most bishops favored getting the young folks back in good standing with the church, but two bishops, Eli J. Hershberger and Mose Miller, supported the minister. Their refusal to back down caused local bishops to "seek counsel" by calling bishops in from other settlements, as had been done for the Sam Yoder conflict. The logic in such cases is that, especially when excommunication is at stake and two sides cannot resolve the issue locally, an outside mediating committee is needed. If the mediating committee's ruling does not lead to reunification, in theory every Swartzentruber church district across the country must decide which side to support so that it can enforce the ban (or not).

As it turned out, two national mediating committee meetings were required. At the first meeting, which Miller and Hershberger did not attend, Joe Troyer, as one of the oldest Swartzentruber bishops in the Holmes County Settlement, represented the majority of church families, who favored reinstating the boys. Troyer secured the crucial consent of Isaac Keim and Andy Weaver from the Lodi Settlement. When these two bishops returned home, however, they discovered that their deacons, ministers, and some church members of the demütig persuasion strongly opposed the Troyer stance. So the bishops ultimately retracted their consent. At the second national meeting, Miller and Hershberger showed up but did not offer a handshake or the kiss of peace, indicating their decision to officially part ways. Their smaller faction became widely known in Amish circles as the Mosey Mosies, or M and Ms (because another ordained leader was also named Mose), and the larger group became known as the Joe Troyer branch, or simply the Joe church.

The church division was bitter, dividing many families, who had to choose between honoring the sanctioning of the boys, sought by the hard-line Mose Miller branch, or supporting the more lenient majority of Swartzentrubers in the Joe Troyer branch. One young man recalls being put out of the house at age twenty-one because his father supported the Mose Miller group while he, the son, wanted to be baptized in the Joe Troyer group. In a sense, the entire incident became a referendum on the demütig attempt to clamp down on rumspringa. From the standpoint of the Joe Troyers, the demütig group was taking a "holier-than-thou" attitude; conversely, the Mose Millers saw the Joe Troyers as tolerating too many worldly excesses.

This 1993 church division did not mark the end of conflict among the Swartzentrubers. About eight years later, the Mose Miller branch split over a disagreement about policy concerning a parochial school in the Lodi Settlement. When the school board did not settle the matter, Bishop Andy Weaver stepped in. But Isaac Keim disagreed with Weaver's handling of the matter. The two men had already been at odds over Keim's attempt to set up a drip line off a garden hose to irrigate his organic farm. In the Holmes County Settlement, the division did not affect the Joe Troyer group, but the Mose Miller churches sided with Keim. The end result is that there are now three nonfellowshipping Swartzentruber branches in the settlement, each of which considers itself the "true" Swartzentruber church.

To outsiders' eyes, the three groups do not differ much in their use of technology. But subtle distinctions exist. The Andy Weaver buggies use only one lantern along with some gray reflective tape instead of the two lanterns, set diagonally, used on the Joe Troyer and Mose Miller buggies. In addition, subtle differences in the length of women's dresses and the number of pleats in their caps and dresses distinguish the groups. In general, the "Joe" church is a bit "higher" than the other two. One Old Order Amish businessman who employs workers from the most conservative groups claims that he can usually tell which of the Swartzentruber branches individuals are from simply by observing their language and comportment. Members of the ultraconservative Andy Weaver faction are the most submissive and unquestioning of authority, the Mose Millers a little less so, and the Joe Troyers least of all.

Moderate Conservatives: The Andy Weaver or "Dan" Churches

About midcentury another conflict within the Old Order over the issue of shunning culminated in the birth of the Andy Weaver affiliation (no relation to the small Andy Weaver branch of the Swartzentruber

Buggy features are a key symbol of affiliation. The steel-clad wooden wheels (no rubber rims) and the lack of windows and reflective triangle on this buggy mark it as belonging to a Swartzentruber family. Photograph by Doyle Yoder.

church just discussed). The name comes from a bishop who led a break-away group, though this affiliation is locally known as the Dan church because all three of the ordained leaders at one church carried the name Dan. In 2009 the Andy Weavers numbered about thirty church districts in the settlement. They are generally distinguished from the Old Orders by more restrictions on technology, a harder line on shunning, and church Ordnung prohibiting parents from allowing their unbaptized children to own cars while living at home. However, they tend to be more tolerant of alcohol and smoking than the Old Order.

The critical issue that led Andy Weaver to withdraw from his Old Order church district was his belief that the church needed to uphold a stricter interpretation of shunning. Weaver was a very confident and articulate young leader, with many supporters among his extended family and in nearby church districts.[21] By the mid-1950s, about five Andy Weaver church districts (out of approximately fifty church districts in the settlement at that time) had formed through splits in Old Order churches and recruitment of like-minded members from more conservative affiliations. A closer analysis of one of these five districts that bordered Weaver's reveals the internal dynamics of the split.

Although the official division came in 1952, the seeds of conflict can be traced all the way back to the late 1930s, when a church member in the more conservative northern part of the settlement stopped attending church and bought a pickup truck. Consequently, he was excommunicated, though his wife and children remained Amish. At that time, the church district did not have a full slate of ordained leaders (called the ministers' bench) and was relying on two ministers and visiting bishops who came to conduct baptisms and communions. In the spring of 1942, two church members "undertook to hold up the council for communion" because they did not agree that the banned member with the truck should be shunned.[22] The two ministers replied that they would have it no other way, believing that they had scriptural backing for the ban and for shunning. A mediating committee of three bishops, two from Indiana and one from Delaware, was called, and they ruled that the shunning should be practiced as soon as one of the ministers became an ordained bishop. The two members did not agree with this decision, or with similar rulings by other mediating councils in the ensuing years. As a result, ill feelings and unrest persisted for the next decade, long after one of the ministers had been ordained bishop.

The issue surfaced again when a second member stopped attending church for a year. The bishop and other leaders went to see this man, who told them that he did not believe in observing the ban except in Communion. Moreover, he noted that others felt this way. The following Sunday the bishop related to the congregation what this man had said. The bishop then took the unprecedented step of asking all members who supported this more lenient interpretation of shunning to leave. In a dramatic showdown, roughly half of the church members stood up and walked out. Those who remained became one of the first Andy Weaver church districts. "I still remember that day in November 1952 like it was yesterday," recalled an Andy Weaver elder who was a young church member at the time. "Who was sitting next to who, what they said, it's still clear as day to me."

In the meantime, controversy swirled around those who had walked out because on the "off Sundays" they began singing and reading Scripture with no ordained leaders. In an attempt to isolate this group, ministers held a meeting and subsequently decided that no ordained leaders should lead church services for the wayward group.[23] But eventually one or two Old Order ministers came up from the southern part of the settlement and preached for the church in defiance of the council's ruling. Because of concern about a possible impending split, a mediating committee of three external bishops, one from Geauga County, one from Indiana, and one from Lancaster County, Pennsylvania, was called in the summer of 1953. They concluded that the bishop had done nothing unscriptural and that no ordained leaders should help this new group. In a meeting on August 18, 1953, the ministers of the original congregation further decided to work together with the disaffected group on the conditions that "the members who have started a separate church shall make a confession . . . and in the future they shall come to church and fill their office of duties as they have promised upon bowed knee."[24] The next day the leaders announced their verdict to all the parties involved. The bishop further explained that the first step in restoring peace was for everyone to come back and attend church regularly. On the following church Sunday, however, only one member from the disaffected group appeared.

Further complicating matters, over the next two years several sympathetic Old Order ministers began giving help to the new group. With the assistance of a visiting bishop, the new group held Communion in the spring and the fall of 1954 and eventually ordained a full slate of leaders. Such dramatic steps toward formalizing a church division led to an all-congregational ministers' gathering on September 27, 1955, in Holmes County that produced the following report: "Much was brought up about the trouble in the Orrville church, which was pitiful. Seemingly several of these members didn't want to go along with the others right anymore, but didn't have any ministers on their side. Much was said of these how they didn't mind the advices of other bishops and finally started gathering together themselves, reading and singing and so forth til finally other ministers came in and held church for them in their dissatisfied position."[25] The report also noted that disagreement over the issue of shunning had spread to other church districts in the area, forcing one bishop to move to another district because he "had much trouble and couldn't keep house like he should while so much disunity and ill feeling were coming."[26]

For nearly thirty years after the split, the Andy Weaver and Old Order churches differed little in the adoption of technology, with a few exceptions, such as restrictions on gas lighting in the homes and storm fronts on the buggies. In the past twenty years, however, the technological gap between the Old Order and the Andy Weavers has widened, as the former adopted milking machines, tractors in the field, portable generators, hydraulic power, and balers. Moreover, the Andy Weavers have resisted the adoption of everyday household conveniences such as bicycles, power lawnmowers, garden tillers, and rental freezers. One other major restriction was imposed in the 1960s when members in one church district were allowing their sons to have cars at age sixteen and members in another district refused to sign for drivers' licenses. The church leadership closed ranks and declared that parents who supported the purchase of cars by their children would be "set back" and refused Communion.[27] Today, all Andy Weaver young people know that the high price they must pay if they buy a car includes leaving home.

Because they share a strict interpretation of shunning, the Andy Weaver churches in Holmes County are in fellowship with the much more technologically progressive Old Order Amish in Lancaster County. This situation has been somewhat uncomfortable from the standpoint of the exchange of ministers at church services. It has also led the younger generation of Andy Weaver Amish in Holmes County to ask why they are in fellowship with the Old Order of Lancaster County if they cannot use similar technologies.[28] However, the arrangement does illustrate that in this case rituals surrounding shunning rank higher on a hierarchy of values than choices about technology.

The "Liberal" Amish: The New Order Schisms

Church divisions in the Holmes County Settlement have not only given rise to the more conservative Andy Weaver and Swartzentruber branches but also to more progressive groups. Chief among these is the New Order affiliation, which split from the Old Order Amish in the 1960s. By 2009 there were eighteen New Order church districts in the Holmes County Settlement, primarily centered in Walnut Creek, Berlin, and Sugarcreek. The New Order Amish share many cultural practices with their Old Order counterparts, but they also differ in some important ways. The dress of both men and women is more colorful; the men have more neatly groomed hair and beards; their buggies have rubber tires, sliding doors, and other accessories; their homes have telephones; and they consider "balloon" (air-filled) tires on farm equipment acceptable. Unlike the "electric" New Order in other states and settlements, Ohio's New Order Amish have retained the ban on electricity from the grid, though most church districts are comfortable with inverters and generators.[29] Many New Order districts permit travel by plane, though none allow ownership of cars.

An analysis of the New Order schism in Ohio reveals that material concerns were somewhat secondary to theological concerns in the eyes of those who led the revitalization movement. From the standpoint of the "lower" churches as well, the most radical innovations of the New Order had less to do with technology than with such practices as Sunday school and Bible study, both of which came to be seen as forms of "resistance" to the Old Order worldview. How and why did this happen?

The sources of the New Order division can be traced back to the 1940s and 1950s, when growing numbers of ministers called for renewal of the spiritual pulse of the Old Order. These calls focused on two main areas. The first was the elimination of "questionable" practices such as tobacco use and bundling,[30] for which most believed there was no scriptural basis. The early leaders of the movement felt strongly that young people should be within the standards of the church at all times and that it should not be permissible to break church rules during the rumspringa period. They argued that parents should closely monitor teenagers' activities.

A second concern was the promotion of spiritual awareness in the sense of a more evangelical understanding of salvation and outreach. The Old Order church teaches "the new birth," but the way it understands religious commitment is quite different from teachings of religious groups that stress "individual liberation from sin more than submission to the corporate community of believers."[31] The early leaders of the New Order movement were critical of what they perceived as the unquestioning adherence to tradition among many Old Order Amish. One leader of the New Order split told us, "I'm ashamed for some of our community. Just because a person dresses Amish, that doesn't mean he's Christian." The leaders of the New Order movement interpreted the New Testament as offering *assurance of* (not *hope of*) salvation, and they saw spiritual awareness as involving a subjective and vocal experience that found expression in mission work.[32]

At the same time, the early leaders of this movement were skeptical of the "emotionalism" in Protestant evangelism and desired to balance the subjective experience with knowledge and with participation in the "brotherhood" of believers (i.e., the church). The hope was to find a "middle way" in which the Amish lifestyle was retained but with some important modifications.[33] "There was a lot of emphasis when our group broke away," noted one New Order businessman, "to try to maintain the technology and the lifestyle as close to the Old Order people as possible." The new group wanted to retain a discipleship that could be seen and evaluated by the community while also emphasizing individual salvation and Christian outreach. As in other schisms, the leaders of the movement saw themselves as regaining an "old" position (held by Jakob Ammann and others) that had been lost over the years; consequently, they were not happy with the name New Order, though they have accepted it.[34]

Precursors of the New Order split can be seen as early as 1944–45, when one young man, upon his ordination in the lower Walnut Creek district, threw his pipe into the stove and said, "That's it for that!" Like some other members, he could not read or understand high German very well, and he and another minister "were burdened that the people should understand what was preached and taught."[35] They began meeting on "off" Sundays to read the Bible and sing. Later, in the 1950s, influential

preachers such as George Brunk and David Miller began promoting missions and stressing the new birth and assurance of salvation. A New Order
deacon reflected on the influence of the latter minister, known as "Oklahoma Dave": "Oh, he was such a good speaker, he just drew everybody's
attention. See, he knew the plan of salvation. One evening they decided
they'll have a meeting for the young people, and I think there was over
1000 people there. Lots of young people came to him and said, 'What can
we do? We are convinced to do something and our church doesn't support
it.' So that's where someone got the idea." The "idea" to which this deacon
referred was the convening of meetings for the explicit purpose of Bible
study. A potential challenge to the church hierarchy, "fellowship meetings" were nevertheless held occasionally in Amish homes in the ensuing
years. Ervin Gingerich organized the meetings, where the Holy Kiss was
used, for the first time ever, as a greeting regardless of age.[36]

By the late 1950s, Bible studies for the young people, or "youth meetings," had become fairly regular, and by the mid-1960s, they were "the
primary point of contention," causing conflict in every congregation that
had supporters.[37] Youth meetings had become symbolic of broader doctrinal disagreements, but even those who were sympathetic to the youth
meetings often differed on the emphasis. One group in the 1960s, for example, accepted youth meetings and stressed strict courtship and nonuse
of tobacco and alcohol but was uncomfortable with mission activism and
emotional preaching. During this time, it was not uncommon for ordained
leaders who supported these activities to be barred from preaching in
some districts; and young people who attended the youth meetings were
denied baptisms or weddings in some churches.

The first New Order congregation split in 1966–67 when minister
Levi Troyer and his brother Noah, a deacon, supported the practice of
greeting with the Holy Kiss among younger members during an official
church service. Many in their congregation, including the bishop, balked
at this practice. A mediating committee was summoned, but they "did not
call Levi and Noah Troyer's position and activities wrong."[38] Still, the local bishops requested that the Troyers not take Communion, whereupon
they solicited the help of a sympathetic bishop, Wallace Byler, in Hart-
ville, Ohio. What finally precipitated the split was a letter Byler received
from nine of the oldest Old Order bishops asking him not to support the
Troyers. After the first official rupture occurred, several other congrega-

tions split in the ensuing years. As New Order church districts became more established, they institutionalized Sunday school, a testimony to the New Order desire to be "much more intentional in discussing and disseminating their religious convictions, both to members and to outsiders."[39]

A related debate over the emphasis on "church *teaching* to eliminate undesirable behavior" versus "church *sanctions* to eliminate undesirable behavior" was at the core of another schism two decades later that produced a small group of five church districts known as the New Order Christian Fellowship, or more commonly the New New Order. The historical context of this split traces to a growing realization in the late 1970s among the New Order Amish that approximately half of their young people were leaving the Amish. Even though most of the defectors were joining Plain churches, some New Order leaders decided they had "gone too far" toward emotionalism and needed to "back up" a little bit to find the proper balance between faith and works. But other individuals interpreted this reconsidered emphasis on the value of the brotherhood of the church as a return to the "Old Order mentality."[40]

The catalyst for the split came when deacon Aden Yoder and minister Alvin Beachy began focusing on each other's doctrinal differences. If salvation rested on one's individual relationship with God, Yoder argued, the church had no right to compel its members to follow rules. According to one former member, Yoder's belief was that "the church should not excommunicate, period!" Yoder's home bishop and others disagreed, likening Yoder's approach to a parent who threatens to spank and threatens to spank, but never spanks. Apart from the bully pulpit, ordained leaders would have little control over the behavior of members of their congregations. In the end, Yoder and his followers walked out of church while the rest of the congregation pleaded for him to reconsider. The birth of the New Order Christian Fellowship, then, occurred when a deacon who thought of himself a visionary espoused ideas that were doctrinally unacceptable to others in his church. Personality conflicts then brought both sides to a crossroads, at which point they chose to part. One member who spent time in both affiliations reflected, "The main reason for the split was differing views of the role of the church in the believer's religious experience." He paused and then added, "But personal differences between the two men also played a dramatic role."

Today the New Order Christian Fellowship accepts a wider range of technology and an even more subjective religious experience than the New Order. Church Ordnung typically allows cell phones, computers, and electricity. Dress patterns are closer to those of the non-Amish. Owning cars, however, is still off limits, a key prohibition that distinguishes this group from the Beachy Amish. In spite of their liberalism (or more likely, because of it), the New New Order has struggled to retain its young people. As of 2005, the retention rate was only 46 percent.[41] Concern about the lack of church discipline and the fate of the young people has led some families to return to the New Order, and some New New Order leaders now admit that more church discipline is needed than Yoder originally advocated.

Nevertheless, the continued viability of the New Order Amish and, to a lesser degree, the New New Order illustrates that calls for renewal can be incorporated, at least to an extent, into the Amish framework.[42] That the New Order Amish are more restrictive than the Old Order Amish on courtship, smoking, and alcohol also stands as an important reminder that placing Amish affiliations on a single conservative-liberal axis is overly simplistic.[43] In this respect, the influence of the New Order Amish on Old Order thinking has been considerable, far greater than would be expected from the relatively small size of this affiliation.

The View from the Center: The Old Order Amish

Through all of these challenges to the viability of the main trunk of the church, the Old Order Amish have not only persisted but prospered. While other groups usually carry the names of their bishops, the main body has been known as the Old Order ever since the historic split in the 1850s to 1860s. The name implies that they are guardians of the "old ways," but the Old Order in the Holmes County Settlement have made numerous compromises with technology. They adopted daylight savings time in the 1960s to accommodate the needs of factories, and their acceptance of new shop and household technologies has proceeded at a steady pace. With the exception of more conservative dress, fewer buggy accessories, and no phones in the house, the differences in technology use between the Old Order and the New Order are relatively minor. In fact, Amish of the Old Order are more likely to use cell phones and to let their young people own automobiles before baptism than are the New Order

Head coverings vary considerably by gender, age, and affiliation. Shown here are hats worn by Swartzentruber (the middle three), Andy Weaver (the one on the right), and Old Order (the two on the left) Amish. Photograph by Doyle Yoder.

Amish. "I have 15 Old Order customers," noted one New Order lumber company owner, "and I can call every one of them by cell phone."

Even though groups on both the conservative and the progressive ends of the Amish spectrum have broken away, the practices sanctioned by the Old Order Ordnung vary in important ways across the Holmes County Settlement. Examining Old Order responses to the schisms described above reveals this diversity as well as the ways in which status rivalries continue to mark relations between the main body and the various branches.

Looking "up" the Anabaptist escalator, the Old Order Amish have generally viewed the New Order with a mixture of consternation and admiration. On the one hand, Old Order Amish are generally not comfortable with the self-conscious theology of the New Order group. An Old Order businessman explained: "You couldn't get the average Old Order man out on the street to give you a strong faith story. They live it easier than they tell it." Many Old Order Amish also see New Order assurance of salvation as a "misguided human attempt to speak for God." Furthermore, most Old Order Amish resent New Order criticism of the Old Order approach to life. An Old Order factory worker remarked: "You know, there's this thing where some Amish will say they've found Christ—and then all of a sudden they condemn the group that they've been with. To us it seems like they're just trying to justify themselves." They believe that such a "holier-than-thou" attitude flies in the face of the biblical injunction that "he that shall endure to the end, the same shall be saved" (Mark 13:13), which many Old Order members still view as a guiding framework for their lives.

The most common Old Order criticism is that New Order church districts as a whole are unstable because their young people are more likely to be lost to other Anabaptist churches. In this respect, Old Order members often wonder if the New Order "talk of spirituality" is simply a cover for their desire to acquire the "material trappings permitted in the more liberal groups."[44]

Importantly, however, a sizable number of Old Order individuals, including church leaders, are quite attracted to the New Order positions on both spirituality and control of the youth. It is no longer uncommon to find Old Order ministers who focus on the New Testament and "the new birth" in their sermons or Old Order parents who take a proactive stance in restricting the activities of their teenagers. One of the founders of the New Order church commented, "When we started the New Order, everybody was against us, you know, they didn't appreciate that at all. After about 30 years, they are changing their minds, little by little." A New Order businessman concurred: "Young Old Order ministers today agree with the New Order on 95 percent of issues, but that was not true in the 1970s and 1980s."

Looking "down" the Anabaptist escalator, how have the Old Order Amish viewed their Andy Weaver counterparts? Initially, the two affiliations were bound together by similar approaches to technology and by cross-affiliation marriages that stemmed from shared circles of courtship in the late 1940s and early 1950s. But the strict Andy Weaver stance on shunning and the controls on church members' lives are viewed as excessive by Old Order families. The more tolerant attitude of the Andy Weavers toward youth behavior, especially drinking and smoking, is also questioned in some Old Order circles. Still, many Old Order individuals and Andy Weavers study, play, and work side by side.

With respect to the Swartzentrubers, most people of the Old Order are less charitable in their assessment. One person who grew up in the Holmes County Settlement writes, "Although they share the same last names . . . often those most unsympathetic to the Swartzentrubers are other Amish who deal with them in practical daily life."[45] Many Old Order Amish comment that the social distance between Old Order Amish and non-Amish is far less than that between Old Order and Swartzentruber Amish. An elderly Old Order Amish man confessed, "We tend to jokingly look down our nose at the Swartzentrubers."[46] Many Old Order Amish sharply criticize the Swartzentruber tendency to withdraw from discussion with other Amish, and the Swartzentruber stance on buggy safety in particular irks many Old Order. "If they don't want to put slow-moving vehicle signs on their buggies, that's fine with me," fumed one Old Order man, "But stay off the road after dark!"

For their part, the Swartzentruber Amish with whom we talked were quite cognizant of the antipathy directed by some non-Amish and even other Amish toward them. "There are people out there who do not like us—we know that," commented a Swartzentruber bishop. Privately, most Swartzentrubers see their nonconformity as a badge of humility, and they feel that the "soud leut" (literally, "south people," referring to the more liberal Amish in the "south" of the settlement) are "not a group that we'd want to live up to" (emulate). But not all Old Order Amish look down on the Swartzentrubers. One successful Old Order businessman notes that even though he has "issues" with the Swartzentrubers, he appreciates their influence. "They help us keep the brakes applied just because they are here."

What Causes Church Schism?

Based on these case studies, we can now venture some tentative conclusions about why there have been so many schisms in a group that is known for the strength of its communal bonds. We begin by noting several structural features that facilitate and mitigate church schism. On the one hand, the decentralized political structure of Amish society and the normative focus on harmony and community encourages "legal informalism" and face-to-face efforts at conflict resolution at the church district level.[47] As we have seen, church schisms typically occur only after multiple attempts to resolve the problems locally and to hear the advice of outside mediating committees. Rather than an abrupt break, most church divisions involve a gradual sorting-out process in which the seeds of discontent and attempts at mediation cycle for years until the occurrence of a catalytic event.

At the same time, the considerable autonomy given to each church district makes it inconceivable that all Amish will see eye-to-eye. One byproduct of this social arrangement is that personalities loom large in Amish religious life, so much so that affiliations are often named after influential bishops or ministers. At the root of many schisms lie at least two strong-willed men whose courage or vanity—depending on one's viewpoint—leads them to construct theological justifications for their positions in a conflict that is, in part, personal. As Hostetler pointed out, the "articulation of differences in belief by an enthusiastic leader" is a precondition for the development of separatism.[48] The magnification of personalities in the Amish religious system is one reason why groups on each side of the aisle usually assert that it was those on the *other* side who broke with tradition.

Doctrine is not inconsequential in church schism, however. The stark dualism of the Amish worldview, wrapped in the imperative of living a virtuous life aloof from the world, provides a fertile ground for theological disagreement. The doctrine of separation from the world requires a never-ending string of judgments about the proper degree of accommodation. The twin facts that the Amish are residentially interspersed with their non-Amish neighbors and are increasingly interdependent economically only heighten the frequency with which Amish of all affiliations encounter worldly situations that are morally ambiguous.

Surveying the landscape of fracture in the Holmes County Settlement, one recognizes that two doctrinal "wedge issues" surface repeatedly: shunning and control of the young people. There are good reasons why these two issues have had a long shelf life at the center of controversy in Amish communities. For one, both are ambiguous in terms of biblical reference and thus are open to intense theological scrutiny and debate: Does the Bible prescribe shunning, and if so, in what form? Are the young people outside the parameters of church Ordnung until baptism, or should they be treated as members? The answers are not clear-cut.

In addition, both issues are proxies for the ongoing debate over access to technology. The connection is indirect but powerful. Former members who are excommunicated, individuals who decide not to join the church, and youth who are in the rumspringa period before baptism all have access to technologies that are forbidden to church members. Except for those few Amish who are childless, every family will have children who could be a valuable conduit to technology during the interval between their sixteenth birthday and baptism. Although it is less common to have relatives who have been excommunicated, most individuals have at least one or two relatives who decided not to join church in the first place. Since church Ordnung typically prohibit *ownership* of technologies by baptized members, it is not unreasonable to argue that there is nothing wrong with using cameras, cell phones, or even cars that are owned by nonmembers.

Whatever the mix of doctrinal dispute and personality clash in church divisions, the resulting application of different standards of technology— from the kinds of games children can play to methods of household refrigeration—is mind-boggling. Why do these differences, which are often nonexistent at the time of a church schism, gradually emerge over the ensuing decades? At the most general level, technology provides a tangible and visible referent to which the prescription to remain "separate from the world" can be anchored and by which obedience can be measured. But displays of technology also serve as powerful symbols of cultural boundaries and potent markers of religious identity. Regardless of whether one actually believes that God's will is tied to the type of restrictions on the use of phones, for example, such visible markers clearly differentiate Amish groups from each other. Different standards of technology grow more pronounced in the aftermath of church schisms precisely for this reason. It is difficult to see technology as the "prime mover" behind church schism, but once adopted, technology drives social change by highlighting and strengthening the differences between affiliations.

Our analysis, then, ultimately suggests a contingency model of church schism. In this framework, the dualistic and sectarian nature of Amish theology, the decentralized nature of Amish social organization, and increasing contact with a rapidly changing non-Amish world form the enabling conditions for church schism. Whether these conditions lead to divisions in any particular instance depends on the presence of precipitating factors such as strong-willed and articulate church leaders, a core doctrinal dispute, and a catalyzing event. Compared to Lancaster County and Elkhart and Lagrange counties, where diversity within the Old Order has grown in the absence of formal schism, the Holmes County Settlement has more often been home to leaders who chose to pursue paths of divergence rather than conciliation.

CHAPTER 3

Coping with Church Schism

Let's face it, when a church splits, there's bound to be hard feelings.
—An Old Order bishop

G iven that church schism inevitably involves hard feelings and even divides extended families, we would expect it to have far-reaching social implications. To what extent do the differences between Amish affiliations shape social life in the Holmes County Settlement? At least one scholar has noted that the Amish affiliations "have regarded each other with suspicion" and "have focused mostly on their differences."[1] This chapter explores three areas—mission work, rumspringa, and excommunication and shunning—in which religious affiliation strongly shapes attitudes and patterns of participation.

Light That Makes No Noise: The Debate over Missions and Proselytizing

One of the most pervasive features of religious movements around the globe is their proselytizing orientation. Most communities of believers are marked not only by internal symbols and rituals of bonding but also by an explicit attempt to project their worldview outward and convince others of the rightness of their position. For Christians, a key teaching is a passage in the Gospel of Matthew, in which the resurrected Jesus instructs his own disciples, "Go ye therefore, and teach all nations, baptizing them in the name of the Father, and of the Son, and of the Holy Ghost: Teaching them to observe all things whatsoever I have commanded you" (Matt. 28:19–20). Known as the Great Commission, this directive is usually interpreted as applying to all Christians around the world.

For most of their history, however, the Amish have been squarely at odds with the proselytizing impulse, favoring an inward orientation that eschews evangelism and activist concern for the spiritual state of the world. Instead, they have preferred to take the course of embodying the life of Christ in their everyday actions. "We don't feel that going into all the world and baptizing people is imperative," commented an Old Order bishop. "It's more the idea that wherever you find yourself, you try to propagate the truth. That puts mission work in a little different light."

The Amish Mission Movement

It thus comes as a surprise to many who are aware of the traditional Amish position to learn that around the middle of the twentieth century, some Old Order Amish started a "mission movement," one that significantly re-shaped the discourse and practice of outreach. Although many Amish were involved, an outside "catalytic figure" named Russell Maniaci pulled them together by organizing the First Amish Mission Conference in Kalona, Iowa, in 1950. The aim of this gathering was to "surrender the desires of security and stability in exchange for going into the world as missionaries and service workers."[2]

As this movement formed organizational structures and funding mechanisms, including the first full-time Amish mission workers in Gulfport, Mississippi, it was met by skepticism and resistance from other Old Order Amish, who feared it would lead to acculturation and the loss of Amish identity. Traveling Mennonite tent evangelists added to the growing tensions, as did the preaching of David Miller, the Old Order minister known as "Oklahoma Dave." According to Nolt, how one responded to this "pulpit pounding" charismatic preacher became something of an "ecclesiastical litmus test" among the Amish.[3] In spite of a backlash, advocates of the mission movement moved cautiously forward, holding conferences, distributing a newsletter called Witnessing, and venturing into several mission projects that required automobiles and challenged other standards of the Amish church as well.[4] Eventually, the influential leaders moved out of Old Order circles and into Conservative Amish Mennonite Churches or Mennonite congregations. Confirming the predictions of Old Order skeptics, their moves were accompanied by the purchase of cars.[5]

The mission movement had lasting effects on Amish identity, however. Today Amish involvement in Christian outreach and relief beyond the confines of the Holmes County Settlement is surprisingly common. Yet the patterns of Amish involvement in mission work are by no means uniform. Church districts take different stances on the validity of proselytizing and outreach and the form they should take. In addition, since Amish outreach usually involves piggybacking on the efforts of Mennonite, Brethren, or Beachy Amish organizations, it reflects the fault lines in a much broader Anabaptist debate over the meaning of the Great Commission.

The Role of Affiliation in Missions and Outreach

Among the horse and buggy Amish of Holmes County, the New Order Amish are clearly the heirs of the contentious midcentury mission movement. Many New Order individuals exhibit a missionary zeal that is sometimes difficult to distinguish from that of the Beachy Amish. It is no accident that these New Order groups reject car ownership but accept flying in airplanes. "We fly freely," remarked a New Order businessman, "and that opens the door for our young people to go to Haiti, to go to Indonesia, to go to the Ukraine on mission projects." In addition to supporting the two largest mission and outreach organizations in Holmes County, the Mennonite Central Committee and Christian Aid Ministries, the New Order Amish support a variety of other "relief ministries," such as Iron Curtain and Freiheit Messengers Prison Ministry.

The New Order Amish have tempered the mission experiment in several ways, though. Most importantly, they have retained a horse and buggy culture rather than adopting automobiles and other conveniences to facilitate outreach. In addition, it is uncommon for New Order Amish to spend substantial time on overseas mission trips. As a general principle, New Order mission work does not try to alter the newly planted church abroad by "making them Amish." They also appear to be more comfortable with spreading the gospel if such efforts are accompanied by disaster relief or poverty reduction. One project supported by the New

COPING WITH CHURCH SCHISM

Order, for example, has provided garden tillers to a Beachy Amish church in the Ukraine. Still, outreach is likely to include sharing of the gospel and preaching against questionable practices such as tobacco, divorce, polygamy, and alcohol. Another example is that youth from several New Order church districts participate in the Barberton Rescue Mission, where they sing and conduct a church service for recovering drug and alcohol addicts.

Among the Old Order Amish, mission and outreach is more likely to be restricted to giving money and volunteering at fund-raisers. Though impossible to estimate, the total annual sum raised by Old Order and New Order churches is a significant amount. "Oh, I can probably think of ten different mission groups that come and have dinner banquets here," commented one New Order businessman. "Why? Because some of their biggest support comes from Holmes County. It's mostly Amish people that support them." A longtime director of the Mennonite Central Committee agreed. "The Old Order Amish have responded much more positively than I was led to believe they would early on in my career. Even though they don't go directly into mission work, they are willing to share what they have with those who are less fortunate." One Old Order Amish man, who served for several years as the state coordinator for the Haiti Relief Auction, described Old Order participation this way: "We're always supportive of the Great Commission, we're sympathetic to that." He quickly added, however, that the Old Order limit their mission activities: "The reason we don't proselytize is that the lifestyle we feel keeps us going from generation to generation is not conducive to outside seekers."

This comment is particularly instructive in illuminating a key aspect of Old Order theology that has implications for mission work. Not only does proselytizing imply an assurance of salvation that does not sit right with many Old Order individuals, it also places them squarely on the horns of a dilemma. "Witnessing" to nonbelievers in the hope of converting them would normally include an invitation to join their church. Such an invitation to outside seekers could seriously disrupt the social viability of Amish church districts. Indeed, so stringent are the demands of the Ordnung that fewer than one hundred outsiders are currently members of Amish church districts in the United States and Canada.[6] In contrast, because New Order Amish are more likely to claim that one can go to heaven even as a member of another church, proselytizing does not imply the necessity of "becoming Amish." This difference in religious logic partially explains why Old Order members of an Amish work team sent to New Orleans after Hurricane Katrina refrained from passing out tracts and gospel CDs as the New Order members did, preferring to focus their energies on relief and rebuilding efforts.

Another reason for the more passive support for mission activities among the Old Order people is precisely the association of these actions with the lifestyle choices that the "higher" groups have made. One Old Order man described mission-oriented evangelical Amish this way: "They come through sounding like heaven is a different doctrine or sounding as a better place. And of course they're offering a lifestyle of more conveniences and technologies and denouncing what we stand for as a separation from the world." According to Nolt, from the start, the Old Order Amish saw that the embrace of missions could entail a need for cars and higher education and lead full tilt into modernity.[7]

Even within the Old Order, however, the emphasis on mission work varies. In general, those Old Order Amish who support the New Order stance on reforming singings and restricting tobacco and alcohol use and car ownership among the young folks are more enthusiastic about it. "We tend to be more mission-oriented," commented an Old Order elder, "because we want to have projects for our youth. They need something to do so we have lots of little fund-raisers and outreach projects."

One fascinating exception to the Old Order inclination to refrain from hands-on mission work is their participation in spiritual and educational aid to Old Colony Mennonites, who moved to northern Mexico from Canada in the 1920s to avoid legal requirements for their schooling.[8] This effort, arranged through the Mennonite Central Committee since 1995, is comprised almost entirely of Old and New Order Amish. The seventeen thousand Old Colony Mennonites still engage in schooling that consists mainly of memorizing and chanting the catechism (a fifty-nine-page series of questions and answers about the Bible and theology) in High German. A longtime Old Order participant reflected: "They're 90 percent illiterate and even their ministers don't understand the German that they have memorized. They're prime targets for business people to take total advantage of them. We helped them understand that being more literate would make a big difference." The Amish not only introduced report cards but have sent teachers to Mexico as well.

These twenty-first-century Amish missionaries intentionally seek to be culturally sensitive change agents. According to one Old Order man, the Old Colony Mennonites realized that "we understand them better than some evangelistic church that would come in there and tear the whole structure down." At the same time, it is interesting that members of a group routinely identified as "backward" by American mainstream society invoke the same terms of discourse to identify the Old Colony Mennonites as spiritually and educationally deficient. "They don't know how to think for themselves," commented one mission worker. Added another, "They have now identified how bad their education was. We want to get them to read and fully understand God's word so that they can have salvation." That at least a handful of Old Order Amish are participating in this endeavor is a striking testimony not only to the economic success of the Amish in North America but also to how the mission impulse and mind-set has grown in the main body of the church.[9]

Moving down the Anabaptist escalator, the stance of the Andy Weaver affiliation and the various Swartzentruber branches toward mission work is much more cautious, if not negative. Nothing restricts an individual from donating to a particular cause, but taking on an administrative or even a volunteer role for mission activities is less common for the Andy Weavers and almost unheard of for Swartzentrubers. One reason is the perceived danger of publicity that comes with supporting mission work. The Andy Weavers may support a fund-raiser for disabled individuals or the heart fund, but they are less likely to support overseas missions. Swartzentrubers may also support "free will" donations for local causes but will balk at supporting overseas missions. In some cases, these more conservative Amish groups do not consciously consider proselytizing in the first place, perhaps because of the lack of universalizing assumptions in their worldviews. One young Swartzentruber man said, "They wouldn't even give it a thought."

Competing Interpretations of the Great Commission

The various stances of Amish groups toward missions and outreach also reflect a much broader debate within the Anabaptist community over the interpretation of the Great Commission. Should "saving souls" and "church planting" be the top priority, or is God's work best accomplished

through relief and development efforts? Supporters of the latter view often cite a different Bible verse as justification for a more social gospel: "For
I was an hungred, and ye gave me meat: I was thirsty, and ye gave me
drink: I was a stranger, and ye took me in" (Matt. 25:35).

The Mennonite Central Committee (MCC) and Christian Aid Ministries (CAM) occupy opposing sides of this fault line in the Holmes
County Settlement. Begun in 1920, MCC is the peace, relief, and development committee of various Mennonite groups and the Brethren in
Christ Church in the United States and Canada. Because it has effectively
joined massive fund-raising with an efficient administrative system, many
aid organizations around the world see MCC as "cutting edge" in terms of
administering fair trade and engaging in relief and development work. In
Holmes and Wayne counties alone, MCC receives roughly a half million
dollars a year in donations from two nonprofit thrift shops, MCC Connections in Kidron and Save and Serve in Millersburg. Approximately half
of the volunteers in the latter shop are Amish. MCC also benefits from a
relief sale in August that is supported by the Amish. In addition, MCC's
meat-canning committee, chaired in 2008 by an Old Order Amish man,
is a finely honed operation. In conjunction with the scheduled arrival of
a mobile canning truck, Amish church districts send volunteers for "work
days" to can massive amounts of turkey for shipment to Burundi, North
Korea, and other sites. MCC coordinators maintain a list of about fifty
Old and New Order Amish bishops who are comfortable with receiving
letters about MCC projects.

The Beachy Amish, however, have long viewed MCC as far too liberal on various social issues, including support for women in the ministry,
a relatively activist stance with respect to peacemaking, and more tolerant views of homosexuality and abortion than the Beachy Amish hold. In
the early 1980s, David N. Troyer founded Christian Aid Ministries as a
conservative alternative to MCC. Out of its worldwide headquarters in
Berlin, Ohio, and offices in Pennsylvania and other states, CAM has thus
far distributed $1.3 billion worth of donated products around the world.
In 2006 alone, it shipped more than 15 million pounds of food, medicine, clothing, and other aid to more than forty countries.[10] CAM's annual
budget is nearly three times that of MCC, and its fund-raising has been so
successful that Beachy church directors became concerned about declining donations to other Beachy Amish mission programs.

Old Order Amish volunteers mingle with Beachy Amish and Mennonites at Save and Serve, a thrift shop that supports the Mennonite Central Committee's outreach projects. Photograph courtesy of David McConnell.

Although CAM receives strong backing from the Beachy Amish community, it also relies heavily on support from New and Old Order Amish. New Order Amish not only populate the ranks of donors and volunteers but also fill three staff positions at CAM headquarters and regularly fly to Indonesia, Pakistan, and other places to provide on-site assistance. "The New Order are very awake, they're top of the line for us in terms of witness and work," noted a CAM administrator. In contrast, Old Order participation comes mostly in the form of "silent support" through monetary donations; however, some Old Order individuals provide in-kind donations and volunteer in the CAM warehouses. Commenting on the growth of Old Order participation, a CAM employee noted that it "has really changed in the 25 years since I've been here, mostly due to ministers who are born-again." As for the Andy Weaver Amish, a few may quietly send in a check. Swartzentruber participation is virtually non-existent.

CAM appeals to the tastes of mission-oriented Amish in a variety of ways. To avoid looking wasteful to Amish contributors, CAM's newsletter, its main fund-raising tool, sent to twenty-five thousand supporters, did not convert to an all-color version until 2007. The newsletter itself is packed with information; it appeals to Amish sensibilities by providing concrete examples of how donations are used for practical projects. "Our style is not 'in your face' proselytizing," commented a CAM administrator.

At the same time, CAM's sharp division of the world into the righteous and the heathen is clearly on display in its literature. A 2006 publication on flood relief to Romania, for example, begins: "It was an area of darkness, the people steeped in witchcraft and superstition. They did not know that a mighty God in heaven cared about them."[11] In 2006 CAM spent nearly $2 million to translate Bibles and Christian literature into local languages. In short, CAM's outreach and relief programs are wrapped in a cloak of Christian theology that is far more explicit than MCC programs reveal.

Amish views of the tension between CAM and MCC are diverse. Some Amish are completely unaware of any competition or philosophical differences between the two organizations; they tend to focus more on the immediate need being met by a fund-raiser and less on the sponsors. Others are aware of the tension but don't understand it. "I hear there's some static between the Mennonites and Christian Aid," commented an Old Order man, "but I don't know why if both programs are helping people in need." "We support both," responded an Old Order businessman when asked whether he prefers to donate to CAM or MCC. "But if I had to guess, I would say most Amish choose to support one but not the other." According to a New Order man with extensive knowledge of both groups, Amish support CAM more readily than MCC because they are not always comfortable with the "social agenda" underlying Mennonite programs. Other Amish resent CAM because they feel that the Beachy Amish are trying to raise money from the very Amish groups that they rejected. When CAM sent calendars to parochial schools in the settlement, for instance, a controversy erupted: "We as teachers were told by the school committee not to get involved in the CAM-MCC conflict," related an Old Order Amish teacher.

Still other Amish, however, reject these bureaucratized mission programs altogether, believing that they run counter to the biblical injunction to embody Christ in one's everyday life. Such views are more common among conservative Amish, but even one New Order bishop confessed to serious misgivings about evangelical outreach. "The danger in mission work," he said pointedly, "is the sin of pride."

Some Amish religious leaders characterize their stance on mission work as "light that makes no noise," a clever metaphor for a nonintrusive approach that focuses on setting an example and providing relief services without seeking to reconstruct the indigenous church. Such a modest formulation of mission work protects Amish from having to engage in questionable activities in the process of outreach. Upon closer scrutiny, however, we have seen that the Holmes County Amish take a variety of stances on how their "light" should be cast, from active involvement in spreading the gospel at home and abroad, to financial support for disaster relief and material aid, to outright rejection of mission work. The mid-century mission movement may have ultimately broken ranks with the Amish community, but its legacy remains in the form of a widespread, if low-key, debate over which mission organizations to support and how. As with other dimensions of Amish interaction with the outside world, specific responses to the Great Commission vary considerably by affiliation, by district, and by individual inclination.

The Changing Form of Rumspringa

Few Amish cultural practices have received as much public scrutiny as rumspringa (literally, "running around"), the liminal period in an Amish teenager's life that begins at age sixteen and ends with a decision whether to be baptized in the church. Outsiders are especially fascinated with these adolescent years because they appear to be so inconsistent with notions of what the Amish believe. Unfortunately, much of the sensationalized media coverage of rumspringa has created the impression that all Amish youth go through a period of wild abandon. Lucy Walker's 2002 documentary film The Devil's Playground, in which Amish youth told their own stories as they partied and experimented with drugs, alcohol, and sex, contributed to this impression by focusing on some of the wildest youth in an Indiana settlement.[12] In reality, enormous variation exists in the form and content of rumspringa across and within Amish settlements.[13]

The Holmes County Amish fully embody this diversity. This one settlement is home both to Amish who reject rumspringa altogether and to young people who attend large parties and participate in non-Amish entertainment and leisure activities on a regular basis. The Holmes County Settlement also includes a significant number of parents and youth who are deeply ambivalent about the prospect of experimentation with the outside world. A balanced examination of this rite of passage reveals much about the interaction between changes in the external environment and internal responses by Amish affiliations, church districts, and families.

The insistence on voluntary adult baptism creates a singular dilemma for Amish parents and church leaders: How can they best instill in their children the desire to remain in the Amish affiliation into which they were born? Is it more effective to enforce firm limits and clamp down on questionable behavior during the teenage years, and run the risk of making their sons and daughters rebellious? Or is it better to take a more permissive approach, turning one's back temporarily on the attendant dangers of experimenting with the English world, in the hopes that the youths will "get it out of their system"? Kraybill leans toward the latter position in describing rumspringa as a "social immunization" by which a small dose of worldliness strengthens Amish young people for the temptations they will face in adulthood.[14] Although the perception of choice (to join the church or not) is partly an illusion because youth have been thoroughly immersed in an Amish world since birth, Kraybill argues persuasively that the very fact of having a choice does make adults more likely to follow the Ordnung. Nevertheless, this "fact of choice" underlies a vigorous debate in Amish communities about the proper approach to the young folks.

In the Holmes County Settlement, several key changes in the external environment over the past several decades have had a dramatic effect on the contours of this debate. One is the ever-expanding size of the settlement itself. Richard Stevick, in *Growing Up Amish: The Teenage Years*, makes a crucial distinction between "adult-centered communities" and "peer-centered communities." The former are generally small, isolated settlements where young people tend to be respectful of church standards even after they turn sixteen. "Wild" behavior for them may consist of playing the game UNO or listening to country music on the radio. In peer-centered communities such as Lancaster County, Elkhart and Lagrange counties, and Holmes County, thousands of youth live close to one another and to urban centers, allowing for participation in large parties (or "band hops") and athletic leagues, as well as trips to professional sporting events, amusement parks, and more.[15] Another crucial dimension of large settlements is that they afford more anonymity and more opportunities for youth to find a critical mass of like-minded peers.

Amish adolescents' increasing access to cash constitutes another key challenge. One ripple effect of the economic transition from farming to wage labor is that most fourteen-year-old boys and girls now get paying jobs as soon as they finish eighth grade. Some families restrict the use of money earned in this way, but even so Amish youth have more cash in their pockets than ever before, and they have a smorgasbord of possibilities for spending it. The frequency of economic exchanges with non-Amish has also led to a more confident posture among youth toward the outside world. "The young people are losing their shyness," noted one elderly Old Order man. "When I was growing up, thinking of talking to a non-Amish, I wouldn't have had a clue where to start." A New Order bishop confessed, "We're seeing a lot of the young folks following the trends of everybody else. It really bothers me, and I think it comes from intermingling. They're getting away from the farm, and that's why you're seeing more of that."

Combating Drugs and Alcohol in the Amish Community

An even more alarming change over the past few decades has been the steadily increasing availability of drugs, alcohol, and pornography. "It used to be that the people who had a wild period in life would come back to the Amish church," noted one New Order businessman. "But now the things they are getting into are addictive." In 2006, for example, Paul Fehr, an Old Order youth who was about to join the church, was sentenced to three years in prison and fined five thousand dollars for selling marijuana and attempting to sell methamphetamines to undercover agents. In the Millersburg courtroom, where his family took up two rows of seats, Fehr apologized and confessed that his habit started small but grew into a monster. Although Fehr's father asked Judge Thomas White to be lenient, Judge White was not moved. "This is a little more than running around," he commented at the sentencing.[16] Partly because hard drugs were making their way into Holmes County, a federal drug task force named Medway (after Medina and Wayne counties) was extended to Holmes County in 2003 to deal with the growing problem. In cooperation with local Amish leaders and local law enforcement, drug and alcohol awareness workshops have been held throughout the settlement.

In October of 2005, we attended one of these seminars, held at night in a small shop southeast of Mount Hope, along with roughly two hundred Amish parents and teenagers. After noting that some Amish had been among the sixteen arrested for drug trafficking in Holmes County between April and October of 2005, the invited guests—the sheriff, a medical doctor, and the head of Medway—described the medical effects of alcohol, marijuana, and the highly addictive crystal methamphetamine and offered tips on how to detect signs of alcohol or drug abuse. After their presentations, anonymous written questions were collected from the audience and answered by the speakers.[17]

It was the religious prelude to this program on the medical effects of alcohol and drugs, however, that especially caught our interest. Following a hymn and a silent, standing prayer, an Old Order Amish minister, who said he had slept only two hours because he was worried about speaking in English, delivered a talk that framed drug and alcohol abuse in the starkest of moral terms. "We're here for the prevention of this terrible sin," he began. "I'll say it again. A three-letter word: S-I-N. We all know that it is among us." Citing 1 Corinthians 3:17, he reminded the audience that anyone who defiles the temple of God will be destroyed, because "we all go back to the sinful nature of Adam." He then posed the question of the hour: How we can make sure that our young people choose the right path?

In answering this question, the minister made several interesting observations. First, he noted that 95 percent of the job must be accomplished at home, not by the church. The first step is for parents to exemplify what they want their children to be: "They have to see that we love this path." Next, parents need to establish firm boundaries and exercise thorough oversight—"We need to know who their friends are and what they're doing"—in order to "bridle" the body and its "raging hormones." The minister then made a plug for sex education at home: "If we don't do our duty and teach our kids what intimate love between man and woman is all about, they'll find out about it in a way that's dirty and lustful." He ended with a plea to fathers. "If I'm a hard, unyielding captain and everything has to go my way, the children will jump ship," he noted. "Be open to your teenagers so that they can come to you and not be ridiculed." This minister's outright rejection of the logic of rumspringa was one that we heard repeatedly from Amish parents and church leaders. "We discourage running around. It's a heartbreak for us to see young people doing that," confessed a Swartzentruber bishop. "It's not like the parents give them permission to go do it," commented an Old Order man.

Complicating the Liberal-Conservative Continuum: New and Old Order Approaches

Within this broad context of changing external circumstances, Amish affiliations, church districts, and families have responded in very different ways. The signature accomplishment of the New Order churches, for instance, has been the extent to which they have been able to gain control over the lives of their young people during this period. The New Order not only adopted the more evangelical position that the world could end at any time (emphasizing that everyone must be prepared, including those who are not yet baptized), they also took several practical steps to eliminate traditional courtship patterns and experimentation with alcohol and tobacco. Over time, the New Order did in fact develop a reputation for "clean living."[18]

The first strategy was an intentional attempt by New Order adults to reform the "singings," which had become synonymous with parties in many Amish church districts. "Singings" are a little-known aspect of Amish life that youth attend on Sunday nights after their sixteenth birthday.[19] The official agenda is religious—to sing hymns in high German—but the unofficial social goal is allowing teens to interact with their peers and eventually find a mate. For many years before the New Order split off from the Old Order, drinking, dancing, and listening to music had become commonplace before and after the prescribed hymn singing. The founding church leaders and parents of the New Order decided their singings

Volleyball is a popular activity whenever young people gather. Some Old Order and New Order singings require more than ten volleyball nets to accommodate the turnout. Photograph by Doyle Yoder.

would be different from what they had experienced. They drew up strict rules for singings and began chaperoning the youth.

In conjunction with increased control over singings, the New Order church districts took the drastic step of requiring that young people become candidates for membership in the church before they could date. The result is that New Order youth tend to join church two or three years earlier than their peers in other affiliations and tend to marry a year or two later. Some Old Order Amish see this approach as problematic because it is not always clear whether New Order youth are joining church out of a desire to keep the Amish lifestyle or to be able to "go with the young folks" and find a "special friend."

Finally, New Order Amish actively abolished the traditional practice of bed courtship, or bundling. Stevick notes that the custom of bundling, brought by European immigrants to the United States, probably originated when couples were courting in houses without heat.[20] From the start, bundling has been controversial in certain areas, and in many settlements it has waned in popularity or been dropped. Where it is still practiced, it retains the basic cultural script followed by the parents and grandparents over the years. Usually on a Sunday night, after a girl's parents have gone to bed, a boy visits the girl in her bedroom, where they lie together, without shoes but fully clothed, until the wee hours of the morning. Stevick estimates that only 10 percent of Amish communities still practice bundling,[21] but the precise figure is difficult to discern. What is clear is that the New Order Amish categorically reject it, as this parent describes: "As for 'keeping company,' this has changed so much. We want to see more communication in daylight, not at night, and we want them to be downstairs, not upstairs in a bedroom. We also discourage dating for an overly long time, like one to two years. You do not ask for a date just for a date. You have to have a goal of searching for a lifelong companion. Some of our young boys, when they desire to keep company with girls, will go to the father and ask his permission to keep steady company." In addition to discouraging "dating around," New Order parents preach "pure courtship," which includes "hands off" in the early stages and no "bodily contact for the purpose of gaining unchristian liberties" before or after the engagement.[22]

How effective have these New Order approaches been? An interesting indicator can be seen in the timing of first births in relation to marriage.

Using data from the *Ohio Amish Directory*, Elizabeth Cooksey and Joseph Donnermeyer found that the percentage of premarital conceptions among New Order women who came of age in the 1970s and 1980s (after the New Order split off) is roughly half that of the overall figure for 1940–59 birth cohorts. In addition, the percentage of premarital conceptions occurring among the New Order youth was less than half the level for the Andy Weaver youth and less than one-third of the level for Old Order youth. Cooksey and Donnermeyer conclude that the New Order Amish are, in fact, doing a better job of protecting their young people from premarital sex.[23] Apart from sexual behavior, there is widespread agreement across the settlement that New Order youth are also less likely to drink, smoke, and do drugs.

To more conservative Amish minds, though, the ultimate indicator of effective socialization is the rate of retention of young people—and by this standard, the New Order group fares poorly in relation to other affiliations. Based on analysis of the 2005 *Ohio Amish Directory*, the New Order retained only 67 percent of its young people overall.[24] The more permissive stance on technology is probably one reason that the New Order loses so many young people and becomes a de facto "feeder system" for the Beachy and Mennonite churches. But, as Kraybill points out, the more individualistic way of thinking about salvation among the New Order may also be significant: young people who move up a step have only to acquire a car and electronics rather than a whole new mind-set.[25] It is worth noting, however, that average retention rates among the "second generation" of New Order families have crept up from a low of 48 percent in the early 1980s.[26]

Old Order attitudes and practices toward rumspringa show much more variation. Even within congregations, there can be sharp disagreement over what is acceptable behavior for the young people. Still, two broad Old Order positions are discernible. On the one hand, some Old Order families have adopted the thinking of the New Order that the young people are within the restrictions of the Ordnung at all times. One Old Order woman put it this way: "The idea of a period of freedom for a teenager is not biblical. Somewhere in past generations it became accepted as normal." An Old Order businessman agreed. "If there's an Ordnung, it should apply in all stages of our lives." In the early years, Old Order families who took this position and restricted the freedoms of their teenage children were known as Midways. Scattered within various Old Order church districts, Midway parents have tried to keep the singings free of alcohol, tobacco, and drugs and ensure that their teenagers court youth from like-minded families. Although a few Midways have joined the New Order, most have not, for several reasons. For one, they believe their position is biblically justified and consistent with Old Order theology. In addition, they are comfortable with Old Order regulations on technology and fear that their children would be more likely to leave the Amish if they switched to the New Order. As a result, the Midway philosophy has taken root in many families in the absence of any official changes in Ordnung across Old Order church districts. Nevertheless, many New Order Amish have cast the growth of this loose network of Old Order families as vindication of their views.

Our interview with an Old Order minister who was an informal leader of the Midways in the early 1980s provided a fascinating glimpse into the origins of this movement. He related that by the 1960s Sunday night singings had become synonymous with partying in many Old Order church districts: "Youth would invade a home and really the parents couldn't or wouldn't do anything about it." As a result, many parents refused to host singings for about a twenty-year period. Finally, fearing that their own teenage children would start going with the "rowdy crowd," this minister and his wife spread the word among like-minded families that they were going to host a singing on Easter evening. "I just decided, 'We're going to do this' because I wanted to see for myself what the conditions at a singing were really like." He continued:

> We had about 30 young people downstairs and had finished supper and were preparing to sing, when just like that, the autos started pulling up in front of our house. It was mostly boys, but some girls, and they hauled the beer out and marched straight upstairs and started drinking. I'd say there were 50 upstairs and 30 downstairs, and then the ones drinking upstairs started rolling bottles down the stairs. So I went upstairs and one of the leaders, bein' as they were real brave, came right up to me and said, "And is there anything you want up here?" I said, "Yes, very much. Apparently, you were never taught what this day represents." They were stunned and didn't know what to say. I said, "It's important that you understand [what Easter means] and repent." Then the leader demanded, "Are you

trying to preach to us?" I said, "No, I'm just telling you the truth." The next day we found any number of bottles that were only half empty, and that was an eye-opener that we needed to talk with our young people. After that, the rowdy ones stopped coming to the singings. We always invite them, they are welcome, but they never come.

This minister estimates that the Midway philosophy has come to be shared by roughly half of the Old Order families in the Holmes County Settlement. One result is that singings and related youth group meetings are not only supervised but coordinated by committees of nonordained parents rather than by individual church districts.[27] Importantly, the Midway movement in the Holmes County Settlement has spread to Pennsylvania and Indiana. Stevick describes the "supervised singings" that have resulted from the Midway movement as "one of the most profound changes that has occurred in the last 25 years."[28]

On the other hand, a sizable proportion of Old Order parents hold firmly to the belief that if young people do not experiment with the world, they will find it difficult to be completely satisfied with the Amish lifestyle. Usually, the parents themselves have gone through rumspringa with no serious side effects and therefore wonder, "How could you not ask the young people to get it out of their system? I did that when I was young." Such Old Order parents view the New Order struggles to retain their youth as a result, in part, of their restrictions on rumspringa. For instance, one Old Order man told us he notices that New Order youth who do not experience a wild rumspringa compensate by "going overboard" in fancying up their buggies. Parents who condone the logic of a wild rumspringa usually provide passive support, but they will occasionally serve as active facilitators. We heard of a mother who bought jeans for her boys and of a father who lent his credit card to a child to pay for a snowboarding trip to upstate New York. In general, these Old Order parents find the attempt to restrict rumspringa by the New Order and the Midways to be somewhat self-righteous, and they are less likely than either group to view the temporary adoption of English practices before baptism as jeopardizing one's prospects of going to heaven.[29]

The most far-reaching practice of these Old Order parents is the permission they give their sons (and much less commonly, daughters) to buy a car once they turn sixteen to eighteen years old. According to several

Old Order leaders, about one-third to one-half of the Old Order church districts in the settlement condone this practice, and as a result cars can be found discreetly parked behind bushes or barns at numerous Amish homes. "I worshipped my car," recalled one forty-year-old Old Order bishop. "Oh yeah, they have the best [cars]," commented a non-Amish businessman whose work force is mostly Amish. "These kids put a lot of money into their cars." Cars driven by Old Order teenage boys have become a fixture on the roads in the settlement as they take Amish construction crews to work, shuttle family members on shopping trips, or carry their peers to ball fields, parties, or other gatherings. Though they are expected to "put the car away" once they join church, the temporary availability of transportation allows some Old Order youth to have a much broader set of experiences than most other Amish young people have.

Does Lower Equal Wilder? Andy Weaver and Swartzentruber Youth

As we move down the Anabaptist escalator, the general view among the Amish is that the lower the group, the wilder the youth. The cultural logic seems to be that the more conservative the affiliation one is joining, the greater the necessity of "sowing one's wild oats" because the restrictions on adult life will be harsher. This generalization does not always hold up, however, as the variation within the Old Order affiliation attests. The Andy Weavers confound the generalization as well, because their affiliation-wide ban on young people living at home if they purchase a car is stricter than the stance of many Old Order church districts. Yet the Andy Weaver young people also have a reputation for drinking that exceeds that of the Old Order. An elderly Andy Weaver man acknowledged outright, "We do have an alcohol problem among our young people."

The Andy Weavers further stand out from most of the Old Order churches in their acceptance of tobacco. The incidence of smoking among Andy Weavers has declined somewhat, however, compared to previous generations, when virtually every man smoked a pipe and every house had a spittoon. According to one Andy Weaver church member, changing public opinion about the negative health effects of smoking and of secondhand smoke, which led to a statewide ban on smoking in all businesses in 2006, has been partially responsible for this change.

The heavy consumption of alcohol by some Old Order and Andy Weaver youth creates challenges for local law enforcement officials, several of whom have an Amish background and speak some Pennsylvania Dutch.[30] "Absolutely, there is more underage drinking among the Amish than the English because that is their pastime," commented one officer. He continued: "In the summer almost every weekend we would get word on where the parties were at. The biggest ones were at the Holmes and Tuscarawas county lines, hundreds of kids from all over. They'd have bands and set up a stage like a semi-trailer. It would be strictly Amish and you just wonder where they get all of the beer. We'd sit there in awe because we'd stop cars going to the party, and they would be loaded to the gills with beer."[31] This officer also noted that they rarely had to worry about being the target of violence from the Amish kids they arrested, though they could be very argumentative and "knew the law." Interestingly, anonymous phone calls from Amish parents often provide the impetus for law enforcement to intervene. "It's shameful that we have to depend on the sheriff to keep our young people in line," admitted an Andy Weaver elder. "But the sheriff's deputies have helped a lot."

The rumspringa experience among the Swartzentruber Amish differs somewhat from its expression among other Holmes County Amish. The continued prominence of farming, coupled with a more restricted lifestyle, has somewhat insulated the Swartzentrubers from outside influences. One result is that courtship still includes the practice of bundling in all three Swartzentruber branches. In bundling the youth retire to the girl's bedroom, where they lie on the bed—the girl in a special, more colorful "night dress" and the boy clothed, but sometimes with his shirt off—until just before the family awakes. An ex-Swartzentruber woman describes the scene: "After the parents are in bed, the guy shows up, and he sneaks in. Even though they know he's there, facing them is supposed to be embarrassing—you know, like when you first date, you're kind of shy meeting the parents the first time—so somehow you're supposed to do this in secret." Sometimes the couples will be joined by friends and will eat snacks and talk until the boys "escape" just before dawn. Hugging and kissing sometimes occur, but sexual involvement is supposed to be off-limits. In addition to the regular dating after Sunday evening singings, the Swartzentrubers practice a special wedding-night custom known as the "midnight table," in which unmarried boys and girls are paired up for dates by middlemen known as "hostlers."[32]

Although more liberal affiliations see bed courtship as immoral, its Swartzentruber defenders argue that it teaches self-discipline. Stevick recounts that a young man who left the Amish to join the armed forces was met with disbelief when he told his barracks buddies that boys in his community went to bed with girls but refrained from sex. "But we didn't," the man insisted.[33] Even within the most conservative groups, however, there is growing disagreement about these issues. Some Swartzentruber affiliations in Wyoming and Tennessee, for example, have "taken a stand" against bed courtship.

The experience of rumspringa can be somewhat different for children from the three Swartzentruber branches, or even depending on family traditions, parental expectations, and sibling behaviors within each branch. Some Swartzentruber parents try to prohibit partying, drinking, and smoking altogether. Among those youth who do experiment with prohibited practices, the wilder ones are more likely to smoke regular cigarettes, whereas the more conservative ones will smoke pipes and cigars. The kinds of card games (poker versus UNO), the extent of hat and dress modifications, and the kinds of music listened to (pop versus country or western) all provide symbolic markers of the reputation of a Swartzentruber peer group as "fast" or "slow."

Since the ideal culmination of the rumspringa period for all Amish groups is baptism into the church, we wanted to learn how the retention rates of the Old Order, Andy Weaver, and Swartzentruber churches compared with those of the New Order. As shown in table 3.1, the most successful affiliation in the Holmes County Settlement is the Andy Weaver church, with an astounding 97 percent retention rate. Insiders estimate that the Swartzentruber retention rate is about 90 percent, though some believe it has dropped slightly in the past five to ten years. "They are having a lot of trouble with their young people, especially at auctions," noted an Old Order businessman who employs Swartzentrubers. "They get more exposure, and lots are leaving. It's a mini-crisis." The Old Order retain well over three-quarters of their young people, whereas the New Order retain just under two-thirds of theirs. What is clear in this comparison is that a more liberal Ordnung does not necessarily correlate with increased likelihood of youth joining the church. At least one sociologist has argued that when church membership demands less commitment, it is easier to drop out; strict churches, however, "can penalize or prohibit alternate activities that compete for members' resources."[34]

**Table 3.1. Rates of retention by major affiliation,
Holmes County Settlement**

Affiliation	Total children born before 1980	Retention rate (%)
Swartzentruber	—	90
Andy Weaver	1,460	97
Old Order	6,930	86
New Order	985	60
New Order Christian Fellowship	282	32
Total	9,657	83

Source: 2005 *Ohio Amish Directory;* because the Schwarzentrubers do not participate in the directory, their retention rate is an estimate by insiders.

Common Threads in the Rumspringa Experience

In spite of variations in rumspringa by affiliation and by family, several constants shape the rumspringa experience across the settlement. One is that the process of coming of age is significantly different for boys than for girls. Boys are typically given more freedom in dress and behavior, including cars for some Old Order males. Boys usually receive a horse and buggy on their sixteenth birthday, whereas girls are more likely to receive furniture or other gifts related to their future roles as wives and mothers. In addition, with the exception of mixed teams in volleyball and the pairing of courting couples after singings or a wedding meal, young people tend to interact in same-sex groups at most social gatherings. For Amish boys, interaction revolves around shared physical activities such as softball, hunting, and fishing, while girls' interactions stress "female intimacy."[35] Among the Old Order Amish, boys are also more likely to play in organized sports leagues with the girls as spectators. A recent trend has given girls more active options, in the shape of competitive girls' softball teams formed in Kidron and elsewhere in the settlement.

A second thread running through the rumspringa years is the fear of getting "caught out." In a distinctive mental twist on the physical hardship that customarily accompanies rites of passage around the world, most Amish view this period of relative freedom as putting young people's souls at risk. If they should die while living in a state of sin, parents and church leaders fear that their souls are "lost" and that they will go to hell. Denise Reiling even argues that the resulting state of angst among young Amish people may be related to high rates of depression and other mental illnesses later in life. She argues that this period of "culturally prescribed deviance" creates an extraordinary dilemma for Amish youth because they are "damned if they do and damned if they don't."[36]

The Amish we interviewed differed in the amount of angst they felt during rumspringa. Unquestionably, the fear of divine retribution is palpable among some Amish youth and their parents. "I was always afraid I would die before I got rid of my record player," recalled one Old Order woman. A New Order woman noted that parents who believe that you have to get your wild oats out "just pray that their boy won't be one that's killed before he settles down." We found some individuals, though, for whom the fear of getting "caught out" was more "background noise" than anything else. One ex-Swartzentruber stated, "The thing that was on my mind was, 'Am I honoring my parents?' " Another confessed, "I was more worried about getting caught by the preacher than by God."

A third constant is that the period of exploration after age sixteen typically occurs in the company of other Amish teens, not as lone individuals or in mixed groups with non-Amish. One's closest friends during the rumspringa period are likely to be Amish friends from school, work, or church. "They're stuck in their own little thing of drinking and cussing and stuff," reflected an ex-Swartzentruber female. "They don't truly understand the outside world." Meyers and Nolt concur: "Even those Amish teens who wish to get a 'taste of the world' do so, paradoxically, in a particularly Amish way."[37] Moreover, Amish parents do not condone the dating of non-Amish youth, because the church makes no exceptions to the policy of marrying only Amish church members.

An often overlooked fact, however, is that marriages are typically endogamous with respect to church affiliation as well. That is, parents not only want their children to remain Amish but to stay Amish *in their own affiliation*. One Old Order man observed, "The main reason we don't intermarry much is because we don't court in the same circles." Pushed as to why courting is restricted, an Andy Weaver elder replied: "It's not that we dislike Amish in other affiliations . . . But if you make one step, you're so likely to take a second and a third step." Such a "slippery slope mentality" pervades the Holmes County Amish. Parents thus erect boundaries between affiliations to try to ward off the temptation to move up or "jump the fence." As a result, dating someone from a more progressive group will usually raise more objections than dating someone from a more conservative affiliation.

To be sure, there have been successful interaffiliation marriages. Most of these occur in the years immediately following a church schism, when the young people have already been courting each other. Among the Holmes County Amish, there are Andy Weaver—Old Order and Old Order—New Order marriages that stem from the shared circles of courtship preceding the schisms of 1952 and 1967.[38] But the fact that most Amish parents actively discourage dating between youth from nonaffiliated groups is a striking testimony to the perceived threat to group integrity. In a large settlement like Holmes County, where numerous opportunities for interaction with Amish from other affiliations exist, the extent to which each religious affiliation monopolizes potential marriage partners is extraordinary.

Excommunication and Shunning: Cracks in the Foundation?

Another issue that marks Amish identity is the *Bann und Meidung*, excommunication and shunning. Kraybill describes this rite of exclusion both as a "potent tool of social control" and as a "ritual of shaming that is used in public occasions and in face-to-face interaction to remind the ostracized that they are outside the moral order."[39] Typically, there is no prohibition on talking with those who are in the ban, but church members may not sell goods to or accept anything directly from the offender. Moreover, if an excommunicated individual visits the home for a funeral or other occasion, that person's meals must be taken at a separate table. Church members see the excommunicated individual as disobedient, and thus they circumscribe all associations with him or her. Upon closer inspection, however, shunning turns out to be a very controversial practice among the Amish. It is therefore an ideal window for evaluating the role of church affiliations in the settlement and for assessing the gap between cultural ideals and actual behavior that can arise when the interests of church and family collide.

The Amish have been surprisingly successful at retaining their young people, but even a 10–20 percent defection rate means that most Amish have experienced the pain of having a child, sibling, or close relative "taken by the world." To date, most of what we know about shunning comes from autobiographical accounts of individuals who have been excommunicated. Addressed to a popular audience, their stories usually follow an "escape to freedom" narrative in which the Amish are depicted as abusive and cultlike, a people who are smothered by tradition, doctrine, and bias.[40] Lost in these sensationalized accounts of resistance are the views both of the silent majority who have faced excommunication and of church members themselves. Although anger and heartbreak are usually inherent in the initial breakup, listening to these voices on both sides of the fence provides a clearer picture of the conditions under which excommunication is applied and how strictly shunning is enforced across Holmes County Amish affiliations.

It is important at the outset to acknowledge two broad structural principles that govern excommunication and shunning. The first is that all Amish make a sharp distinction between those who choose not to join the church and those who leave after they have been baptized. Leaving the Amish without ever taking one's vows is never a cause of excommunication. Most who decide not to join the Amish report that they maintain fairly regular communication with their families. Joining the church and then breaking one's vows, however, is a different story. Such persons will be placed in the ban and subjected to various degrees of shunning from both family and church members.

In addition, there is a standard process for excommunication. Most individuals who are excommunicated have already gone through a series of confessions and punishments. For minor infractions, "free will confessions" or "requested confessions" to church leaders in the privacy of one's home or barn will suffice. More serious infractions usually lead to public confessions in front of church members in which the offender sits or kneels and may receive a six-week ban, depending on the severity of the case. If the offender is contrite, confessing in front of the entire congregation or being temporarily excommunicated, or both, can serve as a powerful mechanism for restoration and healing. Those who refuse to confess generally receive a six-to-twelve-month grace period by the bishop. During this time, church members try to persuade the wayward to have a change of heart or behavior before the final congregational vote, which must be unanimous. Church leaders will then visit the expelled individual to deliver the message and a verse from 1 Corinthians 5:5: "To deliver such an one unto Satan for the destruction of the flesh, that the spirit may be saved in the day of the Lord Jesus."[41] Even after all this, the door of reunification remains open for any wayward member to repent, kneel, and confess his or her error.[42]

In theory, the system of excommunication and shunning illustrates that the authority of the church supersedes family ties. Family members are to shun their wayward relatives just as any other church member would; the baptismal water is expected to be thicker than blood. In practice, however, the system diverges from this ideal in at least two ways. First, the formal stance on shunning, encoded in church Ordnung, varies sharply across affiliations within the settlement; and second, there is often a considerable gap between the professed ideal of shunning and actual practice. Based on a survey we conducted of about fifty ex-Amish individuals, we will examine each of these two in turn, but let us begin with a more basic question: Why do some individuals part ways with their church after they have taken their vows?[43]

Motivations for Leaving

Our survey uncovered two dominant motivations that have led Holmes County Amish to turn their backs on the security of the Amish way of life: the desire for fewer lifestyle restrictions and the desire for a more intense religious experience. One New Order businessman described the former motivation—for more freedom and material conveniences—as the "traditional route" for leaving the Amish, in contrast to what he called the "fantastic emotionalism" underlying the "born again" path of leaving the Amish.

The ex-Amish who leave to gain freedom in lifestyle choices speak of wanting automobiles, further education, and the ability to choose their own style of dress.[44] An ex–New Order woman wrote, "During that time in my life I was planning on going to college . . . also, I was tired of wearing the same clothes all the time." Many Amish with such a predilection come to view the rules governing Amish life as hypocritical, inconsistent, and ambiguous. An ex–Old Order survey respondent's reason for leaving was "all the rules and regulations that did not make sense." An ex–Andy

Weaver woman, who left in her midthirties, told this story: "The day I decided to leave was when my father came over to cut my countertop in two. The countertop was nine or ten feet long, and the church rule was eight feet. So my dad actually came and was measuring it to see where he could cut it. I could have the whole thing, but it had to be in two pieces. So then, in my mind, I was just like, 'Well, if this little piece of counter-top is going to take me to Hell, I'm going to leave the Amish and drive a car and have some fun and go to Hell.' That was my decision." Another ex-Amish survey respondent wrote, "I remember asking Dad why can we use X's phone but we can't have one; why can we ride in his car but we can't have our own . . . what is the difference? Those kinds of things are really why I left." Amish church members view such complaints about use versus ownership as reflecting a superficial understanding of church doctrine, but such sentiments are not uncommon among the ex-Amish.

A second factor that leads some Amish to leave the faith is the desire for a more intense religious experience.[45] In our survey, the majority of those who had been excommunicated after taking their vows said that they were "saved" or "born again." For these individuals, differences over the inter-pretation of the Bible led to their departure. One of our ex–Old Order survey respondents noted, "There were too many rules that didn't line up with the Bible." Another ex–Old Order respondent wrote, "I could not pray and listen to God without first sifting it through the Amish do's and don'ts." An ex–Andy Weaver man commented, "There developed a seri-ous conflict and disagreements between me and my relatives as to what was 'TRUTH'!" Like some non-Amish converts to evangelical Christianity, these ex-Amish "learn to have out-of-the-ordinary experiences and to use them to develop a remarkably intimate, personal God."[46]

From the point of view of most Amish groups, however, the very idea that individuals should read and interpret the Bible for themselves is a "strange belief." They intuitively understand that such an individualistic approach to religion could undermine the very foundation of the Amish lifestyle. An effort to distribute Bibles that had been translated into Penn-sylvania Dutch encountered resistance from conservative Amish church leaders precisely for this reason.[47] Many ex-Amish have experienced this resistance firsthand. "We witnessed to Amish until they drove us out," lamented an ex–New Order man.

It is possible, however, that those who claim they left because of biblical convictions simply desire more of the luxuries and conveniences of a materialistic society. Church leaders often suspect that the real reasons for leaving involve worldly desires, and they will usually observe the life-style choices (especially car ownership and dress) of those who have re-cently left to try to confirm such motivations. Yet when asked which most influenced the decision to leave, the attractiveness of English culture or dissatisfaction with Amish culture, 67 percent of our survey respondents chose dissatisfaction with Amish culture, 12 percent chose the attractive-ness of English culture, and 21 percent said both were equally influential. When directly asked, 66 percent said that attraction to English culture and people played no role in their decision to leave the Amish community. Differences in age, gender, membership status, or education did not sig-nificantly correlate with their responses. Nevertheless, most ex-Amish do embrace more "modern" lifestyles, which suggests that worldly desires—whether to escape Amish restrictions or gain attractive freedoms—might very well play an important role in the decision to leave.

Holmes County Amish who begin to express doubts about their church leaders' interpretations of the Bible can find a powerful local ally in Joe Keim and his organization, Mission to Amish People (MAP), whose goal is to "take the message of hope and eternal life to the Amish people." Keim, an ex-Amish himself who is based in nearby Savannah, Ohio, offers temporary shelter and advice on adjustment to the outside world, as well as "spiritual counseling" to those who are "coming out" of Amish society. MAP's publications include not only practical advice on manners, money management, dating, personal cleanliness, employment, and education for the ex-Amish, but scathing critiques of the "legalism" that underlies Amish society. One publication, for example, asks, "But what about those vows [to the Amish church]? . . . Was I sealing my own condemnation by breaking those vows? The bishops and ministers certainly wanted me to think so . . . Little did I know that you cannot place part of your trust in Jesus, and part of your trust in *your* good Amish life."[48] Keim's open invi-tation to Bible study and his certainty that the Amish are misguided in relying on works strikes a powerful chord with some Amish individuals. However, Keim's activities are quite controversial in the Holmes County Settlement.[49] One New Order man told us that he felt Keim "does not un-derstand the basic Amish concepts of discipleship and brotherhood."

Individuals who leave the Amish church can also participate in the For-

The Mission to Amish People (MAP) assists individuals who want to leave the Amish in making a lifestyle transition to mainstream American society. The MAP building is attached to the Bethel Baptist Church in Savannah, Ohio. Photograph courtesy of Joe Keim.

mer Amish Reunion (FAR), a support group coordinated by Ada Lendon, herself an ex-Amish. The group has a mailing list of more than two hundred individuals and meets twice a year for a picnic and fellowship, usually alternating between sites in Ohio and Indiana. FAR tends to attract ex-Amish who are sympathetic to the theology of born-again Christians. At one picnic we attended in Shreve, Ohio, nearly two hours of quiet but animated informal conversations among a diverse group of ex-Amish attendees was followed by music provided by a local evangelical church.

From Strict Shunning to Opposing the Bann

Regardless of the motivation behind the parting of ways between an individual and his or her congregation, one's church affiliation carries enormous implications for how the separation ultimately unfolds. For serious offenses such as adultery or divorce, agreement about excommunication will be widespread across all affiliations. Most cases, however, are more complicated and may even involve an attempt by those who leave to use the system in order to avoid being placed in the ban. Their approach rests on the knowledge that, first, there is a grace period before the final congregational vote and, second, most church Ordnung do not require excommunication if a member joins a slightly "higher" church. To avoid being placed in the ban, then, individuals who want to leave the Amish can simply join a higher Amish church or a Mennonite church for a year or so before deciding whether to move on to the next step. Responding to a question about whether she was currently excommunicated, one ex–New Order woman drew a smiley face on her survey and wrote, "No, because we went out in stages." This practice has become less common in recent years, and many now go directly to their "final destination."

The Swartzentruber Amish have eliminated this loophole by taking the strict stance that they will excommunicate and shun a member for transferring to *any* other Amish affiliation or Plain church. In addition, the Swartzentrubers tend to refrain from associating much with those who choose to leave without ever being baptized. As a result, Swartzentrubers tend to "go all the way" when they leave the Swartzentruber church rather than joining another Plain church.[50] "It's like going to another country," confessed one ex-Swartzentruber when asked about the process of adjustment to non-Amish society. "I felt so weird, like I'm stupid. And I was stupid in a sense. I didn't understand, let's say non-Amish girls. You know, trying to compare myself with her, I felt like this itty bitty thing. I wanted to just hide and not get involved with the real people out there. That's kind of the mentality that you grew up with. It's just that you don't feel like you qualify." In the eyes of some Amish, this inferiority complex leads Swartzentrubers to go overboard in trying to "do stuff to prove to the English that I can compete on your level," as one individual put it.[51]

In principle, the Andy Weaver affiliation shares the Swartzentruber commitment to strict shunning: the ban will not be lifted until a member returns to the same church district that imposed the ban. In practice, however, there is leeway if one decides simply to move "up" a step or two. According to one Andy Weaver man, "the unwritten rule has been that if you didn't leave for a car church, you would not be placed in the ban." In recent years, one of the most contentious cases of excommunication, though, involved an Andy Weaver bishop who recommended the ban for a church member who transferred to a New Order church. According to a knowledgeable insider, the sister of the excommunicated individual had schizophrenia, and the Andy Weaver bishop, who was ill-informed about mental illness, refused to allow flexibility in the Ordnung for her to care for her sister. This case, however, seems to be an exception to the rule.

The Old Order churches tend to be more lenient in practice. A church member who moves to the New Order or the New New Order will typically avoid the ban altogether, but even if an Old Order person joins the "car Amish" or a Mennonite church, the ban does not always come into play. In a striking testimony to the growing cracks in the Old Order approach to excommunication, some Old Order bishops will lift the ban on Amish who are "born again" if they receive a letter from the new church verifying the person's status as a member "in good standing." The approach of the Old Order Amish to individuals who never joined the church also differentiates them from the Andy Weavers and the Swartzentrubers. None of the three affiliations will take church action against such individuals, but the Andy Weavers and the Swartzentrubers are more likely to "draw back" from interaction with them because of the fear of negative influences. For example, one Old Order man, whose wife is from the Andy Weaver church, told us he does not feel comfortable associating with his in-laws because of the way they turn their backs on their young people who choose not to remain Amish. "Sometimes I feel that they [the Andy Weavers] are arrogant about it. You know, they'll be with their family members [who did not join the Amish] and if they sit at the same table, they'll just get up and leave because of that. So there's no family reunions because of the shunning."

In contrast, apart from flagrant and unrepentant violators of the Ordnung, the New Order Amish typically do not excommunicate or shun at all if the ex-member joins a "Bible-believing church." It is preferable that this church be of Anabaptist origin, but it is not a prerequisite.[52] The New Order rationale is that the ban is a response to sin, and since ministers would not accuse a Beachy or Mennonite church of being unscriptural, they cannot regard a member's transferring into that church as sinful. A New Order minister put it this way: "Not excommunicating is the way we say that we are not the only church, and so you can go to heaven even if you go to another church." In his view, the ban is for maintaining *spiritual* boundaries, not cultural ones. One New Order bishop privately confessed to us that he believes the Amish should get rid of shunning altogether.[53] "It is supposed to be done out of love," he noted, "but more often it turns to spite." Many Old Order Amish see the New Order's reluctance to use excommunication or shunning when members move "up" to car churches as a major reason that they lose a higher proportion of their young people.

The differences across affiliations in the conditions under which excommunication is imposed have important implications for a related issue: the degree to which other church districts honor a ban. In general, when a church district excommunicates an individual, the decision is honored by all churches that are in fellowship with that church *and* by all "lower" churches. This is not an insignificant point because it shows that in spite of their differences, the "lower" affiliations have respect for the ultimate decisions that are made about membership in the "higher" churches. The reverse, however, is not usually true. A Swartzentruber man placed in the ban for breaking his vows will only be shunned by his "higher" neighbors if the offense is so serious that all parties can agree it is worthy of excommunication, such as adultery or dishonest business practices. For other violations, the "higher" church may not agree with the ban issued by a "lower" church, particularly if it involves technology. For instance, a Swartzentruber man who refuses to permanently "put away" his chain saw and an Old Order woman who hooks up a phone in her house might be placed in the ban by their respective churches, but if they are not arrogant or belligerent, they might be welcomed into a "higher" church.

Preserving Flexibility: Gaps between Church Policy and Its Implementation

If divergent church policies toward excommunication represent one "crack" in the foundation, the gap between church policy on shunning and actual implementation is another. After the ban is in place, the severity and duration of shunning depend on a variety of factors: the conservativeness of the church district, the interpretation of family members, the situation in which interaction occurs, the severity of the offense, and the attitude of the offender. Most of our survey respondents said that the severity of enforcement depended primarily upon the particular church and the degree of its conservativeness. But even within a specific affiliation, bishops often have considerable leeway in determining how strictly the ban should be enforced. One bishop turned a blind eye to the fact that an excommunicated single woman was living in the same compound (though not in the same house) with her mother, who was still a church member. In many cases, however, the latitude of the bishops is constrained by the Ordnung and by precedents in the community. In other cases, the subtle behaviors involved in shunning are simply beyond the reach of ordained church leaders.

Because the stakes are so high, a decision to leave the Amish is often a traumatic event, and many of our respondents said their parents and church officials went to great lengths to try to persuade them to return. Parents were often described as being "deeply hurt," "heartbroken," "very disappointed," "very upset," and "very sad." For example, when one Amish woman was packing to move out, her father approached the English man who was helping her move. "How much will it take to keep her at home?" he said. "I'll give you any amount of money. I'll make the check out right now." This woman recalled that her father believed her leaving "was the worst thing that could happen . . . I was the one that broke the perfect family. And I was a girl, I was single, thirty-four years old, and they were, like, you should be satisfied where you're at."

The concern for loss of salvation is another recurrent theme heard from family members by those who have left the Amish fold. One survey respondent wrote, "Father's reaction was preaching at me. Saying that I was already condemned to hell because all English people are going to hell." Another reflected, "Oh, they came in tears and said how I am going to hell, and my father specifically said he has no hope for me to go to Heaven. And we sat up for hours talking about it." In fact, fear of emotional confrontations with family members leads some to leave secretly at night, as this ex-Swartzentruber woman relates: "Oh, I didn't tell them, we just snuck out, and I was thinking, 'Man, the devil's running after me and I'm going to hell.' Because of what they all tell you, you're going out of the driveway, and it's like, 'Oh my gosh, the devil's going to jump out of the corner.'" Several interviewees even recounted visions of damnation that their family members shared with them. One ex-Amish man related that his father had gotten wind of what was "coming down" before his leaving, upon which "he told me he saw me standing at the very edge of the lake of fire with only a thin crust supporting me." According to Reiling, such anxieties about going to hell do not automatically dissipate upon defection.[54]

Not all family members reacted with hellfire and brimstone, however. From the examples given by the participants in our study, it is clear that family members vary in the severity with which they shun. Our respondents included a few whose parents were quietly supportive or who left later or with the child. In one case, the parents moved to a more liberal church, hoping that their son would return, but to no avail. In another case, an ex–Old Order member related, "Mom started searching the Scriptures for herself and concluded that I wasn't living in sin, and therefore, they didn't shun me and this soon got discovered so they excommunicated them, too." An ex–New Order respondent wrote, "Some parents forbid their children from coming to see them with non-Amish clothes and from writing them. Mine don't go that far. Glory hallelujah!"[55]

Inconsistencies in the enforcement of the ban occur in other ways as well. In some cases family and church members are less likely to take the hard line on shunning when no one else is watching, as this ex-Swartzentruber male relates: "I have brothers that'll shun somebody right in front of the whole family, but when they're by themselves, they won't. Obviously they don't feel convicted before God, that that's a sin. It's just because of the family, because they have to." Others may follow the letter of the Ordnung but still exchange gifts by adeptly using nonverbal cues, such as the "finger tap." One ex-Amish woman reports how, without thinking, she started to hand a card to a female friend. "But all at once she was like [taps index finger hard on the table]. So I put it down and she picked it up." In many cases, enforcement of the ban also seems to wane over time. Asked if they had experienced a "thawing" in enforcement of the ban, over half of the respondents in our survey replied in the affirmative.

One of the practical challenges created by the rapid growth of Amish settlements across the United States has been the difficulty of keeping track of who is in the ban. Despite the efficacy of the "Amish grapevine," church officials and members have trouble monitoring excommunicated individuals. The prohibition on selling goods to those in the ban, for example, is hard to enforce in large settlements such as Holmes County. One ex–Old Order woman reported that she quickly learned where to go when she wanted to purchase something from an Amish shop. An Andy Weaver family recounts that a young couple who spoke Pennsylvania

Dutch moved into the area and set up a business driving the Amish. "It was great, we went everywhere with them for nearly two years," the wife commented. "Then we got word that they were actually in the ban from a community out West, so we had to stop riding with them."

Individuals who have committed serious offenses or who are seen as "kickin' up" trouble are usually met with a hardening of the church's position. Church leaders want to see signs of repentance among the excommunicated. In the absence of a public confession, however, those individuals who do not flaunt their new status but respect Amish sensibilities are more likely to be invited to family events and to experience a thaw in shunning. Although most ex-Amish in our survey said they had no misgivings about their decision to leave, approximately 30 percent said they have some regrets—and nearly all affirmed the positive aspects in Amish culture, such as the work ethic and spirit of cooperation.

In spite of inconsistencies in enforcement, the practices of excommunication and shunning continue to work. In our survey, two-thirds of respondents said shunning was enforced completely and consistently, whereas 17 percent said it was enforced somewhat or inconsistently and another 17 percent said it was not enforced much at all. Similarly, two-thirds of our survey respondents believe that their families look down on them rather than seeing them as equals, and the percentage who feel this way is significantly higher among those who left after having joined the church. One ex–Old Order woman summed up her predicament: "The hardest thing to adjust to is all the rejection, people not saying hi to you, just having nothing to do with you." A striking illustration of exclusion was that 73 percent of ex-Amish in our survey said their closest friend was non-Amish, and 24 percent said their closest friend was ex-Amish. Only one individual who was in the ban had a closest friend who was Amish.

The different stances taken by affiliations, church districts, and family members over shunning and excommunication reveal just how complicated the relationship between the individual and the community can be. What does it mean to be a part of or outside of "community"? How should family ties be weighed against church rules? In answering these and related questions, we see a wide range of meanings and behaviors among individuals living in essentially similar structural contexts. For some people, community and regulation mean support and guidance, a sort of security blanket, while for others the blanket represents suffocation and control. Whether these variations represent more than just cracks in the foundation remains to be seen. G. C. Waldrep reports that in the Kalona Settlement in Iowa, for example, retention rates of Amish youth have been high in spite of a comparatively lax attitude toward excommunication, raising the important question of whether the ban really is an essential tool for social control. The vigorous debate about shunning among the Amish themselves, however, shows that they fully believe the stakes are high.

Church Schism in Perspective

Without question, the old and sometimes bitter intra-Amish divisions still loom over the Holmes County Settlement and shape social interaction in important ways. In a close-knit society, conflict is always difficult, especially when repeated attempts to repair the social fabric fall short. Asked about the consequences of church schism, one Amish leader admitted, "I think it's come to a point where you don't give somebody the benefit of the doubt when you are from the other sect." Most Amish view the history of church schism as a sad, if inevitable, by-product of the fallen nature of humanity and also their tendency to take religion so seriously.

The proliferation of Amish affiliations also has the unintended effect of further confusing outsiders, who may already hold an unrealistic image of the Amish. Ironically, the Amish contribute to their own idealization through their reluctance to talk about church schism to outsiders and their tendency to lump the Swartzentrubers, Andy Weavers, and Old Order Amish together under the label "Old Order." The introduction to the 2005 *Ohio Amish Directory*, for example, describes church division as "truly sad," but the directory refrains from labeling church districts by affiliation.

Nevertheless, Amish church leaders are quick to remind critics that religious splintering is not peculiar to their people and that not a single case exists in which church schism has led to violence. In addition, there is probably some truth to Gertrude Huntington's functionalist interpretation that the divisions have served to keep Amish communities strong because they "preserve small face to face units and reduce friction by separating incompatible factions."[56] Moreover, we argue that understanding the role of Amish affiliations is only the starting point in unraveling the complicated relationship between Amish individuals and their communities. As it turns out, other crosscutting forces and contexts, including family and neighborhood, school, and workplace, bring Amish from various walks of life together and help mitigate the effect of church affiliation differences. We now turn to an examination of the crucial roles of these other institutions in social change.

Continuity and Change in Family Life

We have more money than we need to exercise our lifestyle.
—An Old Order man

Two images of Amish families compete in the American public's eye. The first holds up the Amish as a model of family stability and continuity, a carryover from the "ideal traditional family" of years gone by.[1] In this view, the distinctive combination of prescriptions (such as encouragement of large families and intergenerational households) and proscriptions (such as prohibitions on divorce, birth control, and institutionalized day care) has provided a time-tested recipe for healthy family and community life. Such a positive view of Amish family life is promoted not only by the Amish themselves but by other constituencies as well. The tourist industry's promotional literature highlights close-knit Amish families, epitomized by the ubiquitous *dawdi haus* and by the less obvious, but intensely communal, barn raisings.[2] Local and state government officials have also touted the region's family stability in the hopes of attracting economic investment. Even scholars may have unwittingly contributed to this view by casting the family as one of the institutions most resistant to social change and by describing "the impact on family life" as the nonnegotiable litmus test by which Amish decide whether to adopt new practices and technology.

Juxtaposed in the popular imagination to this idyllic view of Amish family "togetherness," is a more negative set of images that purports to expose the dark side. As early as the mid-twentieth century, some depictions of Amish life in the popular media, such as the musical *Plain and Fancy*, portrayed Amish "disciplinary structures to be naïve, misguided and in some respects cruel" and "[identified] the Amish with religious tyranny."[3] More recently, some feminists and ex-Amish have portrayed Amish wives as second-class citizens who are dominated by their husbands. In addition, several prime-time television documentaries and Web sites have alleged that the patriarchal Amish family is a hotbed of unreported child abuse, domestic violence, and sexual exploitation. A 2004 ABC News 20/20 feature on the Amish, for example, created a storm of controversy by giving the impression that abuse is fairly widespread in Amish communities but is shrouded in secrecy and inadequately handled by the rigid and patriarchal church leadership. According to the critics, one need only dig below the surface tranquility to see that Amish families are rife with domestic violence and sexual abuse.

Neither caricature—nostalgic or dehumanizing—captures the realities of Amish family life in the Holmes County Settlement. In spite of the uniformities created by shared religious doctrine, Amish families show a surprising degree of diversity. And Amish family life has not been stuck in a time warp. The Amish have not been immune from the powerful pressures that changing patterns of work, schooling, and health care can exert on the form and substance of family life. Even for the Amish, predicting the effects on family life of new occupations, household products, or leisure opportunities has not always been easy.

At the same time, the shift away from farming has not turned Amish family life and gender identities upside down. But it has introduced changes, some more dramatic than others. As we explore in this chapter how Amish families have followed different moral compasses in navigating new external pressures and opportunities, we begin by looking at the constellation of meanings surrounding *family* and *home*. We then examine the quality of interaction and the tenor of emotional ties between parents and children and between husbands and wives. Finally, we look at how the influx of cash and spare time has re-shaped patterns of leisure and consumption in Amish communities. Throughout the chapter we try to show how kinship intersects with educational, religious, and economic forces in complex ways.

The *Freindschaft*

In spite of the centrality of the church in shaping social life and identity, the family remains the basic building block of Amish society. The size of church districts is always calculated in numbers of families, and when the threshold of approximately thirty to forty families is reached, the leaders begin to discuss how to divide the district so as to maintain small, face-to-face communities. Similarly, Amish private schools are organized in terms of the number of families who send "scholars" to them. Throughout the settlement, the Amish community is held together by the presence of interrelated kinship groups. Individuals from the same extended family often grow up in the same neighborhood and attend school together; sometimes they will end up joining the same church and working for the same employer. And although extended families usually cluster in the same affiliation, the presence of kin who have switched to other affiliations provides a powerful countervailing force against narrow sectarianism. Even with thirty thousand Amish of different affiliations in the Holmes County Settlement, two Amish meeting for the first time will usually be able to "locate" each other vis-à-vis their kin networks.

Compared to non-Amish families in rural Ohio, Amish families retain several distinctive structural features: a taboo on divorce, the near universality of multigenerational households, and large family size. There are cases of single families and widowhood, which we consider later, but most Amish women marry early and for life and see marital conflict as something that should be "worked out." "There are a lot of marriage problems among the Amish," commented a New Order preacher, "but they will not at the drop of a hat say, 'I'm going to divorce you.'" As a result, the large majority of Amish families pass through a prolonged "nuclear family stage" in which father and mother live together with their unmarried children. Although initiating divorce is grounds for excommunication, it does happen on occasion. When one partner initiates divorce and is excommunicated, the spouse and children are allowed to remain Amish, but the Amish spouse may not remarry until the previous partner dies. A small number of Amish (mostly women) in the Holmes County Settlement receive alimony or child support payments from ex-spouses who have been excommunicated.

Children also grow up with grandparents near them. One retired couple we met had sixty-four grandchildren. "The oldest is 18 and the youngest is 12 days—and each one of 'em's special," quipped the grand-mother. For the Amish, the "gift of mass longevity"[4] does not typically in-volve the cultural nightmare of living old and alone. Parents usually retire to the attached dawdi haus after gifting their home to one of the younger children. The notion that with age come experience and wisdom is deeply ingrained in Amish culture, and consultation with one's elderly relatives on matters of health care or business is common even when younger fam-ily members are "running the show." Nevertheless, the Amish use local nursing homes if special care is needed, although this tendency is more pronounced among the "higher" groups.

In spite of the move away from agriculture, the overall fertility rate for Amish women has remained high. According to our analysis of the 2005 *Ohio Amish Directory*, Amish families average 5 children, well above the national average of 2.0.[5] Most Amish still are born into a large family that includes a vast network of extended kin.[6] Consequently, if "the Ameri-can public has lost the art of visiting," as one bishop put it, such is not the case for the Amish, where visiting the freindschaft (extended family) is a dominant pastime. Most Amish children grow up in a world filled with uncles, aunts, cousins, nieces, and nephews; it is not uncommon for an Amish teenager to have forty to fifty first cousins. Paradoxically, the sheer size of Amish kin networks often makes "family reunions" difficult for lo-gistic reasons. One Old Order man noted that his whole family doesn't get together too often because there are "too many little ones that want to eat right away." Instead, the sisters will get together, or the brothers. Ties with same-sex siblings are typically very strong, and such get-togethers often revolve around shared activities such as quilting, cooking, or shopping for the sisters and attending auctions or hunting and fishing for the brothers.

To this general portrait, however, several qualifications must be added. The first is that variations in family size reflect differences in occupations and the affiliations to which members belong.[7] In general, farmers have more children than nonfarmers. In Samson Wasao's study based on the 1988 *Ohio Amish Directory*, Amish farmers averaged 6.2 children, while the mean for nonfarmers was 4.7 children. Our own study of the 2005 directory showed an even larger gap—more than two children—between farm and nonfarm families.[8] These differences stem in part from the de-creased need for labor as the Amish move away from the farm.

Church affiliation also has a dramatic effect on family size. The Swartzentrubers are widely acknowledged to have the largest families, although reliable data is scarce. A study of 144 Amish families in Wayne County in 1984 found that 47 percent of Swartzentruber families had at least nine children, compared to 25 percent of other Amish; thus, it is likely that the Swartzentrubers average at least seven to eight children per family. Of those affiliations included in the 2005 *Ohio Amish Directory*, the Andy Weavers had the largest average number of children (6.2), followed by the New Order Christian Fellowship (6.0) and the New Order (5.3). Surprisingly, the Old Order Amish averaged only 4.6 children.

Why the Old Order Amish have fewer children on average than the more "progressive" New Order Amish is a puzzling question. Perhaps New Order spirituality leads them to take more seriously the active nurturing and centrality of the family. Much of the Christian literature that is read by the New Order Amish, such as the quarterly magazine *Keepers at Home*, glorifies motherhood and celebrates the wife's place in the home. Having multiple offspring is one way to be proactive in creating a generation of Amish individuals who are spiritually enlightened. Another possible explanation is that the New Order Amish are less likely to use birth control because they feel it is morally wrong.

In addition, the average number of children per family in the settlement is slowly declining. The steepest decline occurred for the two cohorts of women born in the 1940s and in the 1950s.[9] Even over the past seventeen years, however, the average number of children for all Amish affiliations has dropped slightly from 5.3 to 5.0. While the move away from farming is likely the primary catalyst for this gradual decline in fertility rates, another factor appears to be the increased use of birth control and attempts by women to limit the number of pregnancies.[10] An Old Order woman commented, "Artificial birth control is wrong if used for selfish reasons, but it's okay for married couples if used for health or emotional reasons, but only barrier methods." A New Order father agreed: "A lot of Amish use birth control even though we have a conscience against it. But most don't use the pill because it's seen as taking away life."

In recent years, some Amish preachers have said publicly that women should be able to say "No" to more children. Most ordained leaders, however, especially those in the Andy Weaver and Swartzentruber affiliations, still maintain that family size is strictly a matter of "God's will."

Even today it is rare to hear a conversation among the Amish centered around the question "How many children do you plan to have?"

Some Amish couples are unable to have biological children (the incidence of infertility [about 3%] is about the same among the Amish as in the general population).[11] In such cases, adoption is acceptable. "My sister adopted four biracial children," noted one New Order bishop. "They just wanted children to lavish love on." At first, adoption agencies balked at Amish requests because "they used to think we had no technology." But attitudes have changed, and now there is a small number of Amish families in the settlement who have adopted children; restrictions on air travel have limited international adoptions.

Naming practices support the idea that the individual is a member of an extended family that is internally differentiated by age and gender and continuous through time. Surnames anchor a person in a patrilineage, they carry the reputation of the extended family, and they even associate a person with a certain settlement. The six most common Amish surnames in the Holmes County Settlement, for instance, are Miller, Yoder, Troyer, Hershberger, Schlabach, and Weaver, whereas in the Lancaster Settlement the list would include Stoltzfus, King, Fisher, Beiler, Esh, and Lapp.[12]

Because many people have the same name within a church district or affiliation, the frequent use of nicknames provides an easy method of keeping track of individuals. In the Holmes County Settlement, for instance, most Amish know that Apple Abe is a quadriplegic who fell out of an apple tree as a boy and that Air Force Mose is the Swartzentruber boy who joined the military and then came back to the Amish and became a bishop. One local Amish factory worker is fondly called Pete by his friends because, while on the job, he liked to listen to caustic sports talk radio host Pete Franklin, who broadcast on WWWE Cleveland from 1972 to 1987.

The increased mobility of some Amish families has created new challenges, however, in keeping track of kin who may be dispersed across dozens of states and settlements. Phone shanties can be used as one option in the attempt, but several other strategies for keeping in touch are common. Local auctions are a popular place to tap into the "Amish grapevine," including news of kin. In addition, approximately two-thirds of Amish in the settlement regularly read the *Budget*, a "correspondence newspaper" based in Sugarcreek, Ohio, that includes weekly letters from 450 "scribes" in Amish church districts all over the United States and Canada. These letters, written mostly by women, serve not only to create an idealized "imagined community" for the Amish, but give detailed information about the life-cycle events of church members.[13] Circle letters, in which successive contributors add their news, are also popular among spread-out families. Funerals, too, provide a useful, if solemn, occasion for keeping up with far-flung kin. One funeral home director told us that the most distinctive aspect of Amish funerals from his point of view was the large number of "memory cards," usually 800–1,500, that a family would typically order from them as an announcement that someone had passed away.

Within this broad context of stable marriages, three-generational households, and large numbers of children and siblings, Amish families are hardly "havens in a heartless world."[14] Rather, they are a crucial nexus of cultural activities. Since "very few life cycle functions have left the home,"[15] the family remains a site not only for births, marriages, and funerals, but for numerous other activities as well, including economic ones. Economic innovations often run through kinship lines, as do particular rumspringa traditions, the use of public schools, and reliance on certain forms of alternative medicines.

The Home: Land, Architecture, and Household Technology

The term *family* invokes not only a set of people who are deemed kin but also a sense of place. For Amish families, over most of the past two hundred years, the constellation of meanings surrounding the "home" orbited the farm. In the farming context, growing up Amish meant having roughly one hundred twenty acres of land, daily chores such as milking cows and feeding chickens, and annual rituals such as threshing rings and cutting ice from the pond. These associations still apply for a small minority of Amish. But increasingly, home means a much smaller plot of land and fewer chores for children, as a result of what David Luthy refers to as the "crowd-in policy."[16] In some cases, the original farmstead has been carved up into smaller ten-to-thirty-acre plots for the children who "work out"; for example, an Old Order man who works at a furniture store uses the thirty acres he received from his dad for deer hunting and bird watching, and he leases part of it to a Swartzentruber man for vegetable farming. In other cases, homes are built on very small plots of land, although one real estate agent who works closely with the Amish noted that most of the time "they're looking for 1.5 acres minimum because they need a house, shop, and barn." There is nothing in Holmes County similar to the "Amish suburbia" (neighborhoods laid out in grids but occupied solely by Amish) found in Elkhart and LaGrange counties, Indiana,[17] but *farmhouse* and *home* are no longer synonymous for most Amish.

The high price of land in Holmes County has prompted several adaptive strategies by Amish families. Some families have moved to the southern edges of the settlement or to other states in search of cheaper land. "If you want to measure the price of land," commented one real estate agent, "you measure it with the center of Holmes County as the hub and the further you go out the price starts dropping. It's just like putting a pin in the middle, and it decelerates." The Amish have also formed an internal market in which they frequently sell to close family members or relatives. "They have an informal appraisal system, three or four guys who are very strong," noted a local real estate agent. If they can afford it, parents may also buy land in southern Ohio as a kind of insurance policy for their children.

Sometimes families, especially young couples, have needed economic help in getting started in life. Backed primarily by three Old Order Amish men, the Amish Helping Fund was started in 1995 to assist young couples purchasing their first homes. In 2008, this nonprofit organization had loans out to eight hundred to nine hundred persons and held more than $80 million in funds.[18] The loans are for home or land purchases, but the land purchase has to be for livelihood, not for hunting purposes. A list of applicants is kept, with those at the top of the list being first-time home buyers. In 2008 they were charged 5 percent variable interest, and investors in the fund got a return of 4.5 percent. The decision to approve a loan is based on the applicant's priority in the list and on an analysis of the applicant's ability to pay back the loan. There has never been a foreclosure on a loan given from the fund. Although Ohio led the nation in the number of foreclosures in 2006, the rate of foreclosures in Holmes County was only half that of nearby Wayne, Tuscarawas, and Ashland counties, a difference that can be attributed to the high number of Amish in the county.[19] According to the fund's administrator, if a family has trouble repaying its loan, church elders will take over the family checkbook for a while to demonstrate sound household management.

Although Amish of all affiliations are allowed to participate in the Helping Fund, the Andy Weaver group has decided not to take part in it, because the fund promotes household design that runs contrary to the Ordnung of most Andy Weaver churches. Most people currently getting loans are Old Order, reflecting, for one thing, the numerical dominance of the Old Order in the Amish population as a whole. Swartzentrubers do not usually go to the Old Order Helping Fund for home loans. "They'll go to an English bank first. Or they'll go to 5–10 other Swartzentrubers and piece together the money," commented a local real estate agent. "And they are adamant about paying back a debt." Convinced of the truth of this statement, at least one bank in Kidron offers "congregationally guaranteed" loans to Swartzentruber Amish who are backed by their church district. A representative of one real estate agency noted that they never asked for a deposit on Amish homes, period. "That's how confident the owner/builder was that they would pay."

The architecture, layout, and landscaping of Amish homes varies considerably by affiliation. New Order houses, some with stone facades, paved driveways, and carefully manicured gardens, may be virtually indistinguishable from neighboring non-Amish dwellings. Even Old Order houses, especially if they are built new by Amish construction crews, can be state-of-the-art. As one Amish homebuyer put it, "How could an excellent Amish carpenter possibly build a sub-standard house?" By contrast, Swartzentruber houses are easily identified by their peeling paint and by dirt driveways, outhouses, and dark red barns on the property. Typically, Swartzentrubers sell to other Swartzentrubers, or else "it's a tear-down job for others." Whereas Amish of "higher" affiliations may drywall over existing electrical outlets to preserve the value of the house, Swartzentruber families will often remove unwanted conveniences, such as indoor plumbing. A local real estate agent commented that he had just sold a house to a "lower" Amish after a "New Order" looked at it and said it wasn't good enough. "There's definitely a difference in tastes," he concluded.

In addition to the dawdi haus, outbuildings are a common feature of Amish homes. Although it is commonly believed that all Amish hold church services "in their homes," these days it is usually more accurate to

The disparity between the stately homes of progressive Amish and the farmhouses of more conservative Amish has become more noticeable in recent years.
Photographs courtesy of Charles Hurst.

say that church is held in the shop or the barn. In farm families, benches that have been transported via the bench wagon will often be set up under the hayloft and amid farm equipment in the barn. For nonfarmers, the "pole barn" is more often a spacious, cement-floored, well-insulated building that is temporarily transformed from shop or buggy parking garage on the Sunday when the family hosts church. Outdoor play equipment for children also varies by family and affiliation. Swartzentruber and Andy Weaver children have few visible playthings in the yard, but some Old and New Order homes sport basketball hoops, trampolines, and swing sets. Reflected one Old Order man, "Sometimes you go by an Amish home and see all those play things out there—different colored playhouses and swings and slides—and it rivals the play area at McDonald's." Most Old and New Order Amish are allowed to use power lawn mowers, weed eaters, bicycles, and electric typewriters, whereas Andy Weaver and Swartzentruber Amish are not.[20]

Regardless of affiliation, the interior of an Amish home evokes quiet warmth and an orderliness that seems to transcend the hustle and bustle of everyday life. The Amish love of fine woodworking is seen in the cabinetry and furniture of most houses. Interior colors are muted, although the younger generation is increasingly comfortable with pastels and bolder decorating schemes. Kitchens are typically very spacious and feature a large, centrally located table, where meals are taken. The living room may include several chairs—upholstered chairs in the more progressive affiliations—where family members congregate to read, sew, play games, and socialize in the evenings. Many homes have a walk-in basement, where the washing machine (usually a Maytag) is kept and where members of the congregation can be fed after a family hosts church. Bedrooms are usually upstairs. Stipulations about curtains for the windows vary by church district and affiliation. A local real estate agent noted, "When they [the Amish] buy a home, they know what they want. A pie safe, a walk-in pantry, a 30-square foot kitchen." One Old Order home we visited even had a wine cellar regulated by solar power and a sauna in the basement.

The use of general household technology varies considerably by affiliation and by church district. Acceptance of telephones is an especially revealing example. Most New Order members have landline phones in their homes, whereas Old Order and Andy Weaver Amish typically use a phone shanty (often shared with neighbors and thus called a "community phone") at the end of a driveway. Swartzentrubers try to avoid phone use except in emergencies. The logic is that the phone must be separate from the house or one's business, but as Diane Zimmerman Umble has shown, most shops now have a phone in an adjacent building or shanty.[21]

The recent diffusion of cell phones into some segments of the Amish community has created further complications. One New Order leader observed that most New Order members do not have cell phones, although some use them for business only, whereas "75 percent of those people [Old Order] have cell phones." Asked why cell phones had proliferated, an Old Order man noted that "everyone was using them" before church leaders realized what was happening. Many districts have forbidden cell phones in the home, but controlling portable, handheld electronic devices has become a real challenge for many church leaders.

The Amish use of household appliances has also changed markedly over the past half century. The discovery and use of natural gas in the 1950s revolutionized Amish home life for Old Order and New Order families. Gas stoves gradually replaced wood-burning and kerosene stoves for all but the Andy Weavers and the Swartzentrubers.[22] Lighting methods have also shifted from the flat-wick kerosene lamps and pressure lamps, still used by the more conservative groups, to centralized gas lights for most Old Order and New Order groups.[23] For plumbing, old-fashioned hand pumps and windmills are still used when possible by the Swartzentrubers, but even they will use diesel engines to pump water from the well at times. A large majority of the Holmes County Amish use pressurized water systems (air that has been compressed by a gas or diesel engine forces water through the pipes), resulting in "indoor bathrooms with flush toilets and built-in bathtubs and showers."[24] Wood-burning, kerosene, or gas water heaters, depending on church Ordnung, allow for hot water as well. And nearly all Amish groups in the settlement use motorized wringer washing machines (usually motorized by a gas engine). Dryers are rarely used, but "spinners" to wring out the water in washed clothes are becoming more common.

Several relatively recent developments have affected Amish home life. One is the electrical inverter, which converts 12-volt direct current from a battery into 110-volt alternating current that is no different from the current supplied by public utility lines. New Order and some Old Order Amish use battery inverters to run mixers, food processors, sewing machines, blenders, and even word processors. A New Order business-man noted, however, that "the church wants people to keep the appliances small."

Home freezers also have come into common use. In most cases, Amish families rent a freezer and space to keep it in the basement of a local store or church. Sometimes, families who live near one another fund construction of a small "freezer barn" (with electrical outlets) that is located some distance away from their homes. A woman who worked for Wayne-Holmes Electric Cooperative remembers that the firm installed more service drops to freezer barns than to homes in the winter of 2003−4, after several Amish bishops approved the use of freezer barns for their congregations. Only the Andy Weavers and the Swartzentrubers still rely on ice for refrigeration. An unintended consequence of the adoption of home freezers is that the traditional wedding months of November and December have, since the mid-1980s, given way to May, June, September, and October. Now that farming is on the wane and food can be kept cold year round, there is no need to coordinate weddings with the harvest.[25]

In addition, as noted above, the increasing availability of handheld, battery-powered devices that can be recharged has created enormous challenges for the Amish. One English owner of a lumber business whose workforce is mostly Old Order Amish had this to say when asked about the image of the Amish families as backward: "And elephants fly! They're not backwards. They'll have a charger in every outlet in our office. And they won't buy any old cell phone. They'll have the cameras and texting. Their kids will have Game Boys and all the games." Many products of the electronics revolution such as iPods, GPS devices, and cell phones are not easily detected by bishops and, in any event, may not have been anticipated when church Ordnung were formulated. In some cases, usage of these devices has been explicitly forbidden, but in other churches and districts, church members and leaders alike simply "look the other way."

In general, if an innovation encourages pursuit of individual interests over those of the church or community, it is discouraged or outlawed. Some New Order churches, for example, decided against ownership of cell phones because they had heard that Mennonite and Beachy Amish youth were using them to text message during church services and were not paying attention to the service. Other church leaders recognize that acceptance of some technology may help to keep youth within the fold.

The introduction of cell phones into some Amish church districts has led to a spirited debate about their pros and cons. Photograph by Doyle Yoder.

Maintaining a balance between concern for youth and concern for community requires continual sensitivity.

If technology that has been permitted is later abused, it may then be banned. In one New Order church, members were using walkie-talkies for necessary communications during hunting, with church approval, but when it was discovered that a few adolescent boys were using them to talk with girls, the church decided to ban the devices.

Taken together, the carefully thought-out use of alternatives to electricity from public power lines has enabled many families to keep technology at arms length while still benefiting from some household comforts. Even though comfort and efficiency are not the overarching values on display in Amish homes, church Ordnung have been surprisingly flexible in accommodating incremental changes. Amish throughout the settlement have drawn the line at televisions, radios, and CD/DVD players, but it only takes one visit to an Amish home to see that the Amish are not living in museums.

How do Amish manage the succession of their homes and belongings from one generation to the next? Unsurprisingly, Amish approaches to inheritance are intensely practical. One might expect a strong patrilineal bias, whereby sons are favored in matters of succession, but land, dwellings, and other assets are usually divided equally among the children or in ways that all family members agree is most pragmatic. Husbands and wives typically own homes or farms jointly, and they tend to be proactive about deeding their assets to their children before they reach old age. In visiting one elderly Amish couple in their home, for example, we were surprised to hear their two daughters describe in great detail, in front of their parents, precisely which pieces of furniture they would inherit when the parents passed away. To avoid inheritance taxes and to preempt any family squabbles, these parents, like many others, had divided up their assets well in advance of declining health. A quick perusal of public filings at the Wayne County Recorder's Office reveals numerous deeds indicating that elderly Amish parents have "gifted" their land and home to their children for a token fee of one dollar or ten dollars, while reserving to the grantors "for and during the term of their natural lifetimes, the right to exclusively possess and occupy the residence on the above-described property."[26]

Amish families are not as residentially segregated from non-Amish families as the frequent references to "Amish Country" in the tourist literature might suggest. Rather, the degree of residential segregation depends a lot on where one lives in the settlement. Asked how many of the 20 homes "closest to your house" are non-Amish, 48 percent of respondents in our survey responded 1−7 homes, while 46 percent indicated that 8−15 of their closest 20 neighbors were non-Amish. Five percent said that all 20 of their closest neighbors were Amish, and 2 percent said all 20 of their closest neighbors were non-Amish. For just over half of the Amish in the settlement, then, the majority of their neighbors are Amish, and as the population grows, the intensification of mostly Amish enclaves is on the rise. Nevertheless, these figures suggest that the Amish and the non-Amish are still interspersed throughout much of the settlement. The occasional prank or hate crime notwithstanding, it is not hard to find English and Amish who highly value each other as neighbors and who share food and advice on a regular basis as well as assistance in times of crisis.[27]

Residential integration between Amish families who belong to different church districts or affiliations is also fairly common. Contrary to popular belief, church districts are not always mutually exclusive geographic units. Particularly in the northern part of the settlement, church districts may be highly interspersed rather than existing in clusters of contiguous farms or homes. Within a several-square-mile block, for instance, there may be families from up to five different church districts and three different affiliations. In these areas, the sharing of schooling and of "frolics" or other events to help neighbors in need acts as a powerful integrative mechanism. In other areas, however, contiguous church districts of one affiliation are the norm. This latter pattern is growing as the geographic size of church districts in the settlement shrinks with population growth and the movement away from farming. Church districts today rarely span more than 2−3 miles compared with 5−10 miles in the recent past.

Discipline and Emotion in Early Child-Rearing

What is it like to grow up in an Amish home? Scholars show remarkable agreement in their assessment of the underlying goals and the emotional tenor of Amish parent-child relationships. All point to a widespread assumption that children have a sinful nature but that they are lovable and teachable. "Training up a child" thus requires the inculcation of obedience and self-control. Kraybill, for example, describes the ultimate goal of socialization as the development of "the yielded self" and argues that Amish work as hard to "lose themselves" as the English work to "find themselves."[28] Meyers and Nolt describe Gelassenheit as submission to God, to others, and to the church, and they note that this quality "emerges in a primary disciplinary task of parents who seek to 'break the will of the child' in order to promote a sense of collective consciousness in place of individual willfulness."[29] Our interviewees expressed very similar sentiments, summed up nicely by a New Order minister: "We don't have to teach them [children] to be angry. They already inherited that carnal nature. So we have to break them of that. A child receives training of his soul. If a child's carnal nature has not been broken at a young age, he'll have problems in school and when he comes to baptism, it's way too late."

Consistent with Hostetler's observations, we found that for the first two years of life, a baby, whose arrival is a cause for joy, is given lots of love by multiple caregivers in a fairly permissive environment.[30] Some mothers breast-feed for a year or more, but others do so for only a few months, leaving one New Order man to lament, "What has happened over the past generation is that all of us completely gave up breastfeeding and went over to bottle feeding, and I don't know why!" As Amish mothers share advice with one another about how to handle colicky babies, co-sleeping is usually not considered as an option. One reader of *Family Life* magazine wrote, "Rarely do I hear someone who is not ashamed to encourage having the baby with the parents at night." Beginning around age two, discipline is given continuously till adolescence. Although the specific dos and don'ts vary from family to family, there is wide agreement on the general approach: "Children are made aware of what behavior is acceptable and what is not, and the line between the two is non-negotiable."[31]

Amish of all affiliations are similarly united in their agreement that this "training of the soul" must be done in the context of the family and that the mother-child bond is the bedrock for a proper upbringing. Women are discouraged from working outside the home for precisely this reason. One New Order man put it this way: "We feel strongly about putting children in daycare centers—we're not saying there are not good daycare centers, but the mother-child bond is so strong that we feel it should not be broken. Our children will not die physically if they're not at home with the mother, but they will die somewhat inside if they've never been

Children, surrounded by extended family members from birth, grow up in a world in which interconnectedness and service to others is still emphasized. Photograph by Doyle Yoder.

taught integrity and responsibility." To our knowledge, there is not a single Amish child enrolled in institutionalized day care in the Holmes County Settlement.

Amish views of the ideal mother and father rest on the assumption that men and women have discrete roles. Regardless of order or age, the Amish we interviewed described the ideal mother and wife as one who is a "keeper at home": she takes care of her family and her husband. Several drew from the Bible, especially the Titus 2:4–5 standard for young women: "to be sober, to love their husbands, to love their children, To be discreet, chaste, keepers at home, good, obedient to their own husbands, that the word of God be not blasphemed." The ideal mother and wife is repeatedly described as being loving, gentle, patient, kind, humble or submissive, and attentive to the needs of others rather than her own. The ideal father complements the ideal mother. He is the head of the home, a "good worker and provider" who "saves time for the family," "spends time with the children," and is consistently "showing leadership." He "pitches in and helps around the house." It is important that he be kind, patient, and "tenderhearted" with his family. Christ, family, and church are more important than his work. One Old Order woman summed it up this way: "It's the kind of father who, when the children can get anything, for example, candy, an orange, they share it with their dad. Usually they'll give him the biggest piece." Together, parents are continually exhorted to be shining examples for their children and to remember that "attitudes are caught, not taught."

In this context, Amish youngsters quickly learn that a "good child" is one who exhibits "a tame, gentle and domesticated self, yielded to the community's larger goals."[32] The specific qualities that are desired are captured in the many aphorisms and moral imperatives that saturate Amish homes, schools, and churches: A truth told with bad intent is worse than any lie. Never belittle those in authority. Don't gossip. Be cheerful. See the cup as always half full. Help the less fortunate. In addition, from a very young age, children are taught to control their bodily impulses. One Old Order man half-jokingly told us that the reason there are so many good deer hunters among the Amish is "because they are used to sitting still for three hours in church."

Consistent with the belief in separate roles for mothers and fathers, the qualities of a "good child" differ somewhat according to gender. Boys are typically given more leeway to engage in rambunctious behavior and to "tag along" with dad in the shop or in town. Girls are expected to be reserved and to show restraint and purity. "Where are your little girls when shop customers come? May they tag along with Dad and their older brothers anytime they choose?" wrote one concerned mother to *Family Life*. Since "a girl with a loud mouth is headed for trouble," she concluded that "they must know they are girls and not boys."[33] Assigning different chores for boys and girls is one way in which this training is achieved. Although the main goal of any chore is teaching responsibility ("One of the grandchildren has to feed the chickens and if he doesn't, no eggs"), the "hidden curriculum" teaches boys and girls their respective roles.

If there is broad agreement on the overall goals of parenting, however, there are varied interpretations of precisely what a "yielded self" is and how it is to be achieved. The dominant "internal conversation" among the Amish over the goals of child-rearing revolves around the dangers of indi-

vidualism. Several Amish scholars have pointed out that, contrary to popular views, the Amish focus on conformity is not a dehumanizing process,
nor is it predicated on a "weak sense of self."[34] According to one of our
interviewees, "It's not that the individual always takes a back seat to the
community. We stress not to be individualistic, but to be an individual."
But this important distinction seems to be lost on more and more Amish,
at least according to an article titled, "The Big 'I'" that was featured prom-
inently in the November 2007 issue of *Family Life*. "Even though there is
more submission and working together in our church communities than
in the world around us," notes the unnamed author, "we all have to admit there is less than there was fifty years ago." Noting that "the 'BIG I' is
the heart of sIn," this article singles out both the "expensive homes people
build and the consumer lifestyles they follow" as examples of overly individualistic behavior.[35]

Many Amish parents we interviewed acknowledged that raising children today involved new challenges and difficult decisions. "When I was
growing up, I built my own pony cart," said one Old Order father, "but we
just bought one for our kids." Another Old Order father complained, "My
kids have way too much money—and I have to buy 'em things that I don't
want to get 'em." Judging from the Amish with whom we talked, there is
considerable variation in the interpretation of what constitutes individualistic behavior. As just one example, although many families lament the
difficulty of finding "hired girls" to help out with young children, they
have no qualms about encouraging their own daughters to work at better-
paying jobs in restaurants, shops, worldly homes, or factories.

A second conversation that the Amish have among themselves is about
the kinds of parenting techniques that best foster the idea that self-will
must be given up in the service of God. Two broad positions are discernible. The first holds that the time-tested standards of right and wrong,
determined by the Bible and interpreted by church leaders, can be up-
held only through strict discipline embodied in the doctrine of "spare the
rod and spoil the child." Strict obedience to parents must be stressed at
church and home, and "smackings" (by hand, switch, buggy whip, etc.)
are the price one pays for being a smart aleck, mocking others, or having a
temper tantrum. In this view, rigid social boundaries must be imposed so
that children don't face the temptations of the world, since they will go
astray if left to their own devices.

A more optimistic view of the individual underlies a competing philosophy, which holds that "given an emotional climate of love, trust, and acceptance in the home, the developing individual will come to accept the values of the social system, not because he is *required* to do so under pain of punishment if he does not, but because he has warm and kindly feelings toward those people (parents, teachers, etc.) who model and teach the system's prevailing values."[36] In this view, parental imposition of values, especially if done in a punitive way, may actually be counterproductive, leading to rebelliousness. Corollaries to these two philosophies can be seen in the Amish debate over excommunication and shunning described in chapter 3. Whereas the New Order Amish emphasize teaching as the most effective approach, the more conservative churches stress that the bottom line has to be firm sanctions.

Although spanking has become a controversial topic in the non-Amish community, it is still uncommon to find Amish parents who reject corporal punishment outright.[37] "We believe in discipline, from Solomon, the rod of reproof," commented one New Order man. An Old Order man agreed that it was important to teach children "to obey authority and obey the laws of the land and if they don't there are consequences." "One of our daughters got more spankings than all the rest—and she's the one who now tells us she's so happy we did that," commented another.

Most members of the Amish community temper their endorsement of corporal punishment with a note of caution, however. "At times the rod needs to be used," explained a New Order bishop, "but it's never right to discipline a child in anger. We had a certain place we'd take them to. If you explain why this has to be, usually by then, you're crying with them. If we have to paddle 'em, then take 'em on your lap, show them love." Another bishop offered this assessment: "Parents who are high on love and low on discipline, or high on discipline and low on love, are not good." A New Order church leader vented his frustration at parents who spank children in church: "The place of worship is a place of reverence. It is not a place where parents should 'practice' their discipline. That begins at home during devotions, etc. Woe unto us if we start to paddle our children loudly during preaching services. It is irreverent, bringing a sense of unholy disturbance into the gathering. It puts the assembly on edge— what next? Have you noticed that perhaps nine times out of ten the parent who was determined to discipline inside ends up going out after all?"[38] Cautioned a bishop who feels that some Amish families rely too heavily on the rod: "You have to be careful not to remove the sparkle in their eyes."

Occasionally, Amish fathers or mothers have been overzealous in their discipline; in the late 1990s an Amish woman even spent time in the Holmes County jail after being convicted of physically abusing her infant by shaking him. According to the director of Job and Family Services in Holmes County, the Amish have "the same types of pathologies as the English." In his estimation, however, the frequency of child abuse and neglect in the county is far less than one would expect given the relatively low average per capita income. He attributes this to the large presence of Amish in the county.

In nearby Geauga County, the assistant director of the Department of Job and Family Services reports that the number of referrals for abuse in the Amish community is about seven to ten a year, far fewer than for the non-Amish. Nevertheless, she has recruited an "Amish liaison" to help mediate accusations of abuse that do arise. In both counties, these administrators feel that the Amish are very cooperative. "When we do have an Amish case, they are ideal to work with because 'best practices' calls for us to work with networks," commented the director in Holmes County. "With the English, it's almost always a broken family, but with the Amish we never need a foster home." Extended family members always step in to help out.

In the socialization of Amish children, the realities of shared history, language, and overarching values come together to create a relatively high degree of "cultural compression."[39] That is, the boundaries of publicly acceptable behavior, thoughts, and emotions become ever narrower, starting at age two for Amish children. It is doubtful, however, that one can speak of an "Amish personality," as if the Amish authority structure "stamped" every child in a cookie-cutter fashion.[40] Amish recognize different parenting styles and personalities and the varying family dynamics that result from differences in occupation and affiliation. As Nolt has suggested, it is probably more accurate to say that Amish parents today "share a conversation." They may disagree about what constitutes individualistic behavior or exactly how and how frequently corporal punishment should be administered, but they all feel strongly that these questions are worth arguing about.

Marriage: Gender Ideology and Practice

The idea that church-sanctioned unions between a man and a woman express the "natural" order of things is so taken for granted by the Amish that marriage is nearly universal. It also occurs early. Although in the general population there was a dramatic rise in the average age of marriage between 1960 and 2000 for both women (from 20.3 to 25.1) and men (from 22.9 to 26.8), in 2000 the median age of marriage for the Amish in the Holmes County Settlement was still just over 21 for women and 22 for men. By age 25, more than 80 percent of Amish men and women are married, and by age 30 only 4 percent of Amish men (compared to 30% in the general population) and 8 percent of Amish women (compared to 26% in the general population) are unmarried.[41] As in other cultures, marriage for the Amish stands as the primary context for the socialization of children and creates alliances between kin networks.

Weddings in Amish society are literally "high times" that bring together two young people and their extended families for a ceremony embedded in a church service, followed by a meal in the bride's home.[42] Once a couple decides to get married, the young man asks his bishop or deacon for a letter saying he is in "good standing." If both the bride and groom say that they have been "free of fornication" and are otherwise in compliance with the Ordnung, they will "get published," or have their intentions to marry announced, in church.[43] Preparations for the wedding are extensive because three hundred to five hundred people may be invited. At one wedding we attended, the family had rented a "wedding trailer," which was parked in the yard and contained multiple stoves and appliances to help with the food preparation. After a two-to-three-hour church service, punctuated by the short, solemn vows of the bride and the groom, the guests enjoy a feast that is followed by singing, the giving of practical gifts, and, in some affiliations, the much-anticipated pairing off of young people for dates. Increasingly, Amish honeymoons involve a short getaway for just the newlyweds, with less emphasis on the traditional practice of making the rounds of kinfolk to establish their identities as "young marrieds."[44]

The institution of marriage provides an ideal window for examining the ways in which gender serves as a fundamental basis for the organization of Amish families and communities. As is well known, the familial, political, religious, and social structures that direct behaviors in Amish society are formally patriarchal. The "relations of ruling," using Dorothy Smith's term, are technically, and most often actually, in the hands of men.[45] The implications of patriarchy among the Amish have been well documented; briefly, they include these restrictions: Amish women may not become ordained leaders in the church, although they do have a vote on most church matters. Only men are allowed to serve on the many special committees that address issues affecting the Amish at the settlement level or the state or national level. For example, members of the three-person education committee that oversees the Amish private schools in the Holmes County Settlement must be men, and the three-person advisory boards for the settlement's more than two hundred private schools are strictly male, even though more than 90 percent of the teachers are women. In the nuclear family, the husband is widely recognized as the head of the household, and his wife is to be a supporter. Furthermore, most church Ordnung discourage women from working outside the home, but exceptions are sometimes made for single women and widows.

At least four dominant images have depicted the "true" place of Amish women in their community. These include: (a) romantic, (b) dominated and downtrodden, (c) separate but equal, and (d) closet feminist. They characterize Amish women as ranging from (a) "walking flowers in full bloom" to (b) women "at the beck and call of their husbands," to (c) being "equal in worth" but different "in calling," to (d) "benevolent feminists who are decisive about their personal worth, determined to realize their full potential."[46]

The most common view held by outsiders is that the role differentiation pervading all aspects of Amish society is unfairly tilted in the man's favor. Amish women are often depicted as being "stuck" in the house to raise large numbers of children, cook food, wash clothes, and generally serve their husbands and families. Popular images of the Amish woman also incorporate a belief that she is dominated by her husband and has little influence. Seen as "quiet, bashful, obsequious,"[47] Amish women appear to be "surrounded by a culture that may seem oppressive to women."[48] As Louise Stoltzfus notes, "Men are called leaders, women are not."[49] Karen Johnson-Weiner mentions a colleague who "lamented the downtrodden state of Amish women, who . . . live at the beck and call of their husbands, work constantly and have children yearly as long as they are able."[50] Soci-

Demand for the "kitchen on wheels" is so high during the wedding season that couples sometimes reserve wedding trailers up to a year in advance. Photographs courtesy of David McConnell.

ety at large tends to think of Amish women as oppressed by a patriarchal and somewhat primitive community.[51] Thus, seen from the outside, the role and position of women within the Amish community has been very controversial.

Our in-depth interviews with thirty Amish women, however, yielded a surprisingly different picture: The women generally voiced deep satisfaction with their roles. All believed strongly that men and women are meant to have different roles to play in life, largely because of perceived basic differences between the sexes. "Well, face it, men and women aren't the same," commented one Old Order woman. "There are things that men are better at and things that women are better at. So I don't really understand what supposedly is the advantage of getting the roles mixed up." Another Old Order woman put it this way: "He should provide the family with income and women should take care of the house. I like housework a lot more; I don't have to worry about making a living."

What personal qualities would bring an Amish woman the most respect in her community or would cause others to view her as a role model? When we asked our respondents, they singled out being gentle, quiet, patient, and hardworking, but also being kind, respectful, and willing to reach out to others. One Old Order woman listed these qualities: "Quiet and not a gossip. Has her house in order. Gets her work done. Not a big spender. Saves what she can." Another elaborated: "Being industrious and being keepers in the home and trying to reach out to others and being helpful in the community when there's a crisis or there's a death . . . anything to help." Wandering away from these qualities brings disrespect: "If one of our women would go out and get a job, and she'd still have children at home, I don't think we'd really respect her for that." An Old Order woman added, "As a whole, in the Amish community, men and women, we don't have too much tolerance for lazy people, very frankly. I know very few that are. But if somebody makes a remark, 'Oh, she'd rather not do much,' it's not considered a badge, really."

These women were also very comfortable with the idea that the "man is the head of the household." They interpreted that statement to mean that men or husbands serve as "leaders" who guide the family spiritually and economically, not that they are the "bosses" in the home. "He's not like a dictator, my husband isn't," reflected an Old Order woman. "He certainly should be in charge, and be here for us, and I feel he is." Another woman reflected, "My husband would not do anything without my okay, and I wouldn't do anything without his okay. But I still think he's got the final say." Some women explicitly based their acceptance of men as leaders in their homes on biblical or religious beliefs: "Naturally, it's the biblical way. . . Everything works better if it's in that order of Christ, husband, and wife." "If I'm submissive to him, I'm a lot happier because I know that's the Lord's rule." Others flatly stated that having the husband as the leader relieves them of a burden and creates a greater sense of security, freedom, and opportunity for them: "To me, it's the way I like it . . . It's a way I have of being protected." Another said, "It means that my husband takes care of the major decisions. I don't have to worry about the bills. I don't have to worry about making a living. And that frees me up to do what I really like to do, that's taking care of my house, washing my windows, and taking care of the kids."

Our survey of New and Old Order Amish also uncovered high levels of agreement on the issue of women working outside the home. Regardless of affiliation, well over 90 percent of survey participants felt that it was more important for wives to help their husbands in their jobs than to have one themselves, and that children and the whole family suffered if the mother worked outside the home. Virtually all respondents felt that being a homemaker could be just as fulfilling as being employed and that working for wages would not make a woman happier. Interviews with Amish women of different ages and from different orders yielded similar results. All of the Old and New Order women believed strongly that men and women were meant to have different roles because of fundamental differences between the sexes and that problems would arise if roles were switched or disturbed. Women were seen as basically "more compassionate" and more "tender-hearted"; they needed to "be in the house," engaged in "very satisfying work with our children, and taking care of the house." If men and women play the appropriate roles, "then things work out." More than two-thirds said that both traditional gender roles were equally respected in their community.

When they compared themselves with English women, many of whom have their own careers, none of these Amish women felt that English women were more fulfilled than they were. How one interprets this response, of course, depends on the meaning of "fulfillment" for a group. When asked about the dreams and aspirations they had had as young girls, all said that their goals had been realized. Regardless of affiliation, most had wanted to get married and have children; some had desired to be, and had been, teachers, nurses, or waitresses for a while before getting married. Subjectively, at least, these women who had chosen the Amish lifestyle appeared to be fully satisfied with their lives. One Amish woman explained that such a sense of fulfillment should be expected: "It's in the air! They see their mother as leading a happy and contented and fulfilled life and that's really what any human being wants, so they never think twice about other options."

Kraybill notes that Amish homemakers actually have more control over their daily affairs than do women in full-time clerical and nonprofessional jobs. This relative autonomy does not mean that Amish women are exempt from "job pressures," though. As an excerpt from a New Order woman's diary shows (see fig. 4.1), much of their time is spent acquiring and preparing food and coordinating meals for family members. Amish women also devote a huge amount of effort to what Micaela di Leonardo refers to as "kinwork," or the "maintenance and ritual celebration of cross-household kin ties" for their large extended families.[52] Such work includes making visits and telephone calls; writing letters; making or obtaining presents and cards; observation of various life-cycle rituals, such as births and birthdays, marriages, and deaths; organizing holiday gatherings; and the mental work of coordinating all these activities and making decisions about whether to intensify or neglect particular ties. One Old Order woman showed us a poem she had composed on a poster board for her brother's birthday; more than fifteen different kinds of candy bars were taped onto the board, their names humorously incorporated into the poem. Reflecting on the ways Amish women expertly manage food and kin relationships, a New Order bishop praised Amish women as the "true keepers of our culture."

In contrast to the mainstream emphasis on romantic and often publicly flaunted love, the ideal Amish relationship between husband and wife is a quiet and sober, but loving, partnership characterized by respect and mutuality. Rather than espousing the "feminized definition [of love that] dominates both contemporary scholarship and public opinion," with its emphasis on feelings, the Amish view of love approximates the colonial-period model of love with its integration of expressive and instrumental components in roles and individuals.[53] While many of our respondents

July 31

I did the laundry, wrote an obituary poem as a favor for a friend who wants to send it into the *Budget* [in] memory of her deceased grandmother. Made supper, mashed potatoes, and bologna gravy for son Paul and ate with them. Dad did not go with me as he went to the youths' Bible Study in eve. Paul's busy, will have church at their place. I did some "fixin" with needle and thread while there.

August 3

We canned 18 quarts peaches. Peter's next door did 90 quarts. The whole family helped. Johns [husband of] our youngest daughter, did 100 quarts! They had 6 helpers. I did weekly cleaning (quick way), rested and got suitcases ready to travel with son Charles and family to their home in North Carolina. First we plan to attend a school meeting, approximately 600 people, where Charles is to have a topic. He is also a minister. A driver of North Carolina, another friend from there and this friend's friend of Rhode Island, will sleep at our house while we're gone.

September 19

Another busy day! Bridget, next door, picked a large wheelbarrow load of sweet corn. We all helped each other and cleaned, blanched and cut it off, ready for the freezers. It is a lot of work, but it is much more tasty than any corn ever is at restaurants etc.! In the eve, we picked some grapes from our arbor and made grape juice to can tomorrow.

December 6

Got up early and helped each other make gelatine custard pudding to take along to visit our widowed sister, Mrs. Deborah Yoder, another relative couple went too, and she brought a delicious casserole. In P.M. we visited a poor young widow, 26 years old, and her 2 lil' boys. After that we went to a Bulk Food Store to order cheese and ham for our church lunch, which we'll need for Sunday in a week. In eve, we baby-sat grandson "Timmy" (1 year old) while Charles's and many others were to Holmes Siding's banquet support at Walnut Creek Inn.

Fig. 4.1. This excerpt from the daily diary of a New Order Amish woman in Holmes County reveals how central the management of food and the maintenance of good family relations are in the lives of Amish women. Names in the diary entries have been changed to maintain anonymity. Courtesy of Charles Hurst.

volunteered that neither the Amish nor their marital relationships were perfect, none of the women indicated dissatisfaction with their marriages. Nor did they interpret "submission" in a negative manner. Virtually all of these women felt that their own marital relationships were "close" or "very close" to the ideal relationship.

Voices of Resistance?

Not all the women we interviewed were uniformly positive about the daily realities of their position in the family. When asked what they thought made the difference in whether or not Amish women were viewed as equal in honor to men, many women predictably replied that it depended on the extent to which women themselves projected the appropriate personality and performed their prescribed roles. But another dominant reason given for the differential respect accorded women, especially by their children, concerned the behavior of the husband: "I would say probably the main thing that makes the difference is the way the husband treats her," noted one New Order woman. "If the husband treats his wife with a high respect, the children will also." Commented another, "Some of the men feel, you know, 'What I say is it.'" An Old Order woman was even more blunt: "Oh, it definitely depends on the husband. Some men just have this idea . . . you know, they interpret the Bible wrong. I think they do. It says the husband should be the head of the household, and they think he should be the lord of the household. And they have no respect for their women, to tell you the truth. And that gets passed down from generation to generation. Whereas in another household the husband might treat his wife like a queen, and that gets passed down too." According to one Old Order woman, "If the husband says, 'Hey, I'm the boss around here, and we'll do what I say,' you usually end up with a browbeaten wife."

Amish women have strategies they can use to negotiate, maneuver, and interpret their "subordinate" position so that they gain leverage and power in everyday relationships. Their extensive knowledge of household affairs and of their children's emotional needs gives them a powerful voice in many decisions. Wives also often become astute observers of their husbands' moods and trigger points and learn how to frame an idea in a way that gets the best possible reception. When angry, a woman may also use the "silent treatment," a technique that carries an especially strong message in Amish society.[54] Reflecting on a difficult decision he had made that angered his wife and daughters, an Old Order bishop confessed, "The worst part of it is dealing with their silence." An Amish midwife noted that from the outside the Amish family looks patriarchal, but from the inside "It doesn't feel that way, it feels more maternal. Many of the controls are in the hands of wives and mothers but not in a controlling way."

Outright resistance by wives is rare. However, one Amish woman sent us a poem that conveys her perspective regarding her role as a domestic worker. The poem describes a woman who one day becomes tired of washing the dishes as she has done for years:

> *Round and round in an endless reel*
> *Getting to nowhere ever more*

But then she revives and upon reflection finds joy in her work:

> *Somehow, slowly, she seemed to see*
> *the humble things as they really were*
> *Each in its own reality*
> *A part of home and a part of her.*

In replacing her resentment and self-pity with the realization of her own egocentric insensitivity and debt of gratitude to others, this woman is following a time-tested Amish recipe for personal therapy that stresses changing one's attitude rather than the circumstances.

To be sure, there is a handful of cases in which Amish wives suffer serious physical and emotional abuse at the hands of their husbands. The Amish are appalled by domestic violence, and the idea of a husband striking his wife runs contrary to Amish teaching and upbringing. When such abuse occurs, the church community usually gets involved right away; however, the Amish may have difficulty addressing the problems because their distance from the world limits the willingness of victims and perpetrators alike to request services from the larger community. We heard of a case in the Geauga Settlement in which an Amish woman became so fed up with the ineffectiveness of the church leaders' intervention strategies (typically, confession or short periods of excommunication for the perpetrator) in stemming her husband's abuse that she went to the police herself and got a restraining order. According to insiders, cases of sexual abuse are more likely to involve an uncle, a brother or some other male relative rather than the husband, and they tend to occur in larger families from the more conservative affiliations.

Recognizing the difficulties in treating the cycle of physical or sexual abuse that can afflict certain families, the Amish in the Holmes County Settlement have formed Hoffnung Heim (literally, Home of Hope), a shelter for those who need psychiatric help or counseling. One board member commented, "At Home of Hope, we see authoritarian husbands, and it's hard for wives to submit to that. We see way too many cases where the husband is the boss, and it just goes from one generation to the next." Noted an Old Order businessman, explaining why the Amish prefer to try to resolve issues of abuse among themselves: "We don't want people to see our underbelly."

Diversity in Women's Roles

In spite of the general agreement among the Amish on the roles that are appropriate for women, there are structural conditions under which the position of Amish women varies in the Holmes County Settlement. The shift out of family farming to employment in a small business, factory, or construction crew, for example, has direct implications for gender roles and family life because it pushes the family in the direction of separating public and private spheres and embracing the traditional English model of gender roles—the man as breadwinner and the woman as domestic worker.[55] This situation in which Amish husbands work away from home, leaving their wives home alone to carry out the tasks of parenting and housework, can generate stress. One Old Order Amish man reflected on the new pattern of "working out": "With the husbands gone all day, the wives go crazy now, all day with lots of kids—her shopping day is an escape." An informant who conducted focus groups with Amish women pointed out: "If you were home all day without another adult there with eight children, that was different than when your husband was there on the farm with you." The Amish belief in separate gender roles only intensifies the association of women with domesticity in the face of the "lunch-pail threat."

Conversely, when men and women work productively together and share tasks, gender inequality is minimized. Such is the case on farms, where women can move toward an androgynous position.[56] While there are gender distinctions in farm work, owning and working on a farm require sharing of tasks, and each person necessarily crosses into the other's prescribed areas. Moreover, involvement in this partnership on the farm is carried out with men and women in close proximity to each other, which also encourages greater equality between the sexes.[57] Still, the gender breakdown of tasks on a farm varies a lot across families. "Some women are very much involved in the farm work. They help in the field; others don't. And it just depends on their capabilities, their interest, the family load, all kinds of things. Even how they decide or agree to divide the work."

While it is common for single Amish women to be employed as teachers in private schools, as housekeepers, as restaurant workers, and as bookkeepers and receptionists at local Amish businesses, some married women work out of necessity, especially if the husband is disabled, or because the woman is childless. A woman may also be "the driving force" behind a business in or near the home, such as a fabric, natural foods, or crafts store. With the high rate of tourism in the Holmes County Settlement, some Amish women are providing home-cooked meals to outside groups brought in by tour guides. This means outsiders come not only into the shop, but into the more intimate setting of the home as well. In addition, certain home-based businesses, such as greenhouses or bakeries, allow Amish wives to play a more central economic role and form a "partnership" with their husbands.[58] The role of an Amish wife in the postfarming era thus depends heavily on the specific form of economic livelihood that she and her husband have embraced.

The Holmes County Settlement lags behind the Lancaster, Pennsylvania, settlement, where fully 20 percent of the Amish businesses are managed by women.[59] Although the Lancaster Settlement has often been a trendsetter among the Amish, most of those with whom we had conversations did not "see that happening" in the Holmes County community. It appears "highly unlikely that the position of women within Amish society will be transformed" in Holmes County.[60] At the same time, a few women do believe that there is more pressure to work outside the home than in the past, especially as farming has become less common as a full-time livelihood. The Amish have been extremely creative and flexible in adapting to the economic pressures they have confronted.

In addition to economic factors, religious differences among the Amish influence gender inequality. Church regulations on the kinds of work women may engage in vary, with Swartzentruber churches being the most limiting. One Amish employer said, "Even working in my office here, you would never have . . . a Swartzentruber girl working here at a full-time job as an Old Order girl might." Since most Swartzentrubers live on farms, however, the scope of women's daily work is actually quite broad—from managing the household and kin network to helping out on the farm and perhaps even a side business. In contrast, when men in the more progressive affiliations begin working away from home, the domestic role may become more differentiated from the public one, and more narrowly defined. Johnson-Weiner explains this counterintuitive finding in terms of the more evangelical nature of the more "liberal" churches. If the church is to demonstrate to potential converts its faithfulness to biblical strictures about women's place, then it must emphasize and enforce the divinely ordained hierarchy of (1) God, (2) Christ, (3) men, (4) women. While all Amish churches require male authority in strictly religious settings, the more liberal churches enforce these requirements in secular settings as well.

Indeed, three-quarters of our female interviewees who believed men's roles were viewed as more important than women's roles in Amish society belonged to the relatively liberal New Order Amish. "In general, I would probably say that men's roles are considered more important in Amish society," commented one of these women. "To the men, anyway [laughs heartily]." By contrast, most of the Old Order Amish said unequivocally that they thought both male and female roles were equally respected in the Amish community. As Johnson-Weiner points out, there is no clear separation between the home and the church for the more conservative Amish, since religious services are held in the home and the families in the community are viewed as constituting the body of Christ on earth. Within that body of Christ, "there is no male or female . . . A woman's equality as a Christian overrules her subordination to men in the earthly hierarchy."[61] Johnson-Weiner concludes that while in the formal hierarchy of the church Amish men have authority over women, in the informal real world of everyday activities women share power with men.

Being Single or Widowed

Although marriage and parenting are the norm for the Amish, a small percentage of individuals remain single or face the early and unexpected death of a spouse. Among the Amish, single women outnumber single men, in part because a higher percentage of young men than women choose not to be baptized, creating a "marriage squeeze."[62] These "single sisters," as they are sometimes called, occupy a liminal position in Amish society. On the one hand, they sometimes feel they are unconsciously excluded from the nuclear-family orientation that drives Amish church and school life, or that they are censored for their strong views. "I have seen nothing in men that would improve my life," commented one thirty-year old New Order woman. Another single Old Order woman agreed: "Amish women are content because they deny their feelings. They wear a lot of masks." She continued, "I went to one 'preparatory service' for communion and had to bite my tongue when the bishop said women were supposed to be quiet in church."

On the other hand, single Amish people often find that the Ordnung is flexibly interpreted so as to accommodate working outside the home or other "fence-crowding" behaviors. "I'm probably the only Amish girl in the settlement that's got carpet," quipped an elderly single woman. "But don't tell the bishop I told you that." This woman participates in an annual reunion for "single sisters" that spans numerous settlements and is sponsored by a group called the Association of Unmarried Amish Women. An Andy Weaver man who had remained single into his thirties also described doing things, such as visiting a coffee shop in Wooster in the evenings, that would be very unusual for a married Amish man.

Divorce is stigmatized for the Amish, but widowhood and remarriage are much less so. Here again, however, a gender imbalance is seen. In the Holmes County Settlement, 5.3 percent of women are widows as compared to 0.4 percent of the men who are widowers.[63] One church district, for example, has eleven widows among thirty-plus families. The reasons for this somewhat skewed state of affairs are not hard to find. Like their non-Amish counterparts, Amish men die earlier, on average, than Amish women, and they are more likely to remarry. According to Gayle Livecchia, there are two kinds of remarriage, "companion marriage" and "family formation marriage."[64] The former typically involves an older widower marrying for companionship a woman (or "old girl") who is roughly his age, either a widow or a woman who has remained single; remarriages between Amish in their seventies or even eighties are not unusual. In "family formation marriages," a widower marries a younger woman, who will have children. One man in the settlement had twenty-two children by four wives; he kept remarrying after each new spouse died. In Levecchia's study, 72 percent of women who married a widower had never been married before, because men were reluctant to get involved in blended families and deal with someone else's children. In both types of remarriage, however, courtship is very private. It is sometimes done through the mail—the couple might not even see each other during their courtship—placing the Amish at the cutting edge of "mail dating."

Leisure, Consumerism, and Signs of Economic Inequalities

For nearly two centuries, the Amish have been defined by their distinctive style of "production" and by the corresponding absence of a "leisure class," the emergence of which is usually considered one of the hallmarks of modernity. Hostetler believed that the values of frugality and thrift ran so deep for the Amish that recreation and leisure were "not entered into as pursuits in themselves."[65] As noted earlier, however, the changing Amish occupational structure has increased two of the key ingredients for leisure activities: time and money. As a result, the Amish are increasingly defined by their styles of consumption and their purchasing patterns. In the Holmes County Settlement, it is no longer a stretch to speak of a consumer revolution among the Amish.

But not all consumer revolutions are alike, nor do they converge toward the same endpoint. The Amish, of course, have long been wary of the self-serving individualism and the potential for social inequality that is inherent in rampant consumerism. Consequently, they exhibit the kind of ambivalence toward consumer culture that "often surfaces when people believe that consumption has become 'excessive'—that is, when it threatens a culturally understood 'balance' with morality, citizenship, production, saving, or the environment."[66] How, then, have the Amish balanced the cultural imperatives of frugality and service to others with their increased access to leisure time and cash?

Transportation provides a good example of the "middle ground" occupied by most Amish. The common reference to the Amish as a "horse and buggy culture" overlooks the complex mixing of modes of transportation used by Amish families. At one end of the spectrum, some Amish families rely almost exclusively on the "Amish haulers" or "Amish taxis" whose advertisements litter public phone booths and community bulletin boards all over the settlement. "I put 100,000 miles on his vehicle last year," quipped one Old Order man in the roofing business when referring to his driver. So lucrative a business has "driving the Amish" become for retirees, ex-Amish, and others that the State of Ohio recently moved to tighten tax regulations on this self-employed group. Some well-to-do Amish businessmen employ as many as three drivers—one for the man's wife, one for him at work, and one for weekends and evenings—and use the horse and buggy only for church services once every two weeks. Concerned about this state of affairs, a December 2007 letter to the editor of *Family Life* complained, "More and more we see where drivers are hired without a second thought, to take us places where our horse and buggy easily takes us."[67] One Old Order man we interviewed predicted, "The horse and buggy will disappear in the next generation." Probably an overstatement given the symbolic importance of this mode of transportation for Amish identity, his comments nonetheless reflect the compression of time and space that has occurred in the shift to market-oriented businesses.

On the other end of the spectrum are the Swartzentrubers, whose Ordnung restricts them from riding in cars except in emergencies. Most of the Amish buggies that ply the towns of Wooster and Orrville en route to shopping or health care facilities are owned by Swartzentrubers. Members of other affiliations prefer to travel to town by hired van. But even the Swartzentrubers are changing, albeit slowly. For example, when they move to another settlement, they now hire a semitruck instead of going by train. The Swartzentrubers in the Holmes County Settlement were also greatly affected when Greyhound Lines Inc. suspended its services in Wooster; the result was that some Swartzentrubers now rely on a county van service. Even the prohibition on riding in a vehicle other than in an emergency is flexible. A knowledgeable insider explained that although "Swartzentrubers can't get a ride just for the sake of getting a ride, . . . [they] don't want to offend someone who offers [them] a ride." Consequently, Swartzentruber Amish will ride in cars if their destination is "on someone's way to somewhere."

For most Amish, however, daily life still involves a complex mix of buggy and car use. In our survey of Amish transportation patterns, 31 percent of respondents indicated that they rode in a car or a van 4—7 times per week, while 21 percent used their horse and buggy 4—7 times per week; 64 percent of respondents said they used their horse and buggy 1—3 times a week, compared with only 32 percent who ride in a car or a van 1—3 times a week. Since buggy types and accessories are partially regulated by church Ordnung, they are not as easily turned into status displays as are automobiles among the English. Nevertheless, a visit to any buggy shop in the settlement will reveal a surprising range of options. One buggy shop, for instance, markets the "Amish minivan," so called because it comes with an extra seat in back that can be folded down for sleeping infants. The four-thousand-dollar sticker price includes a variety of accessories: velvet upholstery, hydraulic brakes, auto steer, mud flaps, dimmer switch, flashing turn signals, windshield wipers, mirrors, windows and curtains, and a cigarette lighter plug. In addition to the rate of taxi use, a fairly reliable measure of wealth in the Amish community is the quality of one's horse and buggy, including how frequently old buggies and horses are traded in for new ones.[68]

New Twists on Old Hobbies and Travel

Another intriguing aspect of the Amish-style consumer revolution has been the increased centrality of hobbies in their lives. Fishing and hunting have long been integral to life on the farm, and Amish today still enjoy these endeavors as sources of food and as forms of recreation.[69] Unlike their predecessors, however, twenty-first-century Amish hunters and fishermen are outfitted in style. An editor of the *Outdoors Section* of a local newspaper commented, "I've hunted and fished with the Amish, and the ones I've gone with all have top-notch equipment (other than camo). They don't mind spending money on their boots, guns, fishing poles and lures. They read the magazines and keep up to date with the latest in tactics and equipment." When a new Cabellas store opened in Dundee, Michigan, the Holmes County Amish community was abuzz with excitement, and vanloads of Amish shoppers regularly traveled between Millersburg and this store located north of Toledo. In February of 2007, nearly two thousand Amish attended the first annual Great Outdoor Sportsman's Show at Keim Lumber Company in Charm, including Amishman

Jon Schmucker, who harvested the famous Amish Lucky Buck.[70] The Ohio Amish also book a lot of Lake Erie fishing charters and week-long fishing vacations in Canada, and they are frequent visitors to state parks in the summer months.

Although life on the farm always included awareness of bird life, many Amish now engage in bird-watching as a serious hobby. Amish birders sport the latest optical equipment, such as Swarovski spotting scopes and binoculars. It is not uncommon for an Amish birder to carry upwards of twenty-five hundred dollars worth of optical equipment into the field. Some Amish are highly regarded in birding circles for their skills in identifying birds by sight and sound and check the local rare bird alerts on a regular basis. Somewhat surprisingly, Amish birders are avid "listers," keeping life lists, state lists, and annual lists of species seen, which serve as the basis for friendly competition. In many cases, birding becomes a family affair, and everyone will contribute to a "yard list" of all species seen around the house. A visit to Crane Creek Wildlife Refuge on Lake Erie in May for the spring warbler migration reveals that dozens of Amish families have made the trek from Holmes County with children, binoculars, field guides, and lunch pails in tow. Perhaps the most passionate birders, however, are the roughly one hundred Amish men and teenage boys who annually brave biting cold and snow to spend thirteen or more hours in a day birding for the local Christmas Bird Count, sponsored by the National Audubon Society. The final tally of species for the Millersburg Count is virtually an all-Amish affair, with much low-key humor and suspense over the sighting of rare species. In 2006 the group tallied the highest number of species ever recorded on a Christmas Bird Count in Ohio.

The main concern surrounding hunting, fishing, and birding has been the amount of time it may lead fathers to be away from their families. Another favorite recreational activity, softball, has raised a different set of issues and reveals the variety of Amish perspectives on organized sports. The enthusiasm for competitive softball among unbaptized Amish boys is hard to overstate. Dozens of Amish teams regularly compete in local leagues throughout the settlement, and the best teams have even competed in national tournaments. But competitive softball also runs counter to many Amish sensibilities such as simplicity, frugality, and meekness. Softball requires a considerable outlay of money and time for equipment and travel, and it calls for uniforms and even haircuts that do not sit well with church members. The custom of playing under the lights or even on

Sundays also runs against Amish beliefs, and there is the fear that exposure to the argumentativeness and showmanship that characterize non-Amish sporting events will undermine the Amish emphasis on cooperation and humility. So concerned were bishops in Lancaster County about the growing competitiveness of softball that they forbade mothers to wash their sons' softball uniforms, creating a storm of controversy![71]

In the Holmes County Settlement, the acceptance of competitive softball varies according to one's baptismal and marital status. Many unbaptized boys still play their hearts out in competitive leagues. Some parents and church leaders want to clamp down further on this activity, but they are opposed by those who see softball as far preferable to other worldly activities that tempt Amish boys in such a large settlement. Once a player is baptized, the pressure grows against playing in organized leagues, though some individuals keep playing until they get married. Even for married men, however, opportunities abound to join teams that play in a wide variety of benefit tournaments, such as an annual tournament "to raise money for a guy who was paralyzed." Teams often carry the name of a bishop or a place of work, such as Ben's Ballpark Team. Reflected one married Old Order third-baseman, "It's not supposed to be competitive, but it's still pretty competitive."[72]

In recent years, softball competition between an Amish and an English team has been an exciting part of the Kidron Community Fun Day. The Amish and English teams split the three-inning affairs in 2005 and 2006, but the 2007 four-inning tie-breaker was a lopsided affair, won 14-2 by the Amish team in front of five hundred fans.[73] And a new wrinkle suggests that the mind-set encouraged by Title IX—that girls should have the same opportunities as boys—may be spilling over into the Amish community. The majority of rosters of the Wayne-Holmes Women's Softball League in 2009 were made up of Amish girls.

Another change that has affected Amish women, "eating out" or "ordering in," has become more common in recent years. Amish families can be seen not only at fast-food restaurants and the Amish theme restaurants, but also at mainstream restaurants such as Bob Evans, Applebee's, or Panera Bread. For more than a few Amish, pizza delivery has become a family custom on Saturday nights. Home-cooked meals with fresh, local ingredients are still the norm, but store-bought and convenience foods are slowly replacing locally grown items. Similarly, "goodwilling," or shopping for clothes at Goodwill or other thrift stores, has become a regular pastime for Amish women. Many scour the *Bargain Hunter* and other local newspapers for the latest yard sales. Commented a Holmes County employee, "They'll use the *Bargain Hunter* to plan their whole week. They'll call shops that stock it and ask when it's in and then send someone to get it." Although most Amish girls still learn how to sew, sewing has "become an option" as more Amish women go to work in family businesses and have less time to sew.[74] Even Amish dresses, which have always been sewn by hand so as to control the color, fabric, and fit, can now be bought off the rack in some Amish-owned stores.

If access to time and money has re-shaped traditional pastimes for adults, it has also given rise to new ways of spending time for young people. Rollerblading and bicycling have become common summer activities, and some youth enjoy waterskiing and wakeboarding (a combination of waterskiing, snowboarding, and surfing). Snowboarding and skiing trips are not unheard of in the winter months. The one outdoor recreational activity that has remained relatively popular and unchanged is volleyball. Since boys and girls of differing abilities can play volleyball together, it is still the main activity at most singings and youth group meetings. Some Amish businesses have even erected volleyball courts for their employees to use at lunchtime or during other break periods. For indoor recreation, "scrapbooking" is an activity that seems to be growing in popularity, but jigsaw puzzles, card games (those that do not use playing cards), and board games such as Monopoly and Scrabble are still mainstays of Amish family life. And in spite of the changes in traditional pastimes, it is worth noting that 74 percent of respondents in our survey about leisure activities ranked "reading" as one of the top three leisure activities in their lives, far outpacing fishing (31%), hunting (25%), volleyball or softball (25% each), sewing or quilting (20%), and bird-watching (9%).

In rural Ohio, the phrase *Amish tourism* usually conjures up images of the multi-million-dollar industry in which nostalgic English descend on the tranquil, rolling hills of Holmes County to acquire Amish furniture or other products. But these days the phrase could just as well describe the thousands of Ohio Amish who travel all over the United States and Canada to see the sights, visit relatives, and seek out alternative health care. In our survey, nearly one-third of Amish had traveled to more than twenty-one states in their lifetimes, and two-thirds had traveled to more than eight states. One measure of the extent of Amish travel is that the Department of Homeland Security policy to require passports and driver's licenses with photo identification for American citizens traveling to Canada in the aftermath of 9/11 quickly made it onto the agenda of the National Amish Steering Committee.[75] The notion of an "Amish vacation" is no longer an oxymoron.

As in the past, many Amish trips still revolve around visiting friends and relatives, but vacations purely for fun and sightseeing have become more common. Popular destinations for the Holmes County Amish include the Great Lakes, Niagara Falls, and the Great Smoky Mountains, but two-week trips out west are not uncommon. The Pinecraft area of Sarasota, Florida, about five hundred bungalows and trailers situated on 120 acres, has also become a winter destination for Amish families and youth. Pioneer Trails buses from Ohio to Pinecraft, called the "gumboot express" by locals, carry more than four thousand people each way during the peak months of January to March. Nearly 75 percent of the passengers are Amish. One New Order Amish bishop described Pinecraft as a "real mission program for the Amish," because all different denominations come together. Another bishop notes, though, that those who frequent Pinecraft are "the more entrepreneurial segment of the Amish." Our survey bore this out. Whereas only 13 percent of Old Order respondents had visited Pinecraft more than two times, 53 percent of the New Order had visited Pinecraft more than twice, with several indicating twelve to fifteen visits. The more conservative groups often associate Pinecraft with the New Order influence and are wary of the weak social controls and the temporary suspension of some church rules there.[76] A young New Order woman, however, had a different take on Pinecraft: "Florida," she quipped, "is for the newlyweds, half-deads and can't-gets."

One dimension of Amish family life is conspicuous for its absence: participation in civic organizations. Amish adults cannot be found at Rotary Club or Kiwanis meetings or serving on school boards or in public office, nor will Amish children join the Boy Scouts or Girl Scouts, the 4-H clubs, or the Little League teams that are so popular in rural Ohio. An exception to this policy, worth noting, is that Old Order and New Order Amish men volunteer in local fire departments throughout the settlement. The Fourth of July parade in Fredericksburg, Ohio, which includes numerous fire trucks and even a few Amish participants, is witnessed by hundreds of Amish and English families, who line the route with folding chairs and then share a chicken barbecue dinner and softball game afterward.

The Amish themselves have very mixed feelings about the changes in

The popularity of softball among Amish boys and girls has forced parents and church leaders to engage in a spirited debate over the appropriate limits of competitive play. Photograph by Doyle Yoder.

leisure activities among their people. They are concerned, for example, about the way time and money are being spent. One Old Order man explained, "As far as vacations, I don't have a problem with people taking vacations. But I have a problem with people spending a lot of money on leisure if families are really in need in the area. If you have a lot of extra money or have the chance to help other people, let's do that." A related concern is that the frequency and type of leisure activities are becoming markers of inequality. "Our differences can be seen in the amount of hunting land they have," pointed out an elderly Old Order man. "[The disparity] is obvious." Extended vacations also run counter to the Amish work ethic. "You know, nothing gets done if somebody takes a trip every summer," commented an Andy Weaver woman. "You shouldn't be spending six weeks out of the year just vacationing or whatever. It has to be something that's done within reason. It's like . . . use your common sense." Attitudes such as these have somewhat tempered consumerism and the adoption of leisure activities among the Amish. Yet in a large and diverse

Old Order Amish tourists on a trip out west view the rock formations at Garden of the Gods in Colorado. Vacations for fun and sightseeing are on the rise among the Amish. Photograph courtesy of Matthew Dilyard.

settlement such as Holmes County, what is "common sense" to one family is increasingly viewed as extravagant to another. As long as the Amish "have more money than we need to exercise our lifestyle," the challenges created by consumerism and leisure opportunities will not soon disappear.

The Shifting Bedrock of Kinship

Unlike kin ties in the wider society, which are relatively narrow in scope and sharply divorced from other institutions,[77] the Amish kinship system is deeply intertwined with social life more generally. The values and behaviors promoted by parents still overlap quite extensively with those supported by the church, the school, and the workplace. Extended family members are not just seen once or twice a year at holidays, but may occupy important and multiple roles—employer, teacher, preacher—in the life of a given individual. In addition, the basic building blocks of strong kin ties among the Amish, such as three-generational households, clearly defined gender roles, the prohibition on divorce, and large families, have with-stood the pressures of change.

Nevertheless, the shift from farming to market-oriented enterprises—and the subsequent influx of cash and free time—has left an indelible mark on Amish family life. New architectural designs for Amish houses, new household appliances, and new electronic "toys" for adults and chil-dren have joined with changes in leisure opportunities to create a spir-ited conversation within and between Amish families about whether the delicate balance between the individual and the community is being uprooted. To be sure, the watchful eyes and thoughtful admonitions of ordained leaders have reined in some potentially detrimental excesses, but many church districts have developed strong pressures against what is known as "nitpickin'." "We don't look for what our neighbor is doing wrong," explained a young Old Order father. "You can't run to the bishop every time you see someone not wearing their bonnet. My preacher says it is more wrong to nitpick and look for things than it is to be the guy who [breaks the rules]." Within this climate of relative tolerance, the contours of Amish family life are being incrementally redefined.

CHAPTER 5

The Changing Landscape of Learning

I have to question why so many of our people still send their children to
public schools.
—A New Order father

For the Amish, no legal decision has had a greater influence on the educational and cultural prospects of their people than the landmark 1972 Supreme Court decision (*State of Wisconsin v. Jonas Yoder et al.*) exempting the Amish from compulsory schooling beyond the eighth grade.[1] Although school conflict between the Amish and the state occurred in Ohio and elsewhere as early as 1914, it was the "final showdown" in Wisconsin that lead to Chief Justice Warren Berger's decisive conclusion: "Almost 300 years of consistent practice, and strong evidence of a sustained faith pervading and regulating respondents' entire mode of life support the claim that the enforcement of the State's compulsory formal education after eighth grade would gravely endanger if not destroy the free exercise of respondents' religious beliefs."[2] As Meyers points out, the legal precedents set in this case now inform the curricula of law schools across the country.[3] The educational implications, however, were equally far-reaching. To outsiders, the one-room schoolhouse now stands alongside the horse and buggy and styles of dress as one of the most visible signs of the Amish rejection of English versions of "modernity." For the Amish themselves, the decision literally opened the door for the proliferation of private schools, paving the way for cultural self-determination through control of education.[4]

Among ethnic and religious minorities, the Amish stand out for the te-
nacity with which they have fought for control of their children's schooling, and yet the social and economic milieu has changed markedly over
the past few decades. How has the shift away from farming and the growing socioeconomic differentiation in Amish communities affected Amish
schooling? How does the considerable internal variation (both between
and within affiliations) that exists among the Amish manifest itself in
schooling? How has the one-room schoolhouse changed over the past
four decades to keep in step with the changing economic requirements of
Amish communities? In this chapter we explore these areas of educational
continuity and change and ask how Amish parents are navigating a world
of proliferating educational options.

We describe the various schooling choices available to Amish parents
in the Holmes County Settlement (parochial school, public school, and
home school), the reasons parents give for choosing among them, and the
constellation of meanings associated with each; address the rationale for
maintaining the eighth-grade limit on schooling and explore the small but
growing numbers of Amish who pursue a GED or seek certification in
a particular trade; discuss the educational options for parents with special-needs children; and consider the rationale and implications for the
"silence" in church Ordnung on the matter of school choice.

Rising Shares: The Growth of Amish Private Schooling

According to our data, the majority of Amish parents in the Holmes
County Settlement send their children to Amish-run private schools. Just
over 80 percent of our respondents said that they *preferred* Amish private
schools over public schools and homeschooling, and this preference stood
regardless of the church affiliation or sex of the respondent. When asked
about actual use, however, only 71 percent of parents of school-aged children said they actually sent their children to parochial schools at some
point while they were growing up. As of 2009, there were approximately
two hundred Amish-run private schools in the Holmes County Settlement, and at least 2−3 new schools were being built each year.[5]

To support the building and maintenance of schools, parents in a
given neighborhood typically have purchased "shares" that remain with
the owner of a parcel of land. When necessary, parents have raised additional money on their own to construct a new building. Concern about

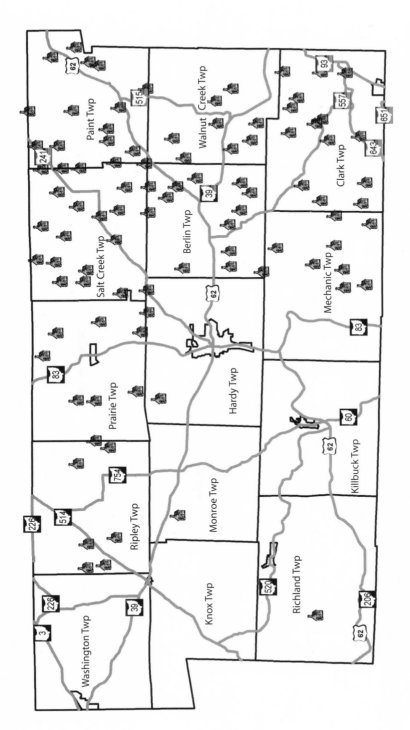

Amish parochial schools in Holmes County in 2008. Amish-run schools have proliferated since a 1972 Supreme Court decision granted the Amish an exemption from compulsory schooling after the eighth grade. Map by Erik Parker.

the ability of young families to cover the $60,000 cost of a new school led to a supplementary fund-raising strategy in 2005. Notices were sent out to all the bishops asking each member of their congregations to contribute approximately $30.[6] "We figured if 60 percent of our membership would pay $6, it would be enough for one school," noted a member of the three-person Amish Advisory Committee for all parochial schools in the settlement. The plan was to give $10,000 each to thirteen schools that had been built within the past three years, and then $40,000 to the new school. Since 2005, the annual collection from church members has ranged from $15 to $50. In addition to this "tax" levied on each family unit once a year, there is a collection later in the year that is tied to a family's income.[7] The result is a settlement-wide pool of money that can be used to augment funds raised locally for a new school building.

Parents we interviewed who sent their children to the private schools cited a wide variety of reasons for doing so, but the overwhelming majority felt that such schools allowed children to engage in activities more directly supportive of the lives they would lead as Amish adults. "We have the freedom of teaching the children what we want them to be taught," noted one parent. Another added, "[In public schools] there is a lot of emphasis on things that really do not fit well with our way of life." A third parent succinctly summed up the problem with public schools: "There's too much we don't need." In our survey as well, parochial schools were evaluated as "effective" or "very effective" by a much higher percentage of respondents than were public schools or homeschooling.

More specifically, over three-quarters of the private school parents we interviewed explicitly mentioned the dangers of technology used in the public schools (computers, videos, and TV). Roughly half offered the opinion that public schools over the years had deteriorated in terms of discipline and that private school students showed more respect for one another. These themes are illustrated in the following responses to the question, Why did you choose private schools for your children?

Because there was too much peer pressure in the elementary school . . . and our kids were not satisfied any more with [the Amish] lifestyle. They were getting into a lot of the computer stuff that we didn't approve of.

Another thing that comes to mind right now is that they don't pick up all these TV characters that I don't care for. Now I don't care if they've heard about [Winnie the] Pooh, the comical ones, but I don't care for the dinosaurs and all those weird-looking animals.

The reason . . . we took them out of public school is because of peer pressure, and we saw all this coming. They [public school students] are a lot more competitive, and I don't believe that goes with the Christian nature. They were really aggressive.

Opportunities for Bible reading and prayer were also mentioned as attractive features of private schools. Several parents mentioned the religious quality of singing at the Amish schools as an important factor in their decision.

Our observations and interviews confirmed many of the distinctive features of Amish-run private schools that have been effectively described elsewhere.[8] These include the small size of the schoolhouse itself (although in Holmes County there are usually two teachers and a retractable curtain between the lower and upper grades); the use of English at all times except for German instruction once a week; a streamlined and pragmatic curriculum focused on the three Rs; and pedagogical approaches that emphasize drilling, memorization of facts, and seatwork. The lack of emphasis on critical thinking was underscored in our survey, which showed that among a variety of desired qualities in a child, "being interested in how and why things happen" was considered among the least important. In fact, among fifteen qualities, this trait was listed as one of the three least important by almost half (49.2%) of the respondents. The qualities of honesty, obedience, and self-control were perceived as being the most important characteristics of a child.

The relative absence of religious instruction in the formal curriculum was a noteworthy feature of most schools as well. As Johnson-Weiner notes, "Perhaps in part because they must accommodate children from different church communities, the Holmes County area Old Order schools leave religious instruction for the church and the home."[9] We also encountered widespread rejection of the idea of homework. One New Order teacher commented that when the Amish see public school students coming home with stacks and stacks of books, "we think life must be really miserable for them nine months of the year." In all of the classes we attended, there was a strong emphasis on the practical applications of schoolwork and on the importance of physical labor.[10]

Because of the focus on seatwork and drills in Amish schools, students eagerly anticipate recess. Cold or inclement weather rarely keeps students indoors. Photograph by Doyle Yoder.

Three other features of the parochial schools stood out in our minds. First, we were struck by the ways in which the formal structure and informal workings of Amish schools both "legitimize[d] and mitigate[d] patriarchal authority."[11] Structurally, the operation of Amish schools is heavily gendered. Each school is administered by an all-male school board (usually three or five fathers), which meets monthly. Teaching, by contrast, is a feminized and temporary occupation; Amish teachers are overwhelmingly young, unmarried women.[12] Of the 330 teachers or teachers' helpers listed in the 2005 *Ohio Amish Directory*, for example, only 6.7 percent (22) were men.

Parental involvement in the upkeep of the school and in special events (providing a hot meal once a month, organizing an end-of-the-year picnic, attending the Christmas play, etc.) also reveals a sharp division of labor. But seating is usually assigned by grade level, with boys and girls mixed together, and all students are expected to learn the same curriculum. Girls regularly joined in the softball games at recess. And every teacher we interviewed was adamant that the academic and extracurricular expectations were equal for both girls and boys.

Second, we noticed the care and intensity with which teachers attended to the socialization of children. Teachers had given much thought to disciplinary strategies and were preoccupied (to our eyes) with minor aspects of misbehavior that signaled nonparticipation in the group or lack of obedience to authority. "Lingering" after the bell had rung and "mocking" other students were viewed by teachers as serious infractions that had to be "nipped in the bud." And although corporal punishment was rarely meted out, Amish teachers were not afraid to levy sanctions (such as writing sentences on the board or, in one case, the administration of cod liver oil) or remove privileges (such as playing softball during recess).

Third, one of the most intriguing features we discovered about Amish-run schools was that, strictly speaking, they are private, neighborhood-based schools run by a group of parents rather than by a particular church district. In the Holmes County Settlement, this means that children from several different church districts or affiliations, including ones not "in fellowship" with each other, may constitute the student body in any given school. Commenting on this arrangement, one father remembered a time when they had children from five different affiliations at the local parochial school. "It's one of the most unexplainable situations you could imagine," he confessed. "They all got along well, but they couldn't take part in each other's sermons!"

The rationale for this arrangement is both pragmatic and ideological. As mentioned earlier, Amish church districts are not residentially segregated but instead overlap to a considerable degree. As a result, it is not economical for each church district to build its own school. The arrangement also ensures that church districts do not become overly self-contained. An elderly bishop recalled: "When Amish schools were started, it was very clear that school problems were not supposed to come to the church." In fact, in Holmes County, bishops rarely serve on the three- or five-person school board. Given that church affiliation has far-reaching implications for individual behavior in Amish communities, parochial schools can serve as an important vehicle for communication and friendships that cut across religious doctrine.[13] Johnson-Weiner describes the private Amish schools as "the best opportunities for bridge building between the different church communities" because they reach a geographically defined population, not one defined by Ordnung.[14] Reflecting on this fact, one Old Order man commented, "I went to school with all of them [the different affiliations]. They looked different and smelled different, but we all played softball together. We don't think, 'Oh, he's Andy Weaver, I'm not going to sit next to him.'"

It is worth noting, however, that a handful of schools in the settlement do cater primarily to children from one church district. Several Swartzentruber districts operate schools specifically for the children of their church members. As mentioned in chapter 1, the most dramatic case involved two schools built to replace one school damaged by fire because Swartzentruber and Old Order parents could not agree on the size of the basement and whether there should be cubbies or hooks and shelves for the students. What looked to outsiders like a relatively minor issue became, for the Amish parents involved, a referendum on worldly "drift," with the result that the two schools now stand only a stone's throw from one another on County Road 77.[15] At the other end of the spectrum, two of the most progressive schools in the settlement cater almost exclusively to the New Order Amish. The tendency for parochial schools to become "church schools" that serve only one district or affiliation is an ongoing concern for some Amish.

Variation among Parochial Schools

To outsiders, Amish schools look strikingly similar. Our school visits and interviews with teachers, however, revealed many differences, both subtle and explicit, in such categories as facilities, curricular emphasis, and disciplinary climate.[16] Because Amish teachers attend regional meetings and regularly visit each other's schools, they are not only aware of these differences but routinely discuss them among themselves.

The most obvious differences lay in the quality of facilities. By chance, the first two schools we visited turned out to have the most marked contrasts in physical amenities of any we encountered. Beech Grove Parochial School contained one small classroom in a very old building with outdoor latrines. The basement was barely large enough to hold one ping-pong table, cubbyholes for the students' gear, and a rusty hand pump for water. The softball field was small and inconveniently sloped downhill. Green Meadow School, by contrast, had four self-contained classrooms, centralized gas lighting, fire alarms, running water and drinking fountains, a merry-go-round, a slide, and two ball fields on an expansive playground, as well as a battery-powered typewriter for the upper grades to practice typing.

To be sure, most Amish schools are more like Beech Grove than Green Meadow, and new school constructions typically follow a standard plan. But schools vary quite a bit depending on the age of the facilities. In addition, schools are typically built on donated land. Depending on the topography of the area and the generosity of the donor, some schools have much larger and more functional sites than others. The extent to which parents are motivated to conduct fund-raisers or to contribute labor and materials to the upkeep of the school also plays a role. Parents and students at one school, for example, had a fund-raiser for a new addition to the building; they made two thousand pizzas and sent out teams to sell them. They brought in ten thousand dollars in one night!

Apart from the buildings themselves, an important factor that differentiates parochial schools is the particular interests, backgrounds, and personalities of the teachers. Given the small scale of Amish schools, it is not surprising that the taught curriculum can vary considerably depending on the teacher's orientation. One male Amish teacher we spoke with commented that "schools are as different as teachers' personalities"; a female teacher noted, "It's kind of what you really love is what the pupils end up loving."

Because teachers are so influential in shaping the identities of their schools and yet are expected to work for relatively low pay, the board members we interviewed considered teacher recruitment the single biggest challenge they faced. Parents, too, spoke of their levels of satisfaction with the parochial schools largely in terms of teacher quality—whether the teachers were firm enough in dealing with discipline problems that arose, especially among the older boys; whether they had good Christian character; or whether they were pedagogically skilled.

While the magnification of teachers' biographies in Amish schools probably does not pose a serious threat to cultural reproduction, it does have implications for curriculum and discipline. At one school we visited, for example, the teacher brought out a microscope and asked the children to view fragments of coal, a venture into the world of science that went well beyond the usual observations of nature in Amish schools. Another teacher had bought a battery-powered talking device from Staples to help her drill students in their math tables. Significantly, all Amish teachers we interviewed had retained some power to choose their own textbooks (Pathway, Schoolaid, and Study Time were popular ones). Some had chosen texts that provided more up-to-date examples of Amish life, while others preferred textbooks that they had used when they were students. "It works better if we have a uniform curriculum but not everyone sees it that way," confessed a member of the Amish Advisory Committee, part of the "homespun bureaucracy" that oversees parochial education in the Holmes County Settlement.[17] "We tried to recommend textbooks but it didn't work." The acceptance of some texts but not others by different school boards and teachers suggests much about how conservative and progressive Amish groups "draw the line between what is acceptable and what is not."[18]

The leeway given to teachers also results in some variation in the degree to which religious teachings enter into the informal curriculum. Although the Golden Rule and other religious sayings are often seen on the walls of parochial schools, most bishops and school committee members recommend that religion be taught in the home and in church but not in school. One Old Order elder put it this way, "We don't want to get away from religion, but do we really want young girls teaching our religion?" He went on to observe, however, that there were "a few New Order teachers [whose classes] are almost on the likes of Sunday School," a reference to the fact that New Order members tend to prefer a more systematic articulation of spiritual convictions than do the Old Order.

A final differentiating force is the type of neighborhood or community in which the school is located. Our data is strictly anecdotal at this point, but we do see evidence that the particular configuration of church affiliations surrounding a given school, as well as the occupations and social class represented among the parents of a given group of schoolchildren, has a discernible effect on the character of the school. One new school we visited, for example, was comprised almost entirely of younger Old Order parents with successful home businesses. Though still a one-room structure, the school had whiteboards instead of chalkboards, gas lighting, indoor plumbing, and other amenities. The school board had gone out of its way to hire two New Order women with excellent reputations as teachers and was paying them salaries that made them the envy of other Amish teachers ("the board asked me to name my price," recalled one of the teachers, "and they pay our transportation, too"). These teachers commented not only on the strong support from parents but on the relative absence of older siblings among the schoolchildren as a key element shaping the "progressive" atmosphere of the school. In another case, a group of mostly New Order parents arranged for construction of a building that far surpassed the guidelines set by the Amish Advisory Committee.

The magnitude of social class variations is still unclear, and their effects are mitigated by the understanding that each parochial school is supposed to serve families from different affiliations. There is nothing akin to "open enrollment" in the parochial school system. But as one Old Order man put it, "if you're buying a home, you want to know what schools are like in that area—so you take it into consideration." And if cases such as the ones described above—in which education-minded parents from one affiliation get together to build their own schools and ensure high-quality teachers and a demanding curriculum—become more frequent, it is possible that the seeds of an emerging class structure will be sown by the differentiation among parochial schools themselves, as well as by the public-private school contrast, to which we now turn.

Swartzentruber Amish "scholars" head for home after a day of study and play at Woodland School. Photograph by Doyle Yoder.

"It's a Rip Van Winkle Kind of Thing": The Public School Alternative

The Amish commitment to adult baptism places enormous pressure on parents to raise children who *want* to be initiated into an exclusive community.[19] The parochial school movement often references the words of Solomon in Proverbs 22:6: "Train up a child in the way he should go: and when he is old he will not depart from it." As Marc Olshan reminds us, the one-room schoolhouse is not a form of primitive social organization but rather is "an indication of the sophistication of a people who understand the need for controlling the socialization of their children."[20] Viewed in this light, the decision of some Amish parents to send their children to public schools takes on special interest.

Approximately half of all children enrolled in the public schools in Holmes County are Amish. In our interview sample, 21 percent of Amish parents had chosen to send their children exclusively to public schools. Another 13 percent had used both public and private schools for their children, and 8 percent had opted for a special charter school that catered to the Amish but employed state-certified teachers. Thus, 42 percent of our Amish interviewees had used public schools at some point, presumably with the full knowledge that the hidden curriculum teaches "competition, individualism, nationalism, scientific modes of thought, hierarchical organization, and the teenage subculture."[21] Given the potential clash with Amish lifestyles and sensibilities, why do some parents choose public over private schooling?

One logical answer would be money: local property taxes paid by all Amish support the public schools, and thus sending one's children to public schools incurs no additional financial burden. The large majority of parents we interviewed, however, indicated that finances had little to do with their decision. Lack of proximity to a parochial school (too far to walk safely) was mentioned by a few parents. But neither money nor distance seemed to be the real issue.

Instead, the reasons given by parents who sent their children to public school had to do with preparing children for a world of ever-increasing contact with the "English." A middle-aged Old Order woman noted, "I really think they need that education to survive in the world. They need to be exposed to some stuff and still survive." An Old Order father who repaired motors for a living put it this way: "I have absolutely no

Amish and English students study and play together at many public elementary schools in Holmes County. Photograph courtesy of Rhoda Mast.

complaints [with the public school our children attend]. Depending on where we were living, there is no way I would send my kids into some of the [parochial] schools that are [out there]. But [Linda] is a great principal, the teachers are great, they're Christians, they teach good values." One of the most vocal Old Order Amish supporters of the public schools did not mince words:

> Just to get to the heart of it, I'll tell you right off the bat I'm not pro-parochial school. It's a great idea, don't get me wrong, but I feel it's misused because our teachers aren't compensated enough and they're too young to be highly qualified ... What's happening in this area is we have very few farmers. We've never faced this situation before. But 8th grade is the end of it for us. I don't agree with that. You need some life skills. You need the minimum of a high school equivalent somehow. Now other parents will disagree with this, but interaction with the English is not always a bad

thing. The more exposure we have to other cultures, and accepting them for what they are, the better off we'll be. It's a Rip Van Winkle kind of thing.

A theme that surfaced numerous times in interviews with Amish parents was the perception that the quality of instruction, particularly in the use of English, is better in public schools. An Old Order bishop commented: "The Amish recommend you send your children to their schools, but I don't know why. What's the reason? I got my education at the Amish school down here. They had two girls from the low, low Swartzentruber, but they weren't good teachers. I never learned my vowels—to this day I can't spell. So we sent our children to public school. I think they learn more how to pronounce English well in public schools." An Old Order parent concurred: "The public school our children go to is a good school. We're very satisfied with the teachers and the education. We think that because they only go to school for 8 years, they should have a good, quality education. Some Amish schools are providing that, but some aren't ... That's the way we feel about it. Now that's not the general Amish way of thinking. I know that; I realize that." Although several parochial school teachers we interviewed were convinced that the quality of instruction they offered was on a par with or better than that found in the public schools, the sentiment that public schools were superior in academics was mentioned frequently by public school teachers and by Amish parents who supported the public schools.

This unusual degree of support for public schooling among the Holmes County Amish can be accounted for in at least two ways. First is the concern that parochial schools might not offer a sound basic education that would allow young people to keep pace with economic changes and to earn a living off the farm.[22] A principal of an East Holmes public school with a student body that is 50 percent Amish gave this explanation: "It's the work scene. I have six families that are farming out of 120 families at this school! That is a huge change and more and more parents want their children to get some skills because they can't assume they'll work on the farm or even work in Dad's business. It's getting more competitive." Amish who support the public schools feel acutely that they must prepare their children for "a world in which they might well be hourly wage earners and not farmers, a world in which, increasingly, the routine of their daily lives is not very different from that of their non-Amish neighbors, and in which innovation, technological change, and the reaction to both will likely yield new definitions of what it means to be . . . Amish."[23]

Second, the strong Mennonite influence in Holmes County has long created a protective cocoon around certain public schools that heavily enroll the Amish. When John Hershberger and other Old Order Amish men were arrested and jailed in 1958 for failing to send their children to public school, a protracted conflict with the Wayne County Court ensued.[24] "We never had the clash with Holmes County in the way we had with Wayne County," commented one Amish elder.[25] Some Amish still feel that public schools in Holmes County are firmly grounded in Christian morals. A male public elementary school teacher described the Amish receptivity to his teaching this way: "They feel they need more education, and they see this as a safe environment because of my background, and because they know I won't cross the line."

Amish enrollment in the public schools is not just a function of "push" from the Amish side; it also involves varying degrees of "pull" from public school principals and superintendents who actively court the Amish. In financially strapped rural school districts in Wayne and Holmes Counties, Ohio, the prospect of losing Amish children to the parochial schools is a palpable concern. One public school principal noted, "We lost about 20 kids last year to parochial schools, though [the parents] are really reluctant to say why they left. This really irks the superintendent because he tends to see dollar signs."[26] An Amish leader reflected, "When this parochial system started coming on, the public system in Holmes County, especially in the Berlin, Wise, Flat Ridge area, changed a lot in being conducive to our needs. And that made a big difference, too. I've heard people in the areas where they were thinking about building a parochial school say, 'Well, the way the public school is working with us, it's not really a big need.'"

At Mount Eaton Elementary School, for example, the principal, Rhoda Mast, whose parents grew up Amish, persuaded her superintendent to construct seventh- and eighth-grade "attached classrooms" so that Amish children could finish out their final two years in the public elementary school. Amish parents, who trusted Mast because of her background and her ability to speak Pennsylvania Dutch, were thrilled that their children could get an additional two years of high-quality education while avoiding the middle school environment of increased athletic competition, peer pressure, and sexual innuendo. Mast went to great lengths to sensitize her teachers to Amish expectations, and she even arranged for a volunteer to come and teach German to the Amish students in the higher grades. For the school as a whole, she was able to introduce portfolio assessment, all-day kindergarten, health screening, and other more mainstream curricular options to her Amish students. When her Amish students complete eighth grade, Mast holds an official graduation ceremony for them, complete with caps and gowns and diplomas signed by the superintendent. As a celebration she has taken students for an overnight stay at a local hotel with a swimming pool. Attendance at the school, which is 70 percent Amish overall, has doubled, and Mount Eaton students score at the "proficient" level on statewide achievement tests.[27]

Yet sending one's children to public schools can be a controversial decision within the Amish community. When asked why some Amish parents would send their children to public schools, one Amish man blurted out, "Most of those would be the 'uppity class' Amish. They want to make sure their children get a better education." Another father agreed that sending their children to public schools required a delicate public-relations balancing act: "You have to be discreet about it. It can be a sore spot. The Amish had a really hard time getting the state to allow it [the parochial school option] so if I don't support them, I have to ask myself, 'Am I doing my part?' But you make a decision and you live with it." Some parents who send their children to public schools also give monetary support to a parochial school. This not only gives them the option of pulling their children out of public schools at any time but demonstrates their support for the principle of parochial schooling. Another example of "straddling" public and parochial options that we discovered was a tendency for some parents to send their children to public schools in kindergarten and the early grades and then switch to parochial schools later on. An Amish teacher told us that a big reason many Amish parents switch their children from public to Amish schools around third or fourth grade is because "the boy-girl talk becomes too much after that."

Variety in the Public School Experience

Does the tenor and quality of the educational experience differ for Amish children in public versus Amish-run schools? There is no question that it

Approximately one-third of the Amish in the Holmes County Settlement send their children to public schools for at least a few years. These Old Order children ride the school bus regularly. Photograph by Doyle Yoder.

An Old Order Amish girl and an English boy at a public elementary school show off their science projects, the girl's farm scene and the boy's gorillas and palm trees. Photograph courtesy of Rhoda Mast.

does, but to varying degrees. For just as the parochial schools exhibit an unexpected degree of internal variation, so too do the public elementary schools in Wayne and Holmes Counties.

At one extreme are several small public elementary schools near Charm, Ohio, that are 100 percent Amish. These schools, which receive Title I funding because of the language barrier, have morning prayer but no pledge of allegiance, maintain an Amish advisory board, teach a curriculum tailored to Amish needs (no evolution), keep homework to an absolute minimum, observe the "old Christmas" holiday on January 6, and have German language and singing classes on Fridays. To some Amish parents, such schools represent "the best of both worlds." At no extra cost (beyond property taxes), they are assured of a high-quality education for their children with certified teachers in a moral environment that is comfortable to them.

Other public schools in the area are more mixed, with Amish pupils constituting 30–60% of the student population. In the mixed schools, the disjuncture between the home and the school environment is sharper. Amish children attending one of these schools, for instance, might have the opportunity to hear a talk by a soldier returned from Iraq, as happened recently in one public school. They will certainly encounter curricular materials that are contrary to their parents' beliefs, leading to dilemmas such as the one described by this Old Order Amish father: "My son . . . at first when he came home with the dinosaur stuff, I told him, 'There might have been dinosaurs, I don't know' . . . He tried to tell me, and I said, 'Maybe there were, but they weren't fifty million years ago.' I said, 'Son, that's OK, you can believe it if you want, but I'm not going to, because it wasn't that long ago. We had a flood. I believe in the Bible, 100 percent. They might have been 5,000 years ago, I won't dispute that.' Maybe there were dinosaurs. They've got records. That's fine. It's part of that school system, science is. If they want to teach them about dinosaurs, have at it, but in my opinion, it's a waste of time." Moreover, the Amish children in public schools are usually exposed to computers and television. One public school principal confessed that his most recent mistake was showing the feature film *Dennis the Menace* at the end-of-the-year party. Several Amish kids left in tears because they were frightened by the character who played the "bum."

To some extent, Amish parents recognize and accept the fact that public schools will not conform to their system. Nevertheless, there is a fine line that public school teachers and principals may cross only at the expense of angering their Amish clientele, who always have the option of leaving if their concerns are not met. The result is a high degree of border work required of faculty and staff, who must be sensitized to Amish issues. According to one public school principal, "the trust level is just huge."[28] At the public Mount Eaton Elementary School's annual Christmas Play, which is eagerly attended by dozens of Amish parents, the principal told us that she had to be careful about how to cast the Amish students. Sheep and shepherd roles were fine, but the roles of the three wise men-turned-rappers, featured in one year's performance, were off-limits to Amish students.

Does public school attendance influence whether or not an Amish young person decides to join the church? We were not able to gather data on this question in this study, but an earlier study in the Elkhart-LaGrange Settlement in Indiana found that the rate of defection was higher for Amish persons who had attended public schools than for those who had attended Amish schools. Meyers argues that Amish schools "not only protect children from non-Amish influences, they reinforce Amish values and help to insure that peer groups will primarily include other Amish children."[29] It is unclear from his study whether the content of the public school experience led to defection, or whether parents who send their children to Amish schools are less committed to being Amish in the first place (and thus less effective in instilling loyalty in their children). It is clear, however, that many Amish parents worry about excessive contact between their children and those of the English. Two-thirds of the respondents in our survey, for example, were against the idea of having their children "sleep over" at an English neighbor's house.

Dissenters? The Homeschooling Option

A third option that is becoming increasingly common among the Amish is homeschooling. Our survey of Amish adults confirmed that this is a relatively new phenomenon. None of the sixty-five adult respondents had been homeschooled themselves, yet nearly 7 percent indicated that it was the preferred method for educating their own children.[30] Of the forty families we interviewed, 5 percent had homeschooled their children. Parents who favored this alternative generally believed that a homeschool education was superior to that given in the parochial schools, in which teachers are not demanding enough, and superior to the public schools, in which the role of the government is too pronounced. One New Order Fellowship parent reflected:

> In our case, we started home schooling because there were no parochial schools in the area, only public schools. That's not the reason we continue to do it today. Most families have begun to home school because they

don't believe the academic level is high enough in the parochial schools. You know, you'll have [mothers] who used to be teachers and they'll say, "Hey, I can do this myself." It's not about the curriculum of the parochial schools, it's a concern about the quality of teachers. And we don't think the state is necessarily the best teacher of our children.

A 34-year old New Order mother added:

We home school mainly because of the bond that it makes. You know, I see our children bonding to me in a way that I never did with my mother because I wasn't there most of the time. I want to hold our children's hearts in my hand in order to guard them, and I see [homeschooling] as a very effective way of doing that. And I also think it's a great protection for them as far as not being exposed to impurity, that sort of thing.

A New New Order father summed up this concern:

Family, control over our own child's education, and personal responsibility—these values undergird home schooling. We see it as a maintainer of Amish culture. To critics, it is seen as a threat to the collective mindset.

To many Amish with whom we talked, the mention of homeschooling evoked much stronger negative comments than did the idea of public schooling. One of the most frequently mentioned arguments against it was that it isolates children from those with whom they will have to learn to live once their education is completed. A second argument suggests a "know-it-all" arrogance on the part of homeschooling parents. "They think we're not reaching out enough to compromise when we have disagreements," noted one parent who homeschools. Another concurred: "Amish generally don't promote home schooling because they're community minded. The home schoolers tend to be more radical—a little extreme on family." In general, we found that the New Order Amish are more likely to homeschool than the Old Order, who tend to see homeschoolers as "dissenters."

Formal Education and Informal Learning after Age Fourteen

An important question to ask as a follow-up to *Wisconsin v. Yoder* is whether the Amish community has held firm on the prohibition against formal education after the age of fourteen. Our research from the Holmes County Settlement suggests that the answer is a qualified yes. We found no Amish family that had enrolled their children in a full-time public or private school after the eighth grade. In addition, the Amish we interviewed gave remarkably consistent responses to our queries about why higher education was prohibited. All emphasized the dangers of "bad" pride that develops when one group of individuals has more schooling than another. Pride is "bad" if it gives you "the sense of feeling that you're better than someone else." A New Order bishop explained, "We don't want people coming back to our community and thinking they're owed a higher standard of living."

But Amish views about education are neither one-dimensional nor simple. When asked, most of our survey respondents did not hold persons with college educations in any higher or lower regard than persons with less education. The Amish are also aware that advanced education may be required for those who have professional jobs: "Doctors have to go through school . . . That's great if they have to do that because I wouldn't want no doctor working on me that's making five bucks an hour." At the same time, given the restrictions on education enforced among the Amish, many of those we interviewed either saw no need in their work for more than an eighth-grade education, or argued that any additional education could be acquired in specific vocational courses or on the job. Implicit is the conviction that real wisdom and know-how come from experience rather than from mere "book knowledge." This is a belief that appears to be most strongly held by the more conservative Amish orders, and it is one that they share with other individuals who have little formal education and who have spent much of their lives in hard physical labor.[31]

The general Amish view of education is very pragmatic: it should teach specific skills required for a job. Simply having a college education with no focus on training for a given occupation is not seen as relevant: "If you're at the workplace, and the guy shows up with a college education, there's a good chance that he won't know how to work . . . Overall, the idea of getting more and more education, and then not being able to find a job, after you've studied for years and years . . . you know, that's kind of a total waste," said a New Order employee. Moreover, a degree itself is not what is important and may not mean you can perform adequately when employed. An Old Order Amish business owner stated directly: "A diploma and a degree in and of itself means nothing to me. Show me what you can do. Show up on time. And do your job. Follow directions. Put out quality work. Give me a day's worth of work. That's what counts. I don't care what your degree says." He went on to say that the Amish consider education just as important as the English, but that it is in the kind of education and the manner and place of its implementation that differences exist. This view is echoed by another Old Order businessman: what's important is "how you treat it, how you administer it . . . if you use it as a tool to do the right things, it's beneficial."

One controversy that erupted when the College of Wooster awarded an honorary degree to a local Amish farmer and author illustrates the complexity of Amish views of higher education. The Amish recipient of the degree, who was recognized for his inspirational efforts to increase faculty and student understanding of the Amish and of how human communities relate to the land, had asked that there be no publicity associated with his receipt of the award. Owing to a miscommunication between the college's public relations office and the local newspaper, however, his photo (in cap and gown) appeared on the front page of the newspaper the morning after the ceremony. Reactions in the Amish community were surprisingly varied, however. Some were aghast that he had accepted the degree in the first place and felt that his participation in the pomp and circumstance of a graduation ceremony was completely incompatible with Amish values. Others, noting the letter of apology from the college president that ran in the paper the following day, said they mostly felt sorry for him and regretted the shame he had to bear because his wishes had not been honored. Still others congratulated him on his achievement, and at least a few privately expressed satisfaction that an Amish individual had been recognized in this way. "That's just [his] work," explained one Old Order man. "We don't look down on him for it." Indeed, a handful of Amish individuals in the Holmes County Settlement and elsewhere have carved out a distinctive niche for themselves as published authors, speakers, and public spokespersons for the Amish.[32]

Part of the problem with receiving an education in a college or university setting is that broad skills such as critical thinking and unwanted values (for example, individualism) and cultural capital (knowledge, experiences, and attitudes) are taught or learned inadvertently that undermine foundational Amish values and contribute nothing directly to job performance. Whereas English adults use higher education as a badge of higher social status, the Amish, like other persons who engage in manual labor, use moral criteria to evaluate what they do for a living. Doing so places a mantle of worthiness on their lives and helps define the cultural and religious boundaries that distinguish them from those who use more secular criteria.[33] One Amish respondent argued that the Amish teach "an alternate set of the 3Rs . . . Respect, Responsibility, Resourcefulness" and that these "are taught by vocational and apprentice-type training."

Upon completing eighth grade, most boys find jobs in woodworking shops or other small businesses, while girls often take positions in restaurants or do office work for a small company. Particularly for the boys, these positions often follow the apprenticeship model. At a time when their English counterparts are just beginning high school, Amish adolescents are working alongside adults on a daily basis. In addition to receiving on-the-job training in a particular skill or craft, they are taught the work ethic, as well as proper attitudes toward one's co-workers and customers. By the age of twenty or twenty-one, these young men are not trying to figure out the "color of their parachute" and to chart the direction of their lives, but are already committed to a job where they make a decent wage and are well versed in a particular craft. The mobilization of knowledge in these Amish small businesses is also formidable. Many woodworking shops and other cottage industries form "communities of practice," where knowledge and experience are intertwined and where "everyday practice is a more powerful source of socialization than intentional pedagogy."[34]

Not all learning after eighth grade involves on-the-job training, however. Accompanying the increased interest in nonfarm occupations is the enrollment of young Amish in short courses aimed at training them for jobs. The Holmes County Amish Vocational Training Program began in 1999 at the request of the Amish Advisory Committee, which oversees parochial schools in the settlement. Since its inception, approximately one hundred Amish students, most of them Old Order, have enrolled in nineteen courses that include welding, engine repair, tractor restoration, book-keeping, and computers. Welding and engine repair have been the most popular, and some students have taken as many as four of the classes.[35] In addition, we met an Amish auctioneer who had attended night classes at Kent State University as well as extended, on-site training in Columbus and in Kansas before getting his state license as an auctioneer. Other Amish persons have participated in training of a shorter duration to become lumber inspectors, accountants, and real estate agents. Differences among the affiliations regarding their views on what constitutes appropriate employment accentuate the economic variations between them and help to shape their future financial fates.

We also found evidence of some slippage around the edges of the prohibition against formal education after age fourteen, in the form of pursuit of the GED (General Equivalency Diploma), the equivalent of a high school diploma. In 2003–4 the Adult Basic and Literacy Education Program in Wayne County counted 23 Amish students enrolled in evening classes to prepare for the GED examination. Almost all of them were working full- or part-time. These were very capable students: 9 of the 23 tested at a grade level of 11.0–12.9 in terms of literacy, and 10 of the 23 tested at a grade level of 9.0–10.9. Their motivations for obtaining the GED were sometimes tied to job prospects (some employers require workers to have at least a high school education) but not necessarily. Several students commented that they were simply curious to know how their Amish education stacked up against state standards. One man we met who belonged to the conservative Andy Weaver affiliation was so intellectually curious (one of his fascinations was particle physics) that he completed several correspondence courses and received college credit.

We found more than a few Amish teachers and parents who truly lamented the end of formal schooling. "I cried the day school was over," commented a former teacher. Perhaps it is this longing that accounts for the voracious appetite for books in the Amish community. The Holmes County Public Library's bookmobile, with an annual circulation of nearly two hundred thousand volumes (predominantly to Amish families), is one of the most active in the nation.[36] It is clearly a mistake to equate the end of formal schooling with the end of learning in the Amish community.

Taking Care of Special-Needs Children

One of the educational challenges facing the Amish community is the comparatively high number of children who have special needs. In the Holmes County Settlement and elsewhere, the general philosophy toward these children is that they can be special blessings who serve as reminders that everyone has a different level of needs.[37] As Mark Dewalt notes, since the Amish do not stress individual achievement, it is easier for them to build a community that supports special-needs children.[38] Nevertheless, the care required of children with physical or mental handicaps can be overwhelming, especially when that care falls disproportionately on the mother. "I've seen a lot of parents struggle with that issue of balancing self-sufficiency versus the burden of care," commented a public school administrator. "The women give their lives to these kids." Until very recently, most Amish families with mildly handicapped children have preferred to send their children to public schools because of the perception that they offered superior services for their children who are "hard to learn."

Over the past decade, however, the Amish have made a concerted effort to increase the accommodation of special-needs children at some of their private schools, with the result that nearly twenty schools in the Holmes County Settlement now offer special-education classes. In addition, there is now a settlement-wide special-education committee that coordinates the hiring of special-education teachers and the provision of services for children with mild handicaps. Usually placements of special-education children will occur without a formal evaluation, because "they don't go by the same rules as public schools." Teachers try to integrate the children with the rest of the class in singing, devotions, recess, and school outings, but they may be pulled aside for separate instruction during the day. At some schools, they are tutored in the basement, while in others a curtain is pulled across the corner of the room where the special-education teacher works with the student(s). Although Amish special-education teachers have no advanced degrees, they do hold regular six-week meetings to share ideas and information about their work. They also avail themselves of print resources and of specialists in the non-Amish community.

The way the Amish schools have gradually taken over aspects of special education that in the past were left to the public schools is illustrative of their openness to learning from the English while developing their own capacity for mastery of a subject. One public school psychologist in the area is regularly asked by the Amish special-education committee to evaluate Amish children and to give seminars to Amish teachers and parents on different types of mental and physical disorders. Reflecting on the first talk he gave on attention deficit disorder, he remembers asking the head of the Amish special-education committee how the audience might react to a recommendation that medication is the best treatment. The man replied that it would be fine, because some Amish children were already taking Ritalin. More than two hundred Amish from three counties showed up for this school psychologist's evening talk in a local Amish shop. "And I will tell you that every single talk I gave, I normally spoke for an hour and then answered written questions that were put in a hat that was passed around. And I was always there another hour after that with people coming up." He concluded, "They're such a wonderful population to speak to . . . Their attention is superb . . . so much better than teachers I talk to in public schools. Ten times better." This Amish capacity to scan the external environment for useful insights is crucial to the successful, if selective, borrowing of "best practices," not only in special education but in economic enterprises as well.

For severely handicapped children, Amish-run private schools are usually not an option. Such children either are placed in multiple handicapped units in the public schools or they attend a county-run educational facility. Even though about one-third of the counties in Ohio "have gotten out of the [special-education] school business because parents can demand services at their local schools," separate public facilities for children and adults who have multiple disabilities still exist in both Wayne and Holmes counties: the Ida Sue School in Wayne County and the Holmes County Training Center. About 60 percent of clients at the Holmes County Training Center are Amish, including both medically fragile adults and children in school programs. To attend, one must live in Holmes County and the disability must have been diagnosed before age twenty-two. Part of the funding for these facilities comes from property taxes, and thus both transportation and the educational programming are free to Amish parents. However, a Parents' Association, composed primarily of Amish members, holds an annual spring festival, including an auction, to raise additional funds for activities like the Special Olympics and horseback riding or facilities such as a handicraft workshop and a pavilion.[39] The Holmes County Training Center also provides medical services, among them therapy, dentistry, and genetic counseling. Therapists even work with families in their homes to help children overcome problems associated with their disabilities. In short, the center has served as a unifier among the Amish, who are deeply involved in its activities.

Meeting the health care needs of these individuals can be very expensive, however, especially since the state government began requiring that families receiving health insurance from the Bureau for Children with Medical Handicaps apply for Medicaid first. This state-run insurance program had covered more than five hundred Amish children with birth defects and special needs such as cystic fibrosis and bleeding disorders. Unwilling to officially sanction enrollment in Medicaid, Amish have had to solicit donations to a newly created Ohio Crippled Children's Fund to offset the loss of funds. Nevertheless, "we do have some bishops who are willing to approve Medicaid," noted the administrator of the Holmes County Training Center. "I would guess about 20 percent of the Amish here at the Center are on Medicaid, and several have done it without the bishop's consent." An Old Order mother whose son was suffering from bipolar disorder told us that it was not impossible for Amish to get government assistance when the bills got too high. She recounted a visit from the bishop about her son's medical bills after the church had recommended they not use Medicaid. "How are you doing financially? Did you get help?" he asked. To her reply that, yes, they were getting assistance, he simply said, "I'm glad."

According to a staff member who makes visits to Amish homes, Amish clients at the Holmes County Training Center are easy to work with because "they have such good genealogy records and because families are so close—we can do the histories very easily." Once in a while the Amish inclination to use alternative treatments strikes staff members as misguided. "We've had infants with seizure conditions that were being treated with herbs and chiropractors," noted one teacher. On the Amish side, support has been very strong, though there have been a few issues around exposure to televisions in the facility or unwanted publicity. "We had a basketball team that went to state for the Special Olympics in 2004, and we had two Amish players," remembered the director. "Their picture was in the paper, and I had to write a letter of apology because one of the kids said his dad was upset." But the support of Amish family members can be inspirational. The director of the center recalled a client whose parents passed away suddenly. "We had to change the bus route every week because his siblings were sharing the burden of taking care of him, one week at a time." In another case, a couple had not had a vacation in all their married life because of taking care of their son. Plans are under way to build a respite home, where families can drop off their loved ones for short-term overnight stays when they need relief from the burden of care.

The Amish approach to education of special-needs children is thus indicative of their ongoing negotiation with the outside world. They are extremely grateful for the public school options for their children and for the care provided by doctors and nurses in area hospitals and clinics. Many avail themselves of these facilities if they are convinced it will make a difference, and a few even accept Medicaid. At the same time, the cost, the distances to travel, and the unwanted outside influences that come with repeated exposure to public institutions have led to a growing attempt within the Amish community to provide services for special-needs children in their own schools. This trend is likely to continue in the foreseeable future, as the Amish nurture a cadre of special-education teachers who are skilled at working with mildly handicapped children.

Diverse Responses to Educational Choice

The Amish have worked to minimize their contact with non-Amish society for the purpose of keeping their community intact and tightly integrated. This high degree of cultural cohesion and insularity is one factor behind the relative success they have had in resisting mainstream schooling compared to other ethnic-religious minorities. The favorable economic environment—access to sizable markets, a large tourist industry, and the positive public perception of Amish products—has also enhanced the attractiveness of Amish schooling and the Amish faith to young people.[40]

But macroeconomic, technological, and legal changes continue to impinge on the Amish community, voluntarily or involuntarily, directly or indirectly. Their infiltration results in the creation of "weak ties" between some Amish and some English, which construct a bridge between the two groups. These ties into a community with strong bonds like the Amish essentially create a conduit through which new ideas and material goods can flow. A bridge that admits outsiders into a tight-knit community, in other words, can create wide diffusion within it. On the micro level, such a bridge emerges when Amish men have to seek out new kinds of employment because of the unavailability of land or the high costs associated with farming. Another bridge is formed when Amish choose to send their children to public schools. While this link creates greater integration, and perhaps greater trust, between the Amish and English communities, it has the potential to lead to fragmentation and dissent within the Amish community.

The increasing number of weak ties appearing in the Amish community encourage the development of numerous internal contradictions, which manifest themselves, in part, in the variety of educational responses elicited among the Amish. In reaction to these contradictions, the Amish have gone down several different educational paths, all of which probably have different levels of effectiveness in keeping the Amish community insulated or, conversely, helping create fissures within it.

At least two of these educational responses are seen by the relevant constituents as promoting continuity among the Amish. Amish parochial schools are controlled by an Amish board, Amish parents, and Amish teachers. It is probably in this situation that the greatest isomorphism exists between schooling and the Amish way of life. Consequently, it is here that the reproduction of Amish social and cultural capital is most likely to occur.[41]

A second major response that encourages perpetuation of the Amish way of life is the public school composed entirely of Amish students. It is worth noting that the Amish exodus from public schools from the 1940s on was primarily a reaction to the consolidation of public schools.[42] When schools remain small, and community values trump individual agency, Amish parents are often happy to keep their children in public schools, because the exposure to non-Amish students and a more varied curriculum occurs in limited doses.

A third response, homeschooling, privileges agency over structure by putting a child's education directly into the hands of his or her parents. It is debatable whether this approach encourages cultural continuity. Parents who homeschool make the argument, consistent with the thinking of many New Order congregations, that this approach allows for a more self-conscious articulation and deeper understanding of the values on which Amish community rests. Criticisms of homeschooling, more common among the Old Order Amish, emphasize that community is a lived experience, which is threatened when families withdraw from the schooling process.

A fourth Amish educational response is to send their children to public schools that also serve significant numbers of English children. This is the response that is most accommodating to the outside pressures that the Amish increasingly face and yet may intensify internal contradictions within their community. For example, in our survey of Amish adults, we found that, on the one hand, "obedience to parents" and "self control" were considered most important as qualities in their children, while "taking the name of the Lord in vain," and "mocking other children" were considered to be the most serious infractions. On the other hand, individuality, free thought, and creativity are cherished in public schools, resulting in a contradiction between Amish and some public school values. The public school also creates another dilemma for the Amish in that the latter desire to retain a certain "ideal" world, whereas the public school's emphasis is on the need to adapt to the "real" world in which they may have to seek employment. A third dilemma follows when Amish adults see the need for new skills and training but want to avoid becoming too "smart." As one Amish woman put it: "We're not into school to get smart ... we can't get too smart if we are to avoid 'bad pride.'" One way that the Amish navigate this dilemma is by selecting courses cafeteria-style or by pursuing a GED. In effect, these actions constitute a fifth educational response to the social, economic, and cultural pressures the Amish have encountered.

Walking an Educational Tightrope

To maintain the integrity of their community, the Amish are walking a very thin tightrope on both sides of which are hazards that can undermine the gemeinschaft quality of their settlement. There is a desire to maintain control over education so as to ensure continuity of Amish lifestyles but also a pragmatic concern to provide for children an education that will serve them well economically in a changing occupational and technological context. Simultaneous emphases on tradition and pragmatism encourage the proliferation of educational choices, including the "straddling approach": sending one's children to public schools in the early years and shifting to the parochial schools in later years—"the best of both worlds," as one Amish parent put it. One outcome of this tendency among Holmes County Amish to use public schools is that it "exerts pressure on the private schools to offer a comparable education."[43]

The diversification of educational strategies is further intensified because Amish of different affiliations view the crosscutting pressures for tradition and economic pragmatism differently. For each group, the question is not whether to change, but which version of change is most acceptable. The Swartzentruber Amish have opted for a "batten down the hatches" approach that allows for only the smallest degree of change. The Andy Weaver, Old Order, and New Order Amish view such an approach as a recipe for cultural and economic obsolescence, preferring instead, to varying degrees, to make greater accommodations to the changing world around them. But since each group has a different view of what counts as "tradition" as well as what counts as "economic pragmatism," their educational strategies necessarily differ.

In this respect, it is worth noting the relative *silence* of Old Order and New Order church leaders on the issue of school choice, a silence that has indirectly allowed these varying modes of accommodation to play out.[44] If the control of their children's socialization is so important to the Amish, why have church leaders refrained from adding to the Ordnung a requirement that parents send their children to private Amish schools? Part of the answer to this question lies in the fact that some Amish parents and many grandparents, including church leaders, were educated in the public schools and had very positive experiences. They value the quality of education they received from certified teachers and the worldly "know-how" and English friends that came from exposure to this outside institution. They see no reason to change course as long as the public schools continue to meet their needs. In addition, practicality and timing undoubtedly play a role. Although a rule to require parochial school attendance would certainly have many supporters, it is much easier for church leaders to ban a new practice than one that has a long history. Ultimately, however, the preservation of the right to school choice among the Amish reflects the recognition that some measure of individual and family autonomy is necessary for the healthy functioning of a collectivist society.

※ CHAPTER 6 ※

Work Within and Outside Tradition

They are the farm. The farm is them.
—An Old Order farmer

The dynamic and shifting nature of the Amish economic structure has been well documented,[1] and the Holmes County Settlement has not been immune to these broad changes. As they work to maintain core cultural values, the Amish are also among those leading in the development of new economic methods and technologies. They struggle to remain true to their Christian beliefs while being buffeted by a storm of economic changes. How have they negotiated the pressures that continually confront them?

This chapter offers an overview of Amish economic activities in Holmes County[2] and how those activities widen and deepen ties with outside society; it then explores in more detail the consequences that have followed the movement out of farming and examines variations that exist among different Amish orders with respect to work choices, wages, and uses of technology. The final two sections of the chapter consider how the Amish have addressed the potential dangers of growing wealth within their community and discuss new areas of enterprise that serve as models for many people in the English community.

The Amish in the Holmes County Context

In 2006 Holmes County had an estimated population of more than forty-one thousand, of which less than 2 percent were members of racial or ethnic minority groups. Just over 70 percent (195,000 acres) of the county's area is composed of farms averaging 109 acres in size. Although the farms in Holmes County are smaller, on average, than those in Ohio as a whole, they have proved to be among the most productive and energy-efficient farms in the United States.[3] In 2002 the average farm in Holmes County yielded sales of $53,645, and total sales for all farms exceeded $97 million.[4]

Despite the past and continuing success of agriculture in the county, the proportion of Amish in full-time farming has dropped significantly. Between 1988 and 2000, the percentage of men who were farmers fell from 33 percent to 17 percent,[5] and it has continued to decline to below 10 percent. The trend away from farming in Holmes County is consistent with that found in Pennsylvania and Indiana Amish communities,[6] but the specific patterns of change have varied among the states. In the Elkhart-LaGrange Settlement in Indiana, a large proportion of Amish have taken factory jobs; in Lancaster, Pennsylvania, because of its proximity to major metropolitan areas, the shift away from farming has been accompanied by greater dependency on tourism, commercialism, and large-scale Amish enterprises.

As land costs have soared, it has become increasingly expensive to farm full time. In discussing how local Amish farmers scramble to survive, an Amish business leader concluded that "the biggest thing that probably has affected us is the price of land. You know, it's really difficult for farmers to survive without it." Land costs have been driven up by business growth and home developers, but in addition, demand by the Amish themselves for land has created higher costs.

A local real estate representative who has worked with the Amish for decades says that the "Amish dictate the land prices in the area," and as a result many of them have sought residences in counties in other parts of the state. Amish "will buy hunting land as a retirement plan . . . they'd rather buy land than stocks . . . A 22-year-old buys land as an investment, buys for $30,000 and sells three years later for $60,000." A young Amish wife agrees, contending that "the reason the land prices are so high is because the Amish have money. They view it as a good investment."

There are some differences among the Amish, however, in the selling and buying of land. Swartzentruber Amish are more likely than others to buy and sell among themselves. Even if they could make more money by selling land to someone else, they will probably keep it in their family if they can. "One Swartzentruber family could have got $1−2 million for their Wayne County farm and moved to southern Ohio and bought eight farms, but they sold it to one of their own for $200,000."[7] Another factor, however, is that the lack of plumbing and septic systems on Swartzentruber properties makes it very difficult to sell them to anyone except another Swartzentruber family.

Consequently, despite the heavily rural nature of Holmes County, 93 percent of the 26,897 employees in the county in 2005 were nonfarm wage or salary workers because of the high cost of land; only about 7 percent of employees worked on farms. The same trend is found among proprietors. Three-fourths of Holmes County's 8,280 proprietors were in nonfarm businesses in 2005. Some Amish churches have no farmers among their ranks, and some families have no farmers among six or more brothers. Referring to three churches with which he is familiar, an Old Order Amish man commented that "most heads of families . . . work in lumber mills, building crews, furniture factories, saw mills and . . . I'll bet there is a dozen that we'd call millionaires." Manufacturing is the dominant employer in the county. In 2005, when just over 12 percent of Ohio's employment was in manufacturing, 28 percent, or 7,530, of the employees in Holmes County worked in manufacturing. Manufacturing was by far the dominant type of industrial employment.[8] Wayne-Dalton Corporation, which produces garage doors and openers; Weaver Leather Goods Inc., which makes custom leather products; and Case Farms Inc., a poultry-processing plant, are among the major manufacturing firms.

Employment in retail trade has also grown as tourism continues to increase. In 2002, for example, retail sales totaled almost $351 million, compared to $242 million just five years earlier. In 2005 visitors alone spent more than $300 million in Wayne and Holmes Counties.[9] Hotel accommodations and restaurants, which cater heavily to visitors, had sales exceeding $34 million in 2002, an increase of about 25 percent over 1997. The number of nonfarm businesses grew in Holmes County from 623 in 1990 to 1,049 in 2004.[10] In the communities of Berlin and Walnut Creek, two of the major tourist hubs in Holmes County, retail trade, manufacturing, hotels, and food establishments constituted more than half of all the industries present in 2005.[11] In that same year, about four thousand people were employed in the tourism industry in Holmes County.[12]

Manufacturing, tourism, and agriculture form the interconnected core of industries in the county: "If we didn't have the agriculture going on, we would not have the tourism, and if we didn't have the tourism, we would not have all that furniture manufacturing going on. So, really, those three here in Holmes County cannot exist without each other."[13] The county even offers awards, funded by local bed taxes, to individuals and organizations that actively promote tourism in some measurable way. Some Amish state plainly that they do not like the tourism, while others see it as almost a necessary evil: "Let's face it; we need the tourists. Unfortunately, they'll only buy stuff they can put in a trunk—'trunkables.'" So although Amish residents of Holmes County have a decidedly mixed reaction to tourism, county officials and some business owners actively promote it. A recent ad in a newsletter for Amish and other readers encouraged visitors to "keep Holmes County green—bring money."[14]

Bringing money has had its effect. Holmes County's 2007 poverty rate was lower than the state's and lower than that of the country as a whole. The poverty rates were also lower for the other counties that are part of the Holmes Settlement (see table 6.1). With one exception, the poverty rates for individuals younger than age eighteen were also lower in the settlement counties. The lower rates of poverty reflect the smaller degree of income inequality in these counties, the historically lower levels of unemployment, and an above-average increase in per capita income in Holmes County. Between 2000 and 2005, for example, the per capita income of the county rose by more than 22 percent, compared to a 13 percent increase for the entire state.

Despite the presence of some poverty, there is low usage of government welfare programs. In 2005 Holmes County had one of the lowest dependency ranks in the state.[15] Table 6.2 shows the amounts spent and participation rates for several public assistance programs in Holmes County in January 2007 and how these compare to the amounts and rates for the state as a whole. Both the amounts spent on participants in Holmes County and the rates of program participation are lower than the county average for the state. The low figures are attributable in a significant way to the high percentage of Amish and Mennonite families in the county

Table 6.1. Poverty and median household income estimates for counties involved in Holmes County Settlement, 2007

County	Median household income ($)	Poverty rate for all persons (%)	Poverty rate for those under 18 (%)
Ashland	46,805	10.0	14.5
Coshocton	38,111	12.8	20.1
Holmes	43,597	10.7	17.7
Knox	44,381	11.3	16.5
Stark	44,950	10.9	15.2
Tuscarawas	41,138	12.0	16.6
Wayne	46,928	8.8	13.4
Ohio	46,645	13.1	18.4
United States	50,740	13.0	18.0

Source: U.S. Census, Small Area Income and Poverty Estimates (SAIPE), www.census.gov/hhes/www/saipe.

who are eligible for food stamps, for example, but do not participate in the program. In 2000 about 20 percent of Amish families in Holmes County had household incomes below 130 percent of the poverty threshold. A 2003 survey in the county further suggested that a greater percentage of Amish than non-Amish household incomes were under $25,000 (50% versus 27%).[16] Despite the lower incomes of many Amish families, they do not apply for governmental assistance. When Amish and Mennonite families are included in a county's population, the food stamp participation rate decreases dramatically. When those families are excluded, the rate increases significantly. For example, in Holmes County, the participation rate among all who are eligible is less than 21 percent when the Amish-Mennonite segment is included in the calculations, but it rises to 53 percent when this segment is excluded, a difference of more than 32 points. This comparison suggests the major influence that the Amish have on decreasing participation in and costs of governmental programs. The map "Estimated Impact of Amish and Mennonite Populations on Food Stamp Participation Rates" shows the differences in each Ohio county. The differences noted in Holmes and surrounding counties, as well as Geauga County, all of which have significant Amish populations, are noticeably higher than those found in other Ohio counties. To increase federal funding to Holmes County, the local government has been urged to

Table 6.2. Amounts spent and participation rates in selected public assistance programs: Holmes County and county average for Ohio, January 2007

	Disability assistance	Ohio Works First	Food and nutrition services
Net amounts spent			
Holmes County	$3,553	$16,326	$91,755
State county average	$46,743	$294,911	$1,223,925[a]
Participation rates[b]			
Holmes County	0.07%	0.3%	2.4%
State	0.12%	1.5%	9.3%

Source: "Public Assistance Monthly Statistics," January 2007, Ohio Department of Jobs and Family Services, Columbus, OH.
[a]Amount for food and nutrition services is the value of the total coupons issued.
[b]Percentage of total population participating in programs.

raise participation rates even though the Amish generally are not willing to participate in government assistance programs.[17]

The growth in Holmes County's income has been fueled by the proliferation of nonfarming businesses and employment that has accompanied the decades-long decline in farming. As Kraybill and Nolt have pointed out, the constraints placed upon Amish individuals by their religious beliefs have forced them to be creative in developing alternatives to farming.[18] Some have been more successful than others. In some cases, less successful enterprises have resulted from ill-advised trust Amish have placed in individuals who have duped them or persuaded them to pursue businesses that were either impractical or unrealistic. A few of these "Ponzi schemes" have included worm and pigeon raising and chinchilla farming.

Broadening Ties and Reinforcing Boundaries

Fortunately, most nonfarm businesses have been more practical and successful. There are approximately four hundred fifty Amish woodworking and furniture manufacturers in the Holmes County Settlement. In 2005 the average Amish furniture manufacturing company in the area had begun in 1994 and employed an average of just over seven workers. Overall, these manufacturers employ almost three thousand individuals, consume

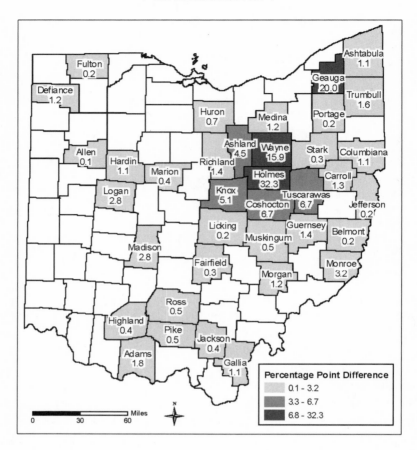

This map presents the percentage point difference in counties' Food Stamp
participation rate that occurs when the Amish and Mennonite residents are included
in the county populations and when they are not included. The 32.3 percentage point
difference for Holmes County indicates that when the Amish/Mennonite population
is included in the calculations, the Food Stamp participation rate decreases from 53
percent to less than 21 percent, a difference of 32.3 points. Data source: "Estimated
Impact of Amish and Mennonite Populations on Food Stamp Participation Rates,"
report prepared for the Ohio Department of Job and Family Services by Ohio
University's Voinovich School (ILGARD), 2005. Reprinted by permission.

roughly 11 percent of Ohio hardwood lumber, and account for about 3
percent of all furniture shipments in the United States.[19]

These firms are complemented by a diverse array of small shops selling
bulk foods, quilts, fabrics, outdoor furniture, horse equipment, storage
barns, fences, hardware, flowers, and lumber. Machine, welding, hydrau-

lics, small engine, and blacksmith shops provide further services. Individual roadside sales offer produce, baskets, birdhouses, custom-made windows, crafts, and sundry other items; these vendors' operations are among the many side businesses that dot the countryside. Many Amish produce individual items, for example, rockers and desks, which are sold to shops that bundle them into sets of furniture. Numerous stores serve as outlets for the wood products made by individual Amish craftspeople who manufacture them in their own shops but do not want to get directly involved in sales or marketing.

The "clustering" of several stages in the manufacture of Amish furniture "helps create a competitive advantage for all" that is "tempered by a sense of cooperation" among the Amish.[20] Such cooperation can occur in the joint design of pieces as well as in individual contributions to an entire furniture collection. Groups of furniture makers in the area have also worked with local stain creators to develop a common set of stains that are shared by several manufacturers. Retail stores that specialize in Amish furniture are also located near the actual manufacturers. These stores sell to customers in almost all fifty states.

Ironically, there are Amish-owned stores whose primary purpose is to serve their Amish neighbors but whose customers are most often tourists, because these stores "are sort of quaint and sort of unique," said a New Order respondent. Tourism thus can have contradictory effects on maintaining a cultural boundary between the Amish and the English. Two elements that feed the tourism are the very uniqueness and separateness of the Amish community; consequently, tourism encourages the Amish to maintain their cultural integrity and reinforces boundaries between the communities. However, tourism increases the social traffic between the English and the Amish communities. The interplay of the two elements helps create a dense web of interconnected economic activity, but it also "congests" and "intensifies" living for the local Amish. Finally, the increased tourism in Holmes County has created more diverse employment opportunities and has fostered Amish businesses catering to tourists.[21]

Increased dependence upon tourism deepens the ties Amish have with outsiders, and some Amish businessmen, especially in furniture sales, have sought to solidify and strengthen their businesses by actively advertising their products. In one effort to compete more effectively with English stores and cheaper imports, almost all of the approximately four hundred fifty furniture makers in the settlement formed the Amish Country Furniture Association, raised more than two hundred thousand dollars, and hired an English advertising firm to promote furniture produced in "the furniture heartland" of the Holmes County Settlement. In 2007 the group created its own brand to make its product better known and expand its market to a larger number of urban areas.

Furniture has been a growing and primary source of revenue in the area. An illustration of its growth is that one of the main stores, which began six years ago with its own manufacturing shop of 2,200 square feet, has since replaced the shop with a 24,000-square-foot facility. There are stores nationwide that now sell this firm's products, and the company just began another furniture business aimed at a more exclusive and international customer base. The owner explained, "We want a global presence." By addressing a higher-income clientele, the owner hopes to reduce the effect of competition from cheaper furniture imports. Two hundred thousand copies of a magazine advertising all the stores in the "heartland" were circulated throughout Ohio, and the plan is to expand the magazine's readership to a five-state region.

The formation of cooperative associations, the cultivation of niche markets, and increased use of advertising are three of the methods used by Amish manufacturers to compete successfully in the global economy. Keeping overhead costs low also helps to maximize competitiveness. To control other costs, Amish manufacturers maintain the traditional values of efficiency and minimum waste in their production of goods, through ingenious use of by-products and energy. As one Amish owner of a furniture store put it: "I'm not a farmer . . . but the idea is still passed on, to be conscious of the environment and not to waste stuff, that we should leave the land as good or better than when we started."[22]

The high demand for their products and the accompanying proliferation of different kinds of Amish businesses have helped to foster a high degree of interdependence within the Amish community, and the high level of communication in that community makes interdependence even denser. As soon as someone makes a new product or changes to a different style, others start to copy it. The large number of small, similar shops all vying for sales makes the search for a competitive edge all the more intense, and since the Amish do not copyright their products, there is little that can be done to restrict this imitating. Moreover, the process is con-

A workshop for a popular furniture business, where pieces for furniture are created and assembled. Photograph courtesy of Charles Hurst.

sistent with Amish beliefs about "brotherhood," which, in the view of one Amish businessman, "promotes the sharing of new products, methods, and markets, rather than hoarding them or being competitive among ourselves."

But being competitive with outsiders "is an entirely different matter." As we have seen with furniture clustering, cooperation among the Amish in the market of durable goods makes competitiveness with others more successful. Paradoxically, they cooperate to compete. These entrepreneurial efforts serve as incubators for new products to be made available to tourists, rendering the Amish economy anything but static.

Another type of interaction between Amish and English is legal business contracts. As Kraybill and Nolt observe, once in a while an Amish businessman will enter into a partnership with an English businessman.[23] Such a partnership makes economic sense because it allows Amish employers to have the advantage of some technology without being accused of using it themselves; it can be argued that it is the English person who owns or uses it. This reasoning does not always work, however.

One prominent English resident of a small town in southern Wayne County has been a lumber-business partner with an Amish man for forty-five years. The men of the Amish partner's extended family own a hardware store, a harness shop, and a furniture store. They argued that the Amish partner owned the land and the lumber, while the English partner owned the technology and the equipment. But the Old Order church did not accept the argument, and the Amish owner was constrained to sell the business "on paper" to his English partner to avoid violating the church's rules. The family has adapted to the new arrangement, which has also worked quite well.

The formation of partnerships with the English makes the Amish less independent and causes concern about the future. An Old Order businessman whose family owns several enterprises admitted, "We're drifting. We're not as self-sufficient as we used to be. The Amish are really very dependent on the English" for their furniture sales and, consequently, their livelihoods. Although these partnerships have served them well economically by helping local Amish adapt to changing circumstances in the immediate economy, they generate uneasiness about the continued inviolability of Amish culture. Being especially wary of such intrusions, the Swartzentruber craftsmen are less likely than others to have close ties with English businessmen.

Sometimes relationships with English businesses are avoided because of concerns about the moral atmosphere at those companies. According to one Old Order business owner, whether the Amish will work for a company depends less on whether the owner is English or Amish than on the morals of the company. In some cases, Amish have left local companies because they found the culture of the firms inconsistent with Amish values. A New Order businessman noted that the Bible's teaching against "an unequal yoke" is still the "official position of the Amish." Because of "friction" caused by differences in values, he argued, "we consider it dangerous to yoke up with English in business."

Even though their work environments are sometimes different, the relationship between English and Amish businesses is often symbiotic, each supporting the other, either directly or indirectly. By overwhelming margins, for example, Amish furniture makers would not use the term *Amish-made* to market their products: "We don't want to market Amish furniture. We want to market quality." But English-owned businesses will put up signs that identify their products as "Amish-made" or "Amish grown" or "Amish crafted," and the Amish make the products for those businesses to sell. Amish reactions to this situation vary and depend on the affiliation's Ordnung as well as the interpretation of when religious-cultural practices must give way to economic necessity.

In general, whether or not to advertise, and to what extent, is a difficult issue because it traps the Amish in a dilemma. While Amish craftsmen value humility and generally do not seek the limelight, their quality-made products draw attention, and advertising increases the volume of customers and profits. When the *Budget*, a local newspaper designed principally for the Amish, began in 1890, the Amish had to be talked into advertising in it.[24]

The products made with traditional craftsmanship by the Amish are attractive to modern English customers; in this case those who are modern want something that is traditional. A conflict Amish workers face is that diligence and careful work result in products that are in demand, resulting in higher profit and more wealth, which in turn pose a threat to the meekness and simplicity that are hallmarks of Amish life. Maintaining the boundary between an acceptable lifestyle and the outside culture in the context of these crosscutting pressures is a constant struggle. In the words of a local Mennonite historian, "When you get the fence fixed here, we're discovering there's a hole over here. So it's a constant work. And we don't believe that . . . you will ever get to a place where you're just rolling free."

Among many ascetic Protestant groups in earlier times, work in a "calling" meant that you not only did your best and did not waste time, but you also took advantage of God-given opportunities that were presented to you to advance your position. Echoing these beliefs, some Amish businesses advertise and actively market their products, because they believe doing so will enhance sales. Others shy away from advertising and are less interested in increasing their profits. Rather than embracing a "purely rational" attitude toward business growth, the latter group espouses a more "traditionalist" approach to their work.[25] "They really just want to earn enough to make a living, because to them, what's really important is being with their family, being in their church, so to them it's not a career goal to be the richest man in Holmes County. They just want to make enough to support their lifestyle," commented a local business representative who has worked with the Amish for more than a decade. The priority of family and the commitment to an integration of and balance between family and work are fundamental axioms of Amish culture. The nature and location of that balance, however, are different for different groups and often even for individuals.

The church may even enforce a lower profit to avoid the cultural, religious, and social dangers that can attend higher profits. In one case a Swartzentruber man had been doing a very good business selling baskets alongside the road, making forty thousand to fifty thousand dollars per year. Representatives of his church had been keeping track of his sales and told him he was making too much money; he had to make some of his money available for lending to other church members at no interest. "In a situation like that, they move in and they do something about it . . . Among the Old Order you wouldn't hear about making too much money but you would hear about the size of business." The Swartzentrubers tend to have a "set law or rule" about these matters, whereas the Old and New Order do not, but have variable and vague teaching on size limits on businesses and on the charging of interest.

Another young Swartzentruber man "had a construction company, and he pushed it and . . . made good money." He was being paid by the hour, and then church representatives "came up with this rule that you can't make more than a certain amount in an hour . . . They try to control your finances if they can." A young man who had grown up in a Swartzentruber family with fifteen brothers and sisters but had left before joining the church told us that there was a belief that people would "rest on their laurels" if they made too much money. The amount one could charge for construction was fixed to avoid the possibility of large profits. He also indicated that there were separate pay scales for those under 21, those over 21 but single, and those who were older than 21 and married. Variations in permitted pay followed variations in perceived need. These practices represent attempts by church leaders to apply church beliefs about community and equality, "principles held dear."

The lower wages paid to nonunionized Amish workers by Amish and non-Amish employers often put them in direct conflict with English unionized workers who see them as competing unfairly. Regardless of affiliation, Amish men have a negative view of unions, as "unreasonable," "a racket," and having "too much power." While some say that unions may have been needed in the past, the Amish believe that even if so, their time is now gone. In their view, the combination of Amish employers' concern for their employees and government regulation of safety and related issues make unions an unnecessary obstacle resulting in higher costs of production. Some church elders have discouraged Amish crews from working in nearby large cities because of the hostility they might face from unionized workers. While it has not been a big issue in the Holmes County Settlement, for Amish work crews who have ventured into large cities, there have even been occasional incidents of English workers sabotaging and destroying Amish construction.

Multiple Benefits of Family Farming

As we have seen, the pressures brought on by population growth, outside competition, and land costs have forced the Amish in the Holmes Settlement to seek out new means of livelihood. "As the world progresses, we have to move on," one said. There is no question that the shift out of farming into other forms of business has brought significant and often worrisome changes to the Holmes Settlement. As Kline and Beachy comment, the movement away from farming creates a challenge for the Amish attempt to maintain a "Christian life" that is "a balanced, sensible experience."[26] A recurrent theme in our conversations with both New and Old Order Amish leaders was the perceived threat to traditional values brought about by the movement away from farming, a refrain voiced by Amish in other settlements as well.

Most of the Amish men in our survey held farming in higher regard than any other occupation. The order of which the respondent was a member made little difference. Farming was seen as being "good for body and soul," an occupation that involved "working closely with nature," and farmers were viewed as workers who were "dedicated to family," "down-to-earth," "practical," "energetic," "hard working," and "ordinary." Farming is considered "the ideal situation"; it "has been the root of the Amish"; and it teaches "better work ethics, responsibility, and moral conduct."

Farming allows everyone to be at home together and to work together, and it creates a situation in which parents can easily teach their children work skills and habits that will serve to maintain Amish culture. It encourages the strong work ethic that is expected in Amish culture: "You know, you realize what work is all about with all the chores and duties on a farm." This value is part of the deeply rooted ethic for life that has long been associated with the ascetic Anabaptist tradition.[27] The strong work ethic is one reason wasting time is to be assiduously avoided. As a 2002 lead article in the *Gemeinde Register* put it, when it comes to time, you either "use it or lose it." "Time is precious because time is life . . . It must be used wisely or it is gone forever."[28]

Some Amish employers mentioned explicitly that they could tell the difference between employees who had been raised on or worked on a farm and those who had not. An Old Order Amish greenhouse and outdoor furniture owner believes the work ethic is different: "When I was young, every Amish man was employed in farming, and that was doing work until it was done, doing it when it had to be done . . . the thoroughness of our work." Family farming requires that everyone pitch in and work together. When hiring employees, "you can tell the difference between those who had chores when they were young."

The absence of a family farm means that children are not as likely to have regular responsibilities and to learn how to organize their time in a useful manner. They develop less discipline and less sense of purpose. An Old Order businessman who had grown up on a farm found that individuals who had not been used to working as young children were less likely to be committed to their jobs when employed as adults. They were not used to the demands of a regular job: "You mean I have to be there at 6:00? I can't get up that early." Moreover, they are less inclined to want to work on the weekend: "On the farm there was no weekend . . . I mean you worked six days a week like the scripture says you should."

In this businessman's view, the lack of commitment to the job is often coupled with an assumption of entitlement on the part of the worker. The sense of individual responsibility is slowly eroded. The worker comes to expect the employer to take care of him by providing pay and other benefits: "And we start acquiring this mentality that someone else is responsible for my welfare from cradle to grave." Simultaneously, since this "someone else" is the business and not one's fellow Amish, the whole process

The Kidron Auction, held every Thursday, is an important means of redistributing animals within the Amish community and between Amish and English farmers. Photograph courtesy of Charles Hurst.

weakens reliance upon members of one's church. For some Amish, moving away from farming also means relying more upon stores for food and other products. This change can produce some undesirable fallout: "Every year the trash pile gets bigger," said an Amish customer at Wal-Mart.[29]

Owning or working in a nonfarm business also removes one from working directly with forces of nature and from the necessity of submission to them. Regularized, fixed hours designated for work foster the notion that the worker controls his or her work and life. This notion can breed an attitude of self-sufficiency, even arrogance, and certainly individualism, worries a young New Order Christian Fellowship Amish man with whom we spoke. It may endanger the selflessness and Gelassenheit demeanor prized in Amish culture. In contrast, farming does not have fixed hours and is as much a holistic way of life as it is an occupation. It nurtures humility and awareness of dependence upon a natural time cycle and forces beyond one's control. "When the sun comes up, it's time to work; when it goes down it is time to go to bed." Thus, the Amish sense of dependence on and interdependence with the environment derives from the capriciousness of weather and the inability to fully control nature.

Whereas the twenty-four-hour routine of farm life makes it difficult to compartmentalize different components of one's lifestyle, the structure of a nine-to-five job away from home fosters mental separations between work and leisure, family and factory. As a local Anabaptist historian commented: "It used to be on the farm, when you got done in the evening, you were ready to eat supper and go to bed. But now they get home at 4:00 to 5:00 in the afternoon, and the big question is, what do you do? This is a real problem and they know it." Having "free time" can be a problem, because it endangers discipline and the work ethic. If you have free time, "it gets filled up with things that are not good in a lot of cases, if there's not real leadership and supervision."

Working for an employer in a business also ties the employee down during his shift, and the nature of his work often makes it difficult for him to leave the job in the event of some family or other emergency. On the farm, observed an Amish owner of a wood-bending business, when there was a family event or emergency, "everybody just dropped everything," but in this business "we have obligations . . . and so sometimes it really makes it tough." He has adapted to the challenge by training his employees so that each can work several machines; this versatility makes it possible for workers to substitute for one another in case of family or other demands. As more Amish encounter the problems associated with these newer ways of making a living, they search out creative solutions that allow them to maintain traditional values and practices.

Family farming on fifty to one hundred acres creates a work environment in which family members freely communicate and learn from one another using their own language. Factory work may result in less communication because of its nature: "Some shops you've got earplugs in, and headphones all the time. They don't do a lot of communicating, and maybe limited interaction. That's not as good as hauling manure, you know, . . . you kind of talk." Amish men often work alongside English workers, and while camaraderie is usual, problems can arise because of language or cultural differences. A New Order lumber owner noted that communication in English may be difficult for the more conservative Amish who have left farming, even temporarily, to work in a factory or a lumber yard. As in any organizational situation, there can be difficulties when token members work with a majority from another group.[30]

While Amish or English workers may not constitute actual formal labor unions, tight-knit cultural groups can make work life easy or difficult for the group that happens to be in the minority. Since each group may have different cultural values and expectations, the minority individuals are often put on the spot to perform, and the boundaries between the groups may be accentuated. Persons in both groups may be hard workers, but their styles may differ: "[The Amish are] not taught, or they're not exposed to, people skills. So they can be beastly blunt with no malice intended. It just comes out that way." This comment by an English businessman who has worked closely with the Amish for decades is an outsider's interpretation of the Amish tendency toward unadorned and unembellished, straightforward language. As in their work, there is an economy of style in their communication, "with no malice intended."

Some Amish groups have replaced farming with other work more than other groups. A member of the National Amish Steering Committee contended, for example, that the Andy Weaver Amish have moved away from farming more than the Old Order Amish have. The Andy Weavers lost their enthusiasm for farming when milking machines and mechanized cooling became a virtual necessity for turning a profit on a dairy farm. Most Old Order churches relaxed the Ordnung on these key pieces of technology, but the Andy Weavers stood firm against it. As a result, there are less than a dozen Andy Weaver full-time dairy farmers in the entire settlement. Nevertheless, in the view of one farmer, the Andy Weavers' overall concern for maintaining smallness and using less technology has meant that "the loss of farming as a 'way of life' is less" and that the Andy Weavers can "better maintain 'Amishness' than groups that adapted more for more farming." Andy Weavers who are farmers are likely to be produce farmers and participate in regular produce auctions. In addition, some of the family breadwinners in this affiliation have become quite successful businessmen, and several are among the biggest furniture makers in the settlement. Some Andy Weaver Amish work in local factories as well. Concern about the loss of farmers among their ranks continues, though, and has led to a serious discussion at present about relaxing the rules on milking machines to try to coax young farmers back.

For those who stick to farming regardless of the difficulties involved, daily issues differ from those faced by Amish workers who enter factories and businesses. For example, the Swartzentruber Amish, who are much more likely to be farmers, encounter problems specific to farmers. An estimated 70 percent of them are involved in family farming.[31] If they cannot afford land for their own farms, some Swartzentrubers rent land from Old Order Amish.

It is estimated that three thousand Swartzentruber Amish live in northern Holmes and southern Wayne Counties.[32] More than the Old or New Order groups, this order considers it very important for men to be at or near home when working. The Swartzentruber restrictions on technology and employment can reduce the work options open to them. A Swartzentruber farmer mentioned, for example, that members of his affiliation will not make pallets because a forklift has to be used to raise them, and "back in Bible times, lifting was by hand." He observed that it may make "Bible sense," but it does not make "common sense."

Another looming problem for the Swartzentrubers is finding employment for their children. Since they cannot work for English employers, we were told that "it's gonna be a bigger problem." Some seek to solve it by helping their children purchase land or moving as a family to another state, or both. In 2007, New York and Missouri were among the most attractive states for those contemplating moving. Rather than seeing these limitations on lifestyle as negative and oppressive, persons within the fold generally interpret them positively as adherence to deeply held beliefs.

The generally poorer economic position of Swartzentruber Amish demonstrates more the effects of their strict rules than it does a weaker work ethic. A young man who grew up in a Swartzentruber household told us that there is less leisure time within this Amish group than in others because work is emphasized so heavily. For example, they "will spread their own gravel rather than having a truck do it, and will put up a pipe to fill the silo and take it down each time."

In addition to their farming, many Swartzentrubers have small side businesses such as making baskets or selling produce. But they don't advertise and don't always participate in the most effective ways to sell their products. As an Old Order bishop told us, if the Swartzentrubers took part in flea markets instead of merely selling by the roadside, they would do a lot better. Their lower sales also reflect the broader problems of small business, which many Amish see as a critical component of our increasingly corporatized economy. One Swartzentruber pointedly argued for the importance of small business in U.S. history: "Small businesses are being crowded out and that's what made America great; small streams made a big river." Benjamin Franklin could not have agreed more.

Working for Others

One of the distinguishing qualities of many Amish businesses in Holmes County is that they employ workers from several different orders; while they may not be in fellowship, they work side by side. One Old Order employer has thirty employees, including his six oldest sons, one daughter, his son-in-law, and a couple of nephews. He has also employed New Order Amish, Andy Weavers, and some English in the past. In 2006, about one-quarter of his employees were Swartzentruber Amish. He considers them very good workers, but he realizes that there are some tasks that they are not allowed to do (for example, drive a forklift or weld) and that there will be turnover in their ranks: "We know . . . upfront that a job like this is never considered as an option to make a career out of it. This is just something until [a Swartzentruber employee] can either farm or do something at home." This employer thinks there is less focus among Old and New Order Amish men on being at home as the children approach their teenage years.

Employing individuals from groups such as the Andy Weaver or Swartzentruber Amish can create some challenges for Amish employers. One Amish business owner, for example, found that teaching safety by using a video is resisted by some of these employees. More conservative employees are more likely to adhere to their traditional ways and not even tolerate an explanation from a member of a different church of why they should accept a change: " 'No, we won't.' I think . . . you will find that mentality a little bit amongst the Swartzentruber Amish. They would say 'no' and just turn their backs and walk away."

Work safety is an issue that became more public in the mid-1990s when a fifteen-year-old Amish boy was injured and killed at an Amish business in southern Holmes County. Representatives from the Occupational Safety and Health Administration (OSHA) came to investigate. A local safety consultant who had worked with businesses that had Amish employees suggested that the Amish community should organize a group or committee to serve as a support group, resource, and liaison between government regulatory agencies and the Amish community. As a consequence of his suggestion, the three-person Amish Safety Committee was created. Representatives from the Old Order, New Order, and Andy Weaver groups are eligible to serve on the committee.

Safety is only one of the concerns when children work. As farms have declined, the question of what to do with children who no longer have farming chores has become more acute. Amish parents worry that their youth may become involved with drugs when they make money and still have time on their hands. According to a girl who left her Old Order church before joining, while working children are supposed to pass along their earnings to their parents for later use, some keep portions of their earnings to purchase "radios and tapes, that kind of stuff, which you're not supposed to have." The Amish believe in keeping their young people active in productive work that serves the community. They also believe in the value of manual labor. "Everyone needs to learn to work with their hands, and you can't learn that too early for children." Fathers and mothers teach their young people skills that will serve them throughout their work lives.

Parents are committed to seeing that their children do not have idle hands. One of the reasons increasing size is not an issue for some Amish businessmen is that they are generating jobs for the younger generation. "We can't just push them out and let them fly," remarked an Old Order employer. Amish have relocated to obtain jobs for their sons in sawmills and woodworking shops, but these include machines that can cause injury. In the past, the Department of Labor has argued that letting boys younger than age eighteen work in these places would constitute a violation of child labor laws. Over several years, attempts were made to pass a bill in Congress that would allow persons exempt from public school beyond eighth grade and at least age fourteen (a definition that would include Amish youth) to work in such businesses under adult supervision as long as the youths themselves did not operate power-driven woodworking machines and if they were protected from flying wood particles, dust, and noise. In 2004 the legislation was passed and signed by President George W. Bush despite arguments against it by the Child Labor Coalition and the United Food and Commercial Workers Union.

When work accidents occur, Old and New Order churches have the Workers' Aid Plan available to pay for treating injuries that occur. Employers provide the funds for the plan, contributing a given amount per employee. They can then seek reimbursement for their costs when there is an injury. The Amish do not use funds from the government's Workers' Compensation program when on-the-job accidents and injuries occur, even though until 2003 Amish employers had been paying into the program. In 2003 the State of Ohio exempted religious groups that are opposed to insurance from paying premiums for the state program. The church plan serves as a substitute and reinforces the Amish beliefs in trusting God, in keeping tight community bonds, and in helping each other rather than relying upon the state. One Amish businessman, however, told us that in rejecting Workers' Compensation, "sometimes I think we take it too far and be too independent." Amish-owned companies with a mix of Amish and English employees often offer a variety of fringe benefits, including group health, 401(k) plans, paid vacations, and profit sharing. Some Amish accept the health insurance, while others refrain: "It's a choice that guys make."

Some mutual-aid programs tend to be exclusive, for example, medical aid programs, but Amish from different orders help each other when fire or some other natural catastrophe occurs. When economic hard times could create an incentive for an employer to protect his or her own and reduce costs by laying off workers, the Amish reaction is more typically to share the burden. An Old Order businessman said he does not see himself as being in business to get rich or because it's "just a job"; rather, the business provides "a sense of purpose," "a way of life." If there are downturns in business, he believes in sharing the economic costs with his workers rather than singling out some workers for layoffs. This response is very different from that found in most English-owned companies, where mass layoffs are likely to result from economic difficulties. But there are differences of opinion within Amish ranks about the equal sharing of aid: some feel that their aid programs should be exclusive to a given order, while others believe aid should be extended to others as well.

Most Amish employers prefer to hire all Amish workers, even if they are of different affiliations, because it makes operations less complicated and strengthens relationships in their community. "The thing with hiring Amish is we take company field trips, . . . we have social events, we all get together in the evening. I'm part of that," muses the owner of a greenhouse and outdoor furniture business. "It blends together better . . . and look at all the cost and the stress that takes out of doing your business." These views are borne out in research that has shown employers to be more comfortable hiring co-workers who are similar to them because they are more predictable and fit into the ongoing company culture.[33] This hiring process enhances the trust employers can place in the employee, and as Kraybill and Nolt point out, trustworthiness is a characteristic that is prized by Amish employers.[34] The fact that recruitment often takes place via word of mouth among acquaintances increases the chances for a homogeneous, like-minded set of employees. In addition to the predictability that comes with hiring fellow Amish workers, issues revolving around social security, workers' compensation, and fringe benefits are greatly simplified.

Amish men who are willing to accept a wide range of manual jobs do not generally have much trouble finding work. Historically, the rate of unemployment in Holmes County is lower than the rate in the state as a whole, and among the Amish unemployment is very low. An Amish businessman who has spent his whole life in the area said that "as far as I know of the thousands of Amish men in this community, I do not know one that is on unemployment or is unemployed . . . I can't really think of anyone that's ever been unemployed." Among the Swartzentruber Amish, however, obtaining long-term employment is more problematic because the range of permissible jobs is much narrower and because they focus heavily on staying at or near home when working.

Occupational Dispersion and Internal Divisions

As noted earlier, the population-land ratio has created heavy pressures within the Holmes County Settlement Amish to diversify their occupations. The cost of farmland in Holmes and neighboring Wayne counties has risen faster than the cost of farmland in the state as a whole.[35] The combination of high birthrates, increasing scarcity and cost of agricultural land, and the continuous growth of tourist-oriented businesses has forced Amish in the Holmes County Settlement to muster all their creativity and strength of will to find new and morally acceptable occupations outside of farming.

Sean Lowery and Allen G. Noble's analysis of data from the 1973 and 1997 editions of the *Ohio Amish Directory* indicates that the percentage of Amish men working in agriculture declined from about 48 percent in 1973 to 21 percent in 1997, while the proportion working in manufacturing, construction, and wood products increased from 25 percent in 1973 to 46 percent in 1997.[36] The percentages of Amish who are farmers vary across affiliations. A higher proportion of New Order than Old Order men were farmers in 1988 and 1997. In the Holmes County Settlement, at least one-third of the men earn their living doing carpentry. Amish of all affiliations are more spread out among a variety of nonfarming occupations than they were two or three decades ago.

As expected, a random sample taken from the 2005 *Ohio Amish Directory* yielded smaller percentages of farmers among all sects, indicating the continuing general decline in farming noted by several commentators. Overall, slightly less than 10 percent of nonretired Amish workers in the sample were farmers. But in contrast to the 1997 figures, a smaller percentage (6%) of Andy Weaver Amish were farmers, reinforcing comments we heard from several Amish respondents that the Andy Weavers were leaving farming at a faster rate, perhaps in part because of the difficulty of competing successfully as dairy farmers without milking machines. Within the New Order churches in the directory, about 15 percent of members were full-time farmers, and in the New Order Christian Fellowship churches, 14 percent were full-time farmers. About 10 percent of the heads of households of the Old Order churches were farmers. The higher proportion of farmers within the New Order may be related to the greater leeway allowed for technology in this group and to the growth of organic farming in the Holmes County Settlement, or both. Among Swartzentruber Amish, who do not appear in the directory, the vast majority are farmers.

A man must be careful in choosing. Occupations are acceptable only if they allow the individual to maintain Amish religious beliefs and maintain a strong family life, and if the job directly or indirectly contributes to the community. Our survey of two New Order and three Old Order churches in the Holmes County Settlement examined members' images of occupational categories. Eight out of ten individuals held the occupation of farming in "higher regard" than either blue-collar or white-collar work, even though most were not farmers themselves. A blue-collar worker was more highly esteemed than one in a white-collar position and was seen as a person who was "faithful," "industrious," "honest," "not afraid to do physical work," and "willing to work for his daily wage"; it was felt that the blue-collar worker "earns his reward."

Only two out of the sixty-five Amish in the survey had more respect for white-collar work than for farming or blue-collar labor. This finding is reinforced by the decidedly mixed image of white-collar workers held by this group. When asked about such workers, many hesitated to judge, hedged their responses, or mixed positive with negative observations: "Most are out to make the big bucks, although we do need some white collar," said one respondent. "I have respect for a person who has the capability to handle such professions if done with a meek spirit," said another. A white-collar worker "may not be energetic enough to 'work' for a living, but still 'brains' are needed!" replied a third.

A strong undercurrent in the responses was a belief that white-collar workers often do not like to work or that what they do is not real work: they "would rather dream and explore new ideas and let someone else do the manual labor." A minority, however, viewed these workers as "more educated" and "business-like" and as engaged in work that "has its place." The mixed rather than wholly negative assessment of white-collar work can be traced in large part to the Gelassenheit value of humility and willingness to give others their due and to the fact that, with their movement into a widening array of occupations and businesses, many Amish realize the inevitability and necessity of white-collar tasks. Some have even accepted white-collar employment. Among the newer occupational areas being entered by Amish in the Holmes County Settlement are real estate, accounting, and auctioneering.

If farming is the benchmark for an ideal occupation among the Amish, then those jobs that are the most similar to farming will be the most acceptable to them. Thus, the most favored occupations are those that are manual in nature, allow one to remain close to home, optimize the opportunity for other family members to participate, and make a measurable contribution to the community. "Your job should consist in making food, making clothing, doing carpentry, that is, doing something that is useful." According to one Old Order leader, the nonfarming occupations most conducive to Amish values are "home-based, small cottage industries where people can still work at home or close to home. And, for lack of a better

A popular view is that the Amish shy away from modern technology, but this is not always the case. For some New Order Amish, the use of computers is permissible for business purposes. Photograph courtesy of Charles Hurst.

term, an Amish environment is most conducive to continuing being able to instill our values and our principles." "The base question is whether the occupation will allow me to be a good Christian, to live with honesty and integrity, and lead a valid life," replied a New Order member.

The pressure to find an acceptable occupation outside of farming would seem to be especially great among the Amish groups who resist change most strenuously but who also have higher birthrates than other orders. Swartzentruber churches have narrower prescriptions than other affiliations on what alternative occupations are allowable.[37] Estimates are that just under three-fourths are farmers. Swartzentruber farms tend to be smaller than those of other Amish. Since Swartzentrubers often work for lower wages than others, some farmers hire them to milk cows and make the hay. Produce growers often hire young Swartzentruber girls, who will work for ten to forty dollars per day. Many Swartzentruber

Amish have side businesses or occupations that allow them to remain near their homes. Woodworking, buggy and harness construction, blacksmithing, carpentry, and working as a general handyman are all acceptable. A job should be physical and require some skill, but it should also keep one humble. Thus, because it suggests modesty, doing construction work on a part of a new house would be preferable to building the whole house. Although Swartzentrubers will work for English customers, they refrain from working for English contractors. Swartzentrubers' tenacious hold on tradition comes at the cost of what outsiders might consider lost business and occupational opportunities. However, these pressures force creative capabilities to come to the foreground, resulting in novel products as sources of income. As they say, necessity is the mother of invention.

Exploring New Enterprises

As Amish people have in recent years sought new ways to make ends meet but at the same time remain close to nature, they have ventured more aggressively into new business arenas. Some of these are closely related to farming and traditional values, while others are less so and more controversial in the community. Dog raising and deer farming are among the more controversial enterprises engaged in by some Amish.

Dog raising has grown as a means of supplementing family income, and dog farms may now be more numerous than dairy farms in Holmes County. In 2006 the county issued 478 kennel licenses; in 2001, only 276 were issued.[38] The central reasons for dog raising are economic: it can be done at home, requires little acreage, and can be a significant source of income. The Buckeye Dog Auction, held about every other month in Holmes County, has been a source of controversy, even among some Amish. Attempts to move the auction to Geauga County have been rebuffed by that county because of negative feedback about the auction and allegations of animal cruelty.

Although there is disagreement between protestors and breeders about the conditions under which dogs are being raised, part of the debate is also rooted in the way Amish and English tend to view the animals. Amish breeders see them pragmatically as a "commodity": "Dogs are livestock, not people."[39] English protestors see them in moral terms, as "pets" with human needs and qualities. There are almost two hundred USDA-licensed breeders in Ohio, and at least half of them are in Berlin, Millersburg, and Sugarcreek, which are all in Holmes County.[40]

In response to the negative publicity that dog raising has generated, a local Amish historian said that he thought the Humane Society and similar groups were focusing on the wrong issue. He argued that these associations should concentrate instead on pet owners who get tired of their pets and then just put them by the roadside. Dog breeders are generally licensed, and Amish take care of their animals, whether they are pigs, cows, horses, or dogs, he said. Nevertheless, several leaders in the Amish community have expressed uneasiness about dog raising as a major source of income, indicating that many have a "negative view on it" and that it is "not a traditional Amish vocation" that would have been "high on our forefathers' list."

Deer farming has also increased among the Amish, as it has in the nation as a whole. A recent study by Texas A&M University estimated that, directly and indirectly, deer farming adds about $3 billion per year to the national economy.[41] Ohio is among the states with the largest number of deer farms, 650–700 in 2007. "For many in the Amish communities, deer breeding is another way to diversify their operations . . . There are a lot of Amish farmers in Holmes and Wayne Counties who are turning to deer farming . . . It doesn't take a whole lot of land . . . You can have a deer farm by dedicating 10 acres of the worst farming land you have."[42] While a disproportionate number of Amish deer farmers in Ohio appear to be clustered in Wayne and Holmes counties, particularly around the communities of Millersburg, Fredericksburg, Dundee, and Apple Creek, Amish deer farmers are also found in Geauga County, and a few are scattered throughout other parts of the state.[43]

By diversifying their farms through deer farming, Amish farmers can help ensure that their land will be passed on to following generations. Many Amish deer farmers, however, take on deer raising only as a hobby. A significant number of Andy Weaver Amish have pursued the endeavor. An Amish farmer may put aside part of his farm to raise deer and then sell them or their products commercially to other ranchers or owners of hunting preserves. Deer farming is attractive because deer require less food, are less taxing on the land than cattle, mature early, and can reproduce for up to twenty years.[44] Not only can more profit often be gained from deer farming than from traditional farming, but it also affords another opportunity for the Amish to gain a livelihood without leaving their farms or their homes. A 2007 two-day deer auction in Wayne County, Ohio, that attracted many Amish brought in over $3 million in sales.[45]

Like dog raising, however, deer farming has elicited mixed reactions in the Amish community. Too often, one Amish farmer observed, "the entire thing comes down to the big trophy deer, to the big rack." "For us to be involved in entertainment for some rich fellow to come out and pay $10,000 to shoot a trophy buck that was raised in a pen—there's something not right about it," said another. It also brings "negative publicity" from the outside. Neither dog raising nor deer farming appears to be "quite consistent with what we pretend to be," said an Old Order businessman. He thinks there are better ways to survive: "Providing good, wholesome nourishing food is something we can all feel good about."

A third somewhat controversial enterprise that some Amish have taken up is establishing salvage stores that sell dented, water-damaged, and expired foods and medicines (but not baby formula). In addition to serving as a source of income, these stores are consistent with Amish values of efficiency and careful use of resources. The Ohio stores, most of which are located in the northeastern part of the state, attract an increasing number of customers who are financially strapped. "We've been amazed, how good we've done," remarked one Amish owner.[46]

Less controversial than deer farming or dog raising, greenhouses and produce auctions are two additional sources of income for the Ohio Amish that are more consistent with their values. Greenhouses, especially those focused on hydroponic technology, are steadily increasing in number because they do not require large areas or quality soil, and they allow intensive production of crops. They are also energy-efficient and can be operated without electricity. Tomatoes, peppers, lettuce, and cucumbers are the vegetables most often grown in them.

Produce auctions have also become more prevalent in Ohio and have made a resurgence nationally, primarily as a way for small-scale farmers, including many Amish, to market their organic goods locally. The auctions occupy an important economic niche because they lie midway between large agribusiness and individual produce road stands. They benefit small local businesses that can purchase fresh products and therefore compete with large grocery chains such as Wal-Mart and Kroger. Small-scale farmers do not produce enough for large chains, but they can satisfy the needs

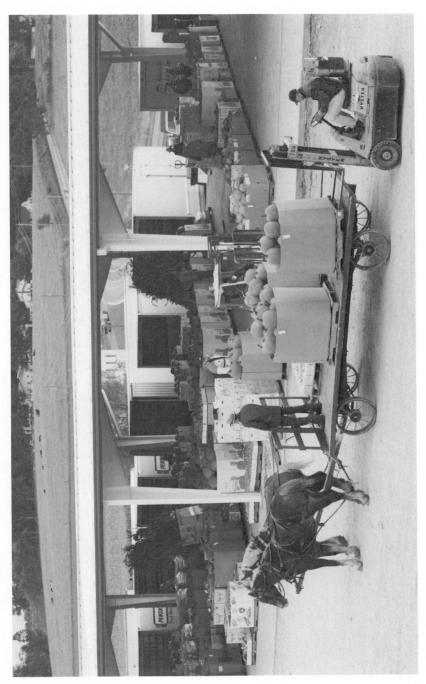

The Mount Hope Produce Auction draws customers from around the area and sellers from around the whole state. Photograph by Doyle Yoder.

of small businesses. As of 2004, there were about a half dozen produce auctions in Ohio, all of them Amish-owned. And all are less than twenty years old.[47] The Mount Hope Produce Auction in Holmes County was the first of its kind in Ohio and is currently one of the largest in the state.

Technology and Pandora's Box

The movement into factory, construction, and manufacturing occupations has exposed Amish employees and entrepreneurs to a variety of new devices and experiences, not the least of which are modern technologies. For example, in 1999 a new woodshop opened every week in the Holmes County Settlement, initiating a demand for more phones, faxes, and computers. Amish efforts to maintain ethical and cultural boundaries between themselves and English society are perhaps most tested when it comes to technology. Because of sensitivity to maintaining the core of their culture, Amish enterprises have had to be judicious in their adoption of new technologies. On the one hand, Amish employers and workers tend to be eminently practical and need to make a living, while on the other hand, they also want to keep their humility and separateness intact. Keeping up with technology allows Amish businesses to compete more successfully. They feel the need to improve their edge especially because they are competing with foreign imports (for example, furniture from China), and of course new mechanical technologies are often more efficient than hand methods of doing things.

Sometimes, however, the Amish fail to anticipate all the consequences associated with adopting technology. To many Amish, new technology is a little like the Greek myth of Pandora's Box, in which Pandora was given a jewel-encrusted box as a wedding gift from Zeus and was told that as long as she did not open the box, her marriage would be successful and happy. But, being curious, Pandora could not resist. She opened the box and loosed all kinds of problems upon herself and others. The possibility of unwanted consequences is the reason groups like the Amish are so selective in their use of "modern" technology.

Technology may be a gift in one sense, but undesirable effects may come with it. The cell phone is an example. Different cell phones have different options. All New Order churches in the Holmes County Settlement have banned the use of cell phones, except under unusual or emergency circumstances, because it may be possible to use them for text messaging, Internet access, and other things, in addition to simply calling someone. For most Amish, these extra functions create a Pandora's Box situation, opening the door to concerns and problems they wish to avoid. If cell phones are accepted in general, how "are you going to keep that in line?" asked a New Order employer. "Cell phones are a touchy subject," commented an Old Order business owner. Young people use them to get together, and then "things happen." As in education, what is important in technology is its effects and how it is used. A related problem is that once a technology comes into general use and people become dependent on it, it is very difficult to ban the item. The cat is already out of the bag.

As a group, the Amish filter out devices that do not meet prescribed criteria. Church leaders and members are involved in making those decisions, and it is possible to find variations not only between affiliations but between individual churches in the same affiliation as well. The potential adoption is clearly discussed and reasons are given for its acceptance or rejection. As one Amish woman said, if asked why church officials made the decision they did, "they could tell you exactly why they decided, what that would lead to, and why we don't have it."

A first criterion is that the technology must not violate the Ordnung of the church. In addition, the Amish are careful to consider the technology's long-term consequences for the coherence and constancy of community life. "If something has a greater potential for harm, we don't own it." Greater efficiency to be gained from a new technology is not a sufficient reason to accept it. Finally, technologies are more likely to be adopted if they make long-term economic sense. It is this set of criteria as an integrated group upon which decisions regarding acceptability of technology are made. For example, the continued use of horses rather than a tractor requires that farmers keep their farms relatively small (75–125 acres), allowing a family to work together side-by-side in maintaining the farm themselves. Horses also need less upkeep and maintenance than tractors and provide free natural fertilizer for the fields. Consequently, in the long run they are less costly, more practical, and indirectly encourage familial togetherness.

There are distinct differences in the usage of technology within the Holmes County Settlement, but these distinctions often become quite complicated. Kraybill's nuanced description of tractor use by the Amish is still largely accurate when applied to the Holmes County Settlement. The tractor is used by Andy Weaver, Old Order, and New Order farmers "in selective and controlled ways," but the New Order is the most liberal in its use.[48] Some New Order churches permit the use of tractors for short-distance road travel. When farming, New and some Old Order farmers can use tractors for hauling crops from the field, but they use horses for traction in the field. The only mechanized equipment used by Swartzentruber Amish in the field is a sprayer powered by a gas motor.

The use of rubber tires and sliding doors on buggies and the use of air tires on equipment are permitted in the New Order, while the Old Order requires steel tires and prohibits sliding curtains on their buggies. The argument is a practical one for the New Order: steel wheels are louder and often rattle bolts loose, and they are more costly in the long run. But the situation can become "complicated," as when some Old Order Amish who must move heavy loads in sawmills put foam in their tires. Old Order Amish can have air tires on their balers for better flotation and on their mowers, but not on their tractors.

And even the distinction of steel versus rubber can become blurred. A new buggy for sale at a recent Holmes County benefit auction featured steel wheels with "new style rubber buffers" that lie just under the ribbon of steel that coats the outside of the tires. Even with the rubber buffers, these wheels would be permissible for Old Order Amish because steel covers the outer edge of the tires. The buggy had numerous other accessories (a hand-controlled windshield wiper, a battery-operated inside reading light, turn signal lights, hydraulic rear brakes, rear and front lights, two rear view mirrors, padded upholstered seats, and a clock). A Mennonite woman remarked that "all it needed is an engine."

The differences in technology use can be seen in the shop, too. All the Amish use diesel power. The Old Order and New Order Amish use electric tools powered by diesel generators and hydraulic and air tools. The Andy Weavers can use air tools and diesel-powered tools, but not hydraulic or electric tools. The Swartzentrubers use only hand tools and line shafts with belts run by diesel—no air, hydraulic or electric tools.

Electricity-powered machines that increase efficiency and productivity for a business may be appropriately changed and redesigned so that their operation is consistent with church rules.[49] One Old Order businessman noted that much of his equipment was effectively converted to use hy-

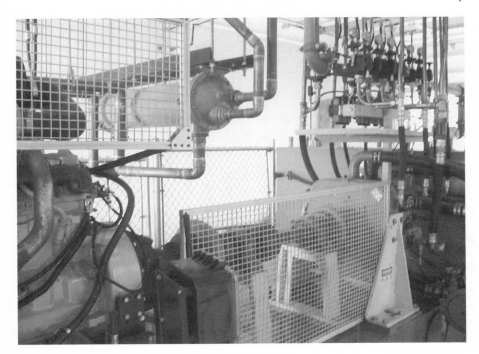

Starting on the left, a diesel is hooked up to a line shaft and then to hydraulics to run all the machines in the shop of a large business. The cylinder just left of center is a heat exchanger used to heat the shop. Photograph courtesy of Charles Hurst.

draulic power; as a result, his Amish employees could run the machines themselves and he did not have to hire English workers. Trying to remain competitive in a marketplace that is often international sometimes leads to conflict between church traditions and the need for increased productivity. Some new technologies can lower labor costs while also increasing production, but they may threaten the "by hand" method traditionally used by many Amish. So pressure is created to reinterpret or adapt a church's Ordnung so that it permits certain technologies. Such alterations are most unlikely within the conservative Swartzentruber affiliation. A recent development has been the use of electricity from the public power grid by some New Order Christian Fellowship businesses.

Technology often sneaks in whether one wants it or not, and often out of necessity. For example, a group of New Order churches decided to accept a particular sewing machine, even though it operated using a computerized program, because "there's too much involved here to do without the computers." Not to change can endanger livelihoods. New technology can also alter the interface between workers and machines as well as social relationships in the workplace. This is as true in the factory as it is in the farm field. The recent adoption of milking machines by the mainline Old Order Amish in Holmes County was seen as needed for the economic survival of their dairy farms. The Andy Weavers decided not to allow milking machines and have, as noted earlier, left dairy farming in larger numbers than Amish of the other orders. The result is that Andy Weaver Amish have had to seek out employment in factories and shops. Affiliations often react differently to the externally driven push for change, but the pressures to adopt newer technologies will never abate.

Our survey results suggest that New Order Amish are much more likely than more conservative orders to own fax and copy machines. Intricate variations also exist with respect to computers; some New Order churches do not allow computers, but others do. Nine percent of the respondents in our survey who are employed said they use computers in their work. Andy Weaver Amish avoid computers, as do the Swartzentrubers. One New Order employer estimated that almost all Andy Weaver and Swartzentruber Amish would be uncomfortable working with a computer in their jobs, compared to about three-quarters of Old Order and one-quarter of New Order Amish.

Complicating the matter is that the definition of "computer" is sometimes debatable. A New Order Christian Fellowship respondent described a "Classic Word Processor" that is used by some New and Old Order individuals because it is not a computer, according to its Old Order Mennonite developer. The ad for it states that the processor is "made specifically for the plain people—Nothing fancy. Just a work horse for your business." Those who would worry about its being converted into a computer need not be concerned, because there is "unequalled safety: No modem, no internet connection, no outside programs, no sound, no games."[50]

These accounts of technology usage demonstrate again the ingenuity and inventiveness of Amish groups as they adapt to changing technological conditions. Technologies are often mixed bags; one part is desirable while another is not. Cell phones with multiple options and sewing machines with computer programs built into them are good examples.

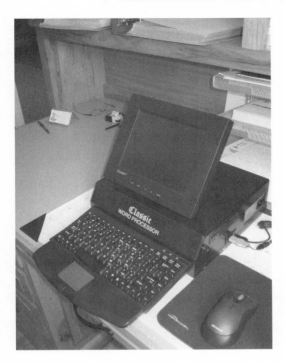

The "Classic Word Processor," used by many Amish businesses, allows word processing, spreadsheet work, and drawing, without providing access to the Internet. Photograph courtesy of Charles Hurst.

The preceding illustrations indicate why it is unwise to make sweeping statements about the Amish community's relationship to technology. As mentioned in previous paragraphs, there are several layers through which technology decisions are funneled: At the broadest level, there is some technology that none of the Amish find acceptable (for example, owning automobiles). Then there are technologies that can be used for some purposes but not for others (for example, tractors), and there are technologies or machines that are defined differently by different Amish affiliations (for example, computers versus word processors). Perhaps most fundamentally, there are differences between affiliations in what technology is acceptable. The different affiliations also face different kinds and levels of pressures to adopt technologies, simply because of their varying distributions among economic niches and occupational categories.

Within the Holmes County Settlement, for example, there is some concern for the discrepancies or inconsistencies about the rules for using technology in farming as compared to nonfarming occupations. Kraybill points out that because farming is embedded in Amish tradition, its technology is more subject to the restrictions of the Ordnung than is technology in the newer, nonfarm enterprises.[51] One Amish employee mused, "If you're a farmer, they expect you to use horses. They expect you to use the old fashioned stuff, and then here you have [a] lumber [yard] . . . and there they actually have a computer which I guess varies a little bit from church to church." Moreover, within affiliations, individual churches may differ, since decisions are made on the church district level. Finally, even within single churches there are occasional differences between individuals in their use of technology. "I could tell you about two local Amish men," commented a New Order woman, "who might as well have a car because they use their tractor like one." As long as there are individuals, anomalies like this will crop up.

All these variations make facile generalizations about technology and the Amish misleading if not flat-out inaccurate, especially for the Holmes County Settlement, because of the diversity of its Amish population. A New Order businessman who has lived in Holmes County all his life warns against such generalizing, pointing out that in some ways the New Order is more conservative than the Old Order, but in other ways it is not.

As more Amish become increasingly involved in nonfarming enterprises, the demands placed upon them to adopt more technologies will probably intensify: "We adopt one thing and there are two more on the horizon. And it's not going to get any simpler." Nine out of ten Amish in our survey believe there are some technologies that are harmful to the stability and integrity of Amish culture regardless of how they are used. The Internet, TV, and computers were singled out most. Concerns about these focused on the impossibility of controlling their proper usage. As one respondent put it, "90% of the people do not have the discipline to use it [the Internet] in only healthy ways." Another saw the computer as a "handy tool" for the devil.

Wealth: Its Danger and Its Promise

The Amish in the Holmes County Settlement have been ingenious and in many cases highly successful in facing the economic pressures attending the decline in availability and the increase in cost of farmland. An inevitable outcome of their success has been an increase in wealth, including the appearance of millionaires within their community. One analyst, who grew up in an Amish-Mennonite home near Holmes County, contends that "the Old Order Amish have become rich. In the eyes of more traditional Amish [for example, Swartzentrubers] they have collaborated with the root of all evil—the love of money."[52] Across the board, however, Amish affiliations are aware of the potential threat wealth poses to their lifestyles. But restrictions are generally not placed on the growth of wealth as long as it is obtained in honest business. "That's not a problem," commented an Old Order respondent.

Possession of wealth in itself, then, is not necessarily an evil. A Swartzentruber bishop told us, "Abraham had money, and it didn't do much harm." An Old Order leader agreed that "prosperity is a blessing and comes from God." But there is no doubt that wealth can be a temptation and a danger. Viewing wealth as ultimately belonging to God rather than to oneself can be "a very, very hard mentality to keep, especially if you work hard and long for your money." But the alternative, seeing money as "mine to use it however I want," is going to get one "in trouble," argued a local Mennonite historian. Wealth is a "challenge," but it "can be used right."

The danger arises when a person wants it too much or consumes it selfishly. Moderation and discipline are required: "It's just like eating . . . we have to eat but if we don't discipline ourselves we become gluttons. Gluttony is wrong. Eating is not." Wealth can encourage its owner to rest on his or her laurels, and it makes it harder to maintain humility, which is stressed the most among the Swartzentrubers. And to seek wealth as an end in itself is to be led into worldly materialism. Wealth can also be a danger for those who do not have it because it can foster feelings of jealousy. "There's always some jealousy for those who do well; it's the same among the English," observed a Swartzentruber man. "Jealousy is a big sickness."

Differences in wealth, of course, exist among the Holmes County Amish; there are millionaires in their midst and, as we have seen, families who are eligible for food stamps. The Swartzentruber church as a whole has the greatest proportion of families who are in or near poverty, in part "because of the limitations that they impose on themselves." At the same time, they do not need as much money as the other Amish, because of their ascetic lifestyle. One New Order member said he knew a Swartzentruber family that was getting by on four thousand dollars per year. But too often, in the long run, a price is paid because such a low income leads to poorer nutrition and less preventive health care.

Opinions differ regarding the extent to which wealth differences are noticeable within the Holmes County Settlement. Swartzentruber churches work hard to moderate such differences among their members and to lead lives that are models of extreme simplicity and lack of adornment. Whereas the Swartzentrubers place and enforce more formal restrictions on possession of wealth, the New and Old Order churches strongly admonish members that the possession of wealth should not affect lifestyle. "Incomes vary but it should not be that a person from the outside can walk into our homes and make a distinction between those who make $50,000 a year and those who make $250,000 a year."

Traditional values also lead to ways to minimize economic discrepancies. If someone is in need, through no fault of his or her own, or if a community needs to have something done, it is expected that those who have more will give more: "You expect to give more because you've been successful, you're more lucky, you're better at business, and you don't resent it." This is a way of leveling out the existing inequality. Despite rigorous attempts to avoid broadcasting one's wealth, however, sometimes wealth is manifested in landscaping, fencing, large homes, standing orders for new buggies, eating out often, and trips for pleasure.

To some extent, the increase in wealth has accompanied the shift out of farming into varied businesses. Both of these have placed pressures on traditional lifestyles, especially in recent years: "Now, if you see their homes, you might see some difference. More so now than it used to be 20 years ago. Because that's one thing that sort of amazes New Order people is the type of houses that [some of] the Old Order are putting up. Because they've got all this money." Despite the inequality that exists within the Amish community and between its affiliations, three-quarters of the Old and New Order respondents in our survey considered the degree of wealth inequality within the Holmes County Settlement to be "about right," with only a small percentage (7%) considering wealth differences unfair. In the opinion of one Old Order Amish source, there is occasional concern that Swartzentruber Amish are sometimes taken advantage of by other Amish who employ them to do their "dirty work." Such employment, he thought, is fostered both by condescending views held by other

Amish toward Swartzentrubers and by the Swartzentrubers' own self-effacement and willingness to work for low wages.

Thus far, the presence of inequality has generated only moderate awareness of distinct social classes in the Holmes County Settlement. Although some are rich while others are poor, and even though one can hear occasional references to "uppity" Amish and status-laden terms like "Swartzies," "noodle pushers," and "wooly lumps," there is little recognition of a class system among the Amish. Nor does there appear to be any pattern of deliberate attempts to encourage children to marry individuals from families of similar wealth. As in English society, especially at the top of its class ladder, there is a conscious concern that one's children marry one's own "kind," but it relates not to wealth but to beliefs. In Amish society the desire is to marry within one's own religious affiliation. If the marrying persons are of similar wealth, this is an accident and "not by design," according to a New Order leader. He also indicated that the attraction of wealth is greatly weakened because individual wealth in the Amish community is "diffused," that is, dispersed, because of aid programs, mission work, and the mandate to live modestly.[53] At least at present, terms like *social class* are generally not part of the mental framework of residents in the Holmes County Settlement. If anything, awareness of status-prestige variations is probably linked more to lifestyle and Ordnung differences than to economic-class divisions.

The German social scientist Max Weber summarized well the secularizing threat that wealth can have within religious groups.[54] The growth of wealth also intensifies the struggle to resist the temptations of individualism and self-aggrandizement that can come with it, and to remain humble and community-oriented in one's lifestyle. In a 1979 *Family Life* survey of the magazine's readers, wealth was seen as the principal danger facing the Amish community, and this view was echoed in our more recent survey. Nine out of ten considered the accumulation of personal material wealth to be a threat to the internal harmony of the community. Still, money's effect depends on whether "you have the money or the money has you."

The Amish believe that wealth should never be sought as an end in itself and that it should be used primarily for the greater good of the community. Like the ascetic Protestants of old, the Amish hold that wealth is a source of moral breakdown when it is a temptation to idleness, waste of time, and indulgent living. Again and again, we were told by our study participants that wealth in itself was not evil if put to good use in the community. And the Holmes County Amish do readily share their wealth with others in need. As noted in chapter 3, they are heavily involved with a variety of aid and mission programs that actively work to improve the daily lives of individuals in different parts of the world.

Is the Future in the Past?

"And some people say, 'Well you're just 50 years behind society.' That's true but at least we have the benefit of looking back and seeing how some of these things are working in general society." This comment by a New Order businessman is a demonstration of the care that the Amish take in considering and making decisions about what technologies to use and what the consequences of those technologies might be. In a real sense, many Amish are ahead of others because they are on the cutting edge of progressive farming and energy usage.

Going back to their practices in Europe, the Amish have always been leaders and innovators in farming. Since farming has always been at the core of their identity as a culture, it should not be surprising that many in the Holmes County Settlement are concerned about the negative fallout for their families that has followed their exodus from farming. In response, some are making a concerted effort to reinvigorate small-scale farming as a central support of Amish culture. In 1997 there were no certified organic dairy farmers in Ohio. But in 2002 a group of about twenty men gathered to discuss the possibility of establishing a cooperative that would consist of farmers who farmed organically. It was an attempt to return to their agricultural roots. As a result of this effort, Green Field Farms was born. In 2008 there were more than one hundred members in the co-op, all of them Amish or Conservative Mennonites. Along with farmers, the co-op's board includes businessmen, who bring their marketing and financial skills to the operation. Most of the members are in Holmes County, but there are also a few in Wayne, Medina, and a couple of southern counties in Ohio.

Green Field Farms (GFF) was set up so that small-scale organic farmers could compete more effectively against larger, technologically advanced, government-supported English farmers. Like the furniture business association, this farm association reflects the Amish belief in cooperation among themselves as a sign of brotherhood and as a method to meet outside competition. The association decided to focus its market on those who are willing to pay a premium for naturally grown farm products. GFF serves as the middleman between the consumer and the farmer by helping to work out the legal, accounting, banking, insurance, transportation, and other logistical issues that have to be addressed. The farmer thus can be left relatively independent to produce his products.

A variety of farmers are included in the co-op, producing eggs, cheese, vegetables, and fruits, which are sold in at least ten states. Specialties are neatly split among the different affiliations. The dairy segment includes mostly New and Old Order organic farmers, while Swartzentruber and Andy Weaver farmers are dominant in the produce area. Andy Weaver members compose the largest proportion of the produce farmers in the area. Neither the Swartzentrubers nor the Andy Weavers use milking machines or bulk tanks, and neither uses mechanical refrigeration. They are therefore unlikely candidates to enter dairy farming; and the Swartzentrubers cannot produce eggs for the co-op because eggs have to be cooled by refrigeration. According to one farmer, the Andy Weaver members of GFF made an exception for egg coolers, which they will use if the GFF owns the cooler rather than the farmer himself.

Less than 10 percent of the produce in Wayne and Holmes Counties is organic, whereas 15–30 percent of all the dairy farmers in the area are organic farmers. The unique challenges of raising organic produce, coupled with the continuing success of farmers' markets, and especially produce auctions, have weakened the incentive to "go organic" in this area. To shift from chemical farming to certified organic farming takes about three years.

According to one Amish organic dairy farmer, organic farming really started growing after grass-based farming gained in prominence. Using grass rather than grain eliminated the need for chemical fertilizers and reduced the number of row crops, which drain nutrients from the soil. Moreover, grass does not need to be seeded every year, as other crops do. In his words, "Once you're in grass-based, you're not in row crops, why, organic is a picnic." The cows are out on the grass, moving around, exercising, not eating "highfalutin'" feed, and as a result, veterinary costs drop dramatically. Not all organic farmers are using grass farming to an equal extent, but the number is growing. The average organic dairy farmer in the area has thirty-five to fifty cows.

In an effort to continually improve the quality of their products and the efficiency of their operations, grass-based farmers in Holmes County get together regularly on certain mornings to walk each other's pastures and discuss problems that arise. This interaction grows naturally out of the heavy emphasis on cooperation in the community. Organic farming has other benefits. According to its practitioners, in the long run organic farming is more economical and more environmentally friendly than chemical farming. Most of the food for animals is grown on the farm, manure is used as a natural enricher of the soil, and the need for artificial fertilizers is eliminated. Organic farmers also use less fossil fuel energy. There is less harmful chemical runoff, because with sod and grass the soil is held in place more effectively. "Seventy years ago, everyone farmed organically," said an organic farmer. Perhaps part of the future lies in going back to the past.

One measure of the resurgence in small-scale organic farms has been the publication of *Farming Magazine*, which was developed and is edited by a local New Order individual. Its focus is to encourage small-scale, environmentally sensitive farming practices and to nurture a love for stewardship of the earth. Inaugurated in 2000, the magazine had about twenty-five hundred subscribers in 2007. Its readership extends across the United States. The editor estimates that no more than one-third of the magazine's readers are Amish, meaning that the rest of the readers are non-Amish persons who are drawn to Amish cutting-edge practices.

The ingenuity involved in finding ways to use resources while minimizing waste is evident not only in organic farming, but in other ways as well. One of the new agricultural products being turned out is "maple water," which is the natural distillate created during the production of maple syrup. The Maple Tree Distillate currently produced by Green Field Farms is sold in health and natural food stores in central and northeastern Ohio. Maple water is considered by some to have medicinal value and reportedly is being used in a local city hospital with patients who have kidney problems.[55] Further niche marketing in small-scale gardening is also a possibility for the future. One Amish man who works in a factory but gardens on the side raises organic garlic and then produces tinctures of reputedly high quality, which are then sold by organic pharmacists.

In addition to these areas, many Amish have been ahead of the national curve in their use of renewal energy sources such as solar energy. Again, the focus is on a natural, renewable technology. The Amish have the high-

Solar panels are used extensively by the Amish as a source of energy. Photograph courtesy of Charles Hurst.

est per capita rate of solar power use in Ohio. Green Energy Ohio estimates that 13 percent of Ohio's solar production comes from the Amish. Just three contractors installed 1,000–1,500 solar units in Amish homes in the past few years.[56] Some among the more conservative orders, such as the Swartzentrubers, still frown on the use of solar power, however. It is used to charge batteries for buggy lights, flashlights, sewing machines, blenders, sweepers, copiers, fax machines, and washing machines. There is thus less reliance on the use of gasoline-powered generators, as gasoline has become more expensive. The most common use of alternators is to charge battery-run floor lamps in homes.[57]

Solar power fits with many Amish values and beliefs: it is natural, economical over the long run, accessible, "free," renewable, efficient, convenient, and safe; it also fosters self-sufficiency and, so far, can supply limited voltage power. It's not that the more progressive Amish reject electricity out of hand; what they reject is being tied into the power grid, where electricity is unlimited. A very small group of New Order Christian Fellowship Amish is an exception. In contrast to Andy Weaver and Swartzentruber Amish, who do not permit use of solar power at all, an estimated 80 percent of Old and New Order Amish families in Holmes County have photovoltaic panels.[58] They are leaders in "green power" in Ohio.

Some Amish businesses are using multiple natural energy sources to power their enterprises. One local company owner told us proudly that his company had been "green certified," noting that, like other Amish, he had been "taught to leave at least whatever we inherited or used . . . in better shape than when we got it." In the new addition this owner is building, everything will be run using solar, air, and hydropower. Moreover, resources continue to be recycled—sawdust is used for animal bedding, wood chips for mulch, engine heat for heating the air. Biofuel will also be used increasingly in the future.

Assessing Economic Change and Its Effect

Over the recent past, the economic changes that have been wrought by the enormous pressures facing the Amish in Holmes and surrounding counties have been widespread and diverse. On the public front, these pressures have altered where many of the Amish work, the way they work, and with whom they work. They have also created a large number and a wide variety of additional ties with groups and societies beyond the community borders. In the private sphere, economic and technological shifts have affected family relationships and sometimes even private attitudes about work and the meaning of individuality. The movement into different kinds of businesses has often pushed differences between and within the affiliations into the foreground and has frequently accentuated them. At the same time, tourism and increased commerce with outside society have also served to highlight Amish sameness and solidarity, underscoring the boundaries between the outside world and themselves.

As for the future, the increasing introduction of new technologies and wealth encourages (or, according to one's viewpoint, threatens) more individualism, even as the members of the Holmes County Settlement are cognizant of and work to maintain a strong sense of community. Wealth can serve both as a badge of individual success and as a resource for the

When compared to their English counterparts, the Amish are less dependent upon gasoline, making them less vulnerable to fluctuations in its availability at a reasonable cost. Reprinted by permission from the *Dayton Daily News*.

community. Walking the tightrope between individualism and a sense of community may become increasingly difficult as change and prosperity continue to infiltrate Amish life. Personal wealth may promise to give more individual freedom, but perhaps at the expense of a reduced sense of reliance upon others, tempting one to believe that security comes from personal wealth and resources rather than from dependence upon the community.

Moreover, the "traditional" Amish way of life has attracted millions of "modern" outsiders, as evidenced in the appeal that "hand-made" Amish furniture holds for tourists. Attraction to Amish life is also based in part on the group's advanced use of more natural, in some ways more traditional, forms of energy. The result is a curious reciprocal interchange between the two worlds, with the traditionalists borrowing from the "modern" society and the modernists seeking to learn from the traditionalists.

CHAPTER 7

Health along the Life Cycle

They don't come in every time they sneeze.
—A local physician

A s Amish individuals confront health decisions throughout their lives, they, like everyone else, are guided by a variety of considerations. Among the most important are moral values and beliefs, cost, knowledge, and accessibility. Whether the person is a member of a New Order, Old Order, or Swartzentruber church can also make a difference. All these factors enter into decisions about how and where to give birth, how to address physical illnesses and injuries during adulthood, what to do about psychological problems and issues of well-being, and how to deal with fatal diseases and near-death dilemmas. In this chapter we explore how these considerations affect health decisions of the Amish at different stages of the life cycle.

Overviews of Amish health care attitudes and practices are already available,[1] but we hope to add to those discussions by focusing more thoroughly on the health care dilemmas faced by the Amish because of (a) new knowledge about alternative techniques, (b) variations in practices of the several orders, (c) pressures exerted by the state and by health care professionals, and (d) increasing health care costs. We also discuss Amish health care from both internal and external vantage points, that is, from the points of view of Amish respondents as well as the various professionals who treat them. In addition, we explore end-of-life issues more completely than previous studies have done and look at the lessons that might be learned from the Amish approach to health care.

It should not be surprising that the distinctiveness and insularity of the Amish community are reflected in their perspective on health care. The differences from English society in Amish cultural beliefs and history and the structural arrangements in the Amish community create "culture care diversities" that are distinctive in some ways when compared to dominant care preferences in English society and also vary within the Holmes County Settlement itself.[2] These factors make it crucial for the health care professional to possess a sympathetic understanding of Amish culture. As members of a "high-context" culture, Amish individuals are deeply connected to each other socially, culturally, and historically. There are mutual understandings that are often unspoken and taken for granted, and nuanced behaviors and language connotations of which outsiders are usually not aware. Being a tight-knit community, the Amish carry a heavy concern for the care of others; they consider themselves first of all members of a close community to which they are accountable.[3] This cultural context and the diversities within the Holmes County Settlement inform health care approaches throughout the life cycle.

Giving Birth

Pregnancy, though a frequent occurrence among the Amish, is not an event that is baldly advertised in local media like the *Budget*. Rather, the subject of giving birth is handled in a more guarded, toned-down fashion. The *Budget*, a newspaper that serves the Amish population and has a national edition with a circulation of about twenty thousand, is made up mostly of letters from Amish people about events in their families. Letters are a major form of communication in the Amish community, and those in the *Budget* come from Amish all over the world, including the nearby population. The editors told us that the term *pregnancy* would not be used in letters; a phrase like *with child* is considered more appropriate. This caution is especially prominent among Old Order and Swartzentruber Amish and appears to be tied to concerns about modesty and privacy. Discussions on the nature of a birth (for example, a Caesarean section) are also frowned upon, as are advertisements of products considered highly personal, such as underwear.

The Amish guardedness in discussing pregnancy is suggested by a story related by a Holmes County chiropractor who has many Amish patients. A "lower" (i.e., Swartzentruber) order Amish woman who was six to seven months pregnant came in to see him, "And she had also brought her 14–15-year-old son in with her. So I had been talking to her about him, and then I turned to her, how's your pregnancy going? She sent him out of the room. She said: 'We don't talk about things like that in front of the children.' I took the opportunity and said: 'What age do you think he should know where babies come from and that kind of thing?' And she said: 'Well, basically, we won't say anything to him' . . . They're not even going to touch that." A rural midwife who has delivered children for Old Order and more conservative Amish families has had similar experiences: "I don't know if you've noticed, but children don't know if [the mothers are] expecting a baby." In visiting pregnant women at "low-church" homes, she said that on occasion she had "been asked to park my car on the other side of the barn so somebody driving by won't see my car when I'm there during pre-natal." The differences among the church orders in their treatment of pregnancy is also noticeable in that New Order mothers are more likely than others to have baby showers before a baby is born.

When an Amish woman is pregnant, one of the decisions the husband and wife have to make is where to give birth to the baby. The main alternatives are a hospital, a birthing center, and home. Occasionally, a woman gives birth in a doctor's office or at another person's home. When asked whether the Amish are more likely than others to home-birth or go to a birthing center rather than a hospital, an employee at a well-established birth center replied, "Yes, definitely." This report is supported by governmental data indicating that while home births composed well under 1 percent of all births in Ohio in 2005, more than 7 percent of all births in Holmes County, which is heavily Amish, took place at home. An earlier survey of 144 Amish families, sponsored by the Wayne County Department of Public Health, obtained similar data.[4] In that study, only 59 percent of the Old Order and New Order Amish births, compared to 84 percent of English births, occurred at a hospital. The results were even more dramatic among the very conservative Swartzentruber Amish; only 18 percent of these mothers gave birth at a hospital. One doctor mentioned that part of the Amish philosophy is that "these things rest in God's hands," so being close to emergency services or in a hospital is not important or a cause for worry.

The literal resignation that one's health rests "in God's hands" was probably most fully espoused when most Amish farmed and did not have the money to seek health care on a regular basis. Now that many Amish are off the farm and work in more lucrative occupations, the reaction to serious health problems is less passive. It is only after seeking medical help to care for the body as God's temple, and finding that the care has proved ineffective and too expensive, that they let go, acknowledging that life is ultimately in God's hands.

Dr. Elton Lehman had this view confirmed in a case involving the transfer of a premature baby to another hospital for additional care. The Amish grandfather stated his position clearly: "Well, as I see it . . . if God is in control of everything that happens, as we believe he is, then why should we try to change what he has allowed to take place? Besides, if heaven is our goal for our families, then why should we struggle so hard and strap ourselves so deep into debt to all stay together down here?"[5] As we will see in a later section, this perspective is perhaps especially noticeable when costly terminal illnesses strike their families. For the Amish, the Bible's message provides guidance and solace for all families, regardless of wealth.

The Amish of the various orders account for the vast majority of births at home and at birthing centers in Wayne and Holmes counties. The birthing center in Mount Eaton recorded 484 live births in 2004, while the care center in Fresno, Ohio, had 113 births in 2004, and the midwifery center in Berlin had 35 births between September 2004 and September 2005, its first year of operation. Almost all of these births involved either Amish or Mennonite mothers.

The mode of operation in some centers in the Holmes County Settlement is more "medicalized" than in others; that is, they vary in the extent to which they follow a mainstream medical model and use licensed doctors or other degreed professionals. The Mount Eaton Care Center, which is the oldest, most popular, and most medicalized center and is licensed by the state, has medical doctors and nurse midwives on its staff who do the deliveries. The center also contains more medical technology available to use in the event of difficulties.[6] The doctors there have delivered babies at area homes as well as at the center. At the next-most-medicalized center, the Doughty View Midwifery Center in Berlin, Ohio, Certified Nurse Midwives conducted the deliveries, and licensed nurses assisted them. The Berlin center closed in late 2008. Births at the New Bedford Care

Center, which is unlicensed and is the least-medicalized center, are supervised by certified professional midwives and lay midwives. The second and third centers are served by boards whose members are primarily Amish and Mennonite. Medical professionals are least likely to be on the board of the third center.

Controversy and strong feelings abound among professionals and the Amish regarding the relative qualifications and desirability of each birthing center. On one side are licensed physicians and nurses, who are concerned about the standard of care that patients are given at an unlicensed center. We interviewed several physicians, both doctors of osteopathy (D.O.'s) and doctors of medicine (M.D.'s) in Holmes and Wayne Counties, who had eight to forty years of experience in working with Amish patients. In speaking about the unlicensed care center, one M.D.'s comment is representative of the medical community's view: "We see a lot of bad cases come out of that one . . . We would blame it of course on the fact that they aren't well-trained midwives there. I suppose just being farther away from the hospital makes it look worse too, because it takes longer to get somewhere."

The concerns of physicians apply as well to the lay midwives who assist at home births, because complications do arise in a small percentage of births, and in a home there is no support structure for dealing with those complications: "In deliveries 90 percent are normal. It's the other 10 percent that you have to know what you're doing." Lay midwives who do not have formal training or education in their field are not recognized by the state of Ohio. The doctors we interviewed believe that there should be one standard of care for all birthing centers, and that the standard should require the presence of licensed and degreed professionals.

The views of certified professional midwives (C.P.M.'s) and lay midwives are quite different, however. They think that many medical doctors fail to fully understand the natural birthing process, "because [they weren't] trained that way, [don't] practice that way, [and don't] see it done, so [they don't] understand it . . . [they] only know how to do protocol one way." One osteopath believes the medical model "has ceased to treat childbirth as a natural process, and this has allowed unlicensed individuals to fill the gap." The workers at the unlicensed birthing center are aware that physicians in Holmes County "don't like this place [New Bedford Care Center]." One of the workers commented, "Ohio does not offer licensure for the type of midwife I am."

They have strong reservations about the need for and benefits of state licensing. "If you *license* it, you *medicalize* it," argued one C.P.M. She feels that a main reason women come to her birthing center is "because they want the midwifery care. And it's about the only place in the state you can get it that's not a home birth midwife." She argued that the whole issue has become politicized by the powerful medical profession, which has dominated, controlled, and held in check the ability of midwives to operate freely and guide those prospective mothers who wish to experience pregnancy and birthing as fully natural processes, "as God intended it to be." In the midwives' view, to medicalize it is to turn the birth process into a problematic and artificial one. "And most doctors never do see normal physiological childbirths. Never." Just because it is natural, however, does not mean childbirth is painless: "Very few women have that . . . [Just like farming,] nobody expects painless farming. So why are we talking about painless childbirth?" Childbirth is one terrain on which the traditional and the modern clash, and one on which disagreements exist about the relative effectiveness and appropriateness of care.

The controversial case of the lay midwife Freida Miller illustrates the conflict between lay midwifery and the medical profession.[7] In 2002 Miller was found guilty of giving a mother two drugs to stem bleeding after she had given birth. Lay midwives are not legally permitted to possess and administer prescription drugs. Her sentence was suspended, but she was then sent to jail for refusing to disclose the source of the drugs to a local grand jury. She was later released on bond. Supporters hailed her as a hero and an example of how the medical profession has oppressed and hassled lay midwives. Opponents from the medical profession, the state, and insurance companies argued that the issues were ones of safety and a consistent, high standard of care for the birthing process.

The Amish themselves appear split on the kind of care they deem desirable. To some extent, location and cost affect their choices of who assists in a birth and where it occurs. While most might prefer a birthing center to a hospital and see birth as a natural process, they differ regarding the specific site they think is best for childbirth. On one end, Swartzentruber Amish are more likely than other Amish to prefer giving birth at home. Some are even hesitant to go to a midwifery center, because "it's not Amish enough." Commenting on how Amish midwives conduct home visits, one English midwife said, "It's actually better for the Amish . . . They can just have someone come in and stay with them." She went on to mention that some members of the Swartzentruber churches "cannot afford" to come to the center, so a midwife may go to their home. So the site chosen for birth is a result of a combination of location, cost, and beliefs. The geographic distribution of different Amish groups affects the professional's practice, while the professional's practice affects the choice made by the Amish.

There are occasional out-of-wedlock births among the Amish, but the rate does not appear to be as high as is found among non-Amish women. An analysis of every fifth church district in the 2005 *Ohio Amish Directory*, covering Holmes, Wayne, Coshocton, and parts of surrounding counties, found that 4.7 percent of households with children (48 out of 1,012) contained a child who was born before the marriage date of the couple.[8] Some of these may have been adoptions, however. As one female physician put it: "It doesn't happen with great frequency. It is much lower among the Amish. I do 250–270 deliveries a year; two or three might be out-of-wedlock. Almost all will marry the father, in contrast with other groups." But she noted that in cases of premarital pregnancy, couples generally wait to be married until after the child's birth, unless it is quite early in the pregnancy and the woman is not "showing" yet.

The percentage of premarital conceptions is more difficult to determine, but review of data from the *Directory* reveals a similarly low percentage of such conceptions, especially if the possibility of premature births is ruled out. Our analysis of every fifth church district in the 2005 Holmes County *Ohio Amish Directory* indicated that just under 2 percent of all children were conceived out of wedlock. Most of these conceptions may be for the first births, since Donnermeyer and Cooksey concluded that more than 10 percent of first births in the Holmes County Settlement occurred either before the parents were married or within seven months after their marriage. In 2006 the percentage of unwed births in Holmes County was less than one-fourth that found in Ohio as a whole.[9] The greater commonality of premarital conceptions among the Old Order Amish as compared with the New Order may be related to the Old Order's greater tolerance of rumspringa among its youth.[10]

In prenatal and preventive care, differences appear to exist between the Amish and the English and also among the Amish. In the 1984 Wayne County study mentioned earlier, fully 100 percent of the English patients saw their doctor, nurse, or midwife sometime during the first three months of pregnancy, compared to 10 percent of Swartzentruber Amish and 28 percent of other Amish. More recently, vital statistics for Ohio revealed that more than half of pregnant women in the state receive prenatal care during their first trimester of pregnancy. However, according to a review of all births in Holmes County during 2003–5, only about 26 percent of women who gave birth received such care, indirectly suggesting that rates of early prenatal care continue to be lower among the Amish, who make up a significant proportion of the Holmes County population. Those most likely not to receive care until after the first trimester in the Holmes study tended to be older married women with no more than an eighth-grade education who had given birth before and had delivered outside a hospital setting. These characteristics are generally associated with Amish women.[11] As one osteopath remarked in a conversation with the authors, "A lot of them tend to come in kind of late in the pregnancy. But it's hard for me to train them to come in earlier . . . Usually if they had a problem previously, they come in earlier the next time . . . But most of them come in rather late compared to non-Amish patients. They're too busy . . . They have to get a driver, pay the driver." But if they can be convinced that they will save money in the long run by coming in early, they will do so, according to the experience of another doctor.

Preventive Care and Genetics

In general, the Amish are less likely than the population at large to seek preventive or dental care or to obtain annual physical examinations and regular immunizations.[12] A 2003 study in Holmes County showed that non-Amish persons were almost twice as likely as Amish individuals to have received a routine examination within the past year. The same research indicated that Amish respondents were less likely than others to have seen a dentist or to have received a flu or pneumonia shot in the past year.[13] As one physician who was raised in an Old Order family put it: "They are more prudent about coming in. They don't come in every time they sneeze." It appears that the more conservative the church, the less likely the Amish are to be proactive in their health care. The most conservative also tend to be poorer, suggesting that a combination of being highly traditional and lacking money largely accounts for the lower rate of health care service usage. In the view of one physician, the Swartzentruber Amish will "take whatever comes." However, they are more likely to get immunized or see a doctor if their English neighbors might be endangered by their reluctance to see a health care provider. Thus, they balance their own concerns against those of their neighbors.

In addition to differences rooted in church affiliation and income, there are gender differences in health care. As in the wider society, Amish men are less likely than women to seek medical help. "Men are usually macho . . . You usually drag them in, you know, when they're just about dying or whatever. Whereas the women, they have a problem, they'll do something about it." A chiropractor explained what he believed to be Amish logic: "If you're not sick, you don't go to the doctor. You don't go to the doctor when you feel good, and we're asking them to do the exact opposite. We're saying 'come to the doctor while you're feeling good.' And you've got this obscure goal of 'we're going to keep you from feeling bad.' But see, that's not tangible . . . So you're kind of working against a lot of human nature there."

Childhood immunizations are also relatively infrequent, especially among the more conservative orders. The Amish population is among those groups that underutilize immunization.[14] Immunization for children "is one area where they do not do well at all," observed a physician. "There is a major distrust with immunizations," said another. Two of the reasons for this distrust are that many of their parents and grandparents did not get immunizations and suffered few, if any, health problems as a consequence; and some Amish people still associate immunizations with other health problems, for example, autism. Swartzentruber Amish are especially likely to avoid immunizations. In the 1984 Wayne County study, only 6 percent of Swartzentruber parents said their children got their "baby shots," compared to 63 percent of Amish parents overall and 85 percent of English parents. In general, Swartzentruber Amish are less likely than others to use any kind of immunization or screening clinic; 87 percent of this order also said they would not use a child immunization clinic either. In addition, location or easy access to health care appears to be more important to more Amish, especially Swartzentrubers, than to English patients.

The hesitancy on the part of some Amish groups to participate in immunization programs opens them up to a greater probability of certain illnesses such as polio and rubella. The Amish also have higher rates of some

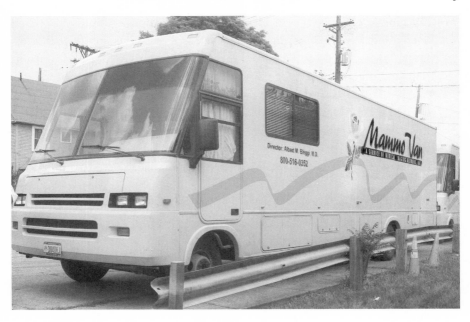

Inside the Mammo Van, which travels around the Amish community, women can be screened for breast cancer and men can receive prostate tests. Photograph courtesy of MammoVan, a division of Medical Imaging Network Inc., Boardman, Ohio.

genetic diseases than the general population. This susceptibility is due to the small size of the founding group, the relatively high level of genetic isolation within that group, and the fact that relevant recessive genes happened, through genetic drift, to have existed in some founders and their offspring. The common ancestry and insularity of the genetic pool creates a "founder effect," which magnifies the effect of certain recessive genes. "Because members keep to themselves and marry within their communities, they rarely get to shuffle their genetic decks, and they are afflicted with a wide variety of rare diseases in far greater frequency than the population as a whole."[15]

Among the genetic diseases found in higher rates among the Amish in general are cystic fibrosis, glutaric aciduria (an enzyme deficiency potentially resulting in brain damage and movement disorder), Crigler-Najjar Syndrome (a result of bilirubin accumulation in the body and creating brain or other organ damage), Ellis-van Creveld Syndrome (a form of dwarfism), nemaline myopathy (a neuromuscular disorder characterized by muscle weakness), and maple syrup urine disease (a protein-related enzyme deficiency). Because of recent changes in the state law that require families to go on Medicaid if their children have high and continuing medical expenses due to birth defects (for example, cystic fibrosis and blood-clotting disorders), a group of Holmes County Amish have initiated the new Ohio Crippled Children's Fund to be run and endowed by the Amish themselves.[16] The fund helps them avoid going on Medicaid.

Some disorders are not evenly distributed among the Amish population but appear to be clustered in particular families or communities. These include Alzheimer's disease and hemophilia B, the latter being often found in the Holmes County Settlement.[17] The Amish in the Holmes County Settlement also have the nation's highest rate of a rare type of hemophilia caused by deficient production of a blood-clotting factor.[18] Brittle Hair Syndrome is also found in unusual numbers among the Holmes County Amish; the rate of Ellis-van Creveld Syndrome is very high among the Lancaster, Pennsylvania, Amish.[19]

When possible, the Amish avoid treatments and care that require involvement in governmental programs. Separate clinics have been established for Amish children who have the diseases mentioned above. The Clinic for Special Children, in Strasburg, Pennsylvania, and the Das Deutsch Center for Special Needs Children (DDC), in Middlefield, Ohio, focus on the diagnosis and treatment of these genetic diseases. The medical director of the DDC says that clinic has encountered more than fifty different genetic diseases that afflict especially the Amish. He noted that the Amish are more accepting of disease than the English, especially diseases about which little can be done, for example, retardation. Because the medical relationship has to do with vital matters and, in this case, involves individuals with different cultural backgrounds, the nurturing of trust is especially important. The Chinese American medical director at the DDC has gained the trust of the Amish by opening an outreach clinic in Holmes County, spending more time than average with his patients, and even making house calls when needed. He has also formed support groups for families of individuals with particular diseases. Members of the Geauga Amish community are deeply committed to the DDC. They helped raise funds for its creation and participated in the selection of the present director. Amish men also currently serve on the DDC's Board of

Directors. And the local Amish population provides significant funding for the continued operation of the clinic.

To further advance the understanding and treatment of genetic diseases among groups with Anabaptist heritage, the Windows of Hope Project was launched in 2000 as an international effort to provide accessible and clear information on the genetics, variety, diagnosis, and treatment of inherited diseases among Anabaptists. The project has been operating in Holmes County since that year and offers a Web site where individuals can find a list and descriptions of genetic disorders that occur in the Plain community. To help facilitate and coordinate understanding and treatment of these diseases, the Holmes County Settlement has established the Windows of Hope Genetics Information Center in Walnut Creek, Ohio.

Early diagnosis of serious treatable diseases is important for their effective treatment. While the genetic diseases mentioned above can be detected early in children, other, more common health problems can also be detected when Amish adults engage in preventive care. Yet, as mentioned, most Amish adults do not do so. A major reason relates to the Amish definition of good "health": "Good appetite. Good work. Then you're healthy." If a person feels okay, can work, and has a hearty appetite, he or she is generally considered healthy, and the Amish see no reason for such a person to go to a physician or other health care provider. A local physician told us that Amish acquaintances often say they do not have to go to the doctor "if nothing is hurting, and I have a good appetite, and the bowels work." In the absence of overt, debilitating symptoms, one is expected to work. In comparison with the English neighbors of the Amish, this perspective on health appears to most closely mirror the attitudes held by English men rather than English women.

One of the most stigmatizing labels that can be placed on an Amish person is that he or she is considered lazy. Keeping busy and doing the chores necessary to maintain one's family is central to the Amish way of life. Taking time out to see a doctor for no apparent health problem is judged unnecessary and, among some Amish, a waste of time. Time is not to be wasted.

Lifestyle and Health

The Amish lifestyle has significant implications for Amish health. If a family lives and works on a farm, positive effects follow from the physical exercise (for example, lower obesity rates), organic food, and early-to-bed, early-to-rise schedule associated with farm life.[20] The farm lifestyle also helps to keep members of the family in close proximity to each other and thus can help maintain the solidarity of the family. But as one Amish bishop observed, "Working with farm machines and horses can be dangerous." Another Amish man mentioned farming and carpentry as leading "the list of injuries." Some doctors, noting the greater frequency of farming and wood-chopping accidents among the Amish, have also observed that "farming is a high-risk occupation."

The kinds of accidents, injuries, and stresses experienced by the Amish become more diverse as an increasing proportion of some groups take up occupations other than farming. The rates of change in employment are noticeably higher among the New Order and Old Order Amish than within the Swartzentruber branch, since the latter have fewer acceptable occupational options and are more likely to doggedly cling to farming. Variations in lifestyle are bound up with variations in the specifics of values, church rules, and adherence to tradition found among the Amish. Consequently, the forms and intensity of work-related mental stresses the Amish encounter will likely also continue to change and vary among them. Because of the great heterogeneity of the Holmes County Amish, it might be expected that these shifts will be especially significant among them.

Like men in general, Amish men tend to go to a physician less often and later in life than women do. In his practice of more than thirty-five years, one M.D. found that, unless there is an emergency, "You don't see many men in the office until they're about 55 years old. From then on, the men come in because they've worked hard. They've got backaches; they've got arthritis. They have abused themselves from physical labor . . . So then they start slowing down and they get less physical activity. [The men and the women] start gaining some weight, they get hypertension, diabetes, and so from 60 on up they have the same problems as everyone else does . . . There isn't much difference where you start and where you end. The in-between is different."

The constant hard physical work associated with the Amish lifestyle can take its toll on women as well as men. The high number of births can itself create challenges. In addition, hard work over the years creates specific problems for many Amish women. Heavy lifting of wet clothes to hang them outdoors can foster prolapse issues and leg problems. Varicose veins are a "huge issue" among Amish women. The use of ringer washers leads to accidents. Among the Swartzentruber Amish, the lack of indoor plumbing requires carrying water in from outside, a task that discourages frequent bathing and results in hygiene problems.

Diet is another element that affects Amish health. Like the non-Amish population, some Amish are very conscious of what they eat, while others are not. One older, semiretired New Order Amish couple, for example, told us that when they were younger and more physically active, they ate large breakfasts and dinners. Now, however, breakfast typically consists of dry toast, a banana, water with vinegar, and a vitamin. There is less use of lard, pork is eaten less frequently, and the wife bakes fewer desserts. More typically, observed a local doctor, especially among Old Order and Swartzentruber Amish, "as a general rule, . . . they like their pork and beef and those kinds of things. A lot of starch. So the diets aren't very good, and that's one of the difficult things . . . to try and change . . . when they have cholesterol trouble or diabetes." Their diet is also high in sugar and fat. The movement away from farming into nonagricultural enterprises and wage labor has possibly accelerated these dietary developments and exacerbated their health consequences as Amish individuals eat out at restaurants more often than in the past and purchase more of their foods, relying less on their own farms and gardens for sustenance. The result is the introduction of more additives, preservatives, and processing into their foods.[21]

Although the typical Amish diet may not have as drastic a set of consequences for the young, its health implications grow as one ages: "When they get up to about 50 and start to slow down then they develop diabetes . . . they are semi-retired . . . still eating well and start to put on weight." Offsetting the problems that might be associated with diet are the relatively low rates of tobacco and alcohol use among the Holmes County Settlement Amish. In comparison to the non-Amish, a greater percentage of these people have never smoked a cigarette, chewed tobacco, or drunk alcohol. Moreover, they are more likely than others to take dietary supplements of some kind.[22]

The values that Amish hold dear are deeply embedded in their decisions about health care. In reflecting upon lessons from his own Amish childhood, a doctor concluded that one of the most significant messages from Amish culture is for all of us "to be mindful of people around us . . . Help neighbors in need, be mindful of what effect your actions will have on somebody else." One manifestation of the sensitivity of the Amish to the larger community is their generous donation of blood to the Red Cross. Self-effacement and sensitivity to others also become important in health care when high costs cause a clash between a sick individual's expensive regimen and the needs of the family. If a case is complicated and involves unknown numbers of tests and procedures, and the patient believes it is unlikely that treatment will be successful, the person will often say something like "[My husband and I have] thought about this, and we've lived a good life, and just give me some pills and I'll do the best I can. I'm not interested in starting that procedure." This sort of decision reflects the belief that little can be done to fully restore one's health, the acceptance of things as they are, and the concern for others found so frequently among the Amish.

Decisions are never straightforward, however. The tensions between individual and community needs created by high costs of complex, unusual, and occasionally unsuccessful medical treatments foster long-term difficulties for cohesion within the Amish community. Individuals make their own medical decisions about care, but it is the community, supporting its members, that provides most of the payment for high medical bills. Although the community spirit is laudable, these costs result in debt and drain funds that would have been available to address other community needs.[23] Moreover, if those who are ill and poor are unable to contribute to church aid, especially as community health costs increase, they may take on an emotional burden and may be forced to accept governmental aid (for example, Medicaid), both of which can threaten long-term cohesion within the community. There can be little doubt that as health care costs rise, so will the intensity of these dilemmas. One form of adaptation to such pressures has been the acceptance by some bishops of commercial health insurance for Amish people who work for English employers.

Alternative Medicine

Often when Amish individuals get sick, they try home remedies and herbs before they seek out a health care professional. More than half of the individuals in our survey of sixty-five Old Order and New Order Amish said that, during an average year, about half of their treatments for health come from home remedies. Part of the reason lies with the generally lower costs of such remedies and the belief that such approaches are more "natural." But another part of the reason is philosophy; "I've had ladies bring in bags of herbs that cost hundreds of dollars," observed one physician, "where the medications would not have cost as much. But they'll believe what they're told as far as how these things are going to work."

In addition, knowing someone in the close community who appears to have been helped by a remedy encourages others to try it. Word of mouth can spread quickly and means a lot when it comes to trying remedies. Advice is especially likely to be followed if it comes from an elder, says another professional: "One big thing about the Amish people is that they really respect their elders . . . Even if they're losing some of their mental capacity, they still respect them. And what they say has a lot more weight than the doctor." As one author who was raised Amish put it, "We believe wisdom is in the ages; most North Americans believe progress is in the new."[24]

Included among the oft-mentioned traditional remedies are kerosene, used as a disinfectant and pain reducer, and various homemade salves and liniments for application to injuries. Dr. Elton Lehman, in the published reminiscences of his more than forty years as a well-known osteopathic physician to Amish families in Mount Eaton, Ohio, relates an incident from early in his career: A farm boy had come in because he had torn his hand on a hay hook. Smelling something, the doctor asked the father what the boy had put on his hand. "Why he soaked his hand in kerosene, of course . . . It helps the pain and slows the bleeding. Why we always bathe our wounds in kerosene, don't you?"[25] Vitamins, vinegar, colonic cleansing liquids, and teas are also used to maintain health, as are by-products such as yeast and bee pollen. Commenting on the frequent use of health supplements by the Amish, one physician said succinctly: "I've always maintained that if you could recover all the vitamins in the urine that Holmes Countians have been marketed, you could retire early."

Before seeking help from mainstream physicians, Amish who are in need of treatment often consult alternative care givers or even unlicensed practitioners. The Amish are frequent users of "complementary and alternative medicine," which includes "mind-body intervention, traditional or folk remedies, special diets or nutrition programs, herbal medicine, manual healing, chemical or pharmacological agents, and bioelectromagnetic applications."[26] Chiropractic is among the alternative approaches that are used extensively. Others are reflexology, which involves manipulation of the feet to relieve stresses and pain in other parts of the body; iridology, in which the practitioner examines the iris to diagnose illness; and chelation therapy, which aims to rid the body of toxic minerals through excretion. A potential danger of medical alternatives lies in the use of unlicensed practitioners. The "worm doctor" was an example given by a few licensed doctors. This local practitioner "basically convinces people, no matter what's wrong with you—you got a headache, heart problems, and diabetes, whatever—you got a parasite. So they call him a worm doctor. You got a worm . . . and he happens to have these potions that will kill the worms. From what I hear, he does a bang-up business."

Such an approach is persuasive to some people because it suggests clear, concrete, and visually accessible explanations for illness. It provides mental images of diseases and cures that appear straightforward and reasonable. The cause of illness is clearly identified and easy to grasp, and the solution appears to make common sense. Sometimes analogies serve as explanations, as when a local care giver tried to explain why a patient has to take high-blood-pressure pills over a period of time and not stop when the patient starts feeling better: "When the fish pulls the bobber under the water it will stay under as long as the fish is staying under, but if he lets go, it's going to come right back up. Your blood pressure is going to come right back up when you stop the pills.' You have to make analogies so they understand sometimes." Many Amish like to fish, so this analogy allows them to easily visualize the issue.

There are many traditional beliefs about cures and manners of diagnosis, most of which are more common among the more conservative Amish. Among them is the belief that one can draw out pain from another with the use of the hands. It is believed that there is a connection between the person ministering and the person suffering. A local chiropractor gave an example of this interpersonal sympathy. He had met with an Old Order mother who had a baby suffering from excess gas. In explaining to the doctor how the baby was cured, the mother said "the other night he was crying really hard, so I just had him close to me, and I passed gas, and then *he* felt better."

The sympathetic connection between the mother and the child in

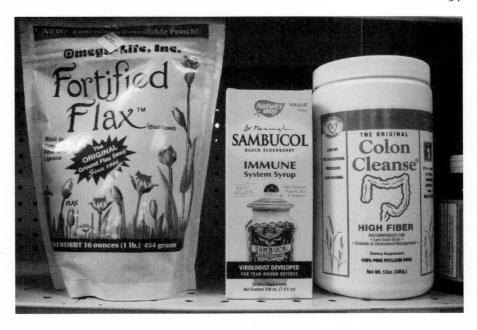

Natural, over-the-counter, multiple-use, unregulated remedies constitute a significant portion of health care treatment among the Amish. Photograph courtesy of Charles Hurst.

that case is also found in powwowing (*brauche* in Pennsylvania Dutch). This pattern is characteristic of "sympathy healing," in which the practitioner recites a chant or sacred words or uses charms or other mysterious rituals to treat the patient. Patients may be suffering from physical or spiritual illnesses; powwowing has been used to remove curses and hexes as well. Some consider the basic *ability* of the *braucher* to be innate, a gift of God, but the secret *techniques* of the practitioner are in most cases learned from a person of the opposite sex. The secrets and recipes of powwowing/brauche are generally passed on by word of mouth rather than documented in formal texts. Powwowing, though controversial for some Amish, shows no signs of completely disappearing because of the increasing cost of mainstream medicine, the rise in acceptance of alternative medicine, and the continued belief by some in the reality of curses and hexes.[27] Sometimes brauche or powwowing is combined with a more professional medical approach, as in the case of Emanuel Stoltzfus, who combined brauche and chiropractic. In this way, Stoltzfus straddled folk and modern medicine.[28]

Another traditional belief was described to us by an M.D. He told of a Swartzentruber man who brought his son in with appendicitis after trying a traditional approach in which he had had "his son crawling down the steps head first." He thought that since the appendix hung below the colon, if the child was turned upside down, the appendix would drain. Puzzled, he told the driver taking him to the hospital: "I don't understand why this is happening; we carried him up and down the stairs backwards all morning." A third traditional belief is the "nail clipper" theory, which holds that if you tie a nail clipper to the end of a string and dangle it above a group of pills in your hand, for example, whether and how the clipper moves will tell the person which pills will or won't work. Many such traditional beliefs are seen as myths or "old wives' fables" by most New Order Amish. Adherence to them is most likely among very conservative groups. Religion is sometimes entangled with healing beliefs as well, as in the following example from the Budget: "To stop bleeding read Ezekiel 16th chapter, verse 6. Repeat 3 times then read it backwards."[29]

When it comes to mainstream medical approaches, commented a physician, "[the Amish] have a healthy skepticism . . . They've seen us prescribe medicines and then five years later say 'No, you don't want to take that medicine.'" Many Amish will try a treatment or medicine if the explanation for its proposed effects sounds logical and if there is someone they know with the same problem who has been helped by the treatment. However, there is a certain amount of general trust and gullibility that makes many Amish susceptible to smooth-talking charlatans, persuasive ads for new treatments, and questionable fads that allege to cure many if not most ailments. They rely more heavily than most others on the honesty of the person treating them. Local physicians say Amish vulnerability is due heavily to their lack of understanding of science and of how medicine really works. Marketing of products is doubly appealing to potential customers if the product is also reasonably priced.

In sum, much of the attractiveness of alternative medical treatments lies in the common sense and understandable manner by which they are explained by practitioners who appear sincere and concerned about their patients. When mainstream treatments are clearly explained by trusted professionals, most Amish have little aversion to using them, especially if they can afford the costs and if some success can be demonstrated. There is no biblical or traditional basis for rejecting mainstream medicine out of hand. Rather, as their knowledge of the usefulness of modern medicine increases, more Amish, especially the less conservative orders, have availed themselves of it. The increased reliance upon local hospital and clinic facilities by the Holmes County and Wayne County Amish is evidenced by their negotiation with these institutions for lower prices (see the subsequent section titled "Paying for Health Care").

Psychological Well-Being among the Amish

More is known about issues of physical health than about psychological difficulties among the Amish. One of the dangers in diagnosing psychological problems is that the standards of what is normal vary between Amish and English communities. Boys and girls are raised differently, are taught different values, and are socialized into different role expectations. The result is that a given attitude or behavior might be considered normal in one context but abnormal in another. The perceptions of issues like confidentiality, counselor-client relationships, sexual abuse, and the objective stance of the therapist can be interpreted differently within the context of Amish culture and religion.

Working effectively with Amish clients "requires a profound shift in perceptions" on the part of English therapists.[30] Misunderstanding Amish culture or imposing one's own mental framework on it can result in the mislabeling of behaviors and demeanor. Some have even argued that mental illness is a social construction, that is, that its existence is determined by differences in cultural definitions of given behaviors.[31] At least there is a danger that diagnoses can be culturally biased. A veteran M.D. who was raised Amish and has served the Amish for several decades noted that English physicians often err in diagnosing because they fail to understand the differences between English and Amish role expectations.

Of course, misdiagnoses related to cultural biases and stereotypes are nothing new and have been found for other groups as well.[32] What might be interpreted as being "withdrawn" by an outsider, for example, would be considered appropriate "reserve" by an Amish person. A good example of such misinterpretation is a case related by a physician who sent an

Amish woman to a psychiatrist. When the physician asked how the visit went, she replied, "Well, he told me that I'm inhibited; I need to get rid of my inhibitions; I need to do this and that." Then she said: "You know, when I sat down, he started telling me about his own life. If you think I have problems, he really has problems." The physician, who has worked with the Amish for forty years and has an Amish background, concluded that "[the psychiatrist] didn't understand her culture at all." In a study of Amish and non-Amish women, Janet Fuchs and her colleagues found that Amish women were more likely to feel depressed and anxious, but they indicated that this result may be due to the greater willingness of Amish women to express some of these feelings because there is little stigma placed upon such expression.[33] Consequently, some of the differences in well-being revealed in their research may not be real differences but rather artifacts of cultural differences. Gender beliefs may also be implicated. A recent study of Amish in Wayne and Holmes counties found that whereas more than three-fourths of the Amish women in the sample felt that the church was supportive when there was a need to seek mental-health treatment, most Amish men disagreed.[34]

Since the early 1980s, there have been several attempts to identify a genetic origin of bipolar disorder within the Old Order Amish population, but these studies have yielded inconclusive results. Whatever genetic roots may exist are very complex and involve more than one gene.

Generally, the rate of psychiatric illness among the Amish does not seem to be significantly different from that found in the general population. Most of the professionals we interviewed agreed with this conclusion. Several mentioned depression as the psychological problem they encounter most among Amish patients. But they did not think the Amish were more widely depressed than the non-Amish. Said a professional whom we asked whether depression rates were higher among the Amish: "No, I don't think they are. I think they're less, but when it happens it becomes kind of a major event . . . They're not stress free; I'll tell you that much." "Depression is the biggest, most common mental illness we see . . . it's not just Amish; it's that generation of English people too," said another physician. "They have the same illnesses everyone else does," noted a veteran psychologist who works with Amish patients. Some research even points to lower levels of stress and depression among Amish women when compared to English women.[35] However, as published studies have indicated, a local psychologist has found that genetics makes a difference in some cases. "There are certain families where the disorders run in the family."

There appear to be some differences tied to the various Amish orders in the kinds of issues raised by patients. Patients who are members of more conservative churches are more likely than other Amish to complain about issues related to authority and oppression. One therapist noted: "We're more likely to hear from the Old Order . . . that they're feeling oppressed by their clergy, or harassed by them. Or by the younger Old Order [members], we'll hear stories about shunning and shaming a lot more . . . It becomes a real difficult struggle for these people, where they have to choose between their own personal beliefs and remaining part of their family. Whereas the Newer Order Amish, they don't tend to shun." Another physician expressed a similar view: "I see a lot more depressed patients in that group [conservative Old Order or Swartzentruber]. And I think because the rules are so strict, that some people just feel crushed underneath them." While some adjust and accept the rules, "I think you have more in that group that struggle with depression and anxiety. There's more of a sense of 'I'm being watched and I don't want to be watched.'"

Further pressure is added because these symptoms also often have religious overtones. Adhering to strongly held beliefs can be difficult. Sarah Weaver, who was an Amish artist and invalid, depicted the choice and struggle associated with the narrow Amish way of life in her painting titled *The Broad and Narrow Way*. The "broad" way is the way of the world—easy, materialistic, hedonistic, immoral. The "narrow" way is the way of the righteous—difficult, Christian, humble, godly. The first leads to "eternal damnation," but the second, though more demanding, leads to "eternal life."

Not surprisingly, behavioral indicators of psychological problems concern areas of central importance to the Amish lifestyle: dissatisfaction with work, religious doctrine, and not being married.[36] Some of the sources of stress among the Amish originate in the discrepancies some feel between their actual behavior and attitudes, on the one hand, and the ideals expressed in their religious doctrines, on the other. "Maybe I feel like this because I haven't submitted myself to Jesus or God enough. Maybe I have sinned," is a refrain often heard by one psychologist. The Amish "think more of depression as a problem with spiritualness and your relationship with God," said another doctor. This traditional interpretation is more likely among those Amish groups that have not changed much in their beliefs and lifestyles. For a church minister, the responsibility to enforce rules and deal with church problems can also cause stress. Other potential sources of anxiety include problems with members of the broader kinship group and economic difficulties. Some outsiders see the patriarchal structure of the Amish family as an added reason for stress among women.

Amish life outside the home generates other stresses. "Farming is always a gamble," noted one Amish man. Most Ohio Amish now work in nonfarm occupations and are often employed by others, a situation that creates different pressures from those encountered by farmers or the self-employed. Sometimes "it's stress at work. Some can't handle deadlines. Like I have one fellow," observes one practitioner. "I think he's the guy in charge of the business. But he's got these phone calls, and he's got people that want this right now, and they want this and they want that. He just goes bananas. He can't handle that unless he's taking some medication that keeps him calmed down." Some see the higher incomes that often come with such work as a growing source of stress and anxiety. A change in the location where one works creates changes at home. Meals, especially breakfasts, for example, may not be taken together because of differences in the work schedules of family members. And other adjustments may need to be made. An Amish businessman also commented that daily devotionals may have to be moved from the morning to the evening because of occupational demands.

The growing diversity of occupations has created some tension within the Holmes County Amish community. According to one source, Amish farmers "have complained a lot [because] people who aren't on the farm have been given a lot more liberty than what they have . . . The guy who has the sawmill has fax machines; he's got telephones . . . He's got a cell phone. He's not lacking much of anything . . . he's been given a lot of freedom. And the farmer hasn't been given all those."

Because the rules and living conditions vary within and between Amish orders, the kinds and degrees of stress and health problems experienced by their members would also be expected to vary. Groups that are more conservative and traditional, for example, the Swartzentruber Amish, may experience difficulties caused by the narrowness and implacable character of their Ordnung. Some Swartzentruber Amish will not work in town or may not go to a health professional if it means interacting with an ex-Amish person. For example, some Swartzentrubers told a well-known doctor who served an Amish community, "If she [an ex-Amish woman] works there, we can't come there." Strict rules place strict limitations on behavior. "I think sometimes too religious or too conservative religious practice can add stress rather than having a calming effect," concludes one physician. For those who accept the rules, however, "there is a firm basis for making decisions that help minimize stress." For those who don't, for example, some youth, there are indicators of rebellion. A local psychiatrist made these comments: "[Old Order and Swartzentruber would say] the generation of people coming up are not as respectful; they're arrogant, they're stupid . . . I've got the new generation talking on the phone . . . And [the parents] know they have a problem, but they don't know what to do with it. [The mixed consequences of] the narrow path and predictable path that their life will follow [is] the strength and weakness of their [Old Order] culture. The predictability is what makes it very comfortable to some people, but it's also what makes it feel too confining to other people who want to break free of that."

New Order Amish, who tend to be more expansive in some cultural practices and who are more likely to have frequent contact with the English community and engage in nonagricultural labor, experience new sources of stress rooted in the changes they have adopted. At the same time, the higher level of flexibility creates an avenue for the reduction of stress. The features that distinguish the orders are thus two-edged swords. Flexibility may create more choices and minimize some sources of stress, but it may also introduce new problems to which individuals are unaccustomed.

Cultural differences and the effort to maintain boundaries separating themselves from outside society sometimes hinder the Amish from seeking help for psychological difficulties.[37] When they do seek help for such difficulties, they may turn to church leaders or Amish counselors before going to a professional outside their community. The training received by Amish counselors most likely has come from Mennonite counselors or Mennonite workshops they have attended. The Amish do not have formal licenses or degrees in psychotherapy. Among Old Order Amish, it has been found that the need to maintain a boundary between their community and the outside has discouraged members from seeking psychological help from mental-health professionals.[38]

Amish counseling is biblically based; that is, there is a belief that following biblical lessons will teach one the truth, and "the truth shall make you free." Most of the problems people have "are the same now as in Eden," observes an Amish counselor. "Now if Christ is on the throne of the heart [instead of one's self], he can control our thoughts and will. Then our feelings fall into place bringing peace . . . The only way one can function properly is to function with God[;] when the conscience is clear, the Spirit controls the will and emotions. This is the ultimate goal of counseling."[39] It is self-centeredness and selfishness that lead to fear, which in turn leads to emotional difficulties like depression and anxiety. To be healed, individuals have to shift their focus from themselves to God and others.[40] In effect, for a person to become mentally healed, his or her own attitude and behavior must change. The source of difficulty is believed to lie within the person rather than in others or in the wider environment.

Few Amish facilities focus on mental-health assistance for the Amish. A Holmes County center for treating emotional problems among the Amish opened in 1999 after one of the bishops realized that a relative needed counseling. The facility itself is unassuming, reflecting Amish values of humility and selflessness, and looks like a typical farm house; it has no sign in front to identify it as a place for counseling. The property also contains a small cabin, where couples can meet to work out problems, and a barn in which hands-on projects are completed by patients. The specific functions of the center, as set forth in its "statement of purpose," are (1) "to support the growth and well-being of the Church"; (2) "to offer guidance and support to those persons and their families who are faced with mental and emotional health needs"; (3) to aid in the recovery of persons who have received medical or psychiatric help, so that they can "continue the healing process in a Christian environment compatible to the ideals of the Church"; and (4) "to offer Biblical guidance for the prevention of serious mental illness."[41] Only four women at a time are taken in as residents, but "walk-ins" also come in for counseling, and these can be men or women. In 2001 the center had sixty-six cases, including walk-ins. A typical day for residents includes attending a Bible session and an advisory or therapeutic session with two counselors, carrying out assigned chores around the property, and working on projects such as making small products that are sold.

The center counsels clients on spiritual issues and in cases of relatively minor emotional and mental problems. It does not provide psychiatric help for serious mental illness. Serious cases are referred to licensed professionals for medication or therapy. But care is taken when making recommendations for referral to a non-Amish professional. A local psychiatrist was invited to tour the facility and meet with its Board of Directors. During the meeting, the psychiatrist explained that while biblical counseling was fine, it was insufficient in some cases because "there are some people where their brains just don't work right . . . And they have to see a doctor who can treat their brain just like some people have to see a doctor who can treat their heart or kidneys." The psychiatrist deliberately used the term "brain" rather than "mind," because it labels the problem as something physical and tangible, for which prescribed medicine might be warranted. The term also helps reduce the stigma that has been associated with "mental" illness. The board thought this explanation made sense and has since used this psychiatrist when help has been needed in serious cases.[42]

Amish Values and Doctor-Patient Relations

Without exception, the professionals we interviewed noted several qualities in their Amish patients that they admired. They consistently mentioned the higher pain tolerance they found among their Amish patients, both men and women. "Oh, they have a higher tolerance," observed a veteran doctor. If you have to do some facial stitching, "that's usually a horrible experience to have to go through. You know, no kid likes that. They're screaming. The Amish kids, the mother will hold them, the mother or father, and tell them, 'It's gonna hurt, you can do it.' The kid will just sit there, might have a tear or two, but he won't move and they do real well. Sometimes, you think, too well for a small kid." One physician told another story of an Amish man who came into his clinic with a thumb off, and the doctor told him he should go to the emergency room to have a specialist treat him. The man replied: "Well, either you're gonna do it, or I'm gonna do it." If at all possible, the Amish generally prefer to be treated in the doctor's office rather than an emergency room, where treatment costs much more.

Another dimension of Amish culture that helps its people adapt to health difficulties and shapes their relationship with caregivers is the fundamental belief that, ultimately, what happens is in God's hands. There is a basic acceptance of what comes. "I don't think they have as high of expectations as the English do. They accept things the way they are . . . if things go sour, it's God's will." Consistently, the doctors we interviewed said that the chances that Amish patients will sue their caregivers are virtually nonexistent. In working with English patients, a psychiatrist found himself having to cope with the mental "background noise" of worry over being sued. The "pretend litigation" in his head has distinct effects in counseling these patients: "I monitor every word I say and write to make sure it is liability proof. I frequently find myself silently answering the questions of pretend lawyers in pretend depositions." The views of another professional encapsulate the general opinions of other caregivers we interviewed:

> I enjoy my Amish patients and one of the reasons I enjoy them is because they come in with a lot fewer strings attached. They don't participate in government programs, they don't have an attorney, and they're often not participating in any formal insurance policy other than their church . . . I feel like in a way because I don't have to worry about all of these third party entities kind of looking over my shoulder, I can be more natural with an Amish patient than with other patients . . . They treat me with more respect than my English patients . . . They don't whine and complain and call their attorney if they don't like me; they just don't come back . . . My other patients are a lot more likely to challenge my opinion.

The Amish tend to trust someone who they believe is working on their behalf. However, remarked a school psychologist, acceptance of God's will makes some Amish less proactive than the English and can exasperate professionals, who become "frustrated with the slowness to react to things and maybe with the feelings amongst the Amish that 'let's not react too fast to this.' "

The Amish are also very pragmatic in their approach to health care. They will continue to come in for help only if they believe they are being helped by the treatment. Whether health care givers are licensed or not is less important than apparent positive results. Many Amish are "not really concerned about licensure. They're concerned about outcomes. And so if they have someone that they feel is communicating with them well, understands their needs, then they'll utilize that person whether or not they're licensed."

As in any society, however, not all Amish think and react the same way. Especially in the Holmes County Settlement, where there is a larger variety of types of Amish than in other settlements, significant variations appear. Members of the more conservative Amish churches generally desire less intervention and tend to delay treatment. They are less likely to go to a hospital to be treated, less likely to get immunized, and more likely to need simplified explanations. Professionals also have to speak more clearly and simply to patients from more conservative churches because they are more likely to have difficulty with English. They are also less "verbal," as one physician put it, suggesting that communication is more difficult for them than, for example, members of the New Order. Consequently, how these churches are distributed affects the experiences of caregivers. One Holmes County physician with an Amish background remarked, "It's hard to generalize about the Amish because of their diversity." In referring to a friend and doctor who works in Wayne County, he noted that "he had a lot more Swartzentruber Amish; his Amish practice is totally different from mine."

Sensitivity to and respect for Amish culture and internal variations are important to patients. A physician who can speak Pennsylvania Dutch or who has an Amish background will be attractive to the Amish. In pediatrics Pennsylvania Dutch may be especially needed because in most cases, Old Order and Swartzentruber children do not speak English before going to school. Being able to "discern" the differences among Amish patients is also important for caregivers: "There are some very subtle things that you look for, that I look for when they come in. For example, you see how they're dressed. And that is one of the biggest things I look for. And you'll see who brings the patient in. Is it the father, is it the mother that comes in?"

Since Amish men tend to have more contact than women with individuals outside their community, female patients are more likely to experience a language barrier or be nervous about their visit to a doctor. So having a female doctor is important for many Amish women. They may discuss issues that they would not be willing to broach with a male caregiver. "Females tend to take more time with the patients as a whole. And so that opens the door for the patient to feel more comfortable," observed a female doctor who has worked with the Amish for eight years and has an Amish background.

Being willing to spend extra time with patients in the office is a quality that doctors notice is appreciated: A physician commented, speaking of the Amish: "I think they're in less of a hurry than the English people are. I mean, they come in and they like to visit with me . . . They want to talk about their kids that you delivered, and all this stuff . . . They also come into the office and if they have to wait an hour, or an hour and a half, most of them are not upset by that. That's part of life."

Paying for Health Care

It is no secret that the costs for health care have been rising in the United States. The reasons are many: advances in technology, malpractice insurance and lawsuits, enhanced preventive care and diagnostic testing, accelerating drug prices, and changes in the nation's demographic profile. Higher costs have a direct and serious effect on many Amish because they generally have tried to avoid participation in governmental health programs like Medicaid and Medicare and most do not carry health insurance from a private employer. Swartzentruber Amish are especially averse to participating in insurance programs. However, the high costs of catastrophic events and chronic illness have pressured some Amish employees working in English-run companies to use the health insurance available from their employers. Some have begun to use Medicaid as well, "and that was unheard of when I started practice just eight years ago; but young families are just strapped," noted a local physician specializing in obstetrics and gynecology.

Some Amish churches limit the range of permissible jobs or prohibit employment in certain organizations, thus increasing the probability that some individuals will be poor and will not be able to afford health care on their own. A family might encounter a difficult time financially because the man is allowed to work only for an Amish employer, who generally pays less than would an English employer. "That's been an issue with some of my pregnant moms. I don't think they're getting enough protein. And I think finances come into play there," concluded a local doctor. A family might be in a real bind because, in general, the more conservative church districts are less likely to provide the amount of aid to a family that might be required to cover their health care costs. A chiropractor who has worked with the Amish for twenty years, and whose father and grandfather also did, suggested that Amish patients who are financially strapped tend to spend more time when visiting a doctor: "I'll tell you one thing the Swartzentrubers do is they want to get their money's worth," and so they will ask about and mention every little physical problem they might have . . . So yeah, I'd say the Swartzentrubers do that more than the New Order."

As a whole, the Amish are very cost-conscious: "They sure flock to the place that's cheapest," pointed out one physician, and it is a refrain mentioned by most other health care givers. Some groups of Amish have bargained with and arranged for lower costs from health care institutions, for example, in Toledo, Akron, and Millersburg. It is not unusual for the Amish to travel outside the state because of the availability of lower-cost health care elsewhere.

To increase its attractiveness to the Holmes County Amish community, one local hospital launched a program that not only offers transportation for patients but also provides housing accommodations for families and friends of Amish patients and a set of pricing packages for a wide variety of services utilized by self-paying patients, such as the Amish, who generally pay at the time of service. This form of payment reduces patient bills by more than one-third. Between 2005 (the year the program was inaugurated) and 2008, the number of Amish patients using the hospital increased 35 percent, according to the Amish advocate at the hospital. The hospital also actively engages in a variety of outreach programs and has an Amish advisory board to help direct hospital-Amish relations.

Another tactic used to reduce health care costs is to first see health care givers who might be able to be of help but will not demand that patients undergo a large battery of expensive tests and who generally treat patients in their offices. In this way Amish patients avoid the high costs of tests and treatments given at a local hospital. Their pragmatism also helps the Amish keep their health care bills down: "If they think that they can spend a reasonable amount of money and that their loved one will be helped, then they'll do it. If they didn't think it would help, or that it costs too much, then they wouldn't do it," says a Wayne County psychologist. Despite the pressures of higher costs, however, virtually all of the health care givers we spoke with noted that, as a group, the Amish are better than their English patients at paying their bills.

Because of the high costs of many medical treatments, most Amish

A Holmes County hospital provides a three-bedroom furnished "Amish House" for Amish families who come from afar and for Amish patients who will undergo surgery soon. Photograph courtesy of Charles Hurst.

churches participate in aid programs that help defray high health care costs encountered by their members. However, the Amish vary in the kinds and availability of church programs with this purpose. In 2009 there were three general health care programs for the Ohio Amish. Old and New Order Amish have separate church funds (Church Fund 1 and Church Fund 2, respectively), into which members pay a monthly fee. For those of each order who do not wish to participate in the relatively new church fund programs, there is the Hospital Aid Program, for which members pay a flat monthly fee. Most of the Hospital Aid Program members are Old Order. Swartzentruber churches are the least likely to have any such programs. When asked about how the Swartzentrubers cover health care costs, a member of the Amish statewide committee on hospital aid replied: "I really don't have any idea how they operate . . . I'm not aware that we have any of those people within our plan." A representative of the Swartzentruber Amish noted that although they do not have a church fund, members get together to provide financial aid. There have been instances when Old Order groups have had fund-raisers to pay off Swartzentruber hospital bills, although the money has not always been accepted.

In a broad sense, the church funds and the Hospital Aid Program are similar in their operation and purpose. In each order there are local church committees of Amish men, and a state committee for each program provides oversight by screening and approving payment of hospital expenses. In the case of the Hospital Aid Program, the choice of the term *aid* is deliberate, since the term *insurance* has negative implications for many Amish: "All join as a brotherhood in trying to help others in need. This is no insurance; it is only an aid in helping each other."[43] In an interview, the first point made by the chair of a local hospital-aid committee was that the guiding principle behind the program was helping others: "Helping each other in need" appears on the cover of a booklet describing the program, and "Love thy neighbor as thyself" appears on its last page. This ethic, which holds for the church funds as well, means that some wealthy members will pay into the program but not draw from its funds because they can afford to pay for many of their own expenses. Members of Old and New Order Amish churches in Ohio may become members of each other's programs by paying into the programs. The idea is to have a fund from which members can draw when they incur heavy health care expenses.

The Hospital Aid Program requires that members pay a monthly fee in addition to a deductible when hospital expenses arise. The monthly fee can fluctuate depending on the demands that are placed on the fund. These demands have increased as health care costs have risen. For example, in 1975 the bimonthly fee for each family in a forty-church plan in Wayne and Holmes counties was $12.00. In 1980 the fee rose to $45.00 per month for a two-person family. In 2004–5, the fee reached $75.00 per month. In 1999 the plan distributed more than $871,000 in payments; in 2004, payments almost doubled, reaching $1.6 million. If costs exceed expectations, additional funds may be requested to cover added costs.

Sometimes money is collected more informally through "showers," which are organized get-togethers to raise funds to help those who have recently experienced a health problem of some kind. Ads for showers regularly appear in the *Gemeinde Register,* a newsletter serving the Amish of Ohio:

Lets have a whatever you wish shower for [name] broke his leg while playing gray wolf . . . lets remember his parents with a Money shower as they had Dr. bills lately.

Lets have a Birthday, Money & Letter shower for [name] . . . while he recovers from surgery to take out his one kidney, due to having a large tumor in his kidney.

Lets have a Get-Well and Money shower for [name]. They had lots and lots of hospital and Dr. bills and still have.[44]

As noted earlier, the economics of health care create complicated ethical and cultural dilemmas for the Amish. The economic pinch caused by high health care costs can catch Amish families in a double bind. For example, a family does not want to be perceived as a burden to other members of their community and thus may hesitate to use the hospital aid plan or a church fund even when the help is needed. Or commercial insurance may be discouraged by the church, but use of it may allow a member to avoid using the Amish Hospital Aid Program, thereby diminishing his "burden" on his community. Neither choice is optimal, because Amish church members frown on *both* use of insurance *and* being a burden to others. Membership fees in the various plans can be afforded better by wealthier church members, who are generally in less need of help from the funds than poorer members, who are less likely to be able to afford the rising fees and in more need of support when facing high medical bills. A separate church collection may cover the bills, but at the same time, this separate approach draws attention to the poor as a burden for the church.

Moreover, the chronic health problems that are found sometimes more frequently among the Amish than in the general population place a very heavy strain upon church programs, resulting in unwelcome pressures to participate in governmental insurance programs such as Medicaid. Historically, participation in governmental programs has been prohibited or at least frowned upon by Amish churches, but the need to properly treat chronic health problems may require it. The dilemma is personified in the case of a three-year-old Amish hemophiliac who suffered internal injuries and needed to be treated. The father "fears he'll be forced to choose between getting help paying for his child's care or following his religious convictions." In the meantime, the state has been paying his bills.[45] The Amish encourage a tight, closed community in which they are expected to marry other Amish, but doing so amplifies the potential for certain chronic inherited health problems, which in turn lead to greater medical expenses and heavier economic burdens on the Amish community.

Confronting Death

"I think the Amish are among the very great minority in our society who know how to die right. I mean, die at home is the way to do it." This observation comes from a retired M.D. who grew up in an Amish family and spent several decades treating Amish patients. One of the recurrent themes in our interviews with a variety of health care professionals in Wayne and Holmes counties was that the Amish see death as a natural process, as an inevitable part of their lives. "Death is a part of life," explained one physician. Another thought "that they [Amish] are gracious in their deaths because they believe. They believe that they're going to go to a better place." The director of a Holmes County funeral home estimated that about 75 percent of Amish die in their homes.

According to local physicians, the Amish also carefully consider others in their decisions regarding the need and desire for expensive health care or extraordinary measures when they have a terminal or life-threatening illness. They have "a healthy realistic theology about life itself," and if the treatment is not a positive cure or if the cost "is going to bankrupt your family [or community], they're going to choose not to do it." "They think about other people. They think about the expense." In recollecting his many experiences with Old Order and Swartzentruber Amish, another doctor observed, "If we told them it's terminal, they would as good as take them home and take care of them and let them die. Rather than starting a treatment and last another six months, a year, two years, and spend all that money." For many of these Amish, "cancer" is the "death word." "If I'm going to die anyway, why spend the money" and take money away from those who need it in their lives. At home, they may get visits from hospice, whose representatives can ease pain and help make arrangements when the patient dies. In general, the Amish seem to be very accepting of ⋅ hospice's mission.

Staff members of hospice in both Wayne and Holmes counties are trained on Amish beliefs, values, and practices, as well as the diversity within the Amish community. They also communicate with Amish bishops about hospice services and provide caregiving classes for potential users. These outreach efforts have led to a greater Amish awareness of the services provided by hospice and have resulted in heavier Amish involvement in the program. Often a nurse from hospice will be called to the home after a person has died to make the formal pronouncement of death.

Acceptance of death appears almost naturally because it is viewed as part of God's divine plan. In a recent book organized by an Amish author, parents and others were asked to write letters about the deaths of family members. The letters relate the events surrounding the deaths as well as family reactions and adjustments to the deaths. The aim of the author was to "help the healing process of the grieving, to preserve family history and food for the soul to the reader."[46] Several common themes running through the letters demonstrate basic Amish beliefs and values.[47] One of these is the refusal to question the deaths involved and the belief that death is part of God's larger plan: "God helped me to see that this is His will and the thought came to me, that I don't want to fight against God's will for me." "The good Lord knows best. We want to put our trust in Him."

There is also a common belief that the deceased is in a better place, is with God, and will be later joined with family members: "How wonderful to know they are safe in the arms of Jesus." "God gives and God gathers His children home again." "Having a family started in heaven gives us a longing to go there and gives us a greater desire to leave this world for a better place, where there will be no parting or tears." Another theme is that God provides signs to help people understand and adjust to the deaths of loved ones: "I dreamed I saw him and he was so happy. I feel God showed me this dream so I could let go and go on." "An angel tapped me this morning . . . God has helped us so much and I trust He will in the future." Pervading the letters are expressions of thanks to friends and relatives who have helped during the viewings and the funerals. There is a clear sense of belonging to a larger community.

The arrangements for funerals and burials have some distinctive features among the Amish. If the person dies at home, the body is embalmed at a funeral home or, in the case of a Swartzentruber death, at home, and is available for a "viewing" at the home to allow friends and

Amish coffins are most often made of cypress and lined in cotton with no ornamentation. Swartzentruber Amish generally use poplar, which is cheaper than cypress. The picture on the bottom shows a buggy that the casket maker has modified to carry coffins. Photographs courtesy of Charles Hurst.

relatives to see the deceased for the last time. Usually a person is designated to escort guests into the room where the body lies. Typically, little cosmetic work has been done on the deceased. How the body is displayed tends to vary with the order of the deceased. Swartzentruber Amish usually place the body on a board stretched over two chairs, whereas the Andy Weaver Amish place the body on a cot. New Order and some Old Order Amish use the wood coffin to display the body. Swartzentruber Amish do not put the body in its coffin until the day of the burial. Coffins are plain on the outside, without handles, but are often given a polyurethane finish. In 2008 there were eight coffin makers in the Holmes County Settlement.

The time between death and the funeral service, held in a shop or other building on the family's property, is usually about three days. The service itself begins about nine in the morning and lasts one to two hours. For Old and New Order services, memory cards are available as mementos or keepsakes. The burial after the service is in an Amish cemetery on someone's property and is usually attended by only the extended family. Located inside the grave is an rough oak box into which the coffin is lowered with the use of cloth straps. Because the box is wood, over time the grave may sink, and so there are some undulations in the ground across the cemetery. A plain Arlington-style headstone is used to mark the grave. After the burial, a light lunch is usually provided for the family by church members, and perhaps an evening meal. Although there are surface variations among the Amish in the trappings used in the funeral and burial process, the process of dying and events associated with death, like most aspects of Amish lives, are treated as parts of the cycle of life. The Amish leave life as they enter it—simply.

Facing Conflicts and Offering Lessons

It should be evident from this survey of health care that there are many variations and disagreements within the Amish community regarding giving birth, getting health care for physical and psychological problems, and accepting remedies from health care givers. Some Amish more readily accept traditional beliefs and practices and are skeptical of modern medicine, although the acceptance and use of modern medicine appears to be increasing, especially among New Order and many Old Order Amish.

Swartzentruber Amish remain steeped in tradition in regard to lifestyle and most health care matters. But in all the churches, there is some mixture of traditional and modern components in the use of health care services, even though the mixture varies.

The differences carry a potential for conflicts within the Ohio Amish community. For example, to what extent should certain birthing centers have to follow state requirements that apply to other such centers? Should a community be allowed to follow its unique beliefs even if professionals believe that a common standard of care should be imposed in these facilities? As health care costs rise, to what extent are lower-income Amish members going to be helped by other Amish who are cost-conscious? And to what extent do they want to be helped, given their desire not to be a burden to others? How can education about health care charlatans, superstitious beliefs, and ineffective and sometimes dangerous remedies be pursued among some groups of Amish without violating their ideas about the role and extent of education needed in life? To what extent does obedience to an authority figure, religious or professional, take precedence over one's own knowledge and concerns? What consequences do differences in "enlightenment" and wealth have for the solidarity within the Amish community? There are significant differences in all these areas. The Ohio Amish are a heterogeneous group about whom broad, meaningful generalizations are hazardous.

General agreement exists among the Amish, however, in certain areas of their overall philosophy about health, about others, and about the place of death in the life cycle. Their views are very pragmatic: health means being able to function properly. It has less to do with "feelings" than with "behavior." In tune with their values of humility and selflessness, there is a prime concern for others. "How will my illness and its treatment affect others?" is a central question when an Amish person is confronted with a life-threatening disease. Finally, the deep religious beliefs of the Amish provide a clear and comforting perspective on death and its meaning.

Although the English community may think of itself as more modern and therefore more advanced or enlightened, there are significant lessons to be learned from the Amish approach to health matters. Among these are parts of their pragmatic philosophy. Being cost-conscious and prudent in the use of health care is important. At the same time, so is preventive care, which, though an expense, can yield long-term benefits. The relationship that exists between Amish patients and doctors also seems worthy of emulation. Honesty, directness, and willingness to follow professional directions are hallmarks of the most effective relationships. In addition, thinking of oneself as only one part of a community whose members are tied together creates a network upon which a sick person can rely for comfort and economic support. Some people simply cannot pay the costs of needed medical care. Moreover, observing the Amish model to reduce costs may provide us with clues about what we need to do to formulate a "sustainable" medical plan for all our citizens,[48] although in the process, difficult choices may need to be made. These are all lessons from which ordinary citizens and national policymakers may be able to benefit.

❈ CHAPTER 8 ❈

Stepping Back and Looking Forward

What will happen to the next generation with the way things are going?
—A New Order Amish man

In the previous chapters, we have discussed numerous dimensions of the Holmes County Settlement as if they were discrete and isolated from each other. But of course they are not. In everyday life and in reality, they are woven into the single tapestry of the Amish lifestyle and culture. In this chapter we present a model that explains the dynamism and diversity among the Amish, and we speculate on how cohesion is maintained in spite of the change and diversity that are so characteristic of the Holmes County Settlement.

Paradoxically, the Amish of Holmes and surrounding counties have had to remain open to connections with English society to preserve the integrity and separateness of their own culture. As a consequence, it is the interplay of internal and external forces that operates to produce the unique character of the Amish community. The complex boundaries that separate Amish and English communities require continual boundary-maintenance work to balance in-group and out-group pressures in different institutional domains. As a result of these pressures on the boundaries, various kinds of tensions are generated to which responses are made. The dialectical processes of change and the seemingly incompatible forces of community and the individual in terms of values and interests, structure and individual agency, and security and freedom, exist as terrains of tension operating through the institutional fields of religion, education, work, family, and health care. But despite the centrifugal forces at work within the Holmes County Settlement, centripetal forces maintain a high level of cohesion. In addition to close ties, these include several mechanisms and interpretations of social control that serve as sources of trust and solidarity in the Amish community. These are the aspects of the Amish paradox examined in the following sections.

We have also identified some consequential trends that suggest lessons from the Amish lifestyle that might serve all of us. And we revisit the issue of trust and the need to find effective solutions to the problems that arise in the relationship between the community and the individual.

Inside the Amish Crucible

A crucible is "a place or situation in which concentrated forces interact to cause or influence change or development." It is also defined as a "severe test or trial."[1] In many ways, the Amish community is a crucible. There is no question that the lifestyles and belief systems chosen by Amish churches and their members are buffeted by powerful, contradictory internal and external forces on a regular basis. These pressures constitute a fundamental test of the mettle of Amish culture and its representatives and provide the immediate context within which decisions about change and constancy are made.

Nolt and Meyers point out that Amish diversity is created by (a) variations in migration histories, Ordnung, and ethnic backgrounds; (b) the use of divergent means to reach common goals within the community; and (c) differences in the local contexts in which Amish groups reside.[2] These contexts vary in their social, economic, and legal features. In other words, both internal and external factors shape the contours of specific Amish settlements. Internally, constancy and change are also conditioned by the differing histories of settlements and demographic variations within them, by the presence of several noncommuning church affiliations with distinctive sets of regulations, and even by the force of individual personalities. The key internal factors that foster Amish diversity are these:

Church district Ordnung
Affiliation

Settlement
  Size
  Age
  History
  Location
Population dynamics
  Growth rate
  Age distribution
Personality conflicts

When these internal elements interact with external pressures such as land availability, tourism, technological developments, and legal issues, they create uneven rates of change within the Amish community, because affiliations frequently react differently to these pressures. For example, as we have noted, while Swartzentruber Amish may react to the lack of land availability by moving to new locations, other groups may pursue new occupations to compensate for the scarcity of available farmland. Differences in the interpretations and weighting of the traditions and core values of Amish culture often lie at the heart of variations in responses.

Sometimes the external economic and political pressures faced by the Amish community are national or even international in scope, as seen in this list of key external forces producing Amish diversity:

Global Forces
Economic competition and markets
Energy resources
Outreach communities and mission work
Flows of outside information
Scholarly work and conferences

National, Regional, and State Forces
Technological innovations
Financial trends
Court cases and legal requirements
Highway safety and funding
Cost and availability of health care

Local Forces
Township and county zoning ordinances
Law enforcement
Health department regulations
Tourism
Local monitoring agencies
Cost and availability of land

An Amish bishop told us of his concern for the many local small wood-working and furniture businesses that have been established in recent years. He worried that the 2008–9 national housing and mortgage crisis might force some of these enterprises out of business because of down-turns in the demand for furniture and other house-related products. One owner of a very successful furniture company indicated that business had indeed dropped because of this national issue. Competition from less-expensive furniture imports from China has also been a concern that has moved some Amish manufacturers to shift their tactics and the markets they target.

More locally, regions vary in numbers and types of employers, ordi-nances, and populations. Individual behaviors in workplaces differ, for example, if in one local area the economy is dominated by English em-ployers who use sophisticated technologies and a particular management philosophy while in others the employers are mostly Amish people who are reluctant to use many new technologies and utilize a different man-agement approach. Work is also conditioned by internal differences in the Holmes County Settlement. In the legal arena, behavioral reactions to external demands like state requirements for buggy safety vary; some affiliations adapt fairly rapidly, and others follow more slowly or resist any departure from tradition. For example, all affiliations in the Holmes County Settlement except the Swartzentrubers display orange triangles on their buggies for safety. Even within the Swartzentruber affiliation, some groups have placed two lights on their buggies while others con-tinue to use only one light. In the workplace, as we've seen, even within a given company, the specific jobs carried out by Amish employees will not be the same because the Ordnung is not the same in all affiliations, nor are the personalities.

The combined pressure created by the interaction of external constraints and internal demands often leads to negotiated settlements that must then be legitimated. For example, internally there may be a concern that an Amish business is becoming too big; externally, there may be a lower demand for some products and consequently a lower demand for labor. What is to be done when a population is growing but the demand for labor is low? Whereas a conservative Swartzentruber response might be to avoid internal change by moving to another region, several Old and New Order Amish businessmen argued that they felt an obligation to provide employment for the next generation; therefore, their enterprises would need to grow, despite the possible dangers of too much growth or success. They would also have to be creative in identifying production areas where demand is still high or growing. Demand may be stimulated by greater amounts of visible, widespread advertising, but then there is the question of how much an Amish employer should advertise. The changes and resulting decisions that need to be made are often interlinked, creating a cascading and ever-present set of quandaries.

The vise created by crosscutting forces from the inside and the outside is not restricted to economic matters. Differences in context and in Ordnung are also manifested in the arena of education. For example, the absence of easily accessible parochial schools in the immediate neighborhood is one factor that helps explain why some Amish children go to public schools even if the family's church prefers for Amish students to attend a parochial school. Others, most likely some in the New Order, may choose to homeschool their children rather than send them to the local public school. As was found in the Sam Yoder and Andy Weaver instances, unique internal events in the histories of different affiliations and disagreements about policies have also instigated divisions in the religious sphere. In health care, the presence or absence of local birthing centers and their relative costs, along with the reputations of given health care givers in the area, interact with internal determinants such as church rules and wealth differences to affect birthing methods. In sum, a battery of shifting external forces act upon changing internal diversity within the Holmes County Settlement to produce a highly complex, sometimes bewildering set of differences, rendering the local Amish community anything but simple.

Boundaries and Border Work: Where Inside and Outside Worlds Meet

Like any open system operating in a turbulent environment, the Holmes County Settlement is a community that is unavoidably influenced by outside forces, but it is a system trying to maintain closure at its boundaries to ensure predictability, smooth operation, and cultural integrity.[3] However, the boundaries involved in Amish social and cultural life are not simple. The boundaries that separate Amish and English communities, for example, are not like the single borderlines that appear on a map. As table 8.1 shows, there are several types of boundaries because there are multiple domains that separate communities, and the permeability of boundaries may vary with the domain.

For example, the boundary with respect to automobiles is very clear and distinct, whereas the boundary that relates to certain technologies and to birthing techniques is more porous and much fuzzier. Some boundaries may be continuously impermeable, that is, set and fixed over time, while others may be malleable and become more or less porous over time. To avoid the military draft during the Civil War and maintain their posture of nonresistance, for example, Holmes County Amish almost always paid an exemption fee or occasionally even found substitutes to serve in the army for them.[4] The continuing impermeability of that boundary is reflected currently in the National Amish Steering Committee's discussion of plans for alternative service in case the draft is reinstated.

Different types of boundaries may also vary in their significance for different affiliations, church districts, and individuals. In addition, some boundaries are more often the sites of controversy or turf battles than others, again suggesting that they vary in their degree of permeability. While some boundaries are defined primarily by external factors (for example, laws regarding safety), others are created more by internal decisions (for example, adoption of technology).

The boundaries within the Holmes County Settlement also vary in strength and in the degree to which they separate groups from each other. The boundary distinguishing the Swartzentruber Amish from other Amish is especially strong and distinctive, while that separating the Old and New Orders appears to be becoming weaker. The separation between the Beachy Amish (a liberal group whom many do not really consider

Table 8.1. Dimensions of boundaries that shape Amish diversity

Type: Economic, Educational, Religious, Kinship, Political
Permeability: Impermeable, Semipermeable, Porous
Location: Between Amish affiliations, Between Amish and Ex-Amish, Between
    Amish and English

Amish) and the English is smaller, because the Beachy Amish drive cars. In sum, the boundaries that impinge upon Amish life are numerous and vary in their complexity and constancy.

The roads traveled across Amish-English boundaries are, more often than not, viewed as if they were one-way streets, with modern and other pressures from the English world imposing themselves on the Amish community, pushing it to adapt. The contacts may involve government-mandated safety requirements, licensing by the mainstream medical establishment, or contract requirements in economic exchanges. This image reflects the dominant view of the modern (for example, as in law or technology) as re-shaping or dissolving the traditional, or tradition collapsing in the face of a more powerful and relentless modernity. Tradition and modernity are seen as antagonistic and mutually exclusive. But this perspective is too simplistic.

The path between modernity and tradition, the English and the Amish communities, goes both ways; it is a two-way rather than a one-way street. When traditions are redefined or negotiations take place with modernity, tradition becomes an amalgamation of the old and the new, and the modern is mixed with traditional elements. In other words, the diffusion of ideas and artifacts works in both directions. We tend to think of modern technology, for example, as a Trojan horse that will undermine traditional Amish culture and identity. But conversely, as more Amish enter modern workshops or become employees in modern factories, it may be that they will re-shape these settings, revamping and reinvigorating traditional values and ways of working within them. The very attractiveness of some aspects of the Amish lifestyle to outsiders suggests that Amish ways of living and working can influence the English.

The Amish may be a "reverse Trojan horse" for many modern institutions, helping to inspire change within them. In some cases, Amish employers may only have "weak" ties with other groups, as when an Amish businessman visited the Kentucky Toyota plant to see how the Japanese operation works. The contacts between them may be infrequent, superficial, and impersonal, as one would find between mere acquaintances rather than between close friends. Nevertheless, these weak ties affect Amish business structures and work arrangements, arrangements that Amish workers, in turn, can then carry along into their jobs in English companies. These workers then become social carriers of new ideas. "When a man changes jobs, he is not only moving from one network of ties to another, but also establishing a link between these."[5]

In addition to the workplace, education is an arena in which amalgamation of ideas and structures between English and Amish cultures has occurred. Each community often has something the other needs or wants. Because of the nature of school funding in the English community, rural public schools have sometimes catered to Amish needs so that their enrollments can remain high enough to receive adequate funding. Since the Amish tradition requires that students go to school through the eighth grade, some local elementary public schools have added on seventh- and eighth-grade "attached classrooms" to allow Amish children to finish out their schooling. In this case, a modern English institution has been dependent upon the more traditional Amish, but both sides have benefited from the arrangement. The site of this negotiated settlement can be seen as a border terrain where representatives of both cultures temporarily meet and conflicts between them are worked out.

In health care as well, there have been mixtures of Amish and English elements to accommodate the needs of Amish patients. Birthing centers provide a clear example of the attempt to blend traditional and more mainstream medical approaches into an effective health care delivery system. While some centers balance the two components more evenly than others, each of those in the Holmes County Settlement contains some proportion of mainstream and traditional elements. Not surprisingly, those that are viewed more positively by the English medical establishment are more likely to have medical doctors and nurses on their staffs and have close ties to local hospitals. The more traditional birthing centers are more likely to be directed and operated by professional or lay midwives, or both, and have weaker ties to hospitals and physicians.

In the political realm, the ties between the Amish and English communities tend to be one-sided, with the Amish generally reacting to legal requirements imposed upon them by local, state, and national governments. But even here, negotiation between the parties often occurs and compromise results. That is, the connection is usually not a reciprocal, voluntary, or frequent one, and thus it is consistent with the broadly held Amish belief that a minimalist and nonintrusive government is best.

As in other Amish communities, citizens of the Holmes County Settlement do not get heavily involved with governmental matters, regardless of their church affiliation. A study of Amish voting patterns in the 2004 presidential election revealed that while 43 percent were registered to vote, only about 13 percent of Amish adults in Holmes County voted. Most endorsed George W. Bush, whose conservative views appeared to be more consistent with Amish values. The low rate of voting among the Amish is linked to their belief in keeping the spiritual and material "kingdoms" separate.

The low rates of voting among Americans in general have been cited by critics as a sign of weakness in our civil society.[6] The fact that most Amish do not vote could easily be construed to mean that they are contributing to weakness in our civil society by not exercising their duty to vote. But in contrast to many English citizens who do not vote, the Amish community and its leaders do tend to get involved in legal matters that have a direct bearing on their culture and lifestyle. Public issues like zoning, safety, and hunting, for example, have drawn Amish voters into the political arena. Their selective involvement suggests that most Amish feel that they can make a difference when it counts.

The desire to remain separate by minimal political involvement in government extends to social relationships with outsiders as well. To measure the extent to which Amish social capital involves outsiders, we asked our survey respondents about the "social distance" they felt with respect to English people and also to racial and ethnic minorities in our society. Only a minority of the Amish individuals in our study spent at least half their time each week with English individuals, but this result varied by order. Of the New Order participants, 41 percent said that they had this much contact with the English, compared to only 21 percent of the Old Order members in our sample. Given the differences in lifestyles and language abilities between these groups, this finding was not very surprising. Moreover, many of these social connections are due to work activities and requirements.

However, very few in any church affiliation had many close relationships with English persons. Only about 10 percent said that one-third of their close relationships were with English individuals. When it comes to their children's contacts with English children, most Amish parents say it would be okay to play at an English child's house but not to have a "sleepover" there. While it may seem counterintuitive, it is especially New Order respondents in our study who appear to be hesitant for their children to cultivate close friendships with English children. However, this position is consistent with that group's deep personal conviction that they need to be directly involved in cultivating their children, as reflected in their greater tendency to homeschool their children.

The wish to remain separate or to establish only superficial or business relationships with outsiders is even greater when racial and ethnic minorities are considered. A 2007 Gallup Poll found that 77 percent of Americans felt that marriages between blacks and whites were okay.[7] In contrast and regardless of affiliation, nine out of ten Amish respondents in our survey said they would not admit a black, Hispanic, or Native American person into their families by marriage. A slightly smaller majority of all affiliations also responded that they would not accept these individuals into their social circles. The differences between the Amish and Americans in general might suggest that the Amish are more prejudiced, but this contrast should be interpreted very carefully, because the principal reason appears to lie elsewhere. A prominent local Amish leader told us that admission of outsiders into Amish families, regardless of their race, would be more likely if "they embraced the Amish faith." In other words, it is more likely the case that the Amish participants in our survey are responding to a desire for their children to marry others of their faith and tradition than that they simply desire to keep individuals of another race out of their families. A comment by one of our respondents further clarifies their position: "In our church fellowship there is an older girl who has adopted an African American boy. If he would grow up and be a faithful member of our church, I would feel he would be eligible to marry my daughter. Now if a Black would come from the outside and want to marry our daughter I would probably be against it. This would go for Hispanics or American Indians [too]. In our area I know of an Amish [who] married [a] Hispanic. My desire would be to see my children marrying faithful Christians in our church fellowship."

This argument indicates that the boundary defining kinship between insiders and outsiders is at least semipermeable. The responses also reflect a desire to keep intimate contact with the English world under control and to maintain an attitude of self-effacement and humility. On numerous occasions during our interviews with Amish men and women, respondents would comment offhandedly that they were "no better than anyone else" or that "they're human like everyone else," or that "they've got problems like everybody." Our survey showed that most would accept blacks, Hispanics, and Native Americans as neighbors and as partners at work. The roads along which Amish-English border clashes occur constitute "bridges" that connect the world outside with the world inside the Amish community. Each bridge is a "weak" tie or narrow road along which travel ideas and artifacts between the two worlds.[8] The road is often narrow or weak because the contacts between representatives of the two cultures are generally one-dimensional, limited in time, and not intimate in nature. It is along these border roads that contradictory pressures surface.

Terrains of Tension on the Border

Regardless of whether or not specific affiliations within the Amish community change or do not change in reaction to these pressures, the intersection of external and internal forces creates dilemmas for the persons who are affected. We call these dilemmas "terrains of tension." Three of the main areas of tension involve (a) conflicts between a community's cultural values and an individual's material interests, (b) control over the behavior of the individual by the community's structure versus control by the individual as the agent of his or her own actions, and (c) the security provided by the community versus the freedom desired by the individual.

As figure 8.1 suggests, because these dilemmas may call forth different responses by individuals, they encourage the development of multiple interpretations of tradition and corresponding variations in behavior. The ultimate result is a dynamic and diverse community.

In the first instance, a delicate dance takes place when the values of the community confront the interests of the individual. The potentially divisive effects of economic inequality and the occasional tense relationship between the individual and the community are tempered by rules that are designed to keep the individual in check. There are clear expecta-

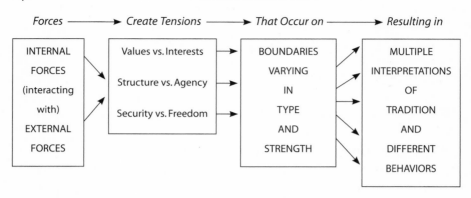

Fig. 8.1. Causes of diversity and change in Amish communities. Different kinds of boundaries with varying permeability and significance separate Amish and English society as well as Amish affiliations from each other. When these different groups come into contact because of the operation of external and internal forces, tensions can arise and border work has to be carried out to address these dilemmas. Courtesy of David McConnell.

tions about behavior and attitudes enunciated by church Ordnung and enforced by church leaders. To borrow a phrase from the social scientist Erving Goffman, the institution of the church creates a "mortification of the self" with the goal of producing a kind of individual who is respectful and hardworking and who humbles himself or herself before the community.[9] In the Amish crucible, individuals "make do" to adjust to pressures and difficulties. Some adjust well to the personal difficulties, while others may withdraw (for example, leave the Amish), rebel (i.e., create schisms), or negotiate or reinterpret their situation in a way that allows them to see it as acceptable or favorable (for example, interpreting some new technologies as consistent with traditional values).

The notion that the relationship between the Amish individual self and his or her community is, by definition, harmful, however, is misleading. Self and community are "twin born"; each grows and maintains its integrity by its connection to the other. Like others, Amish individuals gain their identities and selfhoods by their interaction with others, including those in the English community. To a large extent, who they are depends on how others have acted toward the Amish historically. The *Martyrs' Mirror* surveys a large part of that history. The lengthy text recalls the stories and final testimonies of Christians, largely Anabaptists, who lived

during the sixteenth and seventeenth centuries in Europe and who suffered and were martyred for their faith. The book also recounts the deaths
of earlier Christians, including the first apostles. As part of their past, that
history is also a part of who the Amish are; it is part of their identity.

Personalities are shaped when individuals are tested by outside pressures. That is, the self develops through the community; one's relationship to the community helps define who one is as an individual. Within
an Amish church, the Ordnung suggests how successful individuals are
to define their wealth and dispose of it in ways that make the use of "personal" wealth less selfish. In so doing, the church helps to shape who these
individuals become. The conflicts and pressures imposed on individuals
steel them and help them to grow. Within the Amish community, the interface of the individual and the community has been a locus for both constancy and change.

There has been a long-standing debate among social thinkers about the
relative importance of values versus interests as motivations for decisions
on how to behave. Like many either-or dichotomies, this one fails to accurately reflect the complexity of concrete decision-making. The Amish are
practical and grounded, but also idealistic and traditional. Consequently,
decisions on how to proceed with economic or other alternatives are informed by a mixture of cultural-religious (often communal) values and
material (often individual) interests. Although values and interests can
be compatible and serve each other, they can also be at odds, as in cases
where adherence to a community's values does not serve an individual's
immediate economic interests. The controversy over whether or not to
accept unemployment compensation is one illustration of this dilemma.
This is one terrain upon which external and internal forces collide.

The point on the continuum where the weight tips more heavily toward values or interests as a motivating force depends in part on the nature of the decision being considered. In some cases of economic exigency,
interests may be more important in making a decision than in decisions involving, for example, school curricula or types of family vacations. In most
cases, however, decisions incorporate a blend of motivations based on
values and interests. For example, in trying to adapt to outside economic
pressures, Amish farmers and manufacturers in the Holmes County Settlement have formed cooperative organizations among themselves to compete successfully with non-Amish groups. Amish *values* clearly encourage

cooperation among their own Amish brothers and sisters, while Amish *interests* invite the cooperation so that they can compete effectively.

Greater success in business can mean greater wealth for certain individuals and greater inequality in a community. The hierarchy of wealth and one's place in it is not a primary source of Amish diversity, but rather a product of the interaction of external and internal forces cited in our model. For example, whether or not a church Ordnung (an internal factor) allows certain technologies in response to an external force such as shifts in demand or a newly opened economic opportunity will have an influence on how prosperous an affiliation or a person will be. However, the resulting inequality, in turn, creates a potential seedbed for greater individualism and larger egos, both of which stand in stark contrast to the focus on community and the attitude of Gelassenheit strongly encouraged by the Amish. Like other dilemmas, this one calls attention again to the "crucible" nature of the Amish lifestyle.

The meeting of external and internal pressures takes place also on the terrain where the relative effect of a community's structure and the role of individual agency collide. The "structure" of a community, that is, its traditions, rules, and organization, places limits upon the freely chosen behaviors (the "agency") of its members. This fact is reflected in the kind of border work in which Amish engage. On the one hand, if the owner of a company decides to change by adopting a new technology or exploring a different market, he or she will encounter new elements within the English community. One New Order employer commented that while the style of work with the local Amish and English is "the same," "things change" when the firm branches out to work with English in larger cities in Ohio or surrounding states. Having to work with larger numbers of distant strangers, an employer may have to "change down the road" and hire sales representatives instead of relying on word of mouth for sales or adopt more formal and "stringent guidelines of what you are willing to [do] and what you're not willing to [do]." If, on the other hand, a group chooses not to change but to maintain tradition in response to pressure, they will likely have some change imposed upon them, if only to survive. This appears to be increasingly the case for the more traditional, conservative affiliations, such as the Swartzentrubers. As discussed earlier, many of those families have had to move because of their reluctance to adopt newer technologies or ways of living. Within the Andy Weaver group, there continue to be debates about the adoption of milking machines, which would open up another occupational outlet for them.

Each group provides a sense of security to its members, and the Amish community in general does the same. But to gain that security, one has to adhere to the rules of the community that often restrict and direct an individual's behavior. Consequently, in an objective sense, the individual's freedom becomes limited. But both freedom and security are generally considered desirable. The clash between the freedom of the individual and the security of the community constitutes a third terrain of tension. Freedom in choosing one's lifestyle is restricted if one wants to be a community member in good standing and retain the security that comes from being a part of the larger group. In this sense, the benefits of security may come at the expense of freedom. But as discussed in the next section, this dilemma can be and has been negotiated psychologically through creative interpretations of the meaning of *security* and *freedom*. For most churches, it has also been dealt with behaviorally by granting youth some freedoms through the loosening of restrictions to explore alternative lifestyles before joining the church, so that when they do join the church, they can benefit from the security that comes from being an effective participant in their community.

When faced by dilemmas on several terrains, the Amish have utilized both *interpretive* and *behavioral* techniques to address them. The economic example of market expansion presented above involves a behavioral response to pressures. One example of an interpretive response has been to reinterpret meanings of the terms associated with sources of tension in ways that blunt the stress created by the contradictions. In the dilemmas in which the individual and his or her interests are pitted against those of the community and its values, for example, issues of inequality versus equality arise. They are often dealt with by interpreting *equality* and related concepts in a particular manner. The concept of equality has an ambiguous meaning among the Amish. For example, although they believe that men should be the leaders in the family and the community, men are not supposed to be bosses, because all are considered equal in the eyes of God. When asked about the meaning of the term *equality* to them, Amish women in our interviews frequently asked, "What is that?" or said, "We don't dwell on it as a big deal." The term "doesn't come up in conversations" or was "puzzling" or "didn't make sense," or the term was "a real

hard one" for the respondents. The broad meanings and occasionally contested nature of terms like *equality, freedom, authority,* and *tradition* create
opportunities for variations in interpretations and flexibility in responses.
These, in turn, allow for negotiation and justification of practices.

In reacting to the stresses a group faces, the group may also reinterpret
tradition. Rather than acting against tradition by adopting something
new, or being seen as doing so, a group may redefine or broaden the meaning of tradition to allow incorporation of new elements; or it may focus on
aspects of tradition that its members consider more central to the culture
than others in order to justify change in a less important area. For example, emphasis on the spiritual rather than the material elements of tradition may allow a group such as the New Order to adopt some technologies
that another affiliation, such as the Andy Weaver or Old Order Amish,
would not accept because they believe in honoring the material tradition
at least as much as the spiritual. In education, members of the New Order
are much more likely than others to homeschool their children, because
they argue that, as parents, they are personally responsible for the spiritual enlightenment of their offspring. Old Order Amish are more likely
to stress the importance of the parochial school as a place where, together,
Amish children can learn the traditions of their culture. Homeschooling
would be considered by the Old Order an act of arrogance or individualism, characteristic of "uppity" persons.

As suggested by one Amish historian with whom we spoke, affiliations vary in the significance they place on different traditions. Concern
for maintaining spiritual values as manifested in concrete behavior has
created differences between the New Order and the more conservative
affiliations, for example. New Order members believe that the "rigors of
early pioneer life" led to compromises in the original Amish traditions.
The early Ordnungs Briefe (church disciplines) take a clear stand against
bundling and the use of tobacco and alcohol (except for medicinal purposes), and New Order leaders argue that this position should not change
over time. This historian felt that more conservative churches have lost
some of these traditions and consequently have "lost some of the original
Amish/Anabaptist vision." The New Order Amish consider other traditions listed in the Ordnungs Briefe to be more malleable and relative to
the times, and thus subject to potential change. These would include restrictions on the adornment of houses, styles of buggies, the use of mules,
and other indicators of separation from the outside world.

The division between material and spiritual aspects of tradition calls attention to the multidimensional nature of the contents of tradition and is a reminder that tradition, as in any culture, is not always internally consistent, nor are its individual traits always closely linked with each other. The more open its boundaries are to outside influences, the more the Amish community will have to negotiate and perhaps even redefine its tradition.

At the same time, Amish groups differ in how they experience tradition and modernity. Given variations in the geographic, economic, legal, and demographic contexts in which they must survive, the degree to which each affiliation's traditions are tested is also different. Some groups have to negotiate the meaning of tradition more often: the strains in surviving they experience because of the interaction of forces often appear as a clash between the traditions inside and the modernity outside the culture.

The Ties That Bind

As our discussion thus far has noted, the dynamism and diversity to be found within the Amish community are a function of the meeting of both internal and external forces along boundaries that trigger dilemmas that are then addressed by members and groups within the community. But despite the diversity, the Amish as a whole still maintain much in common and continue to remain somewhat separate from English society. Leaving behind the discussion of diversity, we turn now to some of the primary factors that create cohesion and commonality within the Amish community.

Comparisons between the Amish in our survey and Americans overall, in national surveys, suggest that the Amish feel much more connected to others than Americans in general do. They do not experience the levels of alienation found in national studies of adults. For example, in its 2007 national survey of Americans, the Harris Poll revealed that significant majorities of adults feel that (a) "the rich are getting richer and the poor get poorer," (b) "the people running the country don't really care what happens to you," (c) "most people with power try to take advantage of people like you," and (d) "what you think doesn't count very much any more." More than one-third of those respondents also believed that they were "left out of things going on around [them]."[10] When these questions were put to Amish respondents in our survey, the results were noticeably different. Less than one-quarter felt that people in power tried to take advantage of them or that what they thought didn't count. Less than one-tenth felt they were left out of things around them. Just over one-quarter felt that those running the country did not really care what happened to people. The only question in which a slight majority of Amish sensed some alienation concerned economic inequality. About half did feel that the rich were getting richer and the poor were getting poorer in the country as a whole. Another question asked in the national survey, one that was not part of the alienation measure, addressed the issue of whether politicians in Washington were out of touch with people around the country. Three-fourths said "yes." In contrast, only one out of ten in our Amish survey said that those in the local, state, and federal governments were out of touch with their constituencies. In sum, Amish in the Holmes County Settlement appear to be much less alienated than adults in the society as a whole. Table 8.2 summarizes these differences. Perhaps the lower sense of alienation felt by the Holmes County Amish is due in part to their culture and religion, which foster a perception of their lives as having a clear plan, direction, and meaning.

In a few cases, the particular affiliation to which the Amish person belongs appears to make a difference. Our Amish survey found, for example, that while only 14 percent of the Amish as a whole felt that Washington, DC, is out of touch with the rest of the country, 38 percent of the Old Order participants in our study expressed this feeling. (This finding should be interpreted cautiously because of the small size of our sample.) Members of the Old Order were also more likely to feel that their views didn't count much any more (one-third had this feeling), but still, that proportion was smaller than the majority who had this feeling in the national Harris study. Ironically, then, despite their separation from the rest of society, Amish in the Holmes County Settlement appear to be less alienated than the rest of the population.

However, the lack of alienation does not mean that the Amish believe there ought to be strong connections between themselves and the government. The Amish feel a clear obligation and devotion to their churches, but they do not generally feel that church and state ought to be closely linked. A full 80 percent said that the government and the church should have little or nothing to do with each other; 20 percent said that the two should interact frequently or be closely related to each other. Among these

Table 8.2. Levels of alienation in the nation and in
Holmes County Settlement, 2007

	National sample (%)	Holmes County Amish sample (%)
The rich get richer and the poor get poorer	73	51
Most people with power take advantage	57	16
People running the country don't care what happens to you	59	29
What you think doesn't count very much	55	22
You're left out of things going on around you	36	6

Sources: For national sample, Harris Poll #110, phone interviews conducted with 1,052 adults in October 2007. For Amish sample, a questionnaire survey of 65 Old and New Order Amish adults in the Holmes County Settlement, 2006–7.

respondents, New Order Amish were more likely than Old Order members to state that the two institutions should remain separate (32% versus 13%). In addition, there is not a majority belief that the government is obliged to help minorities like African Americans. Only 26 percent thought the government had this obligation, 40 percent disagreed, and the remaining 34 percent were split in their views. Affiliation of membership made no difference.

The lower levels of alienation among the Amish suggest that they feel more closely connected and trusting than does the general population. Several of our respondents, both Amish and non-Amish, indicated that in some situations the Amish are more gullible and perhaps too trusting of those outside their community. The high level of trust found within the Holmes County Settlement is rooted structurally in the multilevel network of social capital that has been built up in the broadly distinct community, and culturally in the biblically based and traditional belief systems. It is also maintained by the relative stability of the local population and the personal nature and small size of most local businesses.[11] The tight network of social ties consists of relationships that often cut across several institutions, including family, church, school, and work.

At the most basic level, sets of large interrelated kinship groups knit the community together. Individuals in these families often worship together or belong to the same affiliation, grow up and go to school together, and work with each other or for some other Amish employer. The predictable nature of these relationships is nurtured by adherence to a set of shared customs and religious beliefs. Broader cultural values inform the relationships that structure each of the institutions in which the Amish participate. In the parochial school, for example, "the ethos of the classroom accents cooperative activity, obedience, respect, diligence, kindness, and interest in the natural world. Little attention is given to independent thinking and critical analysis."[12]

One of the critical factors that distinguishes traditional from modern communities is the greater permeation of reflexivity in all kinds of behavior among groups of "modern" people, meaning that assessment of one's actions is constantly considered and reconsidered in light of new knowledge and has little to do with what was done in the past, that is, tradition. In Amish communities, by contrast, tradition permeates daily behavior, with reflexivity "still largely limited to the reinterpretation and clarification of tradition, such that in the scales of time the side of the 'past' is much more heavily weighed down than that of the 'future.' "[13]

While the weight and interpretations of tradition vary among the affiliations in the Holmes County Settlement, it is easy to see that the Amish social structure and cultural tradition are developing social beings who feel connected and responsible to others rather than persons who see themselves as isolated, self-sufficient individuals. Even during school recess, the emphasis is placed upon organized group activities, such as softball games involving both girls and boys. This pattern contrasts sharply with the individualized, free-for-all atmosphere that generally permeates outdoor recess activity at public schools. Repeated, regular involvement in group activities of this type reinforces one's belief in commitment to others as a member of a group rather than self-identification as an atomized, autonomous individual who stands apart from everyone else.

The depth at which this message permeates the Amish person is reflected in the meaning and interpretation they give to terms like *autonomy*. When asked in interviews, most Amish women interpreted autonomy as something negative, requiring decisions by oneself or ignoring ties to others. "I really wouldn't want to make my own decisions," said one woman. "I'd rather have someone give me advice," said another. "I don't think it would bring satisfaction to me," said a third participant. As a group, these women feel that "you need to be responsible to someone," that "you have to consider others first," and that they "wouldn't feel right to just live [their] own [lives]."

In essence, arrangements within the social structures of the Amish community are directly and clearly dependent upon important values in their culture, and both the arrangements and the values shape the kinds of individuals produced in the community. One consequence is a set of individuals who share a broadly similar existential and normative worldview. The worldviews held by individuals are "broadly similar" because, as we have mentioned elsewhere, there are variations in the specific interpretations of tradition and beliefs and, as a result, variations in the immediate structures and social relationships in which individuals are involved. The overall consequence is that, within affiliations, there is a dense social network held together by social relationships, mutual help, formal social gatherings, church rules, and a mostly common cultural heritage. Because of the variations between orders, the network of ties between affiliations tends to be looser and less dense.

Nolt and Meyers argue that, in addition to cultural and structural sources that encourage integration, the Amish community is also held together by ongoing conversations with the past, the outside world, and themselves.[14] These conversations shape, renew, and solidify the identities of individuals as members of a distinctive cultural group in society. Their continuing conversation across a variety of venues, even in the form of debate, also helps them to address difficulties of adaptation and the pressures to change that arise. The result is a reproduction of their community.

The intentional and highly organized structures within which Amish individuals grow and mature create a system of control over these individuals that could, under certain circumstances, foment resistance and rebellion on the part of youth and even adults. Like a security blanket, by encouraging loyalty, trust, and a sense of security, this system shelters the individual, but it can also suffocate his or her uniqueness and frustrate the freedom that he or she may seek. The question becomes, How does the Amish community keep its members and grow in the face of this dilemma? How do you keep them "home" when they have seen the temptations of the outside "world"? How do you keep a population "in line" when there are pressures all around to deviate from the narrow path prescribed for them?

Several specific devices and mechanisms are in place to promote appropriate behavior and allegiance of individuals within the Amish community.[15] Monitoring individuals to make sure that they are adhering to community expectations is one of the more informal techniques used. Various committees within the community regulate and advise on matters of safety, education, fire, and other issues. When Swartzentruber representatives find out about a church member's earnings and then instruct him about the proper usage of his wealth, they provide another example of monitoring. A third instance of informal monitoring was uncovered in a conversation with a young Amish mother who noted that her next-door neighbor, who is also Amish, watched her as she did her laundry to see at what time of the morning she hung her clothes outside. The respondent thought the neighbor was watching to measure the woman's work ethic. Hanging the clothes early was interpreted as an indication of a strong work ethic, while doing it later was seen as evidence of a weaker ethic. In a close-knit community, such monitoring provides an easy and accessible mechanism for enforcing community mores.

The dependence of individuals on each other within the Holmes County Settlement further cements ties within the community. Informally, this dependence takes the form of mutual help when a barn burns down or help is needed on the farm. More formal dependence is seen in the several plans that address medical and housing needs. Sanctions also serve as a means to control behavior. In an extreme case among some affiliations, sanction takes the form of shunning.

The use and effects of the mechanisms of monitoring, dependence, and sanctions generally differ among the affiliations, with their effects being greater in the more conservative churches. Within more "liberal" affiliations, such as the New New Order, external mechanisms of these types appear to be less heavily used. Rather, there seems to be more reliance on inner spiritual and mental containment to control behavior. The New Order churches have also created more outlets for their youth to "stretch their wings," releasing some of the pressure that expectations place upon their behavior. These outlets include youth sings, Sunday school, and social gatherings. The softer edges of these control mechanisms direct behavior in a desired direction without the harshness of more overt forms of control.

These numerous sources of control would seem to justify a view of the Amish, especially the more conservative groups among them, as a suppressed and oppressed people. An outsider may assume they have few choices and little freedom in their lives. But the meanings of *choice* and *freedom* have both subjective and objective dimensions. *Objectively*, one could argue that, indeed, Amish men and women are subject to rules and other constraints that limit their behavior. But it is another matter to consider how they experience and interpret their choices and freedom, how they view their situation *subjectively*. It is within the subjective realm that individuals can use their agency to interpret a structural fact in ways that allow comfort or complacency. Since ideas like security and freedom have both subjective and objective meanings, they can be a source of both diversity and cohesion. The position of Amish women provides a good example of how this interpretation works.

Frequently, outsiders view Amish women as being limited in their freedoms and choices. But our interviews with Amish women suggest that they do not see themselves as being either less free or as having fewer meaningful, desirable choices than English women. Almost all of the women we interviewed said that they had at least as much if not more freedom than English women, or that they had all the freedom they wanted. They have the same positive perspective on the choices that are available to them. They are content with the choices they have: "There may be fewer choices [than among English women]," replied one respondent, "but I don't want those choices." "I'm satisfied with what I have and am," said another.

The sense of direction and security that comes from life in the Holmes County Settlement serves as a moral anchor that encourages a particular slant on the meaning of choice and freedom. In the minds of these women, too many choices and too much freedom create confusion and a sense of dissatisfaction and unhappiness. "I think you'd be a lot more miserable actually [with more choices] because you couldn't decide what to do." When people "have so many choices, . . . [their] attention is diverted in so many ways, and it's harder to decide what to do." When it comes to choosing clothes and other material things, the Amish woman "doesn't have to be plagued with that, where that's a main thing in society today." In Alan Ehrenhalt's study of close-knit neighborhoods of the 1950s, he also notes the downside of too many choices: "The worship of choice has brought us a world of restless dissatisfaction, in which nothing we choose seems good enough to be permanent and we are unable to resist the endless pursuit of new selections—in work, in marriage, in front of the television set."[16]

Although there are many differences and potential sources for division among the Amish, being mindful of others, helping those in need, and serving the community are enduring values within the community. Photograph by Doyle Yoder.

The reaction of Amish to their freedom is similar. Like choice, freedom takes on a different meaning in the Amish context. One Amish woman, when asked about the extent of her freedom, responded: "It depends on what you call 'freedom.'" Another replied: "We have just as much freedom, but in a different way." It is a freedom from concerns that still plague English women: "Our freedom is feeling at peace or a happy home . . . We have some freedom from the cares that they [English women] have, and the pressures and everything." "I don't have to worry about any income, or my husband leaving me. I can do whatever I want to; maybe I just don't want to do as much as she wants to do." "[I'm] not a slave to a job like English women." As in the case of choice, too much freedom has its disadvantages: "You probably get more in trouble . . . there's more temptation out there." Constraints on choices and limits on freedom have their benefits, whereas English women "always want more; there's no end to it. The more they have, the more they want." The contentment that seems to characterize life for many Amish is founded in the constraints, meanings, and direction created by their tight relationships and cultural heritage. These features allow an interpretation of freedom and choice that does not threaten cohesion within or separation from their community. Thus they help keep the Holmes County Settlement alive and encourage its growth.

The generally close-knit system of social capital inside the Holmes settlement contrasts sharply with the much looser and superficial set of ties its members have with individuals and groups outside the Amish community. As noted above, this difference is reflected in their feelings about outsiders and the ideal relationships between their own community and institutions like the government. Nevertheless, the ties that are forged with outside elements can also help to maintain the integrity of the Amish community. As we've seen, Amish individuals in the Holmes County Settlement are often tied to English outsiders in multiple ways—through their employment, business contacts, medical needs, technological changes, educational experiences, and legal requirements. While these ties can always potentially introduce novel elements that could undermine Amish tradition, they also serve to help the Holmes County Settlement adapt and survive. In their reading of and experience with the wider economy, for example, the Holmes County Amish have been able to identify and carve out economic niches that have allowed them to prosper. In this way, like the many internal mechanisms we have discussed, outside ties help to reproduce the Amish community over generations.

What the Future Holds and What We Can Learn

How will the next generation in the Holmes County Settlement adapt to change and yet remain Amish at their core? How can Amish culture reproduce itself in the face of unrelenting pressures to change? What does the future hold for this community? We recall a concern about the next generation expressed by an Old Order businessman who worried that the new generation of Amish youth may not have the same work ethic as the present generation of adults and that, as they move out of farming into employment positions with English and Amish companies, they might become too dependent upon their employers to support them. Their sense of self-reliance may become weaker. These concerns are similar to worries that have been harbored by many English parents. Older generations frequently decry the alleged bad habits and lack of grit shown by their youth. As such, this is not an unusual complaint.

But as the Amish have already shown themselves adaptive to the challenges they have confronted, it should be expected that they will find ways to guide their youth into activities and areas that will ensure the reproduction of the Holmes County Amish community. Such guidance is already evident in the organized meetings and workshops in which their youth are involved. It is also found in the kinds of jobs that have been encouraged when the possibility of full-time farming has become more remote. While farming involves directly working with nature and its foibles and has historically occupied a central place in the Amish identity, it is not the only occupation that taps central values in the Amish culture. Engagement in manual labor for the production of goods that have widespread value to the community can still occur in other occupations. Furniture, housing, machines, buggies, clothing, and other products all address fundamental needs. Their production often involves the apprenticing of young workers who are trained by older Amish workers in traditional skills. This on-the-job education allows members of the present generation to pass on not only specific job skills but Amish work habits and attitudes as well. In this way, nonfarm work experiences can contribute to the maintenance of Amish culture.

There are some clouds on the economic horizon for the Amish, how-ever. As for many others, the 2008–9 downturn in the national economy created serious stress for many Amish. In the area around Elkhart County, Indiana, for example, where 60 percent of the country's recreational ve-hicles are manufactured, unemployment rates soared to 20 percent in mid-2009. More than half of the area Amish worked in factories, and so many became unemployed. In the absence of immediate job alterna-tives, pressure grew among the most destitute to accept government aid in the form of unemployment compensation. Some bishops have reluctantly granted permission for especially hard-hit church members to accept this aid. Strong traditions have been severely tested in the face of economic exigency.[17]

A significant part of the reason for this problem is that employment is so concentrated within a small range of industries among the Elkhart-LaGrange Amish. According to an economic leader in the Holmes County Amish community, employment in the Holmes County Settlement is more widely distributed than it is in the Elkhart-LaGrange Amish com-munity. He estimates that only about 30 percent in the Holmes settlement work for English employers, who are more likely than Amish employ-ers to lay off workers. In general, Amish employers feel an obligation not to lay off workers but to share the burdens imposed by tough economic times. More than half of Amish workers are self-employed, for example, in carpentry crews.

One test of the cultural strength and integrity of a community and its members is their reaction to adversity. Amish employees in the Holmes County Settlement have been affected by recent economic problems, with some having their hours reduced and others having to shift from a five-day to a four-day work week. But rather than viewing this predic-ament as wholly negative, some have seen it as an opportunity to work more on their own homes, because prices for many building materials and services are down. The greater self-sufficiency, ingenuity, and group sup-port found among the Amish provides them with resources not as readily found among many English who are left unemployed or underemployed. Ingenuity in job creation, a strong work ethic, and community support will very likely help the Holmes County Amish culture maintain its re-silience.

Economic developments within the Holmes County Settlement also encourage its continuance in some ways while endangering traditional family arrangements in others. Some Amish businesses are actively seeking broader markets through advertising and word of mouth. Broader markets generally mean a more heterogeneous mixture of customers and partners, which in turn necessitate creativity to make such relationships viable. One especially intriguing relationship is the one between the Amish and the Japanese. Both groups prize quality, efficiency, and work commitment. Both seek to eliminate or at least minimize waste in their enterprises. Consequently, both can benefit from their relationship. At least one Amish owner of a large company has visited the Toyota plant in Kentucky to study Japanese manufacturing techniques and methods. Blending the best of both approaches may yield a business model from which English businesses might learn.

The ascetic concern among the Amish for eliminating waste and seeking efficiency extends beyond business to the health field. The Amish actively search for the most cost-effective care, and they are careful not to overdo their use of health care services. This approach can have an obvious downside, but it is a lesson for those English who abuse the use of drugs such as antibiotics and for those who are trying to make the health care system more efficient and effective.

As more Amish men and their children become employed by businesses away from their homes, relationships within their families may become further altered. The distinction between public work and private home spheres may become more accentuated, making the Amish married woman into more of a traditional housewife, one whose life experiences become increasingly different from those of her husband. Historically, this model has been more characteristic of white English families, especially during the 1940s and 1950s, than of Amish families. The tight relationships that exist within the Amish family may become looser if this trend continues.

Although Amish men are less likely than in the past to be farmers, it has been suggested that there is a farming resurgence in the Holmes County Settlement. Organic farming has gained momentum, fed by a desire on the part of many Amish to return more fully to their agricultural roots and by the demand for food that is naturally grown or bred. The theme of working with rather than against nature is found as well in the increased use among the Amish of solar, wind, and similar natural sources of energy.

While they are often thought of as less progressive than their English neighbors, the Amish are national leaders in this area. Traditional peoples are generally thought of as dependent upon nature, subject to the whims of weather and soil conditions, whereas modern individuals are generally seen as independent, "controllers of" rather than "subject to" the forces of nature. But considering the mounting problems of climate change and environmental degradation, one can reasonably ask which approach is the most enlightened. The traditional perspective of the Amish may very well be the most forward-thinking.

Environmental problems are only one of the pressing issues our society faces today. Effective solutions to these and other problems are stalled because of deep suspicions, distrust, and mocking cynicism that bedevil many of our relationships. Evidence from national surveys suggests that Americans' confidence in their institutions has declined since the 1970s, and at least half believe that other people cannot be trusted.[18] This finding is discouraging, because institutions are often a major mechanism through which significant social problems are addressed. Weakened institutions mean weaker attempts to resolve social issues. Ironically, trust has declined at precisely a time when it is most needed. In a "risk society," when problems spill across local and national borders because of globalization and advanced technologies, trust becomes an increasingly crucial requirement for the smooth operation of social relationships.[19]

Why is trust lower in some groups than in others? What fosters higher levels of trust? Research suggests that individuals who are in more secure socioeconomic positions are more trusting.[20] This group would include white people, as opposed to members of racial or ethnic minorities, and persons with higher incomes who are married, older, and living in a rural area. Surrounding conditions that appear to decrease trust are increased numbers of scandals involving corruption, lies, or similar crimes by political or economic leaders. In other words, individuals are more comfortable who live in groups that are better off and are prospering within the structure and culture of our current society. Clearly, those who benefit from current arrangements or are isolated from many contemporary social problems might be expected to have more optimistic outlooks.

As we found in our survey, Amish individuals also tend to be less cynical or negative in their outlooks; interestingly, and perhaps coincidentally, they also happen to fall into many of the categories that characterize those who are most trusting. That is, most tend to be economically secure and married, and they live in rural areas and are usually white. Moreover, being less dependent than most English on national institutions, they are relatively insulated from the corrosive effects of political and economic scandals.

But these socioeconomic features are not the main wellsprings of their trust in others. In large part, trust is built on the experience of one's interactions with others, and in their tight social networks, interaction among the Amish is frequent and often deep and multifaceted. Repeated interactions in social networks provide knowledge of others, whom they can trust or distrust. In addition, trust is fostered by knowledge of and respect for the assumed character of the individuals with whom one is interacting. It is further heightened if there are fundamental similarities in backgrounds and values between the acting parties. All these elements of the trust-building process are found among the Amish. It is a combination of their identification with the similar elements within their history, strong Christian faith, and the broadly predictable behavior that flows from them that nurtures Amish trust in others. These components have also allowed them to forge the tight social networks within which trust and trustworthiness can grow. Trust, in turn, encourages a civic culture, one in which everyone works to the benefit of everyone else and a greater good.

Trust solely within tight social networks like those found among the Amish can foster extreme insularity, however, and can discourage trust across cultural and social boundaries and between social groups. Encouraging everyone to be the same to create more widespread trust would be a dangerous path to follow. Both the community and individuality need to be considered; that is, there needs to be tolerance of diversity. Diverse communication devices appear to be one way to draw on the strengths of both community and individuality.

Within the Amish community, communication between diverse affiliations and churches has been strengthened by a variety of informal and semiformal structural arrangements that continuously bring diverse parties together. Included are everything from widely distributed public letters in the *Budget* and *Die Botschaft* to weddings and funerals, communal work projects, committees, auctions, and mission activities. These various forms of communication knit the community together despite its diversity. As we have seen, the Amish have also built ties across their boundaries with the English. Granted, U.S. society contains much greater diversity than is found within the Holmes County Settlement. But too often the structures of communication lie almost solely within rather than between groups. The Amish example poses the dilemma of how to create and maintain a cohesive society in the midst of diversity. One place to start in the broader society is to address the issue of how to build communication bridges across diverse groups as a means to break down unwarranted stereotypes and increase understanding. The Amish remind us that diversity does not need to result in social isolation for some groups, weak social networks, or a disintegration of trust.

At the same time, the Amish wrestle with many of the same dilemmas that the rest of society faces. For example, despite the generally close-knit nature of relationships within the Holmes County Settlement, which promotes identification with the Amish community, some trends appear to encourage individualistic tendencies. Among them are increased numbers of entrepreneurships, a greater probability of working away from home, increased discrepancies in wealth and education, and the continuing fission of Amish churches. There is an increasing tension between centripetal and centrifugal forces, and therefore between the impulses to put one member of the pairs community or the individual, values or interests, and security or freedom ahead of the other. These conflicts are not unlike those found in the larger society today. The Amish have proved to be adept at balancing these oppositions within their communities. Working through the community to reach goals that are individual in nature suggests that conflicts can be meaningfully resolved, benefiting both the community and the individual. In contrast, the English appear to have become more individualistic, pitting their own goals against those of others and emphasizing their own rights and individual careers over their obligations and responsibilities to others. Perhaps the modern English society that venerates the individual so highly needs to consider more carefully what can be learned from this more traditional society to maintain a sense of community and trust.

Methodology

We used a variety of specific research techniques and samples in seeking understanding of the local Amish community. Here we briefly describe our use of four primary methods: interviews, surveys, observation, and document analysis.

Interviews

During the seven-year period 2001–8, we interviewed almost two hundred individuals for various parts of our study. Interviews were held with representatives of all the major Amish affiliations and covered all the topics discussed in the book. Some of the participants served as key informants on several areas, while others were interviewed for their responses concerning single, narrow topics. Since, for given issues, we wanted both insider and outsider perspectives, we included Amish and non-Amish as well as male and female and professional and nonprofessional respondents. Within the Amish community, our reception and access varied somewhat by affiliation, as might have been expected, given the clear differences in openness to the outside world that exist between orders among the Amish. At one extreme were our attempts to talk with Swartzentruber representatives. We once received permission for an interview with a group of Swartzentruber church leaders, only to have it rescinded and then granted again. But even though the interview was granted, and ten leaders were present, almost all responses came from one Swartzentruber bishop, an obvious leader and spokesperson in his community. Access to the Andy Weaver churches was better but still difficult. Asked about the possibility of an interview with his family, one Andy Weaver man who had asked his family about the request said that his son had blurted out: "An interview? Who does he think I am, Omar Vizquel [a former Cleveland Indians shortshop]?" Over time, however, we were able to meet and talk with more than two dozen individuals from the Swartzentruber and Andy Weaver affiliations. By contrast, the Old Order participants were typically amenable to talking and sometimes to having their conversations tape-recorded. The New Order representatives were most accommodating of all; we even hired two of them as research assistants. And they had few qualms about being tape-recorded if we assured anonymity.

Virtually all of the interviews were conducted in the respondents' homes or business offices, but in a few cases interviews were held in other locations where the participants felt comfortable, such as restaurants. We took care in how we dressed and presented ourselves and always gave respondents the option to not have the interviewed taped. In most cases, individuals expressed willingness to have their responses taped. All the interviews were conducted in English, since neither of the authors speaks Pennsylvania Dutch. While this lack of fluency limited our ability to understand conversations among the Amish themselves, we were able to discuss all topics in depth and in detail in English, because the Amish are functionally bilingual. Interviews generally lasted one to two hours, with a few going over two hours.

Interviews with Amish key informants were used throughout the study. Our sometimes multiple interviews with them usually covered a wide range of topics. We met with most of the central Amish spokespersons and powerbrokers in the Holmes County Settlement, including at least one member of nearly all the major Amish committees (education, safety, helping fund, steering committee, mental health, missions, hospital aid, and workers' aid). Some informants were well-known as leaders in their fields, for example, business and organic farming. We also met with Amish who were board members of birthing centers and business associations, and bishops and ministers of their churches. Often, key informants were able to fill in gaps in our knowledge of local history or provide us with specific details of events or situations of interest. It was not unusual for these informants to ask to see our written drafts, and we were eager to oblige their requests because we wanted to present as complete and accurate a portrait of the Holmes County Settlement as possible. Copies of survey results, papers, full chapters, and excerpts were forwarded to them for their perusal. In several instances, these readers suggested changes in specific words to capture the right nuances and meanings, while in other cases, they pointed out factual errors or added interesting examples and insights.

In addition to the broad use of key informants, we interviewed samples of individuals for specific areas of our study. For the education chapter, we interviewed eight bishops and ministers, twelve parochial school teachers, six teachers and administrators in public schools that cater to the Amish, and the director of the local Adult Basic Literacy Education Program. Since we were interested in parental perspectives on the schools their children attended, we also interviewed parents in forty families, representing a range of occupations, church affiliations, and socioeconomic levels. The latter were procured using a snowball sample technique.

To increase our understanding of the perspectives of Amish women, we systematically canvassed thirty Amish women to solicit their descriptions of gender roles and the relationships that exist between their spouses and themselves, as well as their perception of the ideal marital relationship. To gain access to these women, we followed the advice of an Amish friend who suggested we first interview one or two wives of Amish men we knew. From these women we were able to obtain additional names of women who might be receptive to being interviewed. When asking for potential respondents, we stressed that we wanted to interview a broad range of persons who might have varying opinions, that is, that we sought a representative sample. To help ensure representativeness, we also had two non-Amish female counselors who work with the Amish and two Amish friends confirm that our sample mirrored the broader Amish population in the settlement. The final interview sample of 30 women included 16 Old Order, 11 New Order, 2 Andy Weaver, and 1 Swartzentruber, representing nineteen different church districts. All but one of these women were married. The married women differed in the number of children they had, ranging from 0 to 14. They ranged in age from 27 to 70, the average age being just under 46.

We also interviewed ten individuals who had left their Amish communities. As in other cases, the names were most often obtained by suggestions from others we had met at a Former Amish Reunion (FAR) or elsewhere. They included men and women ranging in age from the early 20s to the mid-60s, and from both Old Order and Swartzentruber communities. As in all the interviews, we explained who we were and what the purposes of our study were, and assured them that their responses would be kept confidential and anonymous. We also explained what would be done with the data we collected. These measures were especially important because of the potential personal repercussions to participants if their names were made public.

In addition to the Amish and formerly Amish persons we interviewed, we spoke with many English individuals who work with or have served the Amish in some way. Some of these were from the business community (e.g., partners with Amish, business owners, real estate agents, and tourist operators), while others represented local government in some capacity (e.g., chamber of commerce employees, law enforcement officials, and a director of job and family services) or worked in nongovernmental groups like the Christian Aid Ministries or Mennonite Central Committee. Agricultural extension agents and the director of the Ohio Agricultural Research and Development Center Sugarcreek Watershed Project were also interviewed. Additional participants included specialized professionals and educational administrators. For example, for our analysis of health care, we sought out medical professionals in the Holmes and Wayne County area who had regularly served all kinds of Amish in the settlement for a long time, often several decades. Included were physicians (both D.O.'s and M.D.'s), nurse practitioners, registered nurses, midwives with varying levels of professional training, chiropractors, psychologists, and counselors. Hospice workers and funeral directors were also interviewed. School principals and administrators of vocational training programs were included to provide information for the education chapter.

One of the valuable benefits of conducting in-depth interviews is the findings that come indirectly from the demeanor and manner of speech of participants, and the general context in which interviews occur. In our interviews, sometimes nearly as revealing as the *content* of the responses were the *form* and *context* in which answers were presented. For example, in our interviews on gender roles, New Order women were more talkative and articulate than women from more conservative churches, who sometimes had more difficulty with the English language and occasionally consulted their husbands about how to say something. Another form that was noted was the frequent use by many participants of the third person when speaking, rather than use of the first person, which would draw attention to themselves. For example, instead of saying "when I come home," the respondent might say "when mother comes home," referring to herself. The context of the interviews was often suggestive of the centrality of family in Amish life. While in many cases, children were present at the kitchen table when we were interviewing, they were always quiet and never seemed to annoy the mother. Occasionally, the husband was also present, but he never dominated or overrode responses by the wife. Without exception, their demeanor suggested a marriage founded on companionship and partnership. Finally, the quiet, slower-paced, relaxed atmosphere of the homes was palpable, conveying a family-centered, home-oriented ambience.

Surveys

Two basic surveys were used to collect data, one given to members of five Amish church districts and another sent to members of a group of individuals who had left the Amish. The first questionnaire was completed by a total of sixty-five Amish members of three Old Order and two New Order Amish churches. The questionnaires were sent to the bishop of each church, who then distributed them to church members. Each member who completed the survey placed it in a separate envelope that was then sealed and returned to the bishop. When all the questionnaires had been submitted, the bishop mailed them to us. A general set of the statistical results was sent to each church that had participated. A profile of the survey sample is provided in table A.1.

The questions in the survey were arranged into several subsets, including several on each of the following topics: leisure activities, media exposure, health care, technology, work-related issues, government, education, rumspringa, family, and Amish-English relationships. A set of demographic questions was also included.

Table A.1. Demographic profile of the church member sample

Age	
Range	23–87
Median age	43
Sex (%)	
Male	82
Female	18
Marital status (%)	
Married	88
Other	12
Male occupation (active or retired) (%)	
Farming	16
Nonfarming	84
Family income	
Range	< $15,000 to > $90,000
Modal income	$31,000–$45,000

Source: Holmes County Settlement survey of Old Order and New Order members, N = 65.

The data from the surveys were analyzed using the Statistical Package for the Social Sciences (SPSS) software program.

The second survey was sent to members of the Former Amish Reunion, a group formed by two persons in Shreve, Ohio, about ten years ago to provide support for individuals who had left their Amish communities. Currently, the mailing list includes more than two hundred individuals from several states and Amish orders who left the Amish either after formally joining the church or without joining. Questionnaires were sent to everyone on the FAR list. Since the final sample for our survey was derived from the master member list kept by the original organizers of FAR, it may not be fully representative of individuals who have left the Amish community. Rather, the list may overrepresent joiners of organizations, those who otherwise have weak social-support networks, or those who have continuing adjustment problems. This population may also be skewed toward persons with a "chip on their shoulder." (This is the view of one former Amish woman who says she has never been invited to FAR and that the group is very negative toward the Amish.) The group may also overrepresent persons who left the Amish for religious reasons, because the FAR organizers are "born again Christians" and the re-unions have sometimes affiliated themselves with evangelical churches and with Joe Keim's Mission to Amish People. So while FAR served as an available means by which to reach a large number of formerly Amish people, the reader should keep in mind that its membership may not represent the entire spectrum of individuals who have left the Amish fold. See table A.2 for a demographic profile of the FAR sample.

Of the 200 questionnaires mailed to this group, approximately 25 percent (49) were completed and returned. A large number of unopened envelopes were re-turned to us because the persons were no longer at the addresses we used, for one reason or another. The small size of our sample does not allow us to answer certain questions, for example, whether Amish from particular affiliations are more likely than others to leave the community. In spite of the limitations of the sample, the survey provided many insights into the varied motivations and experiences of the ex-Amish.

The survey itself consisted of questions covering four main topics: (1) member-ship status when leaving the Amish community and reasons for leaving; (2) reac-tions of family and the Amish church to their leaving; (3) degree of adjustment to post-Amish life and reflections on Amish society; and (4) socio-demographic in-formation on the respondents. As with the survey discussed earlier, data were ana-lyzed using SPSS software.

Observation

Even before formally beginning our study of the Holmes County Settlement, we had occasion to observe Amish families and leaders in operation. In the mid-1990s, Chuck Hurst had served as a consultant for an engineering firm and conducted in-terviews with Amish leaders whose farms and families could be affected by a high-way bypass that was being designed by engineers. David McConnell had had many long conversations with fellow birders in the Amish community; he also has had an abiding interest in Amish schools. In addition, both of us helped Ervin Gingerich distribute forms used in the 1996 and 2005 editions of the *Ohio Amish Directory* to church representatives.

The number and variety of our observations increased as we became more fully involved in our research. We visited at least a dozen Amish parochial schools when they were in session and were able to see different classes and lessons in action. We experienced how male and female teachers and students interacted in this setting and were given time after class to talk with the teachers. We also visited several public elementary schools that cater to Amish students and spoke with their Eng-lish principals. The school observations complemented the interviews and ques-tionnaires we used, so that we could investigate "flows of practice" in diverse edu-

Table A.2. Demographic profile of the Former Amish Reunion sample

Affiliation (%)	
New Order	10
Old Order	76
Andy Weaver	8
Swartzentruber	4
Other	2
Age	
Range	27–76
Mean age	50
Sex (%)	
Male	46
Female	54
Marital status (%)	
Married	79
Divorced/separated	13
Other	8
Education (%)	
8th grade or less	50
GED	25
College degree	8
Other	17
Standard of living now compared to when growing up (%)	
Lower	6
Same	37
Higher	57

Source: Survey of Former Amish Reunion (FAR) Members. $N = 49$.

cational settings.[1] We were able to look "from the families to the school" as well as to work "within the school and [look] from the school outward."[2]

To gain a broader perspective on Amish lifestyles, we also attended church services and went to a wedding, a Christmas play, and a quilting bee. Attending the Haiti Benefit Auction, held yearly, allowed us to examine a wide selection of Amish products, ranging from furniture to buggies. We visited at least a dozen Amish-owned businesses, including those that deal in lumber, farm equipment, woodworking, quilts, furniture, greenhouses, and bulk foods.

Documents

A final source for our data consisted of various publications that serve as windows into Amish culture. Historical documents were available from the Heritage Historical Library in Aylmer, Ontario, Canada, which, with the kind permission of David Luthy, we visited a few years ago, and from the Ohio Amish Library in Berlin, Ohio, administered by Ed Kline, which we visited on several occasions. These libraries gave us access to materials on the roles of women, the activities of the Old Order Steering Committee, and church schisms in the settlement.

Content analyses of representative textbooks in mathematics, health, history, and geography, as well as story books used by Amish teachers and analyses of the *Blackboard Bulletin* (a newsletter for Amish teachers published by Pathway Publishers in Ontario) helped us identify central themes, subjects, and values focused upon in Amish classrooms. *Family Life*, another Pathway publication, provided an additional source for uncovering Amish attitudes about gender roles and family values. The local Amish newsletter, the *Budget*, was used to analyze the content of advertisements of products, such as medical goods, whose market is the Amish community. In addition, a miscellaneous group of newsletters and pamphlets published for the Amish by the Amish on mental health, hospital aid, business listings, and education were used as data sources for particular chapters.

Systematic random samples from the 1996 and 2005 editions of the *Ohio Amish Directory* were used to detect shifts in occupational structure and examine the relationship between occupation and family size on the one hand and occupation and retention on the other. We were interested in overall results on each of these for the Holmes County Settlement as a whole and for each affiliation. The *Directory* allowed us to uncover similarities and differences among the different orders.

Ohio Amish Settlements, 2008

Settlement	Counties	Founded	Districts	Affiliations
Adamsville	Muskingum	1997	1	Tobe
Andover	Ashtabula	1992	1	Nebraska
Ashland-Shiloh	Ashland, Richland	1954	7	Ashland
Barnesville	Belmont	1993	2	Swartzentruber
Beallsville	Monroe	2007	1	Old Order
Beaver	Pike	1994	1	Old Order (Renno)
Belle Center	Logan	1974	3	New Order
Bergholz	Jefferson	1995	1	Sam Mullet
Bremen	Fairfield	1989	1	Kenton
Brinkhaven-Danville	Knox	1990	4	Andy Weaver
Carrollton	Carroll	1981	2	Old Order
Chesterhill-Stockport	Morgan	1978	1	Kenton
Danville-Butler	Knox	1964	4	Tobe, New Order
De Graff	Logan	1994	2	Swiss
Dorsett–Cherry Valley	Ashtabula	1991	1	Old Order
Frazeyburg	Muskingum	2007	1	Old Order
Fredericktown-Bellville	Knox, Richland	1972	8	Andy Weaver
Gallipolis	Gallia	1993	4	Andy Weaver
Geauga	Geauga, Trumbull	1886	85	Old Order
Glenford-Somerset	Perry	2006	1	Kenton
Glenmont-Brinkhaven	Holmes, Knox	1994	2	Old Order
Hicksville	Defiance	1914	1	Old Order
Hillsboro-Leesburg	Highland	2006	1	Ashland

Settlement	Counties	Founded	Districts	Affiliations
Holmes	7 counties	1808	221	11 affiliations
Howard-East Knox	Knox	2000	2	Andy Weaver
Kenton—Mt. Victory	Hardin	1953	7	Kenton
Kilgore	Carroll	2005	1	Old Order
Kinsman	Trumbull	1975	1	New Order
Lakeville—Big Prairie	Holmes	1962	3	Andy Weaver
Laurelville	Hocking, Pickaway	1988	1	Andy Weaver
Lewisville	Monroe	1987	4	Old Order
Lodi-Homerville	Medina, Ashland	1952	14	Swartzentruber
Londonderry	Guernsey	2007	1	Old Order
Loudenville-McKay	Ashland	1991	1	Old Order
Martinsburg-Utica	Knox	1987	3	Swartzentruber
McArthur	Vinton	2003	1	Kenton
Middlebourne	Guernsey	1998	1	Swartzentruber
Oak Hill	Jackson	2001	2	Andy Weaver
Peebles	Adams	2006	1	Swartzentruber
Peoli—Port Washington	Tuscarawas	1969	2	Swartzentruber
Piedmont	Harrison	2001	1	Andy Weaver
Pierpont-Conneaut	Ashtabula	1994	4	Stutzman-Troyer
Plain City	Madison	1896	1	New Order
Pomeroy	Meigs	2006	1	Swartzentruber
Salesville—Quaker City	Guernsey	1991	2	Old Order
Scio	Harrison	2001	1	Old Order, Andy Weaver
Vinton	Gallia	2004	1	Ashland
Walhonding-Warsaw	Coshocton	1990	1	New New Order
West Union—Winchester	Adams	1976	4	Old Order
Williamsfield	Ashtabula	1997	1	Stutzman-Troyer

Sources: Luthy, "Amish Settlements across America"; Stephen Scott, Research Associate, Young Center for Anabaptist and Pietist Studies, Elizabethtown College, Elizabethtown, PA; local Amish historians.

Holmes County Settlement
Amish Church Schisms, 1900–2001

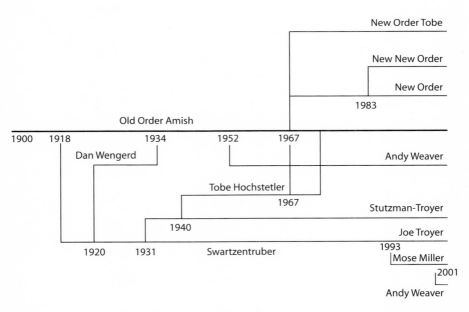

New Order Tobe

New New Order

New Order

1983

Old Order Amish

| 1900 | 1918 | 1934 | 1952 | 1967 |

Dan Wengerd

Andy Weaver

Tobe Hochstetler

1967

Stutzman-Troyer

1940

Joe Troyer

1993

1920   1931   Swartzentruber   Mose Miller

2001

Andy Weaver

Source: Adapted from *Ohio Amish Directory: Holmes County and Vicinity* (Sugarcreek, OH: Carlisle, 1996). Courtesy of Mary Schantz.

Notes

Preface

1. Olshan, "The Opening of Amish Society," 383.
2. All Bible verses quoted in the book are from the King James Version.
3. Comaroff and Comaroff, *Of Revelation and Revolution*, xi–xii.

Chapter 1. Discovering the Holmes County Amish

1. Information on the size and value of the farms comes from the Wayne County Web site, www.waynecountyauditor.org.

2. See Christine Pratt, "Witnesses Recount Night of Cornfield Shooting," *Wooster (Ohio) Daily Record*, March 4, 2004.

3. Yoder was never prosecuted, because the judge in Millersburg said the case would have to be retried in the same county in which it was declared a mistrial, and the original witnesses could not be rounded up. Yoder was temporarily excommunicated by his church district as a punishment but was reinstated based on his confession and apology.

4. In the early nineteenth century, dressing in white, not black, was considered an expression of conservatism, because white more closely resembled the color of natural flax without any dyes. Stutzman's views were considered strange by most Amish, however.

5. Although Mount Hope is an "Amish hub," it is less popular among tourists than Walnut Creek and Berlin, which present an architectural style and "cultural memory" more consistent with tourists' expectations of the Amish as relics from a bygone era. See Biesecker, "Heritage versus History," 122–23.

6. Kraybill and Nolt, *Amish Enterprise*, vii.

7. Kraybill and Nolt, ibid., 22, refer to this set of circumstances as the "demographic squeeze." External forces such as land scarcity, rising land prices, urbaniza-

tion, and tourism combined with internal factors such as high birth and retention rates and attachment to the region to create the need for a solution such as micro-enterprises.

8. Ericksen, Ericksen, and Hostetler, "The Cultivation of the Soil," 50.

9. Kraybill and Nolt use the phrase "from plows to profits" as the subtitle of their book *Amish Enterprise*, which describes the transition away from farming among the Amish.

10. Kraybill and Nolt, *Amish Enterprise*, 191.

11. Greksa and Korbin, "Key Decisions," 388−89.

12. Olshan argues that home businesses expose Amish children and parents to non-Amish strangers with increasing frequency because the "open" or "for sale" sign invites the outsider into a "state of talk" with the Amish seller. Using Erving Goffman's work on "interaction ritual" to describe the difference between an Amish farmer, who was free to remain aloof, indifferent, or contemptuous toward the outside world, and an Amish shop owner, whose "open" sign represents an implicit invitation to enter the Amish world, he concludes that the result of this loss of institutionalized avoidance is that the Amish man must have "a greater concern with how to manage a more or less constant interfacing with the public" ("The Opening of Amish Society," 381).

13. Kraybill and Nolt, for instance, seem somewhat less skeptical than Olshan about the negative influence of micro-enterprises, which they describe as "an ingenious negotiation with modernity" (*Amish Enterprise*, 34).

14. As just one example, Donnermeyer and Cooksey argue that "today, the distance between the Amish and mainstream North American society is much greater [than in the past]" ("Demographic Foundations," 12). In contrast, Stambach sees a rapidly increasing "slippage of non-Amish practices into what has become Amish custom" ("The Silence Is Getting Louder," 39).

15. Kraybill and Nolt, *Amish Enterprise*, x.

16. In *Plain Diversity*, Nolt and Meyers offer a similar account of increasing diversification among the Indiana Amish.

17. Kraybill notes that "there have been surprisingly few studies conducted on the Holmes County Settlement" ("Plotting Social Change," 264n3). His 1994 article is still the best social scientific account of the Holmes County Settlement. Donnermeyer and colleagues have also published several papers from an analysis of the *Ohio Amish Directory*. *A Quiet Moment in Time*, by Kreps, Donnermeyer, and Kreps, focuses on the Holmes County Settlement but is written largely for tourists, as is Miller's *Our People*.

18. We have drawn extensively on both Nolt's *A History of the Amish* and Kraybill's *The Riddle of Amish Culture* in this summary.

19. Ammann's view of shunning was not new; it applied an earlier understand-

ing based on the teachings of Menno Simons and the Dordrecht Confession of Faith in 1632.

20. The Amish share the Anabaptist label with three other groups: the Mennonites, the Hutterites, and the Brethren. Of these four groups, the Mennonites (42%) and the Brethren (34%) make up about two-thirds of the total Anabaptist population in the United States. The Amish account for 22 percent and the Hutterites 2 percent. See Kraybill and Hostetter, *Anabaptist World U.S.A.*, 33.

21. Louden, "Pennsylvania German in the 21st Century." *Pennsylvania German* is the term preferred by linguists, but we use *Pennsylvania Dutch* to reflect common usage. The dialect spoken in the Holmes County Settlement is known as Schwäbisch.

22. Ibid. Ex-Amish who still speak the language on a regular basis are a rapidly aging group. Younger people who leave tend to switch quickly to English as their sole means of communication.

23. The Swiss Amish, the majority of whom live in Indiana, speak a different dialect called Swiss. See Meyers and Nolt, *An Amish Patchwork*, 60–62, for a useful overview of language and dialects. It is also worth noting that the comfort level with speaking English varies somewhat depending on affiliation, school background, occupation, and general exposure to the English-speaking world.

24. Linguists use the term *diglossia* for this situation in which a very prestigious language reserved for formal occasions coexists with a vernacular.

25. Among the New Order Amish and a few "progressive" Old Order church districts, the Holy Kiss is shared between all church members of the same sex. At funerals and weddings attended by Amish of different affiliations, however, the New Order typically refrain from the Holy Kiss to prevent awkwardness. Interestingly, although most church members in conservative affiliations do not exchange the Holy Kiss, elderly members sometimes do, a practice that seems to reinforce the status hierarchy.

26. The use of the lot to choose ordained leaders involves an interesting mixture of divine providence and congregational input. In Ohio, male and female church members whisper the name of a candidate to the deacon, and the men who receive three or more votes (usually a half dozen or less) are placed in the lot. The man who chooses the song book with a slip of paper in it bearing a Bible verse becomes a deacon, a minister, or a bishop. The service is usually very emotional, since being chosen to serve is a heavy burden to be carried (without pay or training) for the rest of one's life.

27. Kraybill, *The Riddle of Amish Culture*, 112.

28. Hostetler, *Amish Society*, 108.

29. Kraybill, *The Riddle of Amish Culture*, 36.

30. In this respect, we follow several Amish scholars, such as Kraybill ("The Amish Encounter with Modernity") and Nolt and Meyers (*Plain Diversity*).

31. The Amish even formed a three-person National Amish Steering Committee (which reports to "state directors" who serve as intermediaries with each settlement) in the 1960s in response to concerns about the effects of the draft. This committee has helped negotiate nationwide compromises favorable to the Amish on such issues as alternative service, occupational safety, education, and federal income tax exemptions for the self-employed. See Olshan, "Homespun Bureaucracy."

32. Property owners installing wastewater systems are required to get permits from the county health commissioner to ensure that runoff does not adversely affect the surrounding environment, but some Swartzentruber Amish have installed systems without obtaining a permit. When they refuse to pay the seventy-five-dollar assessment fee, their tax bills are tagged as delinquent. See Marc Kovak, "Amish Balk at Wastewater System Assessment: Wayne Stands Firm," *Wooster (Ohio) Daily Record*, September 8, 2005, A1.

33. See Stambach, "The Silence Is Getting Louder." We see many parallels between the situation of the Amish and ethnic groups that are struggling to maintain a collective sense of identity in an ever-changing world. We reject the idea that ethnic identity is a never-changing, innately given fact of social life, and agree with Tambiah: "Ethnic identity unites the semantics of primordial and historical claims with the pragmatics of calculated choice and opportunism in dynamic contexts of political and economic competition between interest groups" ("Ethnic Conflict," 336).

34. Weber, "Class, Status, Party," 131.

35. Cohen, *The Symbolic Construction of Community*.

36. Turner, "Betwixt and Between."

37. In *Purity and Danger*, Douglas notes four kinds of social pollution: danger pressing on external boundaries, danger from transgressing the internal lines of the system, danger in the margin of the lines, and internal contradiction, "when some of the basic postulates are denied by other basic postulates, so that at certain points the system seems to be at war with itself" (531). Douglas argues that clearly defined boundaries of purity reinforce a society's common definitions and reduce the stress, helping members know who they are and what is expected of them.

38. William Watson, "The Things That Are More Excellent," in *One Hundred and One Famous Poems*, edited by Roy J. Cook (Chicago: Reilly and Lee, 1958), 132.

39. Quoted in Giddens, *Emile Durkheim*, 115.

40. Appadurai, *Modernity at Large*.

41. Kraybill, "The Amish Encounter with Modernity," 25–32. In contrast, Olshan argues that to the extent that the Amish reject fatalism and "self-consciously manipulate their path of social development," they are more accurately viewed as a "modern people" rather than as a "folk society" ("Modernity, Folk Society, Old

Order Amish," 189). As early as 1956, Huntington described the Amish as a "consciously maintained folk society" ("Dove at the Window," 144) to acknowledge the self-imposed nature of their isolation.

42. Stambach, "The Silence Is Getting Louder."

43. On telephones, see Umble (*Holding the Line*); on bureaucracy, see Olshan ("Homespun Bureaucracy"); on health care, see Huntington ("Health Care"); on tourism, see Luthy ("Amish Tourism"); on transportation, see Zook ("Slow Moving Vehicles"). While awareness of Amish cultural compromises has increased, many observers still mistakenly assume that the Amish reject technological comforts out of a religious asceticism (seeking hardship as a means to redemption). Instead, as Kidder and Hostetler have observed, "each decision about accepting or rejecting a 'modern' convenience is based on a consensus about the effect a new product would have on the social patterning of the community" ("Managing Ideologies," 905).

44. Meyers and Nolt, *An Amish Patchwork*, 2.

45. Nolt and Meyers, *Plain Diversity*.

46. Nolt, *A History of the Amish*, 132–33. Although there are a few accounts of Amish being attacked by Indians, most stories passed down through Amish families about the Indian encounter are ones that emphasize goodwill.

47. *Ohio Amish Directory*, xvi.

48. Nolt, *A History of the Amish*, 158.

49. David Beiler, quoted in Nolt, *A History of the Amish*, 170. Some conservative leaders decided not to attend, and others claimed they were not notified of the meeting.

50. Nolt, *A History of the Amish*, 172.

51. Nolt (ibid., 269) reports on this incident and others. Yoder showed up in civilian clothes the next day, and the officers never carried out their death threat.

52. "Amish Farmer Jailed," *New York Times*, March 19, 1960.

53. See Nolt, *A History of the Amish*, 297–98, for a detailed description of this incident.

54. In *Amish Grace*, Kraybill, Nolt, and Weaver-Zercher provide a compelling account of how forgiveness transcended tragedy in the Nickel Mines shooting.

55. Donnermeyer and Cooksey, "Demographic Foundations," 8.

56. One result of the high fertility rate among the Amish is that Holmes County has the youngest average age of Ohio's eighty-eight counties.

57. "Amish Population Growth 2007–2008: One-Year Highlights," Young Center for Anabaptist and Pietist Studies, Elizabethtown College, www2 .etown.edu/amishstudies/Population_Trends_2007_2008.asp (accessed June 29, 2009).

58. Office of Strategic Research, Ohio Department of Development, "Per Capita Personal Income 2006," www.odod.state.oh.us/cms/uploadedfiles/Research/

g201.pdf (accessed July 29, 2008). It is important to note, however, that in terms of median *household* income, Holmes County ranks 42 among the eighty-eight Ohio counties.

59. Economic Research Service, U.S. Department of Agriculture, "County-Level Unemployment and Median Household Income for Ohio," www.ers.usda.gov/Data/Unemployment/RDList2.asp?ST=OH (accessed March 30, 2009).

60. Shasta Mast, interview by David McConnell, October 27, 2006, Millersburg, OH.

61. Office of Policy, Research, and Strategic Planning, "Ohio County Profiles," http://development.ohio.gov/research/files/so/Holmes.pdf (accessed July 8, 2009).

62. The Brethren branches in the area include the Grace Brethren, the Conservative Grace Brethren, the Church of the Brethren, the Brethren Church, and the Brethren in Christ.

63. Kraybill and Hostetter, *Anabaptist World U.S.A.*, 70. Most Beachy Amish also have Sunday school, use church buildings, and are deeply involved in mission work. Many of the Beachy Amish do consider themselves "Amish" in spite of these differences. According to Nolt, by 2002 the Beachy Amish had expanded to include "more than 150 congregations in 23 states and one province, along with 39 other churches in 10 countries on four continents" (*A History of the Amish*, 330).

64. Kidder, "The Role of Outsiders," 214.

65. Interestingly, however, fundamentalists have had to work a lot harder at affirming male authority and female submission, because there is a long history of women as Sunday school teachers, mission workers, and fund-raisers. The gender rhetoric is stronger because gender relations are so much more contested in these communities (Jennifer Graber, personal communication).

Chapter 2. The Origins of Religious Diversity

1. 2000 *Ohio Amish Directory: Holmes County and Vicinity* (Walnut Creek, OH: Carlisle Press, 2000), xvii.

2. Johnson-Weiner, *Train Up a Child*, 104.

3. Ibid., 105.

4. Byler, "The Geography of Difference."

5. Meyers and Nolt, *An Amish Patchwork*, 50.

6. As a result of the Swartzentrubers' insularity, reliable accounts of their life have been hard to find. Recently, however, several scholars have gained limited access and published informative accounts of Swartzentrubers' lives. In *Plain Secrets*, Mackall provides a sensitive and humanizing account of Swartzentruber life based on a ten-year friendship with one family in the Lodi Settlement in Ohio. Johnson-Weiner's *Train Up a Child* gives a detailed description of Swartzentruber schools

based on site visits and interviews with key informants in several states. In "The Geography of Distance," Byler argues persuasively that there is a high degree of social distance between Swartzentrubers and other Amish in the Holmes County Settlement.

7. Luthy, "The Swartzentruber Amish," 19.

8. Ibid.

9. Notes from Jacob Mast entitled "Of the Yoder Spalt" from the Amish library in Aylmer, Canada, reported, "At that time, he [Yoder] and Dan Wengerd were sweet as honey towards each other, but not long afterwards they were like cats and dogs."

10. The five points raised by Wengerd are summarized in Weaver, "Glimpses of the Amish Church," 9–10. Roy Weaver and Kline ("Research Notes") provide quotes from many of the letters and reports during that difficult time. As for the last grievance, according to local historians, the feeling was that Sam's wife was "running the show" behind the scenes and thus overstepping her calling as an "obedient wife." A related story that has circulated in the settlement as a cautionary tale about motherhood purports that Yoder's wife had an illegitimate child. When the boy was ten or eleven years old, she put him on a train to visit relatives in the West. Apparently, she did not give the boy proper instructions, and without the help of non-Amish on the train, the boy never would have arrived. Some time later, Yoder's wife was on the way to Wooster with visitors when a train hit her buggy. According to the story, it was the same train that she had put her son on. The case of Sam Yoder's wife is the only instance we discovered in which gender played a role, albeit a minor one, in a church schism, but it clearly reveals the social disapproval that awaited women who tried to step out of the confines of their socially prescribed roles.

11. Weaver, "Glimpses of the Amish Church," 10.

12. Ammann, who was known for his strong opinions and quick temper, supported more frequent communions (twice a year) and social avoidance. He shocked many by unilaterally placing a number of ministers under the ban and then dramatically walking out on a meeting that had been called to make peace. See Nolt, *A History of the Amish*, 31–40.

13. Kline and Beachy, "History and Dynamics," 1.

14. Luthy finds that Yoder's death certificate listed "apoplexy" (stroke) as the principal cause, that his obituary in the *Sugarcreek (Ohio) Budget* referred to "stroke of paralysis," and that a letter was written by Old Order deacon John Y. Schlabach and signed by John E. Yoder as a rebuttal to the persistent suicide rumors ("The Swartzentruber Amish," 20).

15. Luthy notes that over the years other families joined the Swartzentrubers, leading to a combined total of twenty Swartzentruber surnames in 1998: Byler,

Gingerich, Glick, Hershberger, Hostetler, Keim, Lehman, Mast, Miller, Peter-sheim, Schrock, Shetler, Slabaugh, Stutzman, Swartzentruber, Troyer, Weaver, Wengerd, Yoder, and Zook (ibid.).

16. According to one New Order bishop familiar with the dispute, the deci-sive issue in this case had to do with courtship practices and the difficulty of pleas-ing a particular bishop when young people wanted to get baptized. Today most of the Troyer Amish have moved out of the Holmes County Settlement, though there is still one church district remaining. The outward differences between the Troy-ers and the Swartzentrubers are visible only to the trained eye. For instance, the Troyer buggies are allowed to have a water-repellant cloth, a kind of rubberized sheet, that snaps to the posts on the side of the buggy's windshield to protect the occupants from rain. One Old Order Amish woman reports that she often sees this sheet snapped up on one side of the Troyer buggies even on sunny days, as a signal to other Amish that they are not Swartzentrubers. The Troyer Amish also now use the slow-moving-vehicle triangle on their buggies.

17. According to knowledgeable insiders, the source of the split revolved around Tobe Hochstetler himself, who had been accused of dishonesty in a business deal-ing. The matter came to a vote in the church to relieve him of his ministerial duties for a while, but because the case was not clear-cut, the vote was not unanimous. Nevertheless, the Troyer church took the very unusual step of proceeding on the issue without a unanimous church vote. In the wake of this action, Hochstetler, with support mostly from his extended family, decided to withdraw. Beyond using distinctive royal blue curtains in their windows, the Tobe have exhibited an inter-esting blend of conservative and progressive practices that defy easy categorization on the Anabaptist escalator. They tolerated tobacco, for example, but adopted some technological innovations. The Tobe church, however, encountered difficulties be-cause it had so few congregations that the young people were having trouble find-ing marriage partners who were not closely related. A common joke among other Amish was that all Tobe Amish looked alike, as there were only five or six extended families represented in their affiliation. Ultimately, the Tobe group decided to re-turn to fellowship with the Old Order, though they have retained distinctive pat-terns of dress and buggy design.

18. The relative isolation of both splinter groups probably drew these unusual bedfellows together.

19. In reference to "acting out" by some Swartzentruber youth in the Holmes County Settlement, for example, one bishop famously stated, "Things like that don't happen in Lodi!"

20. Part of this story is recounted in Stevick, *Growing Up Amish*, 100. The rest of the account has been pieced together through interviews with Old Order Amish who work with Swartzentrubers, ex-Swartzentrubers who left before baptism,

and ex-Swartzentrubers who were members of the church during the incident but later left.

21. In addition, Andy Weaver was able to recruit members of the Dan Wengerd faction, which initially joined the Swartzentrubers but later split with Sam Yoder and rejoined the Old Order.

22. Quoted in "Events That Took Place in the Old Order Amish Churches of Holmes and Wayne County, Ohio, from 1938 to 1958," translated by Peter Yoder in January 1973 and available at the Amish Historical Library in Aylmer, Ontario.

23. In any church dispute, a key distinction for the Amish is whether an or-dained leader joins the dissatisfied group. If one does, then a formal church schism becomes a real possibility. If no ordained leader is part of the group, then the matter involves the excommunication of individual church members.

24. "Events That Took Place," 7.

25. Ibid.,11.

26. Ibid.

27. Kraybill, "Plotting Social Change," 56.

28. The discrepancy is especially great with respect to the church districts in the northern part of the Lancaster County Settlement, which are more progressive than those in the southern half, even though all are in fellowship under the Old Order label.

29. For a detailed discussion of the differences between the "electric" New Order of Lancaster County, Pennsylvania, and the "nonelectric" New Order of Holmes County, Ohio, see Waldrep, "The New Order Amish."

30. Bundling, or bed courtship, is the English rendition of a Pennsylvania Dutch term that literally means "unmarried sleeping together" (Stevick, *Growing Up Amish*, 188).

31. Hostetler, *Amish Society*, 306.

32. Waldrep, "The New Order Amish," 407. In 1978 the New Order founded Iron Curtain Ministries to pursue mission work in Eastern Europe.

33. Ibid., 402.

34. Kline and Beachy, "History and Dynamics," 8. Waldrep ("The New Order Amish") notes that at first the terms "Youth Group Amish" and "Levi R. Troyer people" were informally used in the Holmes County Settlement. He also states that according to Amish historian David Luthy, the term "New Order Amish" entered Holmes County through Stephen Scott, a young seeker present in the mid-1960s, who adapted John Hostetler's use of the term to describe the "car" Amish.

35. Kline and Beachy, "History and Dynamics," 9.

36. Ibid. Extending the Holy Kiss to younger members marked a significant de-parture from the custom that only ordained leaders and elders greeted each other in this way.

37. Ibid., 12.

38. Ibid.

39. Stevick, *Growing Up Amish*, 33. But one indication of just how deep the controversy goes is that there remains one New Order district in the Holmes County Settlement that does *not* have Sunday school. The bishop of the district explained to us that he believes there is no place in the Bible where Jesus separated people for religious teaching, though some in his congregation disagree.

40. This interpretation was related to us by several New Order individuals who were intimately involved in both the New Order and the New New Order splits.

41. Waldrep, "The New Order Amish," 423.

42. Waldrep argues that the New Order movement is best characterized as an unsteady compromise between Amish traditionalism and mainstream evangelicalism rather than as a genuine spiritual renewal that recaptures what was lost by the wayside (ibid., 422).

43. Even the labels *progressive* and *conservative* can be interpreted in different ways, however. Some would argue that allowing smoking (a practice common among the more "conservative" Swartzentruber and Andy Weaver groups) is actually more "progressive" because it is less churchly and is an expression of greater individual freedom.

44. Stevick, *Growing Up Amish*, 37.

45. Byler, "The Geography of Difference," 1.

46. In addition to using the English abbreviation "Swartzie," Old Order Amish sometimes refer to the Swartzentruber Amish with a disparaging Pennsylvania Dutch term: *gnuddel vullahs*, or wooly lumps, because of the lumps of manure, dirt, and grime that adhere to their untrimmed beards when they milk cows by hand.

47. Kidder and Hostetler ("Managing Ideologies," 895) used the term "legal informalism" to describe Amish responses to conflict that are not rule-bound or defined in terms of rights, although they focused mainly on Amish responses to conflict with the non-Amish.

48. Hostetler, *Amish Society*, 48.

Chapter 3. Coping with Church Schism

1. Benedict, book review of *On the Backroad to Heaven*, 104.

2. Nolt, "The Amish 'Mission Movement,'" 17. Maniaci himself was a convert to Mennonitism who took a keen interest in encouraging Amish evangelism.

3. Ibid., 21.

4. The editor of the newsletter, Harvey Graber, was an Old Order church member who challenged Amish custom by attending Eastern Mennonite College (ibid., 23).

5. Ibid., 30.

6. Stephen Scott, personal communication. One of the most famous local converts to the Amish was a Swedish man who fell in love with an Amish girl when he came to the county fair as part of Budweiser's Clydesdale horse tour. Another local convert, Donald G. Beam, is described by Reiheld in "Donald G. Beam," 241–49. Although Beam married and had children, he eventually left because he wanted to take a more active role in promoting environmental issues to the world than the Amish were comfortable with.

7. Nolt, *A History of the Amish*, 315.

8. See Sarah Skylark Bruce, "Mission of Understanding: Amish Take Teaching Tools to Old Colony Mennonites in Mexico," *Wooster (Ohio) Daily Record*, May 31, 2006, A1.

9. The differences in standard of living are similar to those faced by sixteen Amish families who moved to Honduras in 1967 and confronted the fact that they were considered wealthy by their neighbors. See Nolt, *A History of the Amish*, 312–14.

10. Christian Aid Ministries 2006 Annual Report, Christian Aid Ministries, Berlin, OH.

11. Ibid., 29.

12. Many Holmes County Amish are quick to differentiate themselves from the Indiana Amish. One local historian and Amish parent noted that because Amish youth in Indiana can get a job in the mobile home plants for twenty dollars per hour as eighteen-year-olds, the drug and alcohol problem is worse than in Holmes County. "So when we hear that the Old Order Indiana Amish are coming, we think, 'Oh dear!'" The Holmes County Settlement also does not have "gangs" of young people with names and symbols handed down over time, as is common in Lancaster County.

13. Stevick provides a balanced and nuanced treatment of this diversity in *Growing Up Amish*.

14. Kraybill, *The Riddle of Amish Culture*, 186.

15. Stevick, *Growing Up Amish*, 11–13.

16. Matt Tullis, "Amish Man Sentenced for Selling Marijuana," *Wooster (Ohio) Daily Record*, February 24, 2006, A1.

17. The questions submitted included these: What should we do if we know somebody we think is on drugs? Would you comment on parents' liability on hosting a party on your property? What is our responsibility if we know there are drugs in the workplace? Why does the government put pressure on tobacco but not alcohol? What are the things that show up when kids use drugs in secret? What effect does Copenhagen have? Are the drugs available in Holmes County made here? In what form is meth purchased?

18. Meyers and Nolt, *An Amish Patchwork*, 52.

19. The most comprehensive overview of Pennsylvania singings is found in Stevick, *Growing Up Amish*, 129—50.

20. The most comprehensive and balanced treatment of bed courtship to date is ibid.

21. Ibid., 194.

22. The stipulations relating to "pure courtship" are from a four-page brief written by one Holmes County New Order district and quoted ibid., 184.

23. Cooksey and Donnermeyer, "Go Forth and Multiply." The general results of these authors' analysis showed that for Amish women born between 1940 and 1969, 76 percent of all first births were conceived within the first year of marriage, 11 percent occurred either before marriage or within the first seven months of marriage (and therefore in all likelihood conceived before marriage); and 13 percent occurred in either the eighth or ninth month of marriage (some of these babies could also have been premaritally conceived). Also noteworthy is that the Andy Weaver and Old Order Amish show an increase in the percentage of conceptions that are premarital among women who came of age in the 1970s and 1980s when compared with women of the earlier generation.

24. Waldrep, "The New Order Amish," 423.

25. Kraybill, "Plotting Social Change," 73.

26. Waldrep, "The New Order Amish," 423. The New Order average is 73 percent if one church district with a very low retention rate is excluded from the analysis.

27. The committee has divided Old Order church districts in the Holmes County Settlement into four geographic areas and schedules singings and other youth events separately for each of these areas.

28. Richard Stevick, personal communication, March 25, 2008.

29. In reality, the situation among the Old Order Amish is even more complex than a simple division between the Midways and other Old Order groups would suggest. One Old Order father described the 52 young people in his neighborhood (three church districts) as follows: 14 were "over-conformed kids" who went overboard in attending singings and "toeing the line"; 21 attended the singings on a regular basis but were not self-righteous about it; 6 dressed Amish but did not attend singings because their parents were against them; 7 owned vehicles and dressed English but were not full-blown partygoers; and 4 were "borderline" youth who drank heavily, partied, and flirted with breaking the law. In this man's neighborhood, the majority of youth attended singings, but in other neighborhoods the majority of young people may not. "It varies wildly from neighborhood to neighborhood," he concluded.

30. The heavy drinking among some Amish youth typically does not carry over into adulthood if they join the Amish church; however, limited drinking in the pri-

vacy of one's home is not uncommon among the more conservative Amish groups. In fact, some Amish make wine at home, and real wine is used in Communion services in every affiliation, because it is seen as far more symbolic of purity than grape juice.

31. Asked how the Amish youth acquired alcohol, the officer replied, "There'd be English guys that they knew, usually it was the drivers, the 'Amish haulers' are what we call them. They'd make, you know, 100% profit because these Amish kids have money to burn so to pay 10 bucks for a six pack would be nothing to them. A lot of people made money supplying beer to these Amish kids."

32. Mackall, *Plain Secrets*, 84.

33. Stevick, *Growing Up Amish*, 192–93.

34. Iannacconne, "Why Strict Churches Are Strong," 1187.

35. Stevick, *Growing Up Amish*, 52, notes that this difference extends to the decor of boys' and girls' bedrooms. Boys typically display sports gear, hunting trophies, or other souvenirs, while girls' rooms are covered with cards, letters, photos, mementos, and furniture with a theme color.

36. Reiling, "The 'Simmie' Side of Life," 148.

37. Meyers and Nolt, *An Amish Patchwork*, 81.

38. For a while after the 1952 split, a couple could be married by bishops in either affiliation. However, eventually, the Andy Weaver bishops refused to sanction a marriage in which one of their members moved "up," and this decision has had a powerful dampening effect on the frequency of such marriages.

39. Kraybill, *The Riddle of Amish Culture*, 138. The rationale for shunning is contained in the *Dordrecht Confession of Faith*, which notes that if anyone has been expelled from the church, he must be avoided by all members of the church; "in short that we are to have nothing to do with him; so that we may not become defiled by intercourse with him and partakers of his sins, but that he may be made ashamed, be affected in his mind, convinced in his conscience, and thereby induced to amend his ways" (36).

40. Perhaps the most noteworthy example is Ruth Irene Garrett's *Crossing Over*, a tale of "escaping Amish repression," to use the title of a *Glamour* magazine article based on the book. In Garrett's eyes, the Amish are like a "cult": the position of women is equated with "a subservient class," the purpose of the cap on education at eight years is "to keep the Amish people in the dark," and church rules are both "inflexible" and "stifling." In a similar vein is Ottie Garrett's *True Stories of the X-Amish*, a collection of anecdotal accounts by ex-Amish that conveys a very negative view of Amish society. David Yoder's Web-based account of leaving the Swartzentruber Amish (www.amishdeception.com) and Chris Burkholder's *Amish Confidential*, a confessional account of misdeeds by a bishop's son, both contribute to the image of Amish society as riddled with abuse that is typically shielded from the public

eye. All of these accounts convey the very negative message that an overemphasis on rules and conformity limits the freedom of Amish individuals, who are so brainwashed that they do not realize their own state of oppression, fear, or ignorance.

41. When the ordained leaders make this final visit, they try to secure the individual's consent to be placed in the ban. As one ex-Swartzentruber put it, "They really want your rights to put you in the ban." For church leaders, this is a way of emphasizing that excommunication is the result of a sin that remains unconfessed. In practice, however, it is often difficult for church leaders to gain consent from the individual because of the breakdown in communication.

42. Kraybill, *The Riddle of Amish Culture*, 136.

43. The results presented in this section draw on the survey and interviews with ex-Amish described in appendix A. Most of the respondents were working in manual trades; the large majority were married and lived (some on a farm) in a rural area within sixty miles of where they grew up; and their educational backgrounds did not reveal a preoccupation with going back to school to "make up for lost time" (though those who left before they were baptized were more highly educated). However, 13 percent of respondents had divorced, many of the women worked outside the home, and more than half of respondents felt their standard of living was higher than it was when they were growing up.

44. Although no one in our survey mentioned it, an Old Order man we interviewed told us that to his knowledge at least a half dozen Amish young men in the settlement had decided not to be baptized in the church because of their sexual orientation. One of them later brought his partner, unannounced, to a family reunion, which "created a lot of talk."

45. As early as 1968, Hostetler argued that one of the main reasons for leaving the Amish was the desire to have a more intensive religious experience, in contrast to the almost ascetic attitude of the Amish toward religion (*Amish Society*, 306–12). Several complementary factors may underlie the desire for a deeper religious experience. First, the born-again ideology is attractive for its simplicity. Individuals don't have to navigate the maze of church rules to be in good standing with God. Second, the newfound certainty of salvation by God's grace alone may appeal to those who feel the threat of hell and damnation is overemphasized, though it is a testimony to the effectiveness of Amish enculturation that most ex-Amish do not reject the underlying dualistic framework of heaven versus hell. Third, the prospect of emotional intimacy with God may appeal to some individuals who are not satisfied with the emphasis on what they perceive to be the form and ritual in Amish religion. The more common explanations put forward by sociologists and anthropologists of religion for the growth of evangelical churches do not seem to apply well to the Amish case. These include the growing attenuation of relationships and disconnection from friends, family, and neighbors, captured by the metaphor of 'bowling

alone' (Putnam, "Bowling Alone"), and the rise of modern media that enhance the experience of absorption and fantasy, creating a desire for a different subjective reality from the frazzled world around us (Luhrmann, "Metakinesis").

46. Luhrmann, "Metakinesis," 518.

47. One ex-Swartzentruber young woman described the reaction this way: "When they started getting the Pennsylvania Dutch Bibles out, I'm telling you there was an uproar because so many young folks started understanding it. They're like 'Oh my gosh, I can't believe Jesus said this. Well, why are we doing what we're doing?' So it caused revelations for these people. And then the preachers would come in and say 'You do this, blah blah blah,' but they said, 'Well, I just read in the Bible this is . . . da da da.' So they done away with them Bibles, you'll get in trouble if you read 'em. They kind of teach you you're being too smart for your own good."

48. Quoted from a pamphlet authored by Eli Stutzman and Joe Keim, *My Amish Vows to the Church: Are They Binding?* (Savannah, OH: Mission to Amish People, 2005), 1.

49. Keim himself confesses to having been ordered off private property more than once. For their part, Amish church leaders are always on the lookout for proselytizers. "It's ongoing, and they end up taking people away from the Amish," commented an Old Order business leader. "Most of these evangelical churches will go after an area where there's an existing church—it's an easier target for them." In addition to revivals, the recruiting strategies of the evangelicals include putting fliers and magazines in Amish mailboxes and arranging for "Bible study" in the homes of individuals who seem receptive.

50. The Swartzentrubers, however, do have a "grace period" during which they will not shun any individual who leaves the church during the six to twelve months following a church split. One Swartzentruber widower took advantage of this grace year to purchase a chain saw, a tractor, and a small car, for which he did not have a driver's license but which he kept parked in a partially hidden shed next to his house. An ex-Swartzentruber man told us that an unofficial split in 2006 among the Swartzentrubers in Tennessee had some young Ohio Swartzentrubers hoping for an official church division so they could leave and not be shunned.

51. One hypothesis about the Swartzentruber tendency to go "all the way" is that it is related to the strict stance on excommunication taken by the church. Since even a small step "up" is equivalent to the worst apostasy, they might as well "go all the way." Stevick describes this as the big jump–small jump theory: the more conservative the affiliation, the larger the jump. Whereas ex–New Order Amish often become members of other Anabaptist churches, the ex-Swartzentrubers often become truck drivers, circus workers, soldiers, factory workers, or even workers on ranches in the western United States (Richard Stevick, personal communication).

52. In "The New Order Amish," Waldrep refers to this approach as the "Kalona understanding" because it is the practice used by Old Order Amish in Kalona, Iowa.

53. As noted earlier, the New New Order districts do reject the principle of excommunication altogether, seeing it as an unnecessary intrusion of the church into an individual's relationship with God.

54. Reiling, "The 'Simmie' Side of Life," 159.

55. We also found some support for Ericksen, Ericksen, and Hostetler's claim that the probability of leaving the Amish clusters in families ("The Cultivation of the Soil," 61). In our survey, fully 70 percent of respondents reported that more than three of their extended family had left the Amish. Only 9 percent of respondents reported that no other member of their extended family had left the Amish before their own decision to leave. Several of the open-ended responses to our survey and to our follow-up interviews also alluded to the fact that families with a high incidence of "leavers" carried a stigma in the community. The impact of family members on defection rates deserves further study, with closer attention to the distinction between the decision not to join the church and defection after baptism. Meyers, for example, found that the majority of those who do not join the church appear to leave on their own without being influenced by siblings' decisions ("The Old Order Amish," 382–84).

56. Huntington, *Amish in Michigan*, 2.

Chapter 4. Continuity and Change in Family Life

1. Coontz argues persuasively that such images of a golden age of the traditional family evaporate upon closer inspection: they are "an ahistorical amalgam of structures, values and behaviors that never co-existed in the same time and place" (*The Way We Never Were*, 9).

2. When elderly parents "retire" and give the farm or the business over to the children, they typically move into a "grandparents' house" that is right next to or even attached to the home of one of their married children. This is hardly a retirement, since they "help their adult children's new families in whatever way they can" (Kreps, Donnermeyer, and Kreps, *A Quiet Moment in Time*, 73).

3. Weaver-Zercher, *Amish in the American Imagination*, 113.

4. Plath, *Long Engagements*, 1.

5. We sampled every tenth family in the directory; therefore, our figure is an average based on an analysis of all families rather than those who have completed their fertility cycles. The 2.0 figure for the general population is based on a Centers for Disease Control analysis of live births in 2003 (Martin et al., "Births").

6. In 1998 Mrs. Bessie Hostetler of Buffalo, Missouri, was listed in the *Sugar-*

creek (Ohio) Budget as having the largest number of living descendants at the time of her death: 951.

7. Wasao ("Fertility Differentials") also showed that ordained church leaders in the Holmes County Settlement had larger families, on average, than did ordinary church members.

8. The gap between average numbers of children per family was largest for the Andy Weavers (at 3.0 children) and the Old Order Amish (at 2.2 children).

9. According to Wasao, the average number of children plummeted from 9.6 to 6.6 among the Andy Weavers, from 7.6 to 5.8 for the Old Order, and from 6.7 to 4.5 for the New Order ("Fertility Differentials," 108).

10. Unsurprisingly, the majority of respondents in our survey indicated they "strongly disagree" (62 percent) or "disagree" (15 percent) with birth control, but 7 percent said they had no feelings either way and 13 percent indicated they "somewhat agree" with the use of birth control. Another factor related to the declining fertility rate is the corresponding decline in infant mortality, which fell from roughly 59 per thousand live births for a cohort born between 1920 and 1929 to roughly 8 per thousand live births for the 1980–89 cohort, the latter figure being only slightly above the average for Wayne and Holmes counties in 1988 (Wasao, "Fertility Differentials").

11. Greksa and Korbin, "Amish," 561.

12. The list of most common surnames in the Holmes County Settlement is based on our analysis of the 2005 *Ohio Amish Directory*, whereas the list from Lancaster County is taken from Kraybill, *The Riddle of Amish Culture*, 93. Miller and Yoder were also the two most common surnames in each of the four affiliations included in the directory. Our analysis of first names in the Holmes County Settlement shows that Mary and Eli have been consistently at the top; there has been some change in the popularity of names for both boys and girls over the past half century, however, although biblical names are still preferred. For girls born before 1945, the five most popular names were Mary, Anna, Emma, Fannie, and Verna, whereas for those born between 1995 and 2004, the most popular names were Mary, Rachel, Esther, Susan, and Clara. For boys, the five most popular names in the earlier cohort were Eli, Daniel/Dan, Levi, Roy, and John, while the more recent cohort shows Eli, Michael, Joseph, David, and Aaron.

13. Nolt, "Inscribing Community," 181–98.

14. Lasch used "havens in a heartless world" to describe the increasing association of the nuclear family with a private sphere of life that had little overlap with the public sphere of the economy (*Haven in a Heartless World*).

15. Kraybill, *The Riddle of Amish Culture*, 90.

16. Luthy notes that dividing farms into multiple parcels has become commonplace since the 1990s ("Amish Settlements across America," 19).

17. Meyers and Nolt, *An Amish Patchwork*, 76.

18. By 2007 the Amish Helping Fund had become so large that it began to be used for refinancing Amish homes and businesses that had originally been financed with conventional bank loans.

19. Bobby Warren, "Escalation Alarming," *Wooster (Ohio) Daily Record*, December 26, 2007, A1. Holmes County recorded only 81 foreclosures, compared to 426 in nearby Wayne County, 400 in Tuscarawas County, and nearly 250 in Ashland County.

20. Kraybill, "Plotting Social Change," 71.

21. Umble, *Holding the Line*, 152–59.

22. Swartzentruber church rules do not permit use of natural gas, but Swartzentruber Amish are permitted to receive some payment for the natural gas wells on their property. The Andy Weavers allow a gas stove only if there is a natural gas well on one's property.

23. Scott and Pellman, *Living without Electricity*, is a very readable account of exactly how the Amish accomplish "life without electricity."

24. Ibid., 50.

25. The Old Order Amish have retained the custom of holding weddings on Thursdays; however, the New Order Amish have switched to Saturdays to minimize conflicts with business operations.

26. This language is from a deed in which Eli and Iva Troyer "sold" 119 acres to Aaron and Nettie Troyer on December 11, 2001. It is standard language for similar transactions.

27. A few Amish families even open their homes to outsiders on a temporary basis. Ohio State University has a program for German students to spend time in Amish homes. We met one Old Order family who had hosted foreign exchange students for years, including one they jokingly nicknamed "useless Yusuf" because of his penchant for avoiding work.

28. Kraybill, *The Riddle of Amish Culture*, 29–36.

29. Meyers and Nolt, *An Amish Patchwork*, 9.

30. Hostetler, *Amish Society*, 156.

31. Johnson-Weiner, *Train Up a Child*, 46.

32. Kraybill, *The Riddle of Amish Culture*, 30–31.

33. "Teaching Girls to Be Reserved," *Family Life*, December 2007, 14.

34. Korbin and Greksa ("Paradox of Self and Conformity") have argued that the conformity essential to the maintenance of Amish identity, which is usually associated with a weak sense of self that can be bent to the will of others, paradoxically requires a strong sense of self.

35. "The Big 'I,'" *Family Life*, November 2007, 6–8.

36. Regehr, *Mennonites in Canada*, 199.

37. The Amish we interviewed tended to echo the traditional defenses of spanking (a sign of nonpermissiveness, anticipatory socialization, and God's will) rather than sympathizing with emergent criticisms (that spanking is compulsive, demeaning, violent, and abusive). See Davis, "The Changing Meanings of Spanking."

38. "Godly Parenting," *Brotherhood Messenger* 4 (1): 1. The *Brotherhood Messenger* is published by Amish Brotherhood Publications, Millersburg, OH.

39. Spindler described cultural compression as occurring at "any period of time in the life cycle of the individual when he encounters a culturally patterned reduction of alternatives for behavior" (*Fifty Years*, 89).

40. On the basis of the dominant profiles of Amish children who took the Myers-Briggs Personality Test, Hostetler refers to the "Amish personality" as "quiet, friendly, responsible and conscientious" and "loyal, considerate and sympathetic" (*Amish Society*, 186). There are many difficulties in seeing culture as "personality writ large," however, including the danger of overstating the degree of cultural homogeneity. Even in Hostetler's original study, the two dominant personality types made up only 54 percent of the Amish sample.

41. Cooksey and Donnermeyer, "Go Forth and Multiply," 12. The authors, who base their analysis on the 2000 *Ohio Amish Directory*, further note that the average age of marriage for the Amish has actually decreased slightly over the past forty years. In addition, women who are currently either New Order or New New Order Amish marry later, on average, than their Old Order or Andy Weaver peers; and a smaller percentage of New Order Amish have married by age thirty.

42. Stevick notes that the German word for wedding, *Hochzeit*, means "high times" (*Growing Up Amish*, 199).

43. If the couple admit to premarital sex, the bishop must excommunicate them for six weeks, and the wedding ceremony itself is be altered slightly. In practice, it is rare for young couples to admit to having sexual relations before marriage unless, as noted in chapter 3, the woman has become pregnant.

44. In *Growing Up Amish*, Stevick provides a detailed account of the wedding itself, as well as pre- and postwedding events.

45. In Smith's view, the relations of ruling refer to all the sets of activities in a variety of institutional contexts by which society, groups, and individuals are ruled and regulated. These include rules, laws, and expectations that define what are appropriate structures and behaviors (Smith, *Conceptual Practices of Power*, 12–19).

46. The quotes are from Hershberger, *Amish Women*, 11; Johnson-Weiner, "The Role of Women," 231; Stoll, "Views and Values," 8–9; and Stoltzfus, *Traces of Wisdom*, 35, respectively.

47. Schwemmlein, "The Weaker Vessel?" 33.

48. Swander, *Out of This World*, 145.

49. Stoltzfus, *Traces of Wisdom*, 130.

50. Johnson-Weiner, "The Role of Women," 231.

51. Umble, "Who Are You?" 48.

52. di Leonardo, "The Female World of Cards and Holidays," 323.

53. Cancian, "The Feminization of Love," 289–90.

54. Hostetler describes the many functions of silence in Amish life, which he collectively describes as the "silent discourse." He argues that silence takes on great significance in communities where people are deeply involved with one another (*Amish Society*, 388–90).

55. Ericksen and Klein, "Women's Roles and Family Production"; Spain, "Gendered Spaces and Women's Status"; Schwemmlein, "The Weaker Vessel?"; Johnson-Weiner, "The Role of Women."

56. Swander, *Out of This World*; Johnson-Weiner, "The Role of Women."

57. Spain, "Gendered Spaces and Women's Status."

58. Interdependence rather than "hierarchically arranged roles" thus becomes the dominant mode of interaction (Johnson-Weiner, "The Role of Women," 238).

59. Kraybill and Nolt, *Amish Enterprise*.

60. Cooksey and Donnermeyer, "Go Forth and Multiply," 22.

61. Johnson-Weiner, "The Role of Women," 235, 238.

62. Cooksey and Donnermeyer note that the results of the marriage squeeze are more noticeable among older cohorts of Amish women: "Whereas less than 82 per cent of women over age 75 were married by age 30, just over 95 per cent of women in the youngest cohort were married by age 30" ("Go Forth and Multiply," 13). Put another way, among women born before 1940, approximately 10 percent never married, compared to just over 2 percent of women born between 1970 and 1980.

63. Wasao, "Fertility Differentials," 98.

64. Livecchia, "Anabaptist Remarriage."

65. Hostetler, *Amish Society*, 164.

66. Garon and Maclachlan, *The Ambivalent Consumer*, 11.

67. "Good Horsemanship," letter to the editor of *Family Life*, December 2007, 1.

68. The relation between the Amish and the state department of transportation has taken a different path in Ohio than in Indiana, where regulations for horses and buggies differ by county, and where some counties require license plates on buggies. In response to criticism that the Amish were not paying gasoline or license plate fees to offset the wear and tear on the roads created by buggies, Amish leaders formed a committee that took up a voluntary contribution of twenty-five dollars per vehicle from every Amish in the state to contribute to road maintenance. New legislation then had to be passed to form a legal channel for these "voluntary" contributions, which exceeded a quarter of a million dollars.

69. Although hunting tends to be a hobby pursued by teenage boys and men, it is not uncommon for preteens, including girls, to harvest deer. One father we

interviewed described his nine-year-old daughter's first buck, one of six deer his children killed that year. "It was more meat than we could eat," he confessed.

70. This thirty-six-point whitetail deer turned out to be the fourth-largest in the world taken by a crossbow, in terms of antler inches. The term *Lucky* came from a special food source the deer had been eating, which had been planted to maximize the deer's antler growth (Chris Kick, "Several Thousand Attend First Sportman's Show in Charm," *Wooster (Ohio) Daily Record*, February 4, 2007, www.the-daily-record.com [accessed April 20, 2009]).

71. Stevick, *Growing Up Amish*, 113.

72. Basketball is another competitive sport that is popular among young males. On April 13–14, 2007, Hiland High School hosted what was billed as the "first Annual Ohio Amish Basketball Tournament." The teams were mainly from the Holmes County Settlement, and the tournament was publicized by word of mouth; T-shirts were sold at the event.

73. Sarah Skylark Bruce, "Amish Cream English," *Wooster (Ohio) Daily Record*, July 26, 2007.

74. "Stores Sell Clothes for Amish Who Don't Make Their Own," *Wooster (Ohio) Daily Record*, October 15, 2006, D2.

75. At least one Indiana politician has backed Amish attempts to gain an exemption from the Department of Homeland Security policy of requiring photo identification when Amish who are American citizens cross the border to visit family members in Canada. See Sylvia A. Smith, "Souder Backs Amish on IDs," *Fort Wayne Journal Gazette*, www.journalgazette.net/apps/pbcs.dll/article?AID=/20080417/NEWS03/8041703 (accessed June 5, 2008).

76. Stevick *Growing Up Amish*, 122. For a history of Pinecraft, see Gingerich, *The History of Pinecraft*. For a description of Pinecraft in the popular press, see Christopher Evans, "A Piece of Paradise," *Cleveland Plain Dealer Sunday Magazine*, March 14, 2004, 11–18.

77. In their classic article, Schneider and Homans describe the American kinship system as "pushed to the wall" by other institutions and very small in its overall effects on social life ("Kinship Terminology," 1194).

Chapter 5. The Changing Landscape of Learning

1. In *The Yoder Case*, Peters provides a complete account of the meaning and legacy of this legal decision.

2. Quoted in Keim, *Compulsory Education and the Amish*, 159.

3. Meyers, "Education and Schooling," 101.

4. As of 2004–5, schools administered by the Amish numbered approximately 1,345 and served nearly forty thousand students in twenty-four states (*Blackboard Bulletin*, 2005).

5. *Ohio Amish Directory*, xviii–xxi.

6. Amish education committees in most states have drawn up guidelines for the operation of their schools. In Ohio, the guidelines are set forth in a small green, undated pamphlet, which addresses such issues as curriculum, attendance, discipline, ownership of schools, teachers, and administration (Bishops, committeemen, and others, *Minimum Standards for the Amish Parochial or Private Elementary Schools of the State of Ohio as a Form of Regulations*, Henry J. Hershberger, Chair of Committee, Apple Creek, OH).

7. Dewalt, *Amish Education*, 156.

8. See Hostetler and Huntington, *Amish Children*; Huntington, "Persistence and Change"; Harroff, *Amish Schools of Indiana*; Dewalt, *Amish Education*; Johnson-Weiner, *Train Up a Child*.

9. Johnson-Weiner, *Train Up a Child*, 124.

10. One way in which the emphasis on practical applications was manifested was in the case of a teacher who dismissed her students at the end of the day by naming specific chores (swept barn, washed dishes, wiped buckets, fed chickens, etc.) and asking who had done them. The students who said they had were then allowed to leave for home. Students are also assigned to do various classroom chores, such as sweeping, bringing water, monitoring the library, and so forth.

11. Olshan and Schmidt, "Amish Women and the Feminist Conundrum," 229.

12. We did encounter a few teachers who had turned teaching into a career—a middle-aged male teacher who worked in a carpentry shop in the summer to supplement his income and an older widow who was a first-grade teacher in a school attended mostly by New Order Amish.

13. Several teachers acknowledged, however, that they had to monitor their students to make sure that children from one affiliation did not "mock" the dress or hairstyles of another. Overall, though, most felt that the arrangement served a positive purpose.

14. Johnson-Weiner, *Train Up a Child*, 105.

15. Johnson-Weiner (ibid., 26–30) discusses in some detail the fascinating conflict that resulted in two neighboring schools.

16. Dewalt's *Amish Education* gives a detailed description of the variation among schools in each of the states served by Amish parochial schools.

17. Olshan ("Homespun Bureaucracy," 199–213) describes Amish bureaucratic forms as "embryonic" when viewed against the characteristics of bureaucracy outlined by Weber.

18. Johnson-Weiner, *Train Up a Child*, 226. For a discussion of how the two major producers of Amish school texts—the Gordonville Print Shop and the Pathway Publishing Corporation—reflect different notions of what it means to be Amish, see Johnson-Weiner, "Publish or Perish."

19. Huntington, "Persistence and Change," 78.

20. Olshan, "Modernity, Folk Society, Old Order Amish," 193.

21. Meyers, "Education and Schooling," 102.

22. Buchanan ("The Old Paths") notes that this concern was present among the Holmes County Amish from the very start of the parochial school movement.

23. Johnson-Weiner, *Train Up a Child*, 128.

24. Keim, "Chronology of Amish Court Cases," 97.

25. This Amish elder pointed out that one result of that conflict was folk wisdom to the following effect: "If you do something stupid, do it in Holmes, not Wayne [County]."

26. Until recently, public schools could count on being chosen by Amish families who had children with special needs. But this "monopoly" is declining as more and more parochial schools have initiated services for special-needs children. According to a school psychologist who serves a district in Wayne County, parochial school teachers and parents have formed close relationships with public school counselors and local psychologists so that they could add special services to the parochial schools.

27. For her efforts, Mast was chosen as one of six "National Outstanding Principals" in 2006 by the National Association of Elementary School Principals.

28. At times, however, the divergence of Amish and English priorities creates tension in the community. For example, according to one longtime resident of Holmes County, "Hiland High School tried to raise funds for a gym but the Amish voted it down because the levy was for high school." Considerable frustration in the community resulted, but in the end the funds were raised privately.

29. Meyers, "The Old Order Amish," 392.

30. Since New Order families were overrepresented in our survey, this figure is probably higher than the average in the settlement. A member of the Amish Advisory Committee, which oversees parochial schools in the settlement, estimated that forty to fifty families were engaged in homeschooling in the settlement.

31. See, for example, Sennett and Cobb, *The Hidden Injuries of Class*; and Collins, *Black Feminist Thought*.

32. Kraybill ("Amish Informants," 171) describes the complex motivations leading such individuals to speak out despite Amish prohibitions against pride: they enjoy being considered expert sources of Amish wisdom; they fear that journalists and other outsiders will misinterpret Amish culture if they do not speak out; and they themselves lead more progressive lifestyles ("one toe inside the Amish community and two feet out") than most members of their communities.

33. Lamont, in her study of French and American workers (*The Dignity of Working Men*), found that working-class manual workers used moral criteria (being hardworking, responsible, having integrity, etc.) to separate themselves from others, criteria that provided them with a sense of personal worthiness.

34. Lave, *Cognition in Practice*, 14.

35. Classes aimed at the Amish population are part of a larger outreach effort by the Holmes County Educational Foundation, a nonprofit foundation dedicated to helping Holmes County residents pursue further education opportunities.

36. Claudia Zimmerman, interview by David McConnell, January 11, 2005.

37. Johnson-Weiner, *Train Up a Child*, 120–21.

38. Dewalt, *Amish Education*, 135.

39. The festival, celebrating its thirty-second anniversary in 2008, raises about one hundred thousand dollars annually. See Paul Locher, "Serious Shopping, Serious Shoppers: Holmes Training Center Festival Draws Large Crowd," *Wooster (Ohio) Daily Record*, May 13, 2007, B1–2.

40. Dewalt and Troxell's case study of an Old Order Mennonite school in Pennsylvania found that successful resistance to mainstream schooling was largely due to "economic self-sufficiency, residential independence, and complete control of their own schools" ("Mennonite One-Room School," 308).

41. This is precisely the argument Cowles makes in his recent study of an Old Order Mennonite community: that achieving "transformative community" through control of one's own schools represents a "third way" in minority education. Cowles further notes that George Spindler pointed out in 1997 that the Amish "have done exactly what is logical according to the anthropologist viewing the relationship between education and culture" ("Charting a Third Way," 391.

42. Keim, *Compulsory Education and the Amish*.

43. Johnson-Weiner, *Train Up a Child*, 128.

44. Stambach, "The Silence Is Getting Louder." Andy Weaver churches, by contrast, do prohibit public school attendance and homeschooling. It is also extremely rare for the Swartzentruber Amish to engage in these alternatives to parochial schooling.

Chapter 6. Work Within and Outside Tradition

Epigraph: Lisa Abraham, "Keeping It Natural," *Akron Beacon Journal*, May 28, 2008, D2.

1. See, for example, Lowery and Noble, "Changing Occupational Structure"; Donnermeyer and Cooksey, "Demographic Foundations"; Kraybill and Nolt, *Amish Enterprise*; Donnermeyer and Cooksey, "On the Recent Expansion."

2. Holmes County contains a majority of the settlement's population, is the economic hub of the settlement, and is the major site for tourists in "Amish country." Consequently, we have chosen to focus on this county because in many ways it is the heart of the settlement.

3. Bender, "Animal Production."

4. U.S. Department of Agriculture, 2002 *Census of Agriculture* (Washington, DC: U.S. Dept. of Agriculture, National Agricultural Statistics Service, 2003), vol. 1, chap. 2, table 2.

5. Donnermeyer and Cooksey, "Demographic Foundations."

6. Kraybill and Nolt, *Amish Enterprise*; Meyers and Nolt, *An Amish Patchwork*.

7. This report comes from a conversation with a local real estate businessman who has worked with the Amish in the Holmes County Settlement for several decades.

8. Office of Strategic Research, *Ohio County Indicators* (Columbus, OH: Ohio Department of Development, June 2007), 52.

9. See Chris Leonard and Bobby Warren, "Marketing Destinations," *Wooster (Ohio) Daily Record*, February 28, 2008, E12.

10. The demographic data are drawn from Office of Strategic Research, *Ohio County Profiles: Holmes County* (Columbus: Ohio Department of Development, 2004); Office of Strategic Research *Ohio County Indicators* (Columbus: Ohio Department of Development, June 2007); U.S. Census (2007), *USA Counties, General Profile: Holmes, Ohio,* http://censtats.census.gov/cgi-bin/usac/usatable.pl?State =&County=3907 (accessed May 3, 2009).

11. U.S. Census Bureau, "2005 Industry Code Summary, ZipCode Business Patterns," http://censtats.census.gov/cbpnaic/cbpnaic.shtml; click on the "Censtats Databases" site, then in the "Zip Code Business Patterns" enter the appropriate zip codes (44610 and 44687) (accessed July 6, 2009).

12. The statistic is from "Marketing Destinations," *Wooster (Ohio) Daily Record,* February 28, 2008, E12.

13. Shasta Mast, executive director of the Chamber of Commerce, Holmes County, Ohio, interview by Charles Hurst, October 26, 2006.

14. *Vendor,* June 14, 2006, 19. The *Vendor* is an advertising pamphlet published every two weeks by Green Valley Printing, Brinkhaven, Ohio, for the Amish community.

15. The dependency rank is based on the percentage of a county's total personal income that comes from transfer payments. Office of Strategic Research, *Ohio County Indicators,* June 2007.

16. Measuring a family's economic standing can be very tricky, and statements about it must be interpreted carefully. First, in contrast to many eligible English families, whose incomes are increased by money from social security or welfare, Amish families do not receive money from these sources, a factor that depresses their incomes. Second, money income does not include the value of homegrown food, which is a partial substitute for income. Third, when families state household income in a survey, it is not always clear whether they are reporting gross or net income. Fourth, studies by the Internal Revenue Service suggest that wealthy in-

dividuals and those who receive government benefits sometimes underreport their incomes. Fifth, and perhaps most important for assessing Amish economic standing, income is a very narrow measure of a family's "class" or economic position. A significant proportion of Amish economic resources lies in the value of their land and their businesses, assets that are not captured by the income measure. A family may have meager income but possess nonmoney assets that strengthen their "class" position.

17. See John Horton, "Counties Caught in Conundrum: Getting the Amish to Take Food Stamps," *Cleveland Plain Dealer*, October 18, 2006; and Susan Green, "Graduate Researcher Links Amish Demographics, Food Stamp Participation," available at Ohio University's Web site, www.ohio.edu/outlook/05-06/Septem ber/3f-056.cfm.

18. Kraybill and Nolt, *Amish Enterprise.*

19. Bumgardner, Romig, and Luppold, "Wood Use."

20. Ibid., 7.

21. Kreps et al, "The Impact of Tourism."

22. Paula Schleis, "Dreams Given Form in Wood," *Akron Beacon Journal*, September 30, 2007, D3.

23. Kraybill and Nolt, *Amish Enterprise.*

24. This information about Amish reluctance to advertise was learned in a conversation with two of the employees of Graphic Publications in Berlin, Ohio.

25. Max Weber, in *The Protestant Ethic*, discusses the distinction between "rational" and "traditional" approaches to work and profit within capitalism. A businessman with a rational perspective is more aggressive, seeks out markets and customers, and strives to grow, while a tradition-oriented businessman waits for customers to come to him and is interested only in making enough money to maintain his current lifestyle.

26. Kline and Beachy, "History and Dynamics," 17.

27. Max Weber discusses how various branches of Protestant religion perceive work and its proper nature. Weber argues that the more ascetic sects associated with or closest to Calvinism viewed work as a calling from God in which the individual is expected to adopt work as an internalized ethic aimed at serving God and the community (*The Protestant Ethic*).

28. *Gemeinde Register*, October 20, 2002, 1. The *Gemeinde Register* is a biweekly paper for the Ohio Amish community and is published in Baltic, Ohio. It contains church service information, notices about meetings and showers, and classified ads.

29. Quoted in Joe Milica, "Rapid Growth Brings Change to Amish Community," available online at www.oacountry.com/Changing-Amish.html (accessed January 28, 2008).

30. Rosabeth Kanter pioneered research that focused on the effects of being in a minority on boundary creation and performance expectations in organizations. Higher-than-average expectations to perform, increased awareness of and accentuation of cultural and social boundaries between groups, and expectations to fulfill stereotypical roles are some of those consequences. See Rosabeth Moss Kanter, *Men and Women of the Corporation* (New York: Basic Books, 1977).

31. This estimate was given by a Swartzentruber bishop.

32. This information comes from Byler, "The Geography of Difference."

33. Kanter, *Men and Women*; see also Robert Jackall, *Moral Mazes: The World of Corporate Managers* (New York: Oxford University Press, 1988).

34. Kraybill and Nolt, *Amish Enterprise.*

35. Lowery and Noble, "Changing Occupational Structure."

36. Ibid.; Donnermeyer and Cooksey, "Demographic Foundations."

37. Any conclusions about the precise occupational distribution among the Swartzentruber Amish would be largely speculative. Throughout the book, we are using a Swartzentruber bishop's estimate that about 70 percent of Swartzentruber Amish are in family farming. Since Swartzentrubers are not listed in the *Ohio Amish Directory*, there is not as much known about this group as about other Amish orders. As one Swartzentruber bishop commented, "We don't want to put [ourselves] out to the world by putting names in the Directory." A New Order respondent said he thought that the Swartzentrubers also objected to the use of numbers, which is interpreted as a sign of arrogance and pride.

38. John Horton, "Holmes County Breeders, Activists Battle over Kennels," *Cleveland Plain Dealer*, August 13, 2006, A1.

39. Ibid.

40. Holly Zachariah, "Amish Accused of Running Dog Mills," *Columbus (Ohio) Dispatch*, April 22, 2007, C1-C2.

41. Anderson, Frosch, and Outlaw, "Economic Impact."

42. Ibid., 7.

43. This conclusion is based on estimates drawn from membership data of the North American Deer Farmers Association and the Whitetail Deer Farmers of Ohio.

44. Information was obtained from the Web site of the North American Deer Farmers Association, www.nadefa.org/.

45. See Dave Mast, "Deer Auction Draws Buyers from Around the Nation," *Wooster Weekly News*, September 6, 2007, B1.

46. Cited in Meghan Barr, "Hard-Hit Consumers Turn to Amish," Associated Press, www.ar15armory.com/forums/Hard-hit-consumers-turn-t29910.html (accessed July 6, 2009).

47. Hebert, "Progress"; Gray, "Local-Based."

48. Kraybill, "Plotting Social Change," 64.

49. Kraybill, "Plain Reservations."

50. The ad for the processor, from which these statements are drawn, appeared in the *Sugarcreek (Ohio) Budget*, November 28, 2007, 43, national edition.

51. Kraybill, "The Amish Encounter with Modernity."

52. Byler, "The Geography of Difference," 4.

53. Although we have anecdotal evidence for wealth variations based on differences in the conditions of schools, individual ability to pay for health care, quality of housing, and similar measures, we do not have systematic data on family wealth and so cannot specify the nature of a hierarchy of wealth across the affiliations. However, we can speculate: to the extent that some affiliations as a whole are wealthier than others, in part because of differences in use of technology and range of occupations, marriages within affiliations may inadvertently reproduce class positions within the Amish community. This is a fascinating area for future research.

54. Weber, The Protestant Ethic.

55. See Chris Kick, "Maple Drink a Bone, Skin, Joint, Kidney Strengthener, People Say," *Wooster (Ohio) Daily Record*, February 27, 2008, B4.

56. Bob Downing, "Amish Adopt Solar Power at Home, Work," *Akron Beacon Journal*, July 13, 2007.

57. Ibid.

58. "Amish Are Surprise Champions of Solar Technology," available at the *New Scientist* Web site, www.newscientist.com/blog/environment/2007_06_01 _archive.html. Amish use of solar power is also discussed on the Green Energy Ohio Web site.

Chapter 7. Health along the Life Cycle

1. See, for example, Hostetler, *Amish Society*; and Huntington, "Health Care."

2. On culture care diversities and universalities, see George, "Theory of Culture Care"; and Wenger, "The Phenomenon of Care."

3. The concepts of "high-context" and "low-context" cultures were developed by Edward Hall in *Beyond Culture* (Garden City, NY: Anchor Books, 1976). They have been applied to the Amish by, for example, Wenger, "The Phenomenon of Care"; and Hostetler, *Amish Society*.

4. Data for 2005 are from the Center for Vital and Health Statistics of the Ohio Department of Health and from Ohio Families for Safe Birth, both located in Columbus, OH. The 1984 study, which included a face-to-face survey as well as a telephone survey of Amish families in Wayne County, was conducted to determine current usage of health care services and assess deficiencies in services, health care needs of the local Amish, and the extent to which preventive health care was carried out by the Amish. See Health Care Associates, *Amish Questionnaire/Results*.

5. Hoover, *House Calls*, 202–3.

6. See Huntington, "Health Care," for a history of the Mount Eaton Center.

7. The Miller case, which received national attention, pitted traditional Amish and midwifery advocates against the mainstream medical establishment. See the local articles "Before Hundreds of Supporters, Miller Says, 'It's about Their Freedom'"; and "Miller Jailed for Refusing to Name Drug Source," *Wooster (Ohio) Daily Record*, March 12, 2002; October 24, 2002; and Wiker, "Mennonite Midwife behind Bars."

8. *Ohio Amish Directory*.

9. Center for Vital and Health Statistics, "Vital Statistics."

10. Donnermeyer and Cooksey, "Demographic Foundations."

11. The information on Holmes County prenatal care is derived from a study by the Holmes County Health Department.

12. See Huntington, "Health Care." A 2006 study of middle-aged Amish women in Holmes County found that less than one-third had had a mammogram in the previous year. Reported in Chris Leonard, "Dr. Melissa Thomas Travels to Remote Places with the Mammo Van," *Wooster (Ohio) Daily Record*, May 11, 2008, B6.

13. The study of 1,108 individuals, 36 percent of whom were Amish, entitled "The Behavioral Risk Factor Surveillance System Study," was conducted by Holleran Consulting for the Holmes County Health Department. The research also indicated that Amish women were less likely than others to have obtained a breast exam or pap smear within the past year, and Amish men were less likely than others to have been screened for prostate cancer in that period.

14. "Pertussis Outbreak."

15. Lisa Belkin, "A Doctor for the Future," *New York Times Magazine*, November 6, 2005, 70.

16. Cheryl Powell, "New Fund to Aid Sick Amish Kids," *Akron Beacon Journal*, July 6, 2005, A1.

17. Van der Walt et al., "Maternal Lineages."

18. Cheryl Powell, "Amish Families Review Stance on Medicaid," *Akron Beacon Journal*, July 6, 2005, A1.

19. Hostetler, *Amish Society*.

20. Bassett, Schneider, and Huntington, "Physical Activity."

21. We are grateful to Lawrence Greksa for this observation.

22. Data are from the 2003 "Behavioral Risk Factor Surveillance System Survey" conducted for the Holmes County Department of Health by Holleran Consulting. It should be pointed out that this study does not analyze differences between Amish affiliations, although such differences are known to exist. More conservative groups, such as the Swartzentrubers and the Andy Weavers, are more likely than New or Old Order Amish to smoke and use alcohol.

23. Girod, "A Sustainable Medicine."

24. Miller, *Our People*, 6.

25. Hoover, *House Calls*, 32–33.

26. Von Gruenigen et al., "Complementary and Alternative Medicine Use," 232.

27. Although they are usually thought of as the same, a few Amish argue that brauche is very different from powwowing in that they associate the former with Christian words and the latter with witchcraft. For our purposes, we consider the two practices to be the same. An in-depth discussion of the nature and techniques of powwowing (brauche), along with examples of its usage and practitioners, can be found in Kriebel, *Powwowing*.

28. Miller, "The Role of a Braucher-Chiropractor."

29. "Information Please," *Sugarcreek (Ohio) Budget*, April 12, 1995, 25.

30. See Cates, "Facing Away"; and Cates and Graham, "Psychological Assessment" for a fuller discussion of the cultural factors among the Amish that affect therapist-client relationships.

31. Perhaps the best known of those who view mental illness as a social construction is Thomas Szasz, whose *Myth of Mental Illness* set forth the argument that mental illness is defined into existence by our interpretations of behavior. Diagnoses of mental illness appear to be affected by the cultural images and expectations that are placed on different categories of people such as minorities and women (see, for example, Institute of Medicine, *Unequal Treatment*; Kromm, "Feminization of Madness").

32. See the research by Loring and Powell, "Gender, Race, and DSM-III"; and Good et al., "The Culture of Medicine," for illustrations of racial and gender biases in diagnoses.

33. Fuchs et al., "Health Risk Factors."

34. DeRue, Schlegel, and Yoder, "Amish Needs."

35. Miller et al., "Health Status."

36. Hostetler, *Amish Society*.

37. Reiling, "The 'Simmie' Side of Life."

38. Ibid.

39. Amish Mental Health Committee, minutes of the meeting held at the Alvin Beachy residence, April 25, 1996, p. 3.

40. Wenger, *Depression*.

41. *Hoffnung Heim Newsletter*, May 2004, 6. Published in Dundee, Ohio, by Hoffnung Heim.

42. Springhaven is another local Christian-based counseling center that works with Amish clients. About one-third of its clients are Amish. The work of its professional social workers and counselors involves strategies based on both Christian beliefs and behavioral science.

43. Amish Hospital Aid Committee, *The Amish Hospital Aid Program* (Sugarcreek, OH: Amish Hospital Aid Committee, 2003), 3. This is a pamphlet distributed to local church members explaining the eligibility rules and covered services of the program.

44. Many announcements of this kind can be found in each issue of the *Gemeinde Register*, which is published biweekly by Gemeinde Register in Baltic, Ohio, for the Amish in Ohio. For the quoted entries, see *Gemeinde Register*, August 3, 2005; August 17, 2005; August 31, 2005.

45. Powell, "Amish Families Review Stance," A6.

46. Weaver, *My Grace*, vi.

47. The quotes that follow are drawn from Weaver, *My Grace*, 15, 238, 3, 403, 167, 97, and 435.

48. Girod, "A Sustainable Medicine."

Chapter 8. Stepping Back and Looking Forward

1. *Webster's Ninth New Collegiate Dictionary*, s.v. "crucible"; *Oxford Desk Dictionary and Thesaurus*, s.v. "crucible."

2. Nolt and Meyers, *Plain Diversity*.

3. James Thompson, in his classic analysis *Organizations in Action*, characterizes organizations as open systems tending toward closure. Organizations, especially businesses, use several techniques to seal off or control outside influences so that they can operate predictably and efficiently.

4. Lehman and Nolt, *Mennonites, Amish*, 103.

5. Granovetter, "Strength of Weak Ties," 1373.

6. See the study by Kraybill and Kopko, "Bush Fever." Robert Putnam, in "Bowling Alone," is among the most notable of those who are concerned about lack of social capital, declines in trust, and other trends moving us away from a civil society. James Coleman was also concerned with a decline in social trust that accompanies the high rates of mobility, heterogeneity, and corporate dominance in our society. See his "Social Capital"; and *Foundations of Social Theory*.

7. Carroll, "Most Americans Approve."

8. Granovetter, in "Strength of Weak Ties," discusses the nature and importance of weak ties with outside groups and their implications for integration and exclusivity in society. He sees such ties as significant avenues along which new ideas and other changes can travel. In the absence of weak ties between groups, dense networks foster fragmentation rather than integration.

9. Erving Goffman's *Asylums* analyzes the ways in which some institutions totally encapsulate the individuals and maintain total control over their lives with the goal of dismantling their old selves and creating new, more acceptable, ones that are

consistent with the values of the institutions. He also examines the myriad ways by which individuals who want to maintain their personal integrity adjust to the pressures imposed by these institutions.

10. "The Harris Poll's 'Alienation Index' Rises Slightly to Highest Level in Presidency of George W. Bush," *Harris Poll #110*, November 8, 2007, www.harrisin teractive.com.

11. In *Foundations of Social Theory*, James Coleman argues that trust is nurtured best in small, homogeneous, tight-knit groups or communities with high amounts of social capital.

12. Kraybill and Bowman, *On the Backroad*, 115–16.

13. Giddens, "The Reflexivity of Modernity," 423.

14. Nolt and Meyers, in *Plain Diversity*, stress the importance of these ongoing conversations for the continued vigor and distinctiveness of the Amish community. Even when there is disagreement in arguments, there is agreement on the importance of what is being argued.

15. Michael Hechter, in *Principles of Group Solidarity*, reviews the methods of controlling "free riding" by individuals in organizations and communities, that is, mechanisms used to ensure that members or citizens do their part and adhere to organizational or community rules.

16. Ehrenhalt, *The Lost City*, 2.

17. Kim Lawton, "Unemployment puts Churches in a Pinch," *Mennonite Weekly Review*, May 4, 2009, 1; Joshua Boak, "Layoffs Are Driving Change among the Amish," www.latimes.com/news/nationworld/nation/la-na-amish20-2009apr 20,0,5794881.story (accessed April 21, 2009); Associated Press, "Faith or Money: Indiana Amish face Uneasy Dilemma," www.heraldtimesonline.com/ stories/2009/05/11/statenews.qp-3620557.sto (accessed May 14, 2009).

18. Tyler, "The State of Trust Today."

19. In *The Risk Society*, Ulrich Beck has described modern societies as "risk" societies because national borders no longer separate them from one another. Pollution and related environmental problems spread across the globe, their effects not distinguishing rich from poor or large from small societies.

20. Pew Research Center, "Americans and Social Trust."

Appendix A. Methodology

1. Nespor, *Tangled Up in School*.

2. Reed-Donahay, *Education and Identity in France*, 37.

Bibliography

Anderson, David P., Brian J. Frosch, and Joe L. Outlaw. "Economic Impact of the United States Cervid Farming Industry," Agricultural and Food Policy Center Research Report 07-4, Texas A&M University, August 2006.

Appadurai, Arjun. *Modernity at Large: Cultural Dimensions of Globalization.* Minneapolis: University of Minnesota Press, 1996.

Barce, Jennifer Wilson. "Examining Early Childhood Literacy in Cross-Cultural Contexts: A Case Study in the Transition between Amish Home Culture and Public School." Ph.D. diss., Indiana University, 1995.

Bassett, David R., Jr., Patrick L. Schneider, and Gertrude E. Huntington. "Physical Activity in an Old Order Amish Community." *Medicine and Science in Sports and Exercise* 36 (2004): 79–85.

Beachy, Leroy. "The History of the Amish." In *The Amish of Holmes County,* edited by Jon Kinney, 25–36. Orrville, OH: Spectrum, 1996.

Beck, Ulrich. *The Risk Society.* London: Sage, 1992.

Bender, Martin H. "Animal Production and Farm Size in Holmes County, Ohio, and US Agriculture." *American Journal of Alternative Agriculture* 18, no. 2 (2003): 70–79.

Benedict, Fred W. Review of *On the Backroad to Heaven,* by Donald B. Kraybill and Carl F. Bowman. *Old Order Notes* 24 (Fall–Winter 2001): 98–104.

Biesecker, Susan. "Heritage versus History: Amish Tourism in Two Towns." In *The Amish and the Media,* edited by Diane Zimmerman Umble and David L. Weaver-Zercher, 111–30. Baltimore: Johns Hopkins University Press, 2008.

Buchanan, Frederick. "The Old Paths: A Study of the Amish Response to Public Schooling in Ohio." Ph.D. diss., Ohio State University, 1967.

Bumgardner, Matthew, Robert Romig, and William Luppold. "Wood Use by

Ohio's Amish Furniture Cluster." *Forest Products Journal* 57, no. 12 (2007): 6–12.

Burkholder, Chris. *Amish Confidential: The Bishop's Son Shatters the Silence*. Argyle, IA: Argyle Publishing, 2005.

Byler, Darrin T. "The Geography of Difference: Constructing Identity in the Holmes County, Ohio, Amish Community." www.mcusa-archives.org/jhorsch/jhorsch2004/byler_essay.htm (accessed March 26, 2009).

Cancian, Francesca M. "The Feminization of Love." In *Feminist Frontiers III*, edited by Laurel Richardson and Verta Taylor, 288–300. New York: McGraw-Hill, 1993.

Carroll, Joseph. "Most Americans Approve of Interracial Marriages." *Gallup Poll Briefing*, August 16, 2007, 7–10.

Cates, James A. "Facing Away: Mental Health Treatment with the Old Order Amish." *American Journal of Psychotherapy* 59 (2005): 371–83.

Cates, James A., and Linda L. Graham. "Psychological Assessment of the Old Order Amish: Unraveling the Enigma." *Professional Psychology* 33 (2002): 155–61.

Center for Vital and Health Statistics. "Vital Statistics Annual County Birth Summary," 2006, Ohio Department of Health, Columbus, OH.

Cohen, Anthony P. *The Symbolic Construction of Community*. New York: Tavistock, 1985.

Coleman, James S. *Foundations of Social Theory*. Cambridge, MA: Belknap Press of Harvard University Press, 1990.

———. "Social Capital in the Creation of Human Capital." *American Journal of Sociology* 94 (1988): S95-S120.

Collins, Patricia Hill. *Black Feminist Thought: Knowledge, Consciousness, and the Politics of Empowerment*. Boston: Unwin Hyman, 1990.

Comaroff, Jean, and John Comaroff. *Of Revelation and Revolution: Christianity, Colonialism, and Consciousness in South Africa*. Vol. 1. Chicago: University of Chicago Press, 1991.

Cong, Dachang. "Amish Factionalism and Technological Change: A Case Study of Kerosene Refrigerators and Conservatism." *Ethnology* 31 (1991): 205–18.

Cooksey, Elizabeth C., and Joseph F. Donnermeyer. "Go Forth and Multiply: Patterns of Marriage and Childbearing among the Amish of Holmes County, Ohio." Paper presented at the "Amish in America" conference, Elizabethtown College, Elizabethtown, PA, June 8, 2007.

Coontz, Stephanie. *The Way We Never Were: American Families and the Nostalgia Trap*. New York: Basic Books, 1992.

Cowles, Spencer L. "Charting a Third Way in Minority Education: Transformative Community in the Old Order Mennonite Church of Kreider County." *Anthropology and Education Quarterly* 36, no. 4 (2005): 386–404.

Davis, Phillip W. "The Changing Meanings of Spanking." In *Family in Transition*, 9th ed., edited by Arlene S. Skolnick and Jerome H. Skolnick, 278–90. New York: Longman, 1997.

DeRue, Diane S., Rob Schlegel, and Jennifer Yoder. "Amish Needs and Mental Health Care." Available at www.marshall.edu/jrcp/sp2002/amish.htm (accessed March 26, 2009).

Dewalt, Mark W. *Amish Education in the United States and Canada.* Oxford: Rowman and Littlefield, 2006.

Dewalt, Mark W., and Bonnie K. Troxell. "Old Order Mennonite One-Room School: A Case Study." *Anthropology and Education Quarterly* 20, no. 4 (1988): 308–25.

di Leonardo, Micaela. "The Female World of Cards and Holidays: Women, Families, and the Work of Kinship." In *Gender in Cross-Cultural Perspective*, edited by Caroline B. Brattell and Carolyn F. Sargent, 322–31. Englewood Cliffs, NJ: Prentice Hall, 1993.

Donnermeyer, Joseph F., and Elizabeth C. Cooksey, "The Demographic Foundations of Amish Society." Paper presented at the annual meeting of the Rural Sociological Society, Sacramento, CA, August 11–15, 2004.

———. "On the Recent Expansion of Amish Settlements." Paper presented at the "Amish in America" conference, Elizabethtown College, Elizabethtown, PA. June 9, 2007.

Donnermeyer, Joseph F., George Kreps, and Marty Kreps. "The Changing Occupational Structure of the Amish." Paper presented at "Three Hundred Years of Persistence and Change: Amish Society, 1693–1993," a conference at Elizabethtown College, PA, July 22–25, 1993.

Dordrecht Confession of Faith. Aylmer, ON: Pathway, 1976.

Douglas, Mary. *Purity and Danger: An Analysis of Concepts of Pollution and Taboo.* London: Routledge and Kegan Paul, 1966.

Ehrenhalt, Alan. *The Lost City.* New York: Basic Books, 1995.

Ericksen, Eugene P., Julia A. Ericksen, and John A. Hostetler. "The Cultivation of the Soil as a Moral Directive: Population Growth, Family Ties, and the Maintenance of Community among the Old Order Amish." *Rural Sociology* 45 (March 1980): 49–68.

Ericksen, Julia, and Gary Klein. "Women's Roles and Family Production among the Old Order Amish." *Rural Sociology* 46 (1981): 282–96.

Ferketich, Amy K., Mira L. Katz, Ross M. Kauffman, Electra D. Paskett, Stanley Lemeshow, Judith A. Westman, Steven K. Clinton, Clara D. Bloomfield, and Mary Ellen Wewers. "Tobacco Use among the Amish in Holmes County, Ohio." *Journal of Rural Health* 24 (2008): 84–90.

Fuchs, Janet A., Richard M. Levinson, Ronald R. Stoddard, Maurice E. Mullet, and Diane H. Jones. "Health Risk Factors among the Amish: Results of a Survey." *Health Education Quarterly* 17 (1990): 197–211.

Friedrich, Lora J. "To Be or Not to Be: An Examination of Baptism into the Amish Church." Ph.D. diss., Ohio State University, 1978.

Garon, Sheldon, and Patricia L. Maclachlan. *The Ambivalent Consumer: Questioning Consumption in East Asia and the West.* Ithaca, NY: Cornell University Press, 2006.

Garrett, Ottie A. *True Stories of the X-Amish.* Horse Cave, KY: Neu Leben, 1998.

Garrett, Ruth Irene. *Crossing Over.* San Francisco: Harper Collins, 2003.

George, Julia B. "Theory of Culture Care Diversity and Universality: Madeleine M. Leininger." In *Nursing Theories: The Base for Professional Nursing Practice*, edited by Julia B. George, 489–518. Upper Saddle River, NJ: Prentice Hall, 2001.

Giddens, Anthony. *Emile Durkheim: Selected Readings.* Cambridge: Cambridge University Press, 1972.

———. "The Reflexivity of Modernity." In *Social Theory: Roots and Branches*, edited by Peter Kivisto, 423–27. New York: Oxford University Press, 2008.

Gingerich, Noah. *The History of Pinecraft.* Walnut Creek, OH: Carlisle Press, 2006.

Girod, Jennifer. "A Sustainable Medicine: Lessons from the Old Order Amish." *Journal of Medical Humanities* 23 (2002): 31–42.

Goffman, Erving. *Asylums.* Garden City, NY: Anchor, 1961.

Good, Mary-Jo DelVecchio, Cara James, Byron J. Good, and Anne E. Becker. "The Culture of Medicine and Racial, Ethnic, and Class Disparities in Health Care." In *Unequal Treatment: Confronting Racial and Ethnic Disparities in Health Care*, edited by B. D. Smedley, A. Y. Smith, and A. R. Nelson, 594–625 Washington, DC: National Academies Press, 2003.

Granovetter, Mark S. "The Strength of Weak Ties." *American Journal of Sociology* 78 (1972): 1360–80.

Gray, Thomas W. "Local-Based, Alternative Marketing Strategy Could Help Save More Small Farms." *Rural Cooperatives* 72 (May–June 2005): 20–23.

Greksa, Lawrence P. "Birth Seasonality in the Old Order Amish." *Journal of Biosocial Science* 36 (2003): 299–315.

———. "Population Growth and Fertility Patterns in an Old Order Amish Settlement." *Annals of Human Biology* 29 (2002): 192–201.

Greksa, Lawrence P., and Jill E. Korbin. "Amish." In *Encyclopedia of Medical Anthropology: Health and Illness in the World's Cultures*, edited by Carol Ember and Melvin Ember. New York: Springer Science and Business Media, 2004.

———. "Key Decisions in the Lives of Old Order Amish: Joining the Church and Migrating to Another Settlement." *Mennonite Quarterly Review* 76 (October 2002): 373–98.

Harroff, Stephen B. *Amish Schools of Indiana: Faith in Education.* West Lafayette, IN: Purdue University Press, 2004.

Health Care Associates. *Amish Questionnaire/Results.* Wooster, OH: Wayne County Health Department, 1984.

Hebert, Kristy. "Progress: Why All the New Produce Auctions." *Farm and Dairy,* on-line edition, June 1, 2004, www.farmanddairy.com/news/progress-why -all-the-new-produce-auctions/ (accessed March 26, 2009).

Hechter, Michael. *Principles of Group Solidarity.* Berkeley, CA: University of California Press, 1987.

Hershberger, Alma. *Amish Women.* Danville, OH: Art of Amish Taste, 1992.

Hershberger, Noah L. *A Struggle to Be Separate.* Orrville, OH: Noah L. Hershberger, 1985.

Hoover, Dorcas Sharp. *House Calls and Hitching Posts: Stories from Dr. Elton Lehman's Career among the Amish.* Intercourse, PA: Good Books, 2004.

Hostetler, John A. *Amish Society.* 4th ed. Baltimore: Johns Hopkins University Press, 1993.

Hostetler, John, and Gertrude Enders Huntington. *Amish Children: Childhood Socialization and Community.* 2nd ed. New York: Holt, Rinehart, and Winston, 1992.

Huntington, Gertude Enders. *Amish in Michigan.* East Lansing: Michigan State University Press, 2001.

———. "Dove at the Window: A Study of an Old Order Amish Community in Ohio." Ph.D. diss., Yale University, 1956.

———. "Health Care." In *The Amish and the State,* 2nd ed., edited by Donald B. Kraybill, 163–89. Baltimore: Johns Hopkins University Press, 2003.

———. "Persistence and Change in Amish Education." In *The Amish Struggle with Modernity,* edited by Donald B. Kraybill and Marc A. Olshan, 77–96. London: University Press of New England, 1994.

Iannacconne, Laurence. "Why Strict Churches Are Strong." *American Journal of Sociology* 99, no. 5 (1994): 1180–1211.

Institute of Medicine. *Unequal Treatment.* Washington, DC: National Academies Press, 2002.

Jackson, Benita M., Tony Payton, George Horst, Thomas J. Halpin, and B. Kim Mortensen. "An Epidemiologic Investigation of a Rubella Outbreak among the Amish of Northeastern Ohio." *Public Health Reports* 108 (1993): 436–39.

Johnson-Weiner, Karen M. "The Role of Women in Old Order Amish, Beachy Amish, and Fellowship Churches." *Mennonite Quarterly Review,* April 2001, 231–56.

———. "Publish or Perish: Amish Publishing and Old Order Identity." In *The Amish and the Media,* edited by Diane Zimmerman Umble and David Weaver-Zercher, 201–20. Baltimore: Johns Hopkins University Press, 2008.

———. *Train Up a Child: Old Order Amish and Mennonite Schools.* Baltimore: Johns Hopkins University Press, 2007.

Jones, Diane H. "Health Risk Factors among the Amish: Results of a Survey." *Health Education Quarterly* 17 (1990): 197–211.

Keim, Albert N. "A Chronology of Amish Court Cases." In Keim, *Compulsory Education and the Amish,* 93–98.

———, ed. *Compulsory Education and the Amish: The Right NOT to Be Modern.* Boston, MA: Beacon Press, 1975.

Kidder, Robert L. 2003. "The Role of Outsiders." In *The Amish and the State,* 2nd ed., edited by Donald B. Kraybill, 213–33. Baltimore: Johns Hopkins University Press, 2003.

Kidder, Robert L., and John A. Hostetler. "Managing Ideologies: Harmony as Ideology in Amish and Japanese Societies." *Law and Society Review* 24, no. 4 (1994): 895–922.

Kline, Edward A. "Research Notes: Letters Pertaining to the Sam Yoder Division." *Heritage Review* 16 (January 2006): 11–13.

Kline, Edward A., and Monroe L. Beachy. "History and Dynamics of the New Order Amish of Holmes County, Ohio." *Old Order Notes,* Fall–Winter 1998, 7–20.

Korbin, Jill E., and Lawrence P. Greksa. "The Paradox of Self and Conformity in Amish Culture." Paper presented at the "Amish in America" conference, Elizabethtown College, Elizabethtown, PA, June 7, 2007.

Kraybill, Donald B. "The Amish Encounter with Modernity." In *The Amish Struggle with Modernity,* edited by Donald B. Kraybill and Marc A. Olshan, 21–33. Hanover, NH: University Press of New England, 1994.

———. "Amish Informants: Mediating Humility and Publicity." In *The Amish and the Media,* edited by Diane Zimmerman Umble and David Weaver-Zercher, 161–80. Baltimore: Johns Hopkins University Press, 2008.

———. "Plain Reservations: Amish and Mennonite Views of Media and Computers." *Journal of Mass Media Ethics* 13 (June 1998): 99–110.

———. "Plotting Social Change across Four Affiliations." In *The Amish Struggle with Modernity,* edited by Donald B. Kraybill and Marc A. Olshan, 53–74. Hanover, NH: University Press of New England, 1994.

———. *The Riddle of Amish Culture.* Rev. ed. Baltimore: Johns Hopkins University Press, 2001.

Kraybill, Donald B., and Carl F. Bowman. *On the Backroad to Heaven: Old Order Hutterites, Mennonites, Amish, and Brethren.* Baltimore: Johns Hopkins University Press, 2001.

Kraybill, Donald B., and C. Nelson Hostetter. *Anabaptist World USA*. Scottdale, PA: Herald Press, 2001.

Kraybill, Donald B., and Kyle C. Kopko. "Bush Fever: Amish and Old Order Mennonites in the 2004 Presidential Election." *Mennonite Quarterly Review* 81(April 2007): 165–205.

Kraybill, Donald B., and Steven M. Nolt. *Amish Enterprise: From Plows to Profits*. 2nd ed. Baltimore: Johns Hopkins University Press, 2004.

Kraybill, Donald B., Steven M. Nolt, and David L. Weaver-Zercher. *Amish Grace: How Forgiveness Transcended Tragedy*. San Francisco: John Wiley, 2007.

Kreps, George M., Joseph F. Donnermeyer, Charles Hurst, Robert Blair, and Marty Kreps. "The Impact of Tourism on the Amish Subculture: A Case Study." *Community Development Journal* 32, no. 4 (1997): 354–67.

Kreps, George M., Joseph F. Donnermeyer, and Marty W. Kreps. "The Changing Occupational Structure of Amish Males." *Rural Sociology* 59 (Winter 1994): 708–19.

———. *A Quiet Moment in Time: A Contemporary View of Amish Society*. Walnut Creek, OH: Carlisle Press, 1997.

Kriebel, David W. *Powwowing among the Pennsylvania Dutch*. University Park, PA: Pennsylvania State University Press, 2007.

Kromm, Jane E. "The Feminization of Madness in Visual Representation." *Feminist Studies* 20 (1994): 507–35.

Lamont, Michele. *The Dignity of Working Men*. Cambridge, MA: Harvard University Press, 2002.

Lareau, Annette. *Home Advantage: Social Class and Parental Intervention in Elementary Education*. New York: Falmer Press, 2000.

Lasch, Christopher. *Haven in a Heartless World: The Family Besieged*. New York: Basic Books, 1977.

Lave, Jean. *Cognition in Practice*. Cambridge, MA: Cambridge University Press, 1988.

Lehman, James O., and Steven M. Nolt. *Mennonites, Amish, and the American Civil War*. Baltimore: Johns Hopkins University Press, 2007.

Leibman, Robert C., John R. Sutton and Robert Wuthnow. "Exploring the Social Sources of Denominational Schisms in American Protestant Denominations, 1890–1980." *American Sociological Review* 53, no. 3 (1988): 340–52.

Livecchia, Gayle. "Anabaptist Remarriage." Paper presented at the "Amish in America" conference, Elizabethtown, PA. June 8, 2007.

Loring, Marti, and Brian Powell. "Gender, Race, and DSM-III: A Study of the Objectivity of Psychiatric Behavior." *Journal of Health and Social Behavior* 29 (1988): 1–22.

Louden, Mark L. "Pennsylvania German in the 21st Century." Paper presented at the "Amish in America" conference, Elizabethtown, PA, June 8, 2007.

Lowery, Sean, and Allen G. Noble. "The Changing Occupational Structure of the Amish of the Holmes County, Ohio, Settlement." *Great Lakes Geographer* 7 (2000): 26–37.

Luhrmann, Tanya M. "Metakenesis: How God Becomes Intimate in Contemporary U.S. Christianity. *American Anthropologist* 106, no. 3 (2004): 518–28.

Luthy, David. "Amish Settlements across America: 2008." *Family Life*, August–September 2008, 17–23.

———. "The Origin and Growth of Amish Tourism." In *The Amish Struggle with Modernity*, edited by Donald B. Kraybill and Marc A. Olshan, 113–29. Hanover, NH: University Press of New England, 1994.

———. "The Origins and Growth of the Swartzentruber Amish." *Family Life*, August–September 1998, 19–22.

Mackall, Joe. *Plain Secrets: An Outsider among the Amish.* Boston: Beacon Press, 2007.

Martin, Joyce A., Bradley E. Hamilton, Paul D. Sutton, Stephanie J. Ventura, Fay Monacker, and Martha L. Munson. "Births: Final Data for 2003." *National Vital Statistics Reports* 54, no. 2 (2005), Centers for Disease Control, U.S. Department of Health and Human Services, www.cdc.gov/nchs/data/ nvsr/nvsr54/nvsr54_02.pdf (accessed March 26, 2009).

Meyers, Thomas J. "Education and Schooling." In *The Amish and the State*, 2nd ed., edited by Donald B. Kraybill, 87–108. Baltimore: Johns Hopkins University Press, 2003.

———. "The Old Order Amish: To Remain in the Faith or to Leave." *Mennonite Quarterly Review* 68 (July 1994): 378–95.

Meyers, Thomas J., and Steven M. Nolt. *An Amish Patchwork: Indiana's Old Orders in the Modern World.* Bloomington: Indiana University Press, 2005.

Miller, Kirk, Berwood Yost, Sean Flaherty, Marianne M. Hillemeier, Gary A. Chase, Carol S. Weisman, and Anne-Marie Dyer. "Health Status, Health Conditions, and Health Behaviors among Amish Women." *Women's Health Issues* 17 (2007): 162–71.

Miller, Levi. *Our People: The Amish and Mennonites of Ohio.* Rev. Ed. Scottdale, PA: Herald Press, 1992.

———. "The Role of a Braucher-Chiropractor in an Amish Community." *Mennonite Quarterly Review* 55 (1981): 157–71.

Nespor, Jan. *Tangled Up in School: Politics, Space, Bodies, and Signs.* New York: Lawrence Erlbaum, 1997.

Nolt, Steven M. "The Amish 'Mission Movement' and the Reformulation of Amish Identity in the Twentieth Century." *Mennonite Quarterly Review* 75, no. 1 (2001): 7–36.

——. *A History of the Amish*. Intercourse, PA: Good Books, 2003.

——. "Inscribing Community: *The Budget* and *Die Botschaft* in Amish Life." In *The Amish and the Media*, edited by Diane Zimmerman Umble and David L. Weaver-Zercher, 181–200. Baltimore: Johns Hopkins University Press, 2008.

Nolt, Steven M., and Thomas J. Meyers. *Plain Diversity: Amish Cultures and Identities*. Baltimore: Johns Hopkins University Press, 2007.

Ohio Amish Directory: Holmes County and Vicinity. Walnut Creek, OH: Carlisle, 2005.

Olshan, Marc A. "Homespun Bureaucracy: A Case Study in Organizational Evolution." In *The Amish Struggle with Modernity*, edited by Donald B. Kraybill and Marc A. Olshan, 199–214. London: University Press of New England, 1994.

——. "Modernity, the Folk Society, and the Old Order Amish." In *The Amish Struggle with Modernity*, edited by Donald B. Kraybill and Marc A. Olshan, 185–98. London: University Press of New England, 1994.

——. "The National Amish Steering Committee." In *The Amish and the State*, 2nd ed., edited by Donald B. Kraybill, 67–86. Baltimore: Johns Hopkins University Press, 2003.

——. "The Opening of Amish Society: Cottage Industry as Trojan Horse." *Human Organization* 50, no. 4 (1991): 378–84.

Olshan, Marc A., and Kimberley D. Schmidt. "Amish Women and the Feminist Conundrum." In *The Amish Struggle with Modernity*, edited by Donald B. Kraybill and Marc A. Olshan, 215–30. London: University Press of New England, 1994.

"Pertussis Outbreak in an Amish Community—Kent County, Delaware, September 2004–February 2005." *Morbidity and Mortality Weekly Report* 55 (2006): 817–21.

Peters, Shawn Francis. *The Yoder Case: Religious Freedom, Education, and Parental Rights*. Lawrence: University Press of Kansas, 2003.

Pew Research Center. "Americans and Social Trust: Who, Where, and Why." 2007, http://pewresearch.org/assets/social/pdf/SocialTrust.pdf (accessed May 14, 2009).

Plath, David W. *Long Engagements: Maturity in Modern Japan*. Stanford, CA: Stanford University Press, 1980.

Putnam, Robert. "Bowling Alone: America's Declining Social Capital." *Journal of Democracy* 61 (1996): 65–78.

Reed-Donahay, Deborah. *Education and Identity in Rural France: The Politics of Schooling*. Cambridge, MA: Cambridge University Press, 1996.

Regehr, T. D. *Mennonites in Canada: 1930–1970: A People Transformed*. Vol. 3. Toronto: University of Toronto Press, 1996.

Reiheld, Amelia T. "Donald G. Beam." In *The Amish of Holmes County*, edited by Jon Kinney, 241–49. Orrville, OH: Spectrum, 1996.

Reiling, Denise M. "Boundary Maintenance as a Barrier to Mental Health Help-Seeking for Depression among the Old Order Amish." *Journal of Rural Health* 18 (2002): 428–36.

———. "The 'Simmie' Side of Life: Old Order Amish Youths' Affective Response to Culturally Prescribed Deviance. *Youth and Society* 34, no. 2 (2002): 146–71.

Roberts, William Clifford. "The Amish, Body Weight, and Exercise." *American Journal of Cardiology* 94 (2004): 1221.

Schneider, David M., and George C. Homans. "Kinship Terminology and the American Kinship System." *American Anthropologist* 57, no. 6 (December 1955): 1194–1208.

Schwemmlein, Susanne. "The Weaker Vessel? Old Order Amish Women: Tradition and Transition." Master's thesis, Karl-Franzens Universität, Graz, Austria, 1997.

Scott, Stephen. *Plain Buggies: Amish, Mennonite, and Brethren Horse-Drawn Transportation.* Intercourse, PA: Good Books, 1998.

———. "New Comers: English Converts to the Amish." Paper presented at the "Amish in America" conference, Elizabethtown, PA. June 7–9, 2007.

Scott, Stephen, and Kenneth Pelman. *Living without Electricity.* Intercourse, PA: Good Books, 1999.

Sennett, Richard, and Jonathan Cobb. *The Hidden Injuries of Class.* New York: Vintage, 1973.

Smith, Dorothy. *The Conceptual Practices of Power: A Feminist Sociology of Knowledge.* London: Routledge and Kegan Paul, 1990.

Spain, Daphne. "Gendered Spaces and Women's Status." *Sociological Theory* 11 (1993): 137–51.

Spindler, George, ed. *Fifty Years of Anthropology and Education, 1950–2000: A Spindler Anthology.* Mahwah, NJ: Lawrence Erlbaum, 2000.

Stambach, Amy. "The Silence Is Getting Louder: Social Change among the Old Order Amish." *Chicago Anthropology Exchange* 17 (1988): 39–46.

Stevick, Richard A. *Growing Up Amish: The Teenage Years.* Baltimore: Johns Hopkins University Press, 2007.

Stoll, Elmo. "Views and Values: Daughters of Sarah." *Family Life,* March 1977, 8–10.

Stoltzfus, Louise. *Traces of Wisdom: Amish Women and the Pursuit of Life's Simple Pleasures.* New York: Hyperion, 1998.

Swander, Mary. *Out of This World: A Woman's Life among the Amish.* New York: Viking, 1995.

Szasz, Thomas S. *The Myth of Mental Illness.* New York: Harper and Row, 1974.

Tambiah, Stanley. "Ethnic Conflict in the World Today." *American Ethnologist* 16 (June 1989): 335–49.

Thompson, James D. *Organizations in Action.* New York: McGraw-Hill, 1967.

Turner, Victor. "Betwixt and Between: The Liminal Period in Rites de Passage." In *Symposium on New Approaches to the Study of Religion: Proceedings of the 1964 Annual Spring Meeting of the American Ethnological Society,* edited by J. Helm, 4–20. Seattle: American Ethnological Society, 1964.

Tyler, Tom. "The State of Trust Today," 2006, www.forbes.com (accessed March 26, 2009).

Umble, Diane Zimmerman. *Holding the Line: The Telephone in Old Order Mennonite and Amish Life.* Baltimore: Johns Hopkins University Press, 1996.

——. "Who Are You? The Identity of the Outsider Within." In *Strangers at Home: Amish and Mennonite Women in History,* edited by Kimberley D. Schmidt, Diane Z. Umble, and Steven D. Reschly, 39–52. Baltimore: Johns Hopkins University Press, 2002.

Van der Walt, Joelle M., William K. Scott, Susan Slifer, P. C. Gaskell, Eden R. Martin, Kathleen Welsh-Bohmer, Marilyn Creason, Amy Crunk, Denise Fuzzell, Lynne McFarland, Charles C. Kroner, C. E. Jackson, Jonathan L. Haines, and Margaret A. Pericak-Vance. "Maternal Lineages and Alzheimer Disease Risk in the Old Order Amish." *Human Genetics* 118 (2005): 115–22.

Von Gruenigen, V. E., A. L. Showalter, K. M. Gil, H. E. Frasure, M. P. Hopkins, and E. L. Jenison. "Complementary and Alternative Medicine Use in the Amish." *Complementary Therapies in Medicine* 9 (2001): 232–33.

Waldrep, G. C. "The New Order Amish and Para-Amish Groups: Spiritual Renewal within Tradition." *Mennonite Quarterly Review* 82 (July 2008): 395–426.

Wasao, Samson W. "Fertility Differentials among Three Amish Affiliations in Ohio." Ph.D. diss., Ohio State University, 1995.

Wasao, Samson, and Joseph F. Donnermeyer. "An Analysis of Factors Related to Parity among the Amish in Northeast Ohio." *Population Studies* 50, no. 2 (1992): 235–46.

Weaver, Eli I. *My Grace Is Sufficient for Thee.* Walnut Creek, OH: Carlisle, 2003.

Weaver, Roy M. "Glimpses of the Amish Church in Holmes County, Ohio, 1917–1922." *Heritage Review* 16 (January 2007): 9–11.

Weaver-Zercher, David. *The Amish in the American Imagination.* Baltimore: Johns Hopkins University Press, 2005.

Weber, Max. "Class, Status, Party." In *Social Theory: The Multicultural and Classic Readings,* edited by Charles Lemert, 126–36. Oxford: Westview Press, 1993. A 1920 article reprinted.

———. *The Protestant Ethic and the Spirit of Capitalism.* Los Angeles: Roxbury, 2002.

Wenger, Anna Frances Z. "The Phenomenon of Care in a High Context Culture: The Old Order Amish." Ph.D. diss., Wayne State University, 1988.

Wenger, Glenn. *Depression.* Ephrata, PA: Weaverland Mennonite Publications, 2002.

Wiker, Benjamin. "Mennonite Midwife behind Bars." *National Review Online,* December 3 2002, www.nationalreview.com/comment/comment-wiker 120302.asp (accessed April 27, 2009).

Wuthnow, Robert. *After Heaven: Spirituality in America since the 1950s.* Berkeley, CA: University of California Press, 1998.

Zook, Lee. "Slow Moving Vehicles." In *The Amish and the State,* edited by Donald B. Kraybill, 145–62. Baltimore: Johns Hopkins University Press, 2003.

Index